Achebe's Women

To Chidi;

In cherished memory of the
icon and pathfinder your father
was + still is. May God rest him.

Nelen Chukwuma
May 2nd, 2014 at Brown
5th Achebe Colloquium.

ACHEBE'S WOMEN

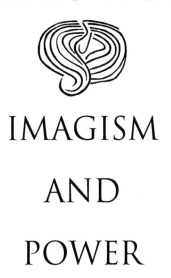

IMAGISM

AND

POWER

EDITED BY
HELEN CHUKWUMA

AFRICA WORLD PRESS

TRENTON | LONDON | CAPE TOWN | NAIROBI | ADDIS ABABA | ASMARA | IBADAN | NEW DELHI

AFRICA WORLD PRESS
541 West Ingham Avenue | Suite B
Trenton, New Jersey 08638

Book and cover design: Saverance Publishing Services
Cover artwork: Uzo Chukwuma

Library of Congress Cataloging-in-Publication Data

Achebe's women : imagism and power / edited by Helen Chukwuma.
   p. cm.
 Includes bibliographical references and index.
 ISBN 978-1-59221-869-1 (hardcover) -- ISBN 978-1-59221-870-7
(pbk.) 1. Achebe, Chinua--Characters--Women. 2. Women in literature. 3. Sex role in literature. 4. Patriarchy in literature. 5. Achebe,
Chinua--Political and social views. I. Chukwuma, Helen.
 PR9387.9.A3Z585 2011
 823'.914--dc23
                    2011028300

To my granddaughters Alexandria Amede Idu and Olivia Ona Ifeoma Ryan Farley, who true to the blood that runs from generations of assertive women in their family, from their great-great-grandmother Amede Olisa Anyaka "Ezeuli Nwanyi", their great-grandmother Cecilia Uyaoke Obba "Okwesili Eze Enyi Bu Odu", and their grandmother Helen Obiagaeli Chukwuma "Gegeli, Odoziaku, Ogene Nwanyi", and lastly, to their mother Catherine Amede Farley "Ezeuli Nwanyi" already show signs of assertive womanhood.

TABLE OF CONTENTS

ACKNOWLEDGEMENTS

To the great Mother of God, the Blessed Virgin Mary, gratitude for her love, protection, and inspiration, through her to her son, God himself, all glory and honor. In the realm of all mortals, I wish to thank His Excellency, Hon Chibuike Rotimi Amaechi, the executive governor of Rivers state for his kind support and encouragement. My thanks to the Obba family, standing tall as always. To my children the Chukwumas under the visionary lead of Nwabunwanne, I thank and cuddle you all for your love and lofty ideals for me still. I wish to register my gratitude to my colleagues Chioma Opara, Blessing Diala-Ogamba, Chinyere Okafor, Christine Ohale, and Angela Fubara for their enduring confidence, support, and encouragement during the formative stages of editing this book. I wish to acknowledge the encouragement and support of the Chair of the Department of English and Modern Foreign Languages at Jackson State University Dr. Jean Chamberlain, and my colleagues Dr. Sakinah Rashied, Ms. Noel Didla, Dr. Doris Ginn, Dr. Brenda K. Anderson, Dr. Preselfannie McDaniels, Dr. Everett Neasman, and the dependable Mr. Herd Graves. My gratitude to Prof. Ernest Emenyonu whose interest in my work is enduring if challenging. I thank you all for being there for me. Special thanks to the visionary master of arts, Chinua Achebe himself for providing us with the ingredients of on-going research and introspection of his works. Thanks to my graduate assistant, Mr. Wynton White, for sharing the rigors of collation and compilation of the text. A book remains what it is, a little slice of the intellect. It is therefore hoped that more intellectual exegeses will follow. After this one, then another, then still another.

H.O.C. 2010

PREFACE

2008 marked the fiftieth-year anniversary of *Things Fall Apart*. The book launched African Literature in the Canon. With its high profile on African Cultural Naturalism, the novel clearly valorized manhood in a pronounced patriarchal society. The general picture is a forest of men, with women as the cool shady spots, few and far between in this forest.

There are indeed some historical and cultural imperatives in Achebe's representation of women in his fiction. These are varied according to the publication dates of these novels. Thus the women characters in *Things Fall Apart* (1958) exist in the rural enclosed society of the Igbo hinterland with its strong patriarchal base. Here, women have no identity except as wives and mothers. Their voices are whimpers when they speak at all. They are the adornment of the home, flowers of the homestead and the engine of the domestic work force.No tales of renown or accomplishments are given to them; their allotted tasks and sole ambition at the time is motherhood and mothers of sons. *Things Fall Apart* is the story of a hero and his community fallen apart and it thus seems that the women are like the ceiling or roof in an Igbo proverb which states: If the house falls, do you ask if the ceiling fell with it? Not quite so, for the women turn out to be the foundation on which the house rests. They survive and live to tell the story. With the demise of Okonkwo, who keeps his household but the women. Therein lies the power of women, the power of the survivor. *Arrow of God*, (1979) still in the rural setting shows that women did not advance much in the society but remained in the background of their husbands' and childrens' advancement. Again it does appear that it is the men's world and the men's story. *No Longer at Ease*

(1969) is a novel that marked Achebe's departure from the rural to the urban setting where we encounter women in relationships with men.Clara the female character here is Beatrice (*Anthills of the Savannah*) in the making. She is educated and accomplished but fell under the yoke of love and cultural inhibitions of the Caste system. *Anthills of the Savannah* (1981) is where Achebe recognizes the true worth and power of women in his characterization of Beatrice the main female character.Through her, women's passivity and limitations are broken and the women come into their own.

The short summary above is to show Achebe's progression in his portrayal of women. For long, literary analysis of Achebe's imaging of women is seen from the widely explicit inferiority that marks their being. In this text, we posit that women, faced with such overwhelming odds of being, do manage to navigate their way through enough to be noticed and yet no songs are made on them. This text is our song for the un-sung, our recognition of the roles of women in the subsuming patriarchal society.

Thus,this text is informed by two considerations: primarily to record the women's tribute to the Eagle on Iroko, our highly esteemed and beloved Chinua Achebe to mark the fifty-year celebration of *Things Fall Apart* and the making of modern African literature. We are proud that the literature has come to its own and we thank God that Chinua Achebe himself has survived to see it happen and to witness the blossoming of African literature.

Secondly, this text is also an interrogation of the image and status of women in Achebe's fiction. The Darwinian notion of the survival of the fittest in nature's ecology still obtains. However, the Igbo remark that it is from the threshold of the weak man's house that we point at the ruins of a brave man's house attests to the virtues of temperance. In other words, the weak man's resilience and fortitude anchor him to survive the rashness which consumes and destroys the strong man. Overriding strength and power are not necessarily an assurance of security, longevity, of life and property. Power and brute force need mediation. This underscores the whole dualistic principle of life where one half melts or yields into the other in meaningful complementarity. Night and day are opposites; day transitionally descends as night transcends in parallel. There is a transitional medium between both which establishes harmony instead of rashness; parity instead of disequilibrium.

This text supplies that middle plain occupied by women and attests quite firmly that women in Achebe's fiction have designated roles that define, mediate and stabilize the home and the society. They are the presumed "weak" who live to tell the story of the brave and rash exploits of the men.

Women are the custodians of culture because they are rooted in their homesteads and on the land. They bear life, nurture life and ensure life continuity despite all odds. This is the power of women, this is the ensuring silver lining veiled by the storm of male machismo. For at the end of the day, it surfaces in its brilliance as seen in *Anthills of the Savannah*.

The power of Achebe's women characters is not given in bold profile nor did he elevate any female character to center stage. This is his patriarchal view of the world which does not admit of female prominence. However the story of *Things Fall Apart* is one of tragic fragmentation because of the negation of the female principle in the life and action of the hero Okonkwo. When the inter-connectivity of life which underlies basic humanity is truncated, so is harmony.

The genius of Achebe the writer shows in his constant effort at upgrading his vision and women characters to reflect modern realities thereby imbuing his work with relevance and grandeur. Thus in his later fiction, women are removed from the shackles of home enclosure and caging motherhood, material dependency, to the wider world of education, professionalism, politics and power. The women have now come into their own. It is indeed not yet Uhuru but this text shows how far Achebe has come and is willing to go in his portrayal and characterization of women in his fiction. This text is our modest contribution to the 50th anniversary celebration of *Things Fall Apart*.

Structurally, the text is divided into three sections. Section 1, exposes the real position of women in households and traditional society where they were not privileged to have a voice or indeed an identity. In this clutter of subsumption, women are still able to have a window in the mystical world and a space in their husbands' homes. In their huts situated tellingly in the back part of the compound, the women hold sway and in that enclosure they nurture children to adulthood as responsible citizens. The writers in this section outline women's power at the mystical level where there is no gender divide.Chinyere Okafor shows how women control the principle of life and existence as is encased in the word "Omumu" Chioma Opara demonstrates the women's strength in weakness and the life-wire mothers throw out to sons in the son's weakest ebb in life. Azodo dwells on female privilege and power as exemplified in the character of Chielo, the priestess of the Oracle of the Caves and Hills. Diala-Ogamba examines the role of children in the home and how Ezinma, Okonkwo's daughter transcends female inferiority and could relate effectively with her parents and especially her father which elicited Okonkwo's frequent lament, "I wish she were a boy, she has the right spirit."

This comment which in that society deemed to be a compliment is actually in the light of modern realization a statement of minimalism and Identitiy loss. Indeed in the world of *Things Fall Apart*, masculinity is defined as zero femininity, an antithesis of it where the one is rough-hewn, violent, quick-tempered, impatient and arrogant and the feminine is peaceful, humane, docile, creative, reasonable, resolute and patient. However, the differences between the sexes, male and female are not absolutes, existing as rigid parallels. There is a certain flexibility in boundary demarcation that attends to the sexes. Thus a woman can indeed be brave, quick, powerful, witty and outspoken, while sitting pretty as a woman (Ezinma) and a man correspondingly can be docile, creative and un-competitive (Nwoye).Thus Okonkwo's world is flawed by the rigidity of his conception of male and female where the male represents the ideal and women a shadow of the substance. His canvas admits of life in two bold colors without shades and blends. Thus to Okonkwo, Ezimma is ill-fitted in the domain of women, she should have been a man. Regardless, Ezinma is beautiful in physique and character and she is FEMALE.

The second section is devoted to the exegesis of the nature of positive female power in Achebe's female characters.I argue that motherhood is supreme and remains in the uppermost level of women's power in its uniqueness. Men and society extol the mother of sons and mothers aspire to that. However, in the char-

PREFACE

acter of Ugoye, Okonkwo's second wife who suffers a high degree
of infant mortality and is able at last to give birth to a daughter
still asserts herself in Okonkwo's compound regardless.She cleverly exploits Okonkwo's love for her as her daughter Ezinma does.

Anthonia Kalu discusses how Achebe's women are caught
in the interplay between modernity and tradition and are always
victims in both cases. She links African women marginalization
as a hindrance to any meaningful development in the continent.
And states "By rejecting the idea that women can and should act
as successful advocates for other women, men and the various
communities, African leaders are embarked on killing Africa's
future." Fubara in her refreshing analogy of the butterfly cycle of
being, shows the various stages of the women's emancipation in
Achebe'es fiction. Mbonu in a kaleidoscope of Judea Christianity
and Igbo philosophies, shows the importance of women's valoriz-
ing impulse.Nwagbara argues from the ideological standpoint of
materialist criticism to show a better understanding of women's
oppression. Ideology indeed mediates literature and offers a better
understanding and appreciation of the notions espoused therein.
Achebe uses Beatrice in Nwagbara's terms "to rid our world of
gender chauvinism".Nutsukpo, Salami-Agunloye, Mbonu all
demonstrate admirably the shift of the power paradigm from the
margin to epi-center of the women characters as exemplified by
Beatrice in *Anthills of the Savannah*.This is seen in the new gender
roles women are entrusted to play.This dovetails to Achebe's assertion in the novel *Anthills of the Savannah*, that "Women as courts
of last resort is a damn sight too far and too late."(91-92) Women
should on the basis of their personal capacities be involved in the
affairs of the polity and not to be fallen back on as the last resort
when all seems lost. This section , because of its concentration on
the paradigm shift in Achebe's portraiture of women, there was
the need to state the position of women before this shift. One
may notice some redundancy but it must be seen as a necessary
launch-pad for the analysis.

In chapter twelve, Udumuku's insightfulness into the veiled
symbol of "the gun that never shot"sheds light into the dilemma
that fueled Okonkwo's brash reaction. Ugoye the beloved wife of
Okonkwo was actually quering the man's virility for which she

nearly paid with her life. However it can indeed be surmised that since Okonkwo's gun misfired, Ugoye has been proved right; the gun is sometimes not effective. We note though that Okonkwo later in his exile in his motherland fathered two children.

Section three, gives some insights into Achebe's craft while questioning the realism of some of his female characters. Patricia Emenyonu, in her discussion of Achebe's short stories, shows how Achebe's portraiture of women incubates in the short stories only to blossom in the novels. Her analysis shows that Achebe, no matter the odds against women, "the essential female voice is never silenced." She calls for a closer study of Achebe's women to reveal their inner strength of character and attributes. Ojukwu wonders how realistic Achebe's portraiture of Okonkwo's wives is when in the extenuating circumstances of their husband's incarceration, their silence remained resoundingly deafening. She wonders whether or not there were real living, talking women in Okonkwo's society. Laura Miller states that women are the foundational structure of African society upon which their children and husbands build. She uses the symbolic image of backbone as a strong pillar of support and irreplaceable part on the human anatomy. But the question is how come this strong pillar i.e. woman is not given corresponding recognition and status in society? How can they be so strong as the backbone, and yet so weak as individual members of society? Wingard posits that the woman must strive to be an individual to be "one's own self." She gives an example of Ona in *Joys of Motherhood* and Ezimma in *Things Fall Apart* of women who are individuals in their own right and whose portraiture comes out as strong and individualistic.. Christine Ohale, in the final chapter, brings together from a variety of sources background information on Achebe's women characters in his works. Achebe's responses to questions are insightful into an appreciation of what informs his portrayal of women.

I hope the reader finds this text interesting and informative and that it helps show the strength of women despite the facade of powerlessness. From 1970 to 1980, with the United Nations declaration of the decade for women to the Beijing declaration of United Nations Platform for Action, so much has happened to bring women into the center of politics, education, and policy-making decisions. However, in 2004 the SDGEA (Solemn Declaration on Gender Equity in Africa) was declared and signed by African nations.[1] The campaign logo and slogan is GMAC (Gender is My Agenda Campaign). The Mozambican success story of gender is my agenda carried out by the FDC (Foundation for Community Development) has six focused commitment areas namely: 1. Peace and Security, 2. Governance, 3. Human Rights, 4. Health, 5. Education, 6. Economic Empowerment. Before that, the AU (African Union) protocol on the rights of women in Africa was declared in 2003. Recently, 2010-2020 has been declared as African Women's Decade Declaration (AWDD). All these declarations and protocols are aimed at promoting gender equality in Africa. For our purposes in literature, woman as subject continues to be pursued to reflect the growing visibility, power, responsibility, and effectiveness of women in modern times.

H.O.C.
October 2010

Note

1.   www.africa-union.org/root/au/conferences-past.

A Tribute to Helen Chukwuma
Frances Orabueze

Like an unsung celebrity you stole in,
Muzzling academic Goliaths,
Who in their self-conceited priggish mien
Had concluded with magisterial certitude:
"There is nothing like feminism."

But having toured the thorny tortuous paths,
Suckled life's sweet berries,
Tasted life's sour grapes,
You smiled at the young men's airs,
Disaffection from the amalgamated strange bedfellows,
For in their egoistic babble,
You are a rebel.

Undeterred but with courage,
You enraptured the mystery sac of knowledge
Making it yield to your relentless assault,
And you heart stout thawed the mines of laziness.

With benign motherly love,
You encircled fragile hands,
Guided the tottering feet,
Molded the malleable minds.

The unborn gazed at your logic,
The youth marveled at your wit,
The aged admired your endless wisdom,
And your critics benumbed into silence

Though the body may be weak,
Yet the heart is as strong as granite,
Through the eyes may be failing,
Yet the vision is clear,
Though the road may be long and tedious,
Yet unwavering determination is your companion.

Oh, nature has been kind
To bless mankind with your presence,
She, who joys in losing herself in others
And others in herself with all joys

In the midst of other constellation,
Your star is the brightest.
Your footsteps are not imprinted on the sandy soil,
Nor is it engraved on marbles,
Nor stored in vaults of banks,
But is written in diamond in the vessels you molded,
Where the vagaries of weather change them not,
Nor the motley moths much their sweetness,
Nor the light-fingered hands touch their beauty.

PART I

CHAPTER 1

WOMANHOOD IN IGBO COSMOLOGY: INTERSECTIONS WITH ACHEBE'S *THINGS FALL APART*

Chinyere Okafor

Introduction

This is an essay on womanhood in Igbo cosmology as it connects with Chinua Achebe's *Things Fall Apart*.[1] Focus is on
the idea of the female-person[2] in the spiritual and material life of
the Igbo as well as in the novel. Achebe has been accused of mini-
mizing the place of women in his novel through an androcentric
portrayal of marriage as enslavement of women and exploitation
of their labor. Mezu sees the world of the novel as one "where
the man is everything and the woman nothing" because they are
considered as part of the man's property along with barns and
social titles (Mezu 1995: 21), and Strong-Leek perceives it as
one where women have no sanctuary either in their homes or in
their husbands' arms (Strong-Leek 2001). Indeed the wives of the
central character, Okonkwo, are abused, beaten and intimidated
by their husband, who derides women as weak. Achebe's main
fictional premise is based on this patriarchal man whose female
hatred bothers on psychosis developed from his childhood hatred
for his father who was regarded as *agbala*, a woman, in the sense

of not meeting the masculine expectation of being a provider. Our discussion of cosmology in this essay will reveal that the fictional portrayal of women in the novel is just what it is: fiction, because it is reflected reality and not reality. We shall see that in actuality, Igbo womanhood is a complex category that derives a lot of its significance from the spiritual and physical dimension of the cosmos, and that the androcentric depiction of womanhood in the novel is largely influenced by the exaggerated masculinity of the hero that ultimately is faulted by the novelist for his overt and self-destructive machismo. His whole life is "dominated by fear, the fear of failure and of weakness" that lies "deep within his soul" (13) and motivates his overt show of male bravado. This kind of bravado in African men has been linked to fear of female control (Awason 2005), and a front for masking anxiety about the real self. Real self has both male and female principles but part of the motivation for male bravado aims at hiding the female one and putting on the guise of masculinity.

A discussion of womanhood necessarily touches on manhood because they operate like complementary, opposing, equal and unequal pairs in cosmological thinking of the people. Moreover the discussion of womanhood in *Things* is mediated by two important male pressures. One is the use of a patriarchal man as the hero, Okonkwo. The other is the male lens of the omniscient narrator. The use of a male person as the central character facilitates the presentation of the fictional world through male lens. The hero, Okonkwo, is represented as a household head, achiever, and a lord with an enviable position, but the author is also able to illustrate the downside of the hero's character through his disdain for the female principle. The contempt for women constitutes a flaw that pilots the hero to a devastating tragedy where he not only dies ignobly but is refused the wholesome embrace of the earth goddess regarded as the prime female principle in the tradition. This is a rejection that no woman in the novel encounters and which puts Okonkwo at the bottom level where it would be insulting to compare his end with that of the lowliest woman or man in the patriarchal world of the novel.

Despite the charge of the narrator's androcentric view of the fictional Umuofia, it is important to point out that the narrator does not project it as the only kind of community because of the references to contrary examples as in the case of Aninta where titled men do domestic chores (73) and other communities where women own the children. This is a realistic portrayal of Igboland or Africa that is not one community with one system or social organization. There are groups with matriarchal inclinations such the matrilineal Afikpo-Igbo and Ohafia-Igbo. Such communities and ethnic groups are also found in the Niger-Benue and Niger-Delta regions of Nigeria as well as countries like Ghana, Ivory Coast, Congo, South Africa, and many other parts of the African continent. It is not surprising that different areas of pre-colonial and postcolonial Igboland had and have structures of female assertiveness (Sofola 1998, Davis 1986: 242), complementality with men (Nnaemeka 2003), rights that surpass those of Western women (Leith-Ross 1939: 230-233) as well as areas of female subjugation (Okeke 2006: 26, Achufusi 1994: 173). Igbo women were kings and warriors (Achebe 2005, Okonjo 1976), titled "Lords" and power brokers (Chuku 2005, Jeffreys 1951), but often misrepresented in reports that are tainted by preconceived views of women's powerlessness. Adimora-Ezeigbo (1990) discusses the case of Basden whose long sojourn in Igboland did not erase his preconceived notions of female inferiority fortified by his association with Igbo male authority. However, a consideration of aspects of Igbo cosmology especially its connection with gender across communities will clarify the place of women in Igbo thinking and also inform Achebe's portrayal of womanhood in *Things* as we discuss the gender of God, female gods and priests, the earth goddess and nurturing, *omumu* theory of begetting, and woman as daughter and mother.

The Gender of God

We shall begin this section by using the name of the author of *Things Fall Apart* as a springboard for delving into the concept of Chi and Chukwu. Chinua in Chinua-Achebe is a short form of Chinualumogu (Chi, fight for me). Like many Igbo theophoric personal names such as Chukwudi (God exists), Chukwuma (God knows), AmaraChi (God's Grace), Ogechukwu (God's time) and many others, Chinualumogu is a short prayer that is based on belief in God and the superiority of the spiritual force. God is denoted by the Igbo word "Chukwu" that translates as Big/Great Spirit and regarded as the creator of all, hence the synonym, "Chineke," which means "the Spirit that creates." Chukwu was not originally gendered in Igbo language but the imposition of Christian categorization of God as male as well as the rendering of a non-gendered category in the gendered English language might have influenced the interpretation of Chukwu as male. The privileging of male power in the Victorian culture of British Colonial rulers in Nigeria as well as the elevated status of maleness in Christian religion might have influenced the translation of Igbo religious culture and concepts. Similar trends have been cited by Okonjo (1976), and Sofola (1998) in their discussion of the marginalization and erasure of the Omu, seat of female simultaneous rulership with a male Obi, in western Igbo areas and the strengthening of male privileging by colonial powers that favored Victorian patriarchy.

Igbo and African religions were disregarded by colonial authority and great effort was made to destroy them, on the pretext of any misconduct by a priest or priests, rather than attempt at correction or punishment. The wanton destruction of shrines and traditional museums notoriously called *Igbu mmuo* or "killing of the spirits" (Amankulor and Okafor 1988) was common in the early colonial period in Igboland. Archival records indicate letters concerning the proposed destruction of the shrines, the quality of ritual objects, and their value for British museums.[3] All these were part of the effort to destroy African culture and impose the culture of the conquerors; a tendency that was enforced through British education. What Robin Horton regards as the "devout approach" (2008: 169), whereby researchers who are influenced by the Christian education and religion bring such influence into their study of African religion, dominates current research on African spirituality. Seeking commonalities with the British was a way that the colonized used to show their equality and reestablish their damaged dignity, but this has had its toll on the Anglicization of aspects of African culture. Agbasiere refers to this tendency in her critique of equating the Igbo Chi to Christian guardian angel and even though she does not totally dismiss the comparison, she insists that it derives "from Judaeo-Christian or Graeco-Roman categories of supernatural beings" that is not based on the study of Igbo context (Agbasiere 2000: 54).

During my field work in Arochukwu in 1983, my questions about the gender of God were overlooked or politely ignored by informants but my field-representative, John Aghabanti, later explained that it was not very respectful to think of God in human terms. The use of the Igbo gender neutral pronoun "o" made it easy for him to talk about God without implying any gender. In 1991, during my field work in Izzi, I tried to use indirection to get at the people's notion of the gender of God. I began with questions about the gender of the mask-spirit that was enacted by the women and was bluntly told by the woman impersonator that "It is not a woman or a man;" but a spirit. The Chi concept would have assumed masculinity if not that it was initially equated to the Christian guardian angel that is open to all genders. In spite of this, scholars have tended to evoke masculinity in their explanation of the idea in English by using masculine nouns and pronouns that may arguably represent the generic man, but their use can nonetheless be misleading for non-insiders of the culture. Such references to Chi as the "divine particle in man by which he shares in the Supreme Being" (Ilogu 1974: 45) and "inner man" (Idowu 1976:87) tend to connote maleness even if it is not the intention of the writers who are constrained by lack of gender neutral pronouns in the English language. The Igbo believe that every individual has the *chi* essence that connects with the Ultimate Spirit. Chi, therefore, includes all in a common spiritual field and also equalizes through a common linkage to the Ultimate Spiritual Essence. The word *chi* denotes the guiding essence, spirit, energy; and vector of providence. According to Ikenga-Metuh,

> Every event in man's life, whether it be success or failure, is "Onatara chi" – destiny imprinted on his palm. *Chi* whether it be personal god, or personal destiny, finally derives from Chukwu – God … Chi could in fact be said to be the Igbo expression of God's providential care for each individual person. Chi is God's own representative in man … However, man can pray to his chi at any time to give him only good fortunes, or to withhold misfortune (Ikenga-Metuh 1982: 18).

The above delineation of *Chi* shows that the writer used "man" in generic terms to denote the Igbo word *mmadu* (person) and might not necessarily have intended to exclude women through the use. It is, therefore, important to clarify the presence of the *Chi* essence in every human being regardless of gender, class and other dichotomies because it is the divine quintessence from God's essence as Chi-ukwu (Big/Great God). The godly essence is invested on humans at creation and performs functions that are comparable though not analogous to the Christian guardian angel. Cardinal Arinze describes it as the spiritual-double of divine essence that God invests on every sentient being (Arinze 1970). It is the most powerful personal concept and driving force with achievement, guardian, and guiding principles. Malevolent spirits can weave misfortune so an individual constantly works with Chi to ensure success. The idea permeates the practices, roles, behavior and all aspects of Igbo system. It is expected to keep an individual on the right path where s/he reveres not just the Ultimate Spirit but human and other living things created by God.

There is constant communion with Chi through very short prayers that sometimes occur several times a day. There is also elaborate veneration at the shrine of Chi usually marked by the *oha* tree, whose leaves constitute the main substance of a special soup. In some areas such as among the Aro,[4] the shrine of Chi is marked by the *ogirinsi* tree whose leaves have special medicinal qualities and are used for ritual purposes. There are communal ceremonies and festivals that focus on Chi. Called Ime-Chi during the Ikeji festival of the Aro, Ogugo Chi in the Ezeagu clan in the northern Igbo, and Ilo Chi in Awka-Etiti and parts of Anambra, veneration of Chi is central in Igbo worship system, because it is the individual's immediate link to God.

Women take the veneration of Chi to heart because of gender subordination particularly when separated from their natal families and ancestral worship. The patri-local arrangement of many Igbo communities requires women to leave their natal homes at marriage to live in their husband's houses or family's households where they have little or no connection with the husband's family's ancestral spirits that are called upon in family prayers. In *Things*, Okonkwo officiates at the family shrine where he keeps "the wooden symbols of his personal god and of his ancestral spirits" and offers prayers to them "on behalf of himself, his three wives and eight children" (14). In situations as reflected in the novel, the women have spiritual recourse through their Chi even though they may partake of the family prayers. Women's personal spirits facilitate their engagement of daily problems. It is common to hear women refer to Chineke-umunwanyi (God of women, God who created women or God who is special to women) in discussing their luck or misfortune. Prayer to the godly essence is important in feelings of subordination because of God's compassion and inclusiveness of all in the godly fold. This is an equalizing and empowering concept that cancels class, gender and other barriers created by society. It enables a poor person or a woman to look at the rich man, challenge him and affirm "*Ibughi Chi m*" (You are not my God), which implies that both have equal claim to God and that the agency of Chi can avert any impending misfortune concocted by the powerful and can also reverse earthly fortunes. Chi is the basis of Igbo confidence and drive. This is reflected in *Things* through the affirmation of the boy from very poor background who "said yes very strongly; so his chi agreed" (27), and helped him to surpass his poor class situation. When the powerful Okonkwo shot at his wife, Ekwefi, her survival was attributed to the vigilance of her Chi as the priestess said: "Your chi is very much awake ..." (48).

Female Gods and Priests

There are Nigerian and African nations and communities with female Supreme Spirits. Awomekaso is the national goddess of Kalabari people (Nigeria) that helped the principality of Elem Kalabari to extend its suzerainty over about twenty three neighboring towns. The influence of the goddess facilitated the peaceful expansion of Kalabari through cultural and religious affiliations rather than warfare (Gabriel 1999: 35), which was the main path of the male gods of war. In the Delta region (Nigeria), the Supreme Deity and creator of Ogoni people is Waa Bari who is regarded as female. Her role and position stems from traditional thinking about creativity and motherhood. According to Paul Bedey,

> ... the Ogoni people have the implicit belief that this
> female creator resides in the earth and that man and
> all animals and plants are created out of the earth. All
> libations and incarnation to Waa Bari are poured on
> the earth and it is believed she receives it as the wine
> or water sinks down into the earth. The dead are buried
> in the earth to return to Waa Bari Ogoni from where
> they come. It is clear in the traditional belief of the
> people that Waa Bari Ogoni is omnipotent and omni-
> scient (84).

Unlike the Ogoni, many Igbo sub-groups did not gender God. The
non-gendered nature of God, however, does not exclude the institution of patriarchal gender power in Igbo societies, but it explains the
empowerment of women in spiritual practices; a situation that has
been noted in other African societies (Kilson 1976). In Igboland,
women and men function as priests, mediums, oracles and other
agents of the supernatural. They therefore have authority in spiritual
matters and this is linked to their non-gendered spiritual endow-
ment from God unlike many other world religions where priesthood
is strictly reserved for men. Spiritual signs from possession, prediction, reincarnation, dreams, and fortune-telling usually indicate the
one chosen for sacred orders. That person then goes into training to
learn the character of the divinity, its relation and particular servitude to God, as well as the laws, taboos, dances, and songs that go
with performance of functions that include offering of prayers and
sacrifices. Allied to the profession of priesthood is that of divination
and mediumship where women excel in varied functions as revealers,
fortune-tellers, and counselors. Compared to some other religions,
women are not marginalized in traditional African religions and
professions. Anti sums this up when he says that:

> The Jews had a rigid masculine concept of God who
> was the 'God of Abraham, Isaac, and Jacob', but not
> the God of Sarah, Rebecca, and Rachael ... In Islam,
> women could only lead prayers for a congregation of
> women. And in the mosque women are not to stand in
> the same row with the men but separately behind the
> rows of men. The situation is, however, not the same in
> Africa (Anti 2009).

From elevated positions in traditional religions, women encountered a dilemma in Islamic and Christian religions that were introduced to African societies, because they lost their preeminence as priests of the gods in religions that reserve priesthood for men only. Diop (1989) maintains that the Islamic incursion into Africa initiated cultural changes that were exacerbated by European colonialism and imperialism. The elevated position of African women through traditional religion is depicted in *Things* through the engagement of two priestesses of the Oracle. Our first glimpse of a priestess in the novel was at the visit of Okonkwo's father to the oracle, Agbala, for consultation about his unending poverty. The priestess, Chika, admonished him with great authority as she delivered the verdict, "You have offended neither the gods nor your fathers ... go home and work like a man!" (17-18). The next priestess we encounter is Chielo of Okonkwo's generation. The author describes her as an ordinary person; a widow with two children and a woman that shares a market shed with Ekwefi. In the world of the novel particularly from the perspective of the central character, Okonkwo, Chielo's female gender would have made her inferior to him. However, based on the principle of God's connection to all irrespective of human dichotomies like gender, Chielo is the one chosen as the voice of the oracle; an elevated spiritual position.

The oracle of the hills and caves is delineated as male, but the human power that drives it and proclaims its wishes is female. Chielo's spiritual power makes her superior to Okonkwo in her role as the priestess who deciphers and enforces the will of the unseen divine essence of the hills and caves. This is illustrated when she comes to Okonkwo's house to take away his favorite daughter, Ezinma. Okonkwo does not react in his usual overbearing manner towards women. He pleads with her, but she responds with godly authority as she evokes her power as the servant of the god and cows him to silence: "Does a man speak when a god speaks? Beware!" (101). Her treatment of Okonkwo is harsh and echoes Okonkwo's rough treatment of women. One can read her disdain for Okonkwo who in the past has shown disrespect for the earth goddess through his rash actions such as shooting at his wife and violence during the peace week (30). Her treatment of Ekwefi, Okonkwo's wife and Ezinma's mother, is different. She has a brief dialogue with Ekwefi, understands her anxiety as a mother and tries to assuage her fears by addressing Ezinma as her own daughter: "Come, my daughter ... I shall carry you on my back. A baby on its mother's back does not know that the way is long" (101).

The Earth Goddess and Omumu

Another important aspect of Igbo cosmology that connotes womanhood is Ani, the earth goddess. This is expressed in male personal names such as Nwale (child of the land), Ani-kwere (the land agrees) and Aniamalu (the land knows) as well as female names like Ana-ezi (bare earth) and Animma (beautiful earth). These names allude to the omnipresence, omniscience, strength and beauty of Ani. The use of Ani in both male and female names indicates some kind of neutrality, yet many communities conceive of Ani as a female spirit because of its nurturing aspects that coincide with traditional ideas of female fecundity, birthing, and creativity. From the physical earth, Ani is conceived of as the mother of human beings, food crops, trees, hills, caves, rivers and other things that stand on it. She is higher than other spirits such as the hills and streams because she is the mother of all. The mothering quality of Ani is used to build a huge ideology of reverence that permeates the conduct of the society. Like a mother, she is the nurturer, the regulator of codes of conduct of her children, and the enforcer of the laws though sanctions. Ilogu itemizes over twenty prohibitions or *nso-ala* in the moral and social codes of Ani (Ilogu 1974:38). The belief that nobody can hide an offence because of the omnipresence of the earth controls social behavior. The influence of Ani permeates the world of *Things* where she is portrayed as the goddess that is responsible for public morality, homicide, kidnapping, violence and many other crimes and offences. Iwe argues that any serious research on the foundations and principles of Igbo ethics must be based on the Igbo philosophy and theology of the earth goddess (Iwe 1988). He anchors his argument on the centrality of the goddess in the regulation of conduct and her superiority to other deities:

> One divinity, however, was beyond the capriciousness
> of Igbo men: that divinity is neither Igwe, nor even
> Chukwu, but Ala, the goddess of the earth. She was
> the one deity which no man or woman and no com-

munity could afford to offend, much less discard. If ever there was a supreme god among the Igbo it was Ala. A crisis in our institutions has obscured this fact (Iwe 1988).

Achebe's portrayal of Okonkwo's encounter with the earth goddess principle seems to concur with Iwe's idea above. We may applaud Okonkwo's rejection of weakness but his equation of that quality with women is unreasonable when he has strong wives that are largely responsible for his wealth and the running of his household. His fixation on exaggerated masculinity to the extent of showing disdain for womanhood is ill-conceived and even naïve for a lord of Umuofia who should understand the principle of omumu and reverence for the goddess as his contemporaries Ogbuefi Ezeudu and Obierika do. Conflict is unavoidable in human affairs, so the Igbo has a sacred week dedicated to Ani when altercation is not tolerated just as the Christians have a holy week before Easter replete with reconciliation and spiritual upliftment. Growing up, every child knows the severity of telling lies and can always ascertain his or her innocence by touching the earth and swearing by her. Okonkwo grew up in an Igbo community, albeit fictional, and should know the laws of Ani as well as the repercussions for contravening the moral codes of the sacred week. For him to show anger and go to the extent of beating someone is an offence against the earth goddess and more so when that person is a woman and mother that fully signifies *omumu*, in addition to being his wife.

Omumu is the principle of fecundity, begetting, and creativity. It is a life-giving essence that is also associated with the earth goddess concept. The ideology derives from gynecology and connects with diverse ideas evoked by the presence, being, sexuality, performance and function of a female-person and motherbeing. It permeates social psychology and inspires human action. It is the most important principle because of its function in continuity, nurturing, birth and death rites as well as connection with the supreme mother, earth. The ideology influences Chiweizu's idea of the womb as the seat of female power used to control men's access to food, sex, and continuity (Chiweizu 1990: 171). Chiweizu does not articulate the enabling stance of the motherbeing that indulges the childbeing, so his thesis appears to nullify the feminist agenda

13

as articulated by Ozumba believes (Ozumba 2005). Ironically, Chiweizu's notion unintentionally calls attention to the predicament of women, which Okonjo and Amadiume have tried to engage in their work on colonial and postcolonial transformations (Amadiume 2000, Okonjo 1976). Women are subordinated in contemporary Igbo and Nigeria affairs, and Nigeria continues to decline in world affairs for varied complex reasons, but the abuse of *omumu* through exaggerated negative masculinity and its negative effect on development is an issue that has not been addressed, but which is reflected in *Things* though Okonkwo's tragedy.

Okonkwo is a performer of masculinity who suppresses the female principle. His neurotic need to demonstrate continually his narrow conception of masculinity is not shared by other male characters such as Obierika and Ezeudu that criticize him for his lack of respect for the principle of *omumu*. He goes against the advice of the great lord of the land, Ogbuefi Ezeudu, by killing his foster son, Ikemefuna, in order to prove his bravery since he is "afraid of being thought weak" (61). He thereby commits a crime for which "the earth goddess wipes out whole families" (67). Okonkwo and his first wife have fostered Ikemefuna and Okonkwo loves him and takes him along to communal meetings "like a son, carrying his stool and his goat-skin bag" (28). This loving relationship is nurtured and cemented in the *usokwu*[5] of Okonkwo's wife. Regarded as the surrounding of the hearth, *usokwu* is the site of his primary bonding with other children while eating, joking, playing, and enjoying mother's stories. *Usokwu* bonding is the most reliable kin connection and it is based on the mothering culture. It is so important that it is simulated where physical women are absent as in men's masking cults where *omumu* is represented through a physical or abstract connection of the female essence such as ascribing the origin of the mask cult to a mother, invoking the mother essence in its inauguration, and incarnating a mother figure in mask-form (Okafor 1992). In *Things*, the *omumu* essence is reflected through oral saga that attributes the birth of the mask-spirits of ancestors to the earth goddess (88). At the funeral rites of passage ushering to earth the same Ezeudu who advised Okonkwo not to have a hand in killing Ikemefuna because "He calls you his father" (57), while the earth sends out ancestral spirits (represented in the mask-figures) to welcome him back to her bosom, Okonkwo is rejected by the earth. He inadvertently kills the dead man's son thereby committing a *female ochu* or manslaughter regarded as a serious offence against the earth goddess for which he is banished for seven years in accordance with the laws of the goddess.

Woman as Daughter and Mother

The gender hierarchy implied in the Western construction of woman (Eve) from man (Adam) is semantically encoded in the word "woman" comprising of "wo," which has no identity without the base "man" that has an independent identity. On the contrary, the Igbo terms for woman *(nwanyi)* and man *(nwoke)* have a common base, *nwa*, (child). The suffixes *anyi* and *oke* denote their biological differentiation while the base denotes commonality and equality just as the spiritual concept of *chi* does. In addition to this equality, the concept of *omumu* and its connection with the goddess principle give preeminence to the female in the tradition, but this superiority is mediated by patriarchal construction of the female as something that should be controlled. The basis of this thinking lies in the mystery of woman denoted in the term *anyi. Anyi* connotes *nwa-nyiri-anyi,* which refers to a child that is impossible or unworkable. It implies a problem that should be solved and the process of solution has given rise to varied arrangements that support female valuation and devaluation. This is similar to the Mandinka (Gambia and Senegal) belief that women are born with "immense creativity and energy" and are "unpredictable and mystically very hot, while men were stable and cool" (Weil 1998: 2). They therefore think that it is important to socialize women to become gentle like men. The Yoruba of Nigeria also believe in women's magical power that Gelede maskers try to appease and celebrate (Abiodun 1976:1-2). According to Gelede elders, "Women posses the secret of life itself, the knowledge and special power to bring human beings into the world and remove them" (Drewal and Drewal 1983: 8); this is their reason for trying to appease and negotiate female power through the mask ritual.

The Igbo woman has freedom and power that is her right from her Chi and enjoyed in her natal home, but a lot of this power is mediated during her relocation to a marital abode where she is faced with problems of adaptation and submission to new ways of her marital family. This is a situation that her husband does not face because he already understands his family's ways that he was nurtured in. In the novel, Achebe depicts womanhood that is enjoyable especially in the early years when a daughter is in her parental home without the constraints and demands of married life as seen from the relative independence of Ezinma and Obiageli; a freedom that is not allowed the boy, Nwoye, who is constrained by demands of becoming masculine. His humane, gentle and compassionate nature is ridiculed by his father who genders him to become masculine and this puts so much pressure on the boy that he eventually runs to the Christian mission. Unlike the son, Ezinma's feminine and masculine principles are encouraged to develop. She has some of her father's temperament but hers shows up in rare moments when she snaps at everyone "like an angry dog" (173). Okonkwo continually wishes that "she were a boy" (173), because of her intelligence, perception, and quickness that he regards as masculine traits. In spite of their father's domineering stance, the girls have liberties with him; they can correct, console, and admonish him in ways that most people cannot. Ezinma can command him to "finish" his food and Obiageli can tell him not to speak when he is eating but his son does not show such liberties. Ezinma grows up to be very beautiful and called "Crystal of Beauty as her mother had been called in her youth" (172). We are not shown her life as a married woman but the experiences of the wives depicted in the novel indicate that wifehood can be a joyful phase of a woman's life that goes with expectations and responsibilities, but also a challenging situation with levels of intimidation and subordination.

The first daughter in an Igbo family is usually designated as *ada*, but in usage, the term extends to all daughters or girls and women. The collective of daughters of a family or lineage is referred to as umu-ada. The group wields tremendous powers through its social and political roles at weddings, burials, family disputes and other occasions. Umu-ada is a positive association with authority and responsibilities that elicit reverence. However, the group sometimes abuses its power such as when it oppresses wives of the families. Marginalized from the center of power in their marital families, these women fare better in their natal families where some of them control their brothers and their wives. In *Things*, the daughters of

Uchendu's family return from their marital homes to celebrate their brother's marriage ceremony. They also try to enforce the expectation of womanhood through a ceremony of virtue during which they try to browbeat the new bride with questions about her virginity and faithfulness. People usually try not to get involved in the affairs of or incur the anger of the tough group. This is why the men and the wives of Uchendu's extended family watch from a distance (132).

Marriage is an expectation in Igboland and the full grown daughter in her prime is the pride of her family because of the promise of *omumu*. *Omumu* brings honor that is realized through the agency of the physical woman. This helps us to appreciate why Okonkwo persuades his daughters not to marry in exile so that he will benefit from the honor that their marriage will bring. The greatest expectation is that of motherhood that brings the new generation and ensures continuity. Motherhood is usually attained through wifehood, but there are communities where mother-hood can be attained without wifehood in special circumstances such as where a woman refuses to marry, does not get her desired spouse, or becomes the husband of another woman for reasons of continuity. In traditional societies, there are rituals associated with the process of enabling a woman to transcend gender and marry a woman (Amadiume 1997:163). This situation widens the roles and expectation of the woman-husband, who takes on the responsibilities of a son that retains the family's name and ensures continuity. It also guarantees the maintenance of family property, old people, and family traditions. This practice is found in other patrilineal African societies such as among the Kikuyu of Kenya (Ngaruiya 2005), Fon of Benin and Lovedu of Southern Africa (Greene 1998). The arrangement centers the woman as the house-hold head and promotes matriarchal control but it is based on patrilineal concerns for the continuation of the family through a male hair that the woman's wife is expected to produce. Thus, women's subordination is not eliminated but assumes another patriarchal guise. It is driven by patriarchy as the woman-husband dictates the sexual partner of the wife and owns the children of the wife. The female husband is also the senior mother of the children born by her wife thereby expressing *omumu* nurturance through her wife's children even when she also realizes the same through her own biological children.

In modern African societies, many women do operate like men by taking on masculine responsibilities even though they have not gone through any ritual of incorporation to manhood and do not need to, because many (not all) barriers are officially lifted even though gender constraints still operate through patriarchal customs and practices. They do not necessarily marry wives, but can expand their social, political, and economic positions to become great mothers in their natal households and communities. Modern exigencies necessitate this unprecedented expansion of women's roles and expectations outside wifehood. Abstract, biological and sociological mothering gives daughters tremendous power as they express the care-giving quality of *omumu*. Omumu power derives from mother's blood and/ or the socializing influence of the nurturer. It is a huge concept in Igbo psychology because of its function as the cohesive glue that binds siblings and families. According to Nzegwu:

> Every *usokwu* is a nodal point of power that derives not from the spiritual *ofo*(authority) of a mother's husband but from her own natal family. It is the center of child socialization activities ... Mother's blood provides the cohesive glue that binds siblings, which men's blood oaths attempt to mimic ... The basis of a mother's power is her provision of the critical organ that housed all children during their most vulnerable state of life (Nzegwu 2005).

We contend that it is not just the provision of the critical organ but the belief in that organ as well as actions that are perceived to be based on that organ that binds. Igbo people recognize biology but emphasize caring for a child like *nwa omuru na afo* (a child of her womb), which underlines nurturing and socialization. Similarly, they recognize the sociological father of a child when the biological is not the mother's husband and the official provider. Thus, even though the reproductive principle in *omumu* finds its bearing from the bio-logic of *nne* or mother, it is not limited to it. Mother-being is conceptualized in terms of function-performance as well as spiritual and creative terms or what Opara and Eboh regard as the "palpable panegyrics of creative mothering" (2005). They argue that biological mothering is similar to creative mothering which is artistic mothering and that both are women's vehicles for transcendence and freedom. This partly explains why creative groups such as dance ensembles and mask cults frequently require mother figures that provide the binding principle of identity and oneness. Whether creative, biological or function-performing, the physical woman or daughter is implicated in the philosophy of *omumu*.

Conclusion

Our discussion of womanhood in *Things* has intersected with the hero's characterization in order to create more understanding of womanhood by engaging his naive view of womanhood that contributed to his predicament in the novel. In Umuofia community where the spiritual and biological principle of *omumu* is elevated and revered in spite of the patriarchal organization of the community, Okonkwo appears immature because of his actions that show disregard for *omumu*. He has a fixation on narrow masculinity and this often drives him to negativity. He looks down on women, is scornful of humane qualities in his son, beats his wife, kills his foster son, kills his friend's son, kills himself, and incurs the wrath of the goddess. His masculinity is a guise to hide his fear of being perceived as a weak person, but he is weak. He puts on a guise of arrogance to hide his weakness and exhibits bravado and intimidation of those he perceives as weak or under his authority. This is in utter disregard of the spiritual principle of the land and this drives his tragedy. The author seems to send a warning to those who lack understanding of Igbo womanhood and the centrality of *omumu*, and therefore tend to deride the female essence in ways that connote self derision. It is self delusion for anyone to deride *omumu* because everyone springs from and benefits from *omumu* largesse. Okonkwo's denial and suppression of whatever he considers female be it a human trait, a physical woman or a man with feminine qualities signify his inability to accept the totality of his selfhood that sprung from a woman's *omumu* and embodies female principles.

Igbo womanhood manifests in various ways, but we have concentrated on the salient commonalities that connect with the *omumu* principle of fecundity, begetting, and creativity. As a principle evoked by gynecological presence and expectation, *omumu* bestows power on women. As daughter, wife, and mother, women are revered because of that principle that extends to the goddess but patriarchal social organization tends to constrain this power while matriarchal organization tends to facilitate it. Both of these organizations are reflected in *Things* even though the patriarchal is the focus of the novel. Another important concept that factors in womanhood is the Chi principle that equalizes all irrespective of hierarchies created by human beings. It is a principle that helps individuals to transcend boundaries as the hero of the novel does in transcending his poor class background and as the widow, Chielo, does in transcending gender barrier to have spiritual authority that makes her superior to the indomitable man of the novel.

Unlike Chi that is common to all, the *omumu* principle is special to women. It is a huge principle that drives the psychology of traditional people and motivates their valuation of women. *Omumu* concept privileges women, but in practice the advantage is mediated by the same essence of its power. *Omumu* essence makes possible the devaluation of the human female by patriarchal power because of the inclusive stances of the mother being. The motherbeing has the power to dominate but it rules by benevolence and inclusiveness. It makes possible the sharing of power with childbeings particularly the type that are directly excluded from the ownership of omumu essence, but who nonetheless can exploit its benevolence because of their kin connection. In the end, Igbo womanhood is profound, complex, and the rock of Igbo communities, but it remains a kind of paradox because of *omumu* nature that has led researchers to conflicting conclusions about women's power, powerlessness, compliancy, and assertiveness. Igbo womanhood is an enigma because of its basis on this significant Igbo philosophical concept.

Notes

1. Referred to as *Things and the novel* in this essay.
2. "Female-person" is deliberately used to delineate the equality of man and woman in the Igbo language signification.
3. CSE 36/1/11 MINLOC 17/1/18, Enugu, National Archives.
4. Arochukwu is a kingdom in Abia State, Nigeria with satellite towns, villages, and lineages in other States. Citizens of the original and satellite locations are regarded as Aro people.
5. "Around the cooking stove" is comparable to the kitchen table culture of western societies.

Primary Source

Achebe, Chinua. *Things Fall Apart.* New York: Anchor Books, 1994.

Works Cited

Abiodun, Roland. "The Concept of Women in Traditional Yoruba Religion and Art." Paper presented at the Conference on Nigerian Women and Development. University of Ibadan, 1976, 26-30.

Achebe, Nwando. *Farmers, Traders, Warriors, and Kings Female Power and Authority in Northern Igboland, 1900-1960.* Portsmouth NH: Greenwood, 2005.

Achufusi, G. I. "Female Individuality and Assertiveness in the Novels of Ifeoma Okoye." In *Feminism in African Literature.* Ed. Helen Chukwuma. Enugu, Nigeria: New Generation Ventures, 1994, 159-175.

Adams, Don, and Arlene Goldbard. *Creative community: the art of cultural development.* New York, NY: Rockefeller Foundation, Creativity & Culture Division, 2001.

Agbasiere, Joseph Theresa. *Women in Igbo Life and thought.* New York, NY: Routledge, 2000.

Aja, Egbeke. "Changing moral values in Africa: An essay in ethical relativism." *The Journal of Value Inquiry* 31.4 (2004): 531-543.

Arinze, Francis A. *Sacrifice in Ibo Religion.* Ibadan, Nigeria: Ibadan University Press, 1970.

Akachi Ezeigbo, Theodora. Traditional Women's Institutions in Igbo Society: Implications for the Igbo Female Writer." *African Languages and Cultures* 3.2 (1990):149-165.

Akers, Ronald L. and Gary F. Jensen. *Social learning theory and the explanation of crime: a guide for the new century.* New Brunswick, NJ: Transaction, 2003.

Amadiume, Ifi. *Daughter of the Goddess, Daughters of Imperialism. African Women Struggle for Culture, Power and Democracy.* New York, NY: Zed Books, 2000.

_____. *Re-inventing Africa: matriarchy, religion, and culture.* London: Zed Books, 1997.

_____. *Male Daughters, Female Husbands: Gender and Sex in an African Society.* London, UK: Zed books, 1987.

Amankulor, J. N. and Okafor, Chinyere G. "Continuity and Change in Traditional Nigerian Theatre among the Igbo in the Era of Colonial Politics." *Ufahamu* 26.3 (1988): 35-50.

Anti, Kenneth Kojo. "Women In African Traditional Religions." Paper presented at Eastern Washington University, 2009. http://www. mamiwata.com/women.html

Awason, Susanna. Yene. "Hegemonic Masculinity as a Distorted Development Paradigm for Africa. *Codesria Bulletin* 3 & 4 (2005).

Chinweizu *Anatomy of female power*. Lagos, Nigeria: Pero Press, 1990.

Chuku, Gloria. *Igbo Women and Economic Transformation in Southeastern Nigeria, 1900-1960*. New York, NY: Routledge 2005.

Chukwuma, Helen. "Introduction: The Identity of Self." In *Feminism in African Literature*. Ed. Helen Chukwuma. Enugu, Nigeria: New Generation Ventures, 1994. 1-21.

Davies, Carole Boyce. "Motherhood in the Works of Male and Female Igbo Writers: Achebe, Emecheta, Nwapa, and Nzekwu." *Ngambika: Studies of Women in African Literature*. Ed: Carole Boyce Davies and Anne Adams Graves. Trenton, NJ: Africa World Press, 1986. 241-56.

Diop, Cheikh A. *The Cultural Unity of Black Africa: The Domains of Matriarchy and Patriarchy in Classical Antiquity*. London: Karnak House, 1989.

Drewal, Henry John and Margaret Drewal. *Gelede: Art and Female Power Among the Yoruba*. Bloomiongton: Indiana University Press, 1983.

Egbujie, Ihemalol I. *The Hermeneutics of the African Traditional Culture*. Boston: Omenana Publishers, 1985.

Greene, B. "The institution of woman-marriage in Africa : A cross-cultural analysis." *Ethnology* 37.4 (1998): 395-412

Idowu, Bolaji. *African Traditional Religion: A Definition*.1976.

Idowu, E. B. *African Traditional Religion: A Definition*. London, S. C. M. Press Limited, 1976.

Ifeka-Moller, Caroline. 1975. "Female Militancy and Colonial Revolt: The Women's War of 1929." In *Perceiving Women,* ed. Shirley Ardener. New York, NY: John Wiley, 1975. 127- 157.

Ifemesia, Emmanuel, I. "Prayer in Traditional Religion: Some Traditional Models" (A case study) in *Religion and African Culture* ed. Elochukwu E. Uzoukwu. Enugu: Spiritan Publishers, 1988.

Ikenga-Metuh, Emefie. "Religious Concepts in West African Cosmogonies: A Problem of Interpretation." *Journal of Religion in Africa*, Vol. 13, Fasc. 1 (1982), pp. 11-24

Ilogu, Edmund. *Christianity and Ibo Culture*. Brill Archive, 1974. 262 pages. Brill.

Iwe, N. S. S. "Igbo Deities." Paper presented at the 1988 Ahịajọkụ Lecture (Onugaotu). http://ahiajoku.igbonet.com/1988/

Iwuka, Alosius Emeka. *Aspects of Ibo Cosmological Ideas.* Lagos, Nigeria: Ambix Publishers, 2002.

Jeffreys, M. J. W. "The winged solar disk or The Itci Facial Scarification." *Journal of the International African Institute* 21.2 (1951): 93-111.

Kalu, Ogbu U. *The Embattled Gods: Christianization of Igboland 1841-1991.* Lagos: MINAJ Publishers, 1996.

Kilson, Marion. "Women In African Traditional Religions." *Journal of Religion in Africa* 8.2 (1976): 133-143.

Leith-Ross, Sylvia. *African Women: A Study of the Ibo in Nigeria.* London, UK: Routledge and Kegan Paul, 1939.

Mbiti, John S. *African Religions and Philosophy.* London: Heinemann, 1969.

_____. "the Role of Women In African Traditional Religion." *Cahiers des Religions Africaines* 22 (1988), 69-82.

Ngaruiya, Wairimu and William O'Brien, "Revisiting "Woman-Woman Marriage": Notes on Gikuyu Women." In *African Gender Studies.* Ed. Oyeroke Oyewumi. New York: Palgrave Macmillan, 2005. 145-166.

Nnaemeka, Obi, "Nego-Feminism: Theorizing, Practicing, and Pruning Africa's Way." SIGNS v29n2, 2003, 1-29.

Nwapa, Flora. "Women and Creative Writing in Africa." In *Sisterhood: Feminisms and Power from Africa to the Diaspora.* Ed. Obi Nnaemeka. Trenton: Africa World Press, 1998. 89-100.

Nzegwu, Nkiru. "The Epistemological Challenge of Motherhood to Patriliny" *JENdA: A Journal of Culture and African Women Studies,* 5 (2004) jendajournal.com (accessed March 20, 2008).

Obiezu, Emeka. *Towards a Politics of Compassion: Socio-political Dimensions of Christian Responses to Suffering.* AuthorHouse, 2008.

Okafor, Chinyere G. "From the Heart of Masculinity: Ogbodo Uke Women's Masking." *Research in African Literatures* (The Ohio State University), 25. 4, (1994): 7-17.

_____. "The Rejected Corner Stone: Women In Igbo Mask Theater." *Africana Studies and Research Center Newsletter* (Cornell University), 4, 1 (1992B): 19-23, 27-31.

Okeke, Phil E. Reconfiguring traditional women's rights and social status in contemporary Nigeria." *Africa Today,* 47.1 (2000): 30-49.

Okonjo, Kamene. "The Dual-Sex Political System in Operation: Igbo Women and Community Politics in Midweatem Nigeria" In *Women In Africa: Studies in Social and Economic Change.* Ed. Hafkin,

Nancy and Edna g. Bay. Stanford, CA: Stanford University Press, 1976, 45-57.

Omoyajowo, Joseph A. "The Role of Women in African Traditional Religion and Among the Yoruba." In Olupona, Jacob, Ed. *African Traditional Religions in Contemporary Society*, New Era Books, January 1991.

Opara, Chioma and M P. Eboh. "On the African Concept of Transcendence: Conflicting Nature, Nurture and Female Creativity." Paper presented at the International Society for Universal Dialogue – 6th Congress, Helsinki, Finland, 2005.

Ozumba, Goddy. "Gender-Sensitivity In Igbo Culture: A Philosophical Re-appraisal." *Quodlibet Journal.* 7.2 (2005). http://www.Quodlibet.net (assessed March 26, 2008).

Sofola, Z. "Feminism and African Womanhood," In *Sisterhood: Feminisms and Power from Africa to the Diaspora.* Nnaemeka, obioma. Trenton, NJ: Africa World Press. 1998. 51-64.

Steady, Philomina C. "An Investigative Framework for Gender Research in Africa in the New Millennium" In *African Gender Studies.* Oyewumi, Oyeronke. New York, NY: Palgrave Macmillan, 2005. 313-332.

Strong-Leek Linda "Reading as a Woman: Chinua Achebe's '*Things Fall Apart*' and feminist criticism". *African Studies Quarterly* 5.2 (2001) [online] URL:http://web.africa.ufl.edu/asq/v5/v5:2a2.htm

Uchem, Rose N. *Overcoming Women's Subordination in the Igbo African Culture and in the Catholic Church: Envisioning an Inclusive Theology with Reference to Women.* Universal-Publishers, 2001.

Weil, Peter. "African women's masking customs documented." *University of Delaware UpDate.* 17.35 (1998).

Zahan, D. "Ornament and color in Black Africa." In *Beauty by Design.* Ed. M. T. Brincard. Miami, 1984.

CHAPTER 2

AND THE TRUTH IS MADE MANIFEST: THE STRONG ONES BEHIND OKONKWO

Chioma Opara

"Truth can break a bow poised to shoot"

Ngugi, *Devil on the Cross*, 215

Truth in literature has over the years been controversial and in its wake have arisen other contentions on realism, idealism, fact, what is and what should be. This essay touches on the ramifications of truth. It argues that the truth which Achebe set out to tell in *Things Fall Apart* about Africa may not be the entire truth. It argues that the women in Okonkwo's life both on the mundane and ethereal levels appear to be a shade stronger than him. Basing our discourse on Alfred Adler's basic factors of human behavior, we shall conclude that Okonkwo is not only obsessed by the fear of being thought weak but by the fear of some of these women whom he had assaulted publicly. This is a distinct function of his inferiority complex and the incessant drive to lead as Subject and Absolute.

Things Fall Apart is a putative item of 'rebranding'.[1] Africa had been branded dark, immature, inhuman and primitive by white colonialists on a civilizing mission. Chinua Achebe maintains that he felt impelled to write the novel after reading the negative portraiture of Africa in colonial literary works by Joyce Cary and Joseph Conrad. He articulates his strong belief in the moral power of fiction thus: "It began to dawn on me that although fiction was undoubtedly fictitious; it could also be true or false, not with the truth or falsehood of a news item but as to its disinterestedness, its intention, its integrity" (Ruth Franklin) Achebe thus set out to make his fiction true with a measure of "disinterestedness" and "integrity", depicting the heartland of Africa which is not in the least darkened.

Nigerian female writer, Akachi Adimora Ezeigbo, who incidentally hails from the same geographical area as Achebe – Anambra State in South Eastern Nigeria – does not totally agree with him. Convinced that Achebe's story is not entirely true, she put pen to paper. According to Susan Arndt:

> In an interview, Akachi Adimora Ezeigbo stressed that she began to write only because she was worried about Achebe's power to define the "true Africa". In search of the place where the rain began to beat the Igbo, she brings women back into history in the first volume of her trilogy, *The Last of the Strong Ones* (48).

Ezeigbo, it would seem, tries to tell the "true" story through the notes of female narrators interwoven by a captivating herstory in a historical novel (Opara "Fleshing",2008). Achebe's controlling purpose, his truth, which strove to debunk colonial myth, was in effect debunked by the feminist–conscious Ezeigbo thirty-eight years later.

A writer is, in the main, seen as "the persuasive purveyor of the truth". The truth is synonymous with accuracy, integrity, sincerity. Max Eastman contends that the real function of the writer is to make his reader perceive what he sees and imagine what he already knows. In his own words:

> The 'literary mind' is simply the unspecialized amateur mind of pre-scientific days attempting to persist and taking advantage of its verbal facility to create the impression that it is uttering the really important

'truths'. Truth in literature is the same as truth outside of literature i.e. systematic and publicly verifiable knowledge. The novelist has no magic short cut to that present state of knowledge in the social sciences which constitutes the 'truth' against which his world, his fictional reality, is to be checked (Wellek and Warren 33).

The primary responsibility of the writer who seeks to inform and teach, is to tell the truth. Aestheticians, in their quest for the purity of art do not believe in the extrinsic values of literature. Macleish in *Ars Poetica* proffers the following formula:" A poem is equal to: not true" (Wellek and Warren 35).

Distinctions have been drawn between true and the truth. A poem may not be true but it is truth-like. The opposite of fiction is not truth but fact or time and space existence. (Wellek and Warren 34). The dialectic of fact and truth is quite expansive. The axiom that truth is stronger than fiction has spawned faction. While Plato frowned upon "second-hand reflection" of truth by the poet, Aristotle defended the poet. He asserts that the object of poetry is universal truth. It is his conviction that the poet delineates a "more significant kind of probability than the mere factual recording of the historian" (Daiches 129). Surely, probability, possibility, truth and true not only co-exist but coalesce in the polemics of accuracy and reality in literature.

We shall in this essay make a modest attempt at plumbing the depths of gender relations and relatedness in *Things Fall Apart* to extract the truth while accenting the centrality rather than marginality of women. These women who are the strong ones will be categorized according to the space or *Ilo*. They will include Okonkwo's wives in the patriarchal space, his deceased mother's presence in his motherland and the overarching figure of the earth goddess, Ani in the ethereal space. Okonkwo's chequered life will be linked to his frayed nerves, a corollary of his inferiority complex and his incessant drive to lead as Subject and Absolute. We shall conclude that the tragic hero's fear of some of these women as well as his obsession with unwomanly acts constitutes the matrix of weakness which glaringly haunts his entire life.

The anthropological significance of *Things Fall Apart* cannot be underestimated. The gaps however reside in patent inaccuracies as regards power-sharing and gender relations. 'Zulu Sofola has emphatically stated that the world view of the African is rooted in a philosophy of holistic harmony and communalism rather than in the individualistic isolationism characteristic of European thought (54). This is hinged on relatedness and co-rulership. She cites Kamene Okonjo to underscore the principle of relatedness:

> The African woman has not been inactive, irrelevant and silent. Rather, African tradition has seen the wisdom of a healthy social organization where all its citizens are seen to be vital channels for a healthy and harmonious society. Hence the establishment of a dual-sex power structure which is lacking in European and Arab cultures (54).

It would seem that the neatly structured Umuofia society is denuded of a "dual-sex power structure". This gap is promptly filled in Ezeigbo's The *Last of the Strong Ones* where we are presented with the inner council – Obuofo – comprising four women and twelve men that focused on governance in Umuga.

Much as Achebe has failed to include relatedness and co-leadership in his "truth", the dominance of the dynamic female self in the vital essence of Okonkwo is palpable. He is introduced to us as a celebrity in the nine villages and even beyond. "Okonkwo's fame had grown like bush fire in the harmattan... When he walked his heels hardly touched the ground" (3). This larger than life figure with a very humble beginning towered above his peers in every *Ilo* or space. He was industrious as he was successful. The famed wrestler had thrown Amalinze the Cat in the wrestling *ilo*. He ranked quite high in the spiritual realm of the nine *egwugwu* or masked spirits who administered justice in the clan. He was according to existentialist philosophy, the Subject, the One, who wielded enormous authority over his children and his three wives, – the Other. The patriarch, Okonkwo, was high-handed and insensitive in his patrilocal, patrilineal and patriarchal household where his word was law. Beneath the veneer of brashness and intransigence was a vein of inferiority complex as well as weakness. Austrian psychologist, psychiatrist and founder of the school of individual psychology, Alfred Adler, cited by Zahar avers that, "Human beings in general try to compensate their inferiority complexes by mani-festing a fictitious superiority vis-à-vis others" (Zahar 49). In his will to power, the ambitious Okonkwo, overwhelmed by daunting social realities surrounding his lowly circumstances and embar-rassing parentage, suffers from a vitiating inferiority complex.

Okonkwo invariably displays fitful bouts of aggression which may be misplaced. When Obierika told Okonkwo that the deceased Ndulue and his wife Ozoemena were so close that he could not take any decision without consulting her, Okonkwo retorted, "I did not know that... I thought he was a strong man in his youth (48). The reply implies that Okonkwo doubted Ndulue's strength and firmness of character as a man[2]. This explains why Okonkwo is not in the least demonstrative in his marital affairs. He is indeed loath to express emotions of love for his women. Uxorious proclivities, in his opinion, verge on weakness. This also explains his excessive use of sexist terms. He would rather argue that Nwoye resembles his mother, his first wife, than his lazy father Unoka. Like a vicious circle, the very weakness he abhors dogs him and sticks out like a sore thumb in his own character enmeshed in a maze of fear. This psychological dent which festers in Okonkwo is glaring in his exhibition of "human behaviour – the will to power and a concomitant inferiority, complex" (see Opara, "The Concept of Otherness 201). The incessant urge to acquire titles is power-related and borders on an attempt to hide his inadequacies. His impatience with less successful men is an index to his subconscious severance with any reminder of his past. His brusqueness with Osugu whom he addressed as a woman simply because he had no titles reeks of misogyny laced with sadism. I have stated elsewhere that "Okonkwo's tragic flaws reside in his misogyny, machismo and hubris which tend to manifest in streaks of violence" ("Woman" 153). Obi Nnaemeka on her own part opines that Okonkwo is not an 'ideal' Igbo man. As she puts it, 'Okonkwo is a flawed man, a marginal character, because he is excessive – excess is an aberration that his culture relegates to the margins of society" (141).

Accordingly, Okonkwo's psychological blotches constitute a patent chink in his armour. He was, however, subtly assisted by the quintessential mother of the family – Nwoye's mother who lent him a hand whenever it was necessary. She is unarguably the mother of the entire family including the overweening Okonkwo. This strong female character was never named in the novel because she is an icon of maternal nurturance and vitality. When Ogbuefi Udo's wife was killed in Mbaino, Ikemefuna and a young virgin were offered to Umuofia clan in propitiation. Ikemefuna thus joined the Okonkwo household and he was in Nwoye's mother's custody for three years. Directly Nwoye's mother heard that Ikemefuna was about to be taken away to be killed, "she immediately dropped the pestle with which she was grinding pepper, folded her arms across her breast and sighed, "poor child" (41). Ekwefi and Ezinma communicated with similar kinetics or body language – arms folded against their breasts (p.75; p.116). This gesture falls under the semiotics unique to the African woman. It represents productivity as well as nurturance and fellow-feeling. Where Ezeigbo employs the womb in *The Last of the Strong Ones* as a metaphor of dynamic motherhood, Achebe accents the breast as a symbol of maternal dynamics and nature. The proverb, "looking at a king's mouth one would think that he never sucked at his mother's breast" (19) underpins the indispensability of this vital female organ in human development. Jungian analyst, Eric Neumann, cited in Andrienne Rich postulates:

> The feminine, the giver of nourishment becomes everywhere a revered principle of nature, on which man is dependent in pleasure and pain. It is from this eternal experience of man who is as helpless in his dependence on nature as the infant in his dependence on his mother that the mother-child figure is inspired forever anew (34).

The appellation Nwoye's mother stands out as a mother-child figurine emblemizing filial dependence and evoking the umbilical cord that has joined two bodies together. The breast, womb, navel, pregnancy and suckling are all symbols which represent nurturing female principle that controls and sustains man and the entire humankind.

By virtue of Nwoye's mother's position as the first wife in Okonkwo's household, she takes the most important position in the hierarchy of wives. Achebe deftly limns this fact in his graphic portraiture of Anasi – Nwoye's mother's counterpart in Nwakibie's household. Anasi is the first of Nwakibie's nine wives. In the social drinking of palmwine, the other wives stand waiting for her to drink before they can take their own drink. She is described as:

> a middle-aged woman, tall and strongly built. There was authority in her bearing and she looked every inch the ruler of the womenfolk in a large and prosperous family. She wore the anklet of her husband's titles, which the first wife alone can wear (14).

This implies that it is only Nwoye's mother who can wear the anklets of Okonkwo's titles. She is, as a matter of course, invested with an inviolable aura of authority and the attendant substratum of invigorating matriarchal ambience.

Her potency lies in her maternal role both in her hut and in the wider *ilo*. Her timely intervention in Ojiugo's case is quite spectacular. In a bid to protect Ojiugo, she lied to Okonkwo that Ojiugo had asked her to take charge of her children before going out to plait her hair. She also took Ojiugo's children to her own hut and fed them along with her own children.

Next in the hierarchy of wives is Achebe's second wife Ekwefi who could be described as the most assertive and dauntless of the three. The village belle, Ekwefi, had admired Okonkwo greatly as he excelled in her favourite sport, wrestling, which is a traditionally male sport. Since Okonkwo was too poor to pay her bride price, she was married off to another man, Anene. In the vein of Flora Nwapa's eponymous heroine, Efuru, Ekwefi defied the bride price tradition, fled her home and headed for Okonkwo's household:

> It has been early in the morning. The moon was shining. She was going to the stream to fetch water. Okonkwo's house was on the way to the stream. She went in and knocked on the door and he came out. Even in those days he was not a man of many words. He just carried her into his bed and in the darkness began to feel around her waist for the loose end of her cloth (76).

Their marriage was thus contracted, consummated and sealed by the bold step she took that early morning.

Clearly Ekwefi was one of the few people who could dare the daunting Okonkwo. He conceded that, "Of his three wives, Ekwefi was the only one who would have the audacity to bang on his door" (53). Ekwefi's courage is graphically dramatized on the night that the priestess, Chielo, carried Ekwefi's only daughter, Ezinma, away at the instance of Agbala, the Oracle of the Hills and Caves. Much as Chielo threatened anyone who should follow her, Ekwefi trudged along on a long, dreary and weary walk. Okonkwo could not dare call Chielo's bluff and only met Ekwefi at the entrance of the cave after her long walk which could be likened to an epic march. They both waited there until their child was eventually released and taken back to her room. Ekwefi had even sworn that, "If she heard Ezinma cry she would rush into the cave to defend her against all the gods…" (76). Such a fearless and focused woman stood her ground whenever the need arose. It would seem that she and her daughter Ekwefi had a way with Okonkwo. He had forbidden Ekwefi to give Ezinma eggs because children were traditionally not allowed to eat eggs. Mother and child conspired to eat the egg in the privacy of their bedroom. Ezinma in defiance then developed a "keener appetite for eggs" and enjoyed above all "the secrecy with which she now ate them" (54).

Surely Ezinma had a hold on Okonkwo. This mystery child or *Ogbanje* whom the priestess Chielo refers to as her child and who could also be summoned by Agbala the Oracle of the Hills and Caves, had an aura of mystique about her. Although Ezinma and her two half-sisters, Obiageli and Nkechi served Okonkwo's meals, she alone could order him to eat. In the wake of the brutal murder of Ikemefuna, Okonkwo lost his appetite for food. Ezinma forced him to eat by insisting, "You have not eaten for two days… so you must finish this" (44). She also wielded a strong influence over her half-sister Obiageli (122).

Okonkwo revered and even feared this precocious child whom he viewed as iconic. Little wonder he wished on several occasions that she were a boy:

> Okonkwo was very lucky with his daughters. He never stopped regretting that Ezinma was a girl. Of all his children she alone understood his every mood. A bond

of sympathy had grown between them as the years had
passed (122).

The bond which was non-existent between Okonkwo and his
sons became very strong between Okonkwo and Ezinma. She was
quite relevant in Okonkwo's most depressing moments. At the
peak of the political crisis, during his incarceration, she went to
Obierika's compound to discuss possible remedies from Umuofia.
Obierika had attended a secret meeting and his wives were not
privy to the meeting probably because it was gender-specific.
Ezeigbo has faulted Achebe in this regard. In her historical novel,
The Last of the Strong Ones she demonstrated that women were
part of the decision-making process in the course of the colonial
invasion. Not only did women lend their support through the
Inner Council – Obuofo, other female groups such as Alutaradi
(Association of married women); Umuada (Association of daughters); Oluada (Voice of Women); played visible roles in the wider
system. Achebe on the contrary tells an important story without
involving women politically. Female voices are in the main stifled.
We are introduced to Okonkwo's third wife, Ojiugo, by her wail
and whimper which are non-verbal, vocal forms of communication. She had been beaten "very heavily" by her fiery husband for
coming home late. He consequently broke the Week of Peace in
his anger. "But Okonkwo was not the man to stop beating somebody half-way through, not even for fear of a goddess" (21).

The fear of a goddess is expressly secondary to the fear of being
thought weak. The beating of Ojiugo is redolent of his assault on
Ekwefi during the season of the New Yam Festival. Okonkwo had
given her a "sound beating" for cutting a few leaves off the banana
tree. Okonkwo, who had never killed a rat with his gun, shot at
Ekwefi for taunting him about guns that never shot. That was a
sore point because Okonkwo has always had a heavy chip on his
shoulder as a result of his father's laziness and weakness, which he
never wanted to be associated with.

His impatience and fury against these two women, whom
he definitely loves, obviously stem from his desperate attempt to
couch his emotions and attendant weakness for them, in sense-
less violence. He would rather be castigated for brutality than be

associated with unmasculine sentiments. These are nuances of encrusted inferiority complex.

Although Ojiugo may not be as assertive and bold as Ekwefi, her name evokes aquiline beauty. The appellation Ojiugo is an amalgam of beauty and strength. In Igbo, *Oji* means Kolanut and *Ugo* denotes the eagle. Accordingly Ojiugo symbolizes nurturant beauty and aquiline strength laced with grace and delicacy. Ojiugo's implicit strength, as a matter of course, lies in her nurturant and aesthetic essence. The youngest wives in African families are in most cases their husbands' favourites. Achebe has definitely not cast Ojiugo as her husband's toy. In spite of her age, beauty and position she exudes poise, integrity and selflessness. She altruistically offers to come home from Obierika's wedding feast to serve Okonkwo's meal. It is pertinent to note that Okonkwo's wives are diametrically opposed to Ezeulu's wives in *Arrow of God.* The women in the polygynous set up in *Things Fall Apart* hold together in female solidarity unlike Ezeulu's wives who continually dwell on bickering and gossips. It is pertinent to note that the female bonding depicted by Achebe extends beyond wives' relationship to mother-daughter bond. We are told that Ezinma is "the centre of her mother's world" (53). In the words of Adrienne Rich, mother-daughter bond is "resonant with charges... the flow of energy between two biologically alike bodies, one of which has lain in amniotic bliss inside the other, one of which has labored to give birth to the other" (*Of Women* 226). Evidently the various facets of female bonding – wives, sisters, mother-daughter – have in no small measure bolstered up the valour, confidence and dynamics of the women who maintain Okonkwo's *ilo* and build a moral hedge around his figure. This enables them to cushion his blows and outbursts as well as face up to his caprices and incongruities.

There can be no doubt that inspite of Okonkwo's emotional weakness, he was very physically strong. A very successful farmer, he arduously tilled the ground while Ani, the earth goddess fertilized his crops. Okonkwo had said yes, his *chi* had said yes and Ani had concurred. He consequently received the blessings of the goddess in his copious harvests. The bumptious Okonkwo, however, overstepped the divine bounds by treading on the toes of the goddess. It is salient to note that the earth goddess, Ani, is endowed with symbols of strength inherent in womanhood. The goddess represents the rhythm of the soil, nature, life and death. In her approbation of goddess religion, Starhawk asserts that:

> The image of the Goddess inspires women to see themselves as sacred, the changing phases of our lives as holy, our aggression as healthy, our anger as purifying, and our power to nurture and create but also to limit and destroy when necessary the very force that sustains all life. Through the Goddess we can discover our strength, enlighten our minds, own our bodies and celebrate our emotions. We can move beyond narrow constricting rules and become whole. The Goddess is also important for men (51).

The importance of the earth goddess in Umuofia community can be gleaned from the institutionalization of normative patterns. Mores were standardized and any aberration was strongly frowned upon and sanctioned. When Okonkwo offended the great goddess by battering Ojiugo's "sacred" body in the Week of Peace, he was asked by Ezeani, the priest of Ani, to appease the goddess. He had, indeed, committed on abomination or *nso ani*. He took to the shrine of Ani the next day, a she-goat, a hen, a length of cloth and a hundred cowries.

Again, Okonkwo earned the wrath of Ani by killing Ikemefuna, the boy who had been placed in his care. Ogbuefi Ezeudu, the oldest man in that quarter of Umuofia, had warned Okonkwo that although Agbala, the Oracle, of the Hills and Caves had pronounced that Ikemefuna should be killed, he should not have a hand in the death of the boy that called him father. Okonkwo went ahead and slew Ikemefuna because of the lurking fear in him.

> He heard Ikemefuna cry, 'My father' they have killed me! as he ran towards him. *Dazed with fear,* Okonkwo drew his matchet and cut him down. *He was afraid* of being thought *weak* (43; emphasis supplied).

This is on obvious example of weakness rather than gallantry. The macho man would rather fly in the face of the goddess whom he obviously feared than be seen as a coward. Overwhelmed by his inferiority complex he was convinced that his inability to kill the child would be analogous to behaving like a woman. Such an abnormal behaviour reeks of a grave weakness hinged on a mental/emotional flaw. Haunted by his wicked action a few days later, he cringed at the thought of becoming "a shivering woman" (45). Chikwenye Ogunyemi has rightly observed that Okonkwo's sexist attitude borders on a "state of denial about his feminine side" (18).

Okonkwo's machismo and his slaying of Ikemefuna set in motion a chain of divinely unleashed cosmic forces, which hounded him till the end. His great friend Obierika had flayed him for his brutal act and added, "What you have done will not please the Earth. It is the kind of action for which the goodness wipes out whole families" (46). Obierika's apocalyptic prediction was virtually fulfilled shortly after: Okonkwo unwittingly felled Ezeudu's teenage son at the old man's funeral. We are told that, "Violent deaths were frequent, but nothing like this had ever happened" (87). In the wake of this unprecedented manslaughter which was a female crime against the earth goddess, the justice of the goddess demanded that Okonkwo's house should be razed to the ground and that he should be banished for seven years with his entire family.

Forced out of his *ilo*, Okonkwo sought another abode in his motherland, Mbanta. In the exiled Okonkwo's opinion, Mbanta is deemed 'female' (Opara "From Stereotype" 11). He is ironically rooted to his "feminine side" for seven years under the auspices and aegis of his late mother's spirit. He had said the traditional farewell to his mother thirty years earlier at her obsequies when he cried, "Mother, mother, mother is going" (91). Her presence remained a strong driving force those long tedious years in Mbanta. As his maternal uncle, Uchendu deftly noted, "Your mother is there to protect you. She is buried there. And that is why we say that Mother is supreme: (94). Her presence provided the solace which cushioned Okonkwo's agony, solitude and grief. She also offered the goodwill and largesse which Ani had provided in Umuofia. This enabled Okonkwo to prosper in that land. His mixed feelings as an exile in Mbanta are articulated in the two names he gave two of the children born there – Nneka (Mother is Supreme) and Nwofia (Begotten in the wilderness).

During this period, the colonial masters invaded both Mbanta and Umuofia. By the time Okonkwo went back to Umuofia, his own *Ilo* and the wider communal *Ilo* had been polluted by Western beliefs and change. Umuofia clan has been blatantly challenged by both the colonial administration and missionaries: the clan was slowly disintegrating. Adler's school of individual psychology views the desire for power as the fundamental human driving force. The power tussle was hinged on the insidious shifting position of the African man who was gradually being reduced from the status of the One to that of the Other. The unmasking of an *egwugwu* by one of the new converts, Enoch, was analogous to laying bare a deflated manhood. There can be no doubt that the Christian church has utterly disempowered the custodians of tradition including the masked spirits, priestesses and deities. Chielo, the priestess of Agbala called the converts "the excrement of the clan", and the new faith, "a mad dog that had come to eat it up" (101). On the contrary, the new faith had, rather than eating up the so-called worthless men or *efulefu* whom Okonkwo considered as woman-like, it amply empowered them and consumed the cosmologic essence of the world of Umuofia. Merlin Stone has stated that the ancient goddess religion and its social customs were designated as pagan and "obliterated by early Christian emperors, medieval inquisitions and witch burnings" (65). The traditional religion of Umuofia now viewed as paganism began to lose its luster and ebb away. Okika laments, "All our gods are weeping, Idemili is weeping, Ogwugwu is weeping. Agbala is weeping, and all the others. Our dead fathers are weeping because of the shameful sacrilege they are suffering and the abomination we have all seen with our eyes" (143). Okonkwo and five other elders had been imprisoned because the desecrated *egwugwu* had burnt down the new church.

It has now become evident that Umuofia leaders have been disempowered in "the new dispensation". Exhibiting the third Adlerian elemental factor of the human drama, Okonkwo in his neurotic flight from reality, balks at his new status as the Other and decapitates the leader of the court messengers – an agent of his obnoxious degradation and concomitant relegation to the sub-category status of the Other. It is also an illusory decapitation of the despicable colonial institution which ultimately consumes Okonkwo. The emasculated Umuofia clan loses the zeal to fight and Okonkwo hangs himself, desecrating the land and the earth goddess. This completes the cycle of flagrant abominations he committed against a powerful female deity whom he had undoubtedly revered and who had meteorically elevated him from a very lowly beginning and dramatically reduced him to a marginal cipher that is finally cast off like a pariah.

Truth as well as beauty is said to be in the eye of the beholder Achebe has tried to tell the truth using "systematic and publicly verifiable" materials such as the historical fact of colonization, the realities of African socio-cultural institutions, sexist proverbs and sayings to punctuate his story. The truth, however, is that the writer has in the inflation of the assets of his flawed hero, glossed over his vulnerabilities while practically playing down on the strength and spark of the women who have continually lent him substantial support. It is evident that the spiritual, material, physical and moral dynamics of these women both at the mundane and ethereal levels are all merged and artistically infused into the veins of the total woman, Beatrice – a lucid antonym of Okonkwo – in his subsequent novel, *Anthills of the Savannah* (1981).

Notes

1. Re-branding is a term that has recently been made popular in Nigeria by the immediate past Minister of Information, Prof. Dora Akunyeli. Re-branding Nigeria simply means giving the country a new image antithetical to sterility and grime. Likewise Achebe has tried to rebrand Africa – giving it an image that is totally different from that of immaturity, evil, inanity and darkness.

2. In contemporary Nigerian society, a man who behaves like Ndulue, confiding in his wife and openly showing conjugal love, is called a woman wrapper. This is a derogatory term for a woman's underdog.

Works Cited

Achebe, Chinua. *Anthills of the Savannah*. Nigeria: Heinemann, Frontline Series, 1998.

_____, *Arrow of God*. London: Heinemann, 1964.

_____, *Things Fall Apart*. London: Heinemann, 1958.

Arndt, Susan: "Paradigms of intertextuality: Orature and Writing Back in the Fiction of Akachi Adimora Ezeigbo". In Patrick Oloko ed. *The Fiction of Akachi Adimora Ezeigbo*. Lagos: African Cultural Institute, 2008: 17-65.

Daiches, David. *Critical Approaches to Literature* 2nd ed. London and New York: Longman, 1981.

Ezeigbo, Akachi Adimora. *The Last of the Strong Ones*. Lagos: Vista Books, 1996.

Franklin Ruth. "After Empire: Chinua Achebe and the Great African Novel." *The New Yorker*. May 26, 2008.

Nnaemeka, Obioma: "Gender Relations and Critical Mediations: From *Things Fall Apart* to *Anthills of the Savannah*". In Leodard A. Podis and Yakubu Saaka *Challenging Hierarchies: Issues and Themes in Colonial and Post Colonial African Literature*. New York: Peter Lang. 1988:137-160.

Nwapa, Flora. *Efuru*, London: Heinemann, 1966.

Ogunyemi, Chikwenye Okonjo. *Africa Woman Palava: The Nigerian Novel by Women*. Chicago and London: Univ. of Chicago Press, 1996.

Opara Chioma. "The Concept of Otherness in African Feminist Thought." In Marie Pauline Eboh. ed. *Philosophical Criticisms*. Port Harcourt, Nigeria: Pearl Publishers, 2000: 197 – 207.

_____. "Fleshing Out Memory: History and Politics in Ezeigbo's *The Last of the Strong Ones*". Paper presented at the 7th ISOLA conference, University of Salento, Lecce, Italy, 11 – 15 June, 2008.

_____, "From Stereotype to Individuality: Womanhood in Chinua Achebe's Novels". In Leonard A. Podis and Yakubu Saaka eds. *Challenging Hierarchies*. New York: Peter Lang, 1988:113 – 123.

_____, "Woman in a Chequered Nigerian History: A Re-reading of Chinua Achebe's Novels". In Chioma Opara. ed. *Beyond the Marginal Land: Gender Perspective in African Writing*. Port Harcourt, Nigeria: Belpot (Nig) Co, 1999:151 – 170.

Rich, Adrienne. "Prepatriarchal Female/Goddess Images". In Charlene Spretnak. ed. *The Politics of Women's Spirituality*. New York: Anchor Books, 1982: 32 – 38.

_____, *Of Woman Born*. New York: Bantam Books, 1977.

Sofola, 'Zulu. "*Feminism and African Womanhood*" In Obioma Nnaemeka ed. *Sisterhood, Feminisms and Power*. Trenton, N.J: Africa World Press, 1998:51-64.

Starhawk. "Witchcraft as Goddess Religion". In Charlene Spretnak. ed. *The Politics of Women's Spirituality*. New York: Anchor Books, 1982:49 – 56.

Wellek Rene and Austin Warren. *Theory of Literature*. Middlesex, England: 1978.

Zahar, Zenate. *Colonialism and Alienation*. Trans Wilfred F. Feuser. Benin, Nigeria: Ethiope Publishing Co, 1974.

CHAPTER 3

FEMALE PRIVILEGE AND POWER IN CHINUA ACHEBE'S *THINGS FALL APART*: THE ROLE AND IMPACT OF THE PRIESTESS CHIELO AS AGENT OF AGBALA, THE ORACLE OF THE HILLS AND VALES

Ada Uzoamaka Azodo

Rather than conflict, there exists a dialectic, a duality and an element of totality among the male-female clusters of relationship in *Things Fall Apart*: Ezeani, a male character, is the chief priest of Ani, the earth goddess; and Chielo, the priestess, whose name means "the mind of god," is the human interpreter of Agbala, the god of the Oracle of the Hills and Caves.

—Ousseynou B. Traore, "The Narrative Grammar of *Things Fall Apart*: Gender and Structural Functions of the Mosquito Myth" (*Eagle on the Iroko* 327).

L iterary critics rarely try to prove that the subject of their analysis and interpretation is the truth,. However, quite frequently, a pattern does emerge that shows a particular critic's trend of thought. In this study of Chinua Achebe's *Things Fall Apart*, two patterns emerge. It is possible to see the female principle as a communal stabilizing force in Igbo cosmology, first, through a look at roles played in religious rituals, and second, through engagement in political governance.. Thus, there is the nurturing cum protecting and guiding power of Chielo, the priestess of Agbala, the god of the Oracle of the Hills and Vales. As a powerful medicine-woman with secret and supernatural powers, Chielo conjures the jinn and abjures the evil spirits. Then, as a professional interpreter, agent and powerful practitioner of specialist medicine, Chielo cures sickness and controls occult arts and powers. She is in possession of second sight, that is, exceptional psychic abilities and is double-headed. It might be problematic to see these qualities upfront, but a closer look will betray them at play at religious rites, language, rituals, ancestry, and signifying practices.

Chielo's privilege and power become all the more glaring when she is compared with Ezeani, a prominent male and masculine agent of the goddess of the earth, Ani. It is through this comparison that her role and impact on the community of Umuofia will be highlighted. Beginning with the premise that as a woman she is a subaltern and that Ezeani belongs to the norm and the center as part of the patriarchal group in the Umuofia community, this essay shall examine how Chielo's role in her community is hardly the one a victimized or powerless woman would play. On the contrary, her leadership and power abilities show that she can make and unmake women and men alike, thanks to her pronouncements of the will of the oracle. As a medium when possessed, she is the voice of the ancestors from the underworld, voices which may not be contradicted without serious repercussions.

The 1996 selected papers of the 1990 international symposium on Chinua Achebe, Eagle *on the Iroko*, edited by Edith Ihekweazu, will allow us to evaluate past literature on the images of women in Chinua Achebe, due to its relevance to the current analysis and interpretation of the role and impact of Priestess Chielo in *Things Fall Apart*. I shall first analyze the limitations that earlier critics have placed in the evaluation of the power and privilege of the priestess Chielo. Then, I shall demonstrate the uplift and empowerment of women in the community, despite male hegemony and the peripheral communal existence of women in particular, and females in general.

Eagle on the Iroko notes that women's power appears illusory, is lacking in reality and is only apparent in rituals, where and when women are considered as mothers, priestesses, young urban professionals, outsiders and insiders. Grace Okereke's paper, "Speech as an Index of Woman's Self-Concept in Chinua Achebe's Novels," which is an analysis of the male-female relationship in two novels by Chinua Achebe based on traditional Igbo society, *Things Fall Apart* and *Arrow of God*, is relevant here, because it holds that it is nothing less than a power tussle with men in which the marginalized women are the losers. Okereke writes:

> In their relationship to their husbands, the women are shown to be constantly on the defensive while their husbands are on the offensive. The men's constant bickering over their wives' shortcomings in everything, places the women eternally on the defensive either justifying their actions or trying to exonerate themselves. This is evident in the relationship between Okonkwo and his wives in *Things Fall Apart* and that between Ezeulu and his wives in *Arrow of God*. This leads to constant tension in everybody around when the man of the house is angry and screams accusations and insults on his wives. This is psychologically eroding for the woman and she is automatically cowed by the man who in turn feels virile in his bullying attitude, from the manner of communication of the partners. Achebe shows the marital relationship to be a power structure with the man as the superior, the master and the woman as the inferior, the servant, who not only serves the man but is also afraid of his tantrums (301).

Furthermore, Okereke states that women's power appears to reside categorically only in religious rituals:

The only occasion when woman is shown to be superior to man is when she possesses supernatural powers. Thus Chielo, the

Priestess of Agbala, in her supernatural states, possessed by her god is raised above the ordinary man and can thus assume an offensive position in her speech to Okonkwo when she asks for Ezinma, his daughter. She warns Okonkwo. "Beware of exchanging words with Agbala. Does a man speak when a god speaks? Beware!" (86).

Okereke also points out that Igbo proverbs used by males talk about lofty philosophical ideas, the human condition and valor, such as discussing Okonkwo's early rise to power and eminence in his Umuofia clan: "As the elders said, if a child washed his hands he could eat with kings" (7). Proverbs used by females, on the contrary, deal with kitchen talk and domestic chores, such as Adaeze in *Arrow of God* talking about the reconciliation between Akueke and her husband: "He did not know that you and he had suddenly become palm oil and salt again." (qtd. in "Speech as an Index of Woman's Self-Concept" ... 300). If Okereke's article was the only one considered, it would tend to foster women's inferior status in male-female relationships. Even in religious ritual activities in which Okereke sees women's power, one could still see women as inferior, if one accepted her implied argument that the power Chielo exercises is not really hers but her god's.

Other critics also see traditional women as subordinated, powerless and without privilege, due to authorial focus on men and masculinity and the male authority system of the Umuofia community. Catherine Bicknell, for example ,opines like Okereke that women have less power than they do in reality, except for those women engaged in religious rituals, such as Chielo. Rose Acholonu talking about Achebe's art in his novels set in the past, again reinforces Okereke's stand, stating that "Achebe's conception of womanhood is generally quite limited both in scope and profundity," due to "the author's commitment to the sacred duty of rehabilitating the battered image of the traditional manhood" (312). Acholonu continues:

> Thus in Achebe's earlier works, whether set in the urban or rural environments, the women are invariably made to live, be seen, and appreciated essentially through their husbands, lovers or children. The resultant artistic invisibility, coupled with the disability of inferiorized and stereotyped characterization, is a necessary tech-

nique for proving the man's undisputed superiority and masculinity. This conscious marginalization of the womenfolk cannot but result in the creation of women who are more of outsiders than insiders in the complex drama of existence (ibid.).

In other words, Achebe shows male superiority over the female as part of the design of his work, which is to respond to the denigration of the African man by the white man in particular, and in general the ills of colonization in running down the values and worth of the cultures of his people.

Nonetheless, one Igbo traditional value seems to have escaped Achebe's design, in spite of himself. The value of Igbo belief in dualism is presented by a few critics in *Eagle on the Iroko*. Obioma Nnaemeka's paper cites Bill Moyers' interview with Achebe in which the famous author illustrated the Igbo concept of dualism with a poignant proverb: "Whenever something stands, something else will stand beside it." However, two other critics, Judith Van Allen and Kamene Okonjo, believe Achebe neglected this intrinsic Igbo dual-sex authority, that is, the duality paradigm that constitutes a check and balance system, ensuring that no one sex lords it over the other unduly both in religious and government practices. The two illustrious women critics state that there is usually a gender balance in Igbo thought system. In *Things Fall Apart*, there may be the male agent of the Earth Goddess, Ani, and the female agent of Agbala, the Oracle of the Hills and Vales, but Achebe appears to have overlooked the female communal power, the *umuada* (daughters of the land), who can counteract the order of masculine power, that is, the *ndichie* (council of elders) and *umunna* (sons of the soil). Again, the implication here is that Achebe has given undue weight to male power and privilege without equal weight to the female counterpart. Catherine Bicknell notes some balance in the existence of the female principles, Ani, and Nneka, a name that says that in Igboland the Mother is Supreme. In Chielo's role as the priestess of the oracle, the authority of the woman is not completely submerged, for it acts as a check on the male principle, she also notes.(267; *Things Fall Apart* 71).

It is then from the angle of the Igbo concept of duality that *Things Fall Apart* would seem to fail, for not giving equal weight to male and female cultural items, given that in the world of Achebe, most, if not all, men are rough and tough, strong, possessors of heavy egos and identities, boisterous and vociferous, standing tall, very tall in their social statuses and prosperity along with their homesteads of multiple wives and children, not to mention overflowing barns of the king of crops, yam. On the contrary, the women are silenced, lacking in identity. As wives, they bicker all day long with their co-wives of the common husband. As mothers, they must not control their male children, but are bugged down with daily domestic chores, are allowed only to cultivate inconsequential female crops, such as cassava and cocoyam, are belittled and depersonalized. Their primary value resides in their roles as sex objects, farm hands, baby-making, baby-rearing and baby-nurturing machines. As women, they are not allowed to 'sit' on erring husbands, according to custom, but nonetheless do sit at the periphery in their husband's compound and indeed in the entire clan or community. Chinua Achebe himself said it very eloquently, when relating his hero Okonkwo's reflections and musings on his life and legacy in relation to his effeminate first son, Nwoye:

> He [Okonkwo] wanted him [Nwoye] to be a pros-
> perous man, having enough in his barn to feed the
> ancestors with regular sacrifices. And so he was always
> happy when he heard him grumbling about women.
> That showed that in time he would be able to *control*
> his women-folk. No matter how prosperous a man
> was, if he was unable to *rule* his women and his chil-
> dren (and especially women) he was not really a man.
> He was like the man in the song who had ten and
> one wives and not enough soup for his foo-foo (45;
> *my emphasis*).

Clearly, more women than men in *Things Fall Apart* have been presented as inferior human beings, stock taken of the critics' reception above, and the likes of Nwoye and Unoka, who are somewhat seen as females, at least by Okonkwo the extra masculine. Second, the few women with privilege and power appear to be only the ones vested with religious authority in the community. Third, it is evident that the Igbo community as presented falls short of the traditional society in reality, because it fails to

46

take into account the age and achievement of a menopausal or post-menopausal women, which would normally elevate her to the status of a man. I have already noted above that political societies of women with power, daughters of the extended family are not heard of in Achebe's *Things Fall Apart*. What is also lacking is the Igbo duality of thought, according to which issues and matters are always looked at from the outside and the inside, up and down, forwards and backwards, and askance and sideways, in order to ensure equality, complementarity, fairness and justice.

Before examining the role and impact of Chielo in *Things Fall Apart*, it is important to explore Chinua Achebe's own ideas about his writing. In a 1964 essay, "The Role of the Writer in a New Nation," Achebe states his perception of his role as a Nigerian writer and a novelist:

> The worst thing that can happen to any people is the loss of their dignity and self-respect. The writer's duty is to help them regain it by showing them in human terms what happened to them, what they lost. There is a saying in Ibo [sic!] that a man who can't tell where the rain began to beat him cannot know where he dried his body. The writer can tell the people where the rain began to beat them (160).

Chinua Achebe's *Things Fall Apart* portrays extremely masculine men to undercut or counter the weak, caricature ones fielded by Western writers, such as Joseph Conrad of the novel, *Heart of Darkness*, and *Mister Johnson* by Joyce Cary. The novel is inherently masculine and flaunts male strength in the face of the Western mind that belittles it as weak and inferior. However, in constructing his female characters, perhaps unbeknown to him (and his critics before us), Achebe is positive as to the privilege and power exercised by the assertive women who prove to be the mainstay of a harmonious, peaceful and stable community. Was Achebe then inadvertently mirroring the Igbo community in reality?

This study will stress Chielo's leadership role in ritual celebrations, well beyond what critics before us have seen merely as her ability to oppose men. When possessed, Chielo is different from her normal, ordinary self as an ordinary woman and female community member. She is not merely a widow and a mother of two; she is adept at psychic ability and an expert in interpreting the psychology of her clients, that is, those who approach her for help through the oracle she serves. As a diviner and a medium, she is one of the spiritual heads of the Umuofia clan. It is possible to see that Chielo's power is not merely ceremonial, virtual, occasional and contextual; she has real power to transform and reshape the lives of those who consult the oracle through her in times of need. Hence one can say that she is the oracle herself. After all, nobody has ever said he or she had seen the Oracle of the Hills and Vales. All interactions with this oracle are through her priestess Chielo or Chika, the one before her (11). Her authority in Umuofia is therefore not merely symbolic, it is also legitimate.[1]

๛

Definitely, Chielo is a manifest link between religion and politics, through Agbala, the Oracle of the Hills and Vales, and her works of intervention for the edification of the community. First, as noted above, no one else but Chielo as priestess ever beholds Agbala (11). Then, it is Agbala, who would advise the community, guided by its dreaded medicine *agadinwanyi* (old woman), to go to war only when their case is "clear and just" and never to fight a *fight of blame*, or face defeat (ibid). Like her predecessor, Chika, Chielo is feared, because she is full of the power extended to her by her god. She is a great interpreter and medium, in one word a great diviner priestess. Chielo's voice is respected in all community affairs, although in normal life she is a widow with two children, who would chat with other women about banal community affairs and issues. She goes to the market four days a week like any other woman, and relates with other women in doing chores, such as cooking for community events and the mothering of community children. Thanks to Chielo's timely intervention one time, a whole group of women might have abandoned their chores to chase a cow that broke loose, leaving the food to burn on the fire: "We cannot all rush out like that, leaving what we are cooking to burn in the fire," shouted Chielo, the priestess. Three or four of us should stay behind" (97). Once possessed by the life-force of her god, Chielo transforms into a medium, and according to the narrative voice: "Anyone seeing Chielo in ordinary life would hardly believe she was the same person who prophesied when the spirit of Agbala was upon her" (42). And when Okonkwo's second wife, Ekwefi, declares her intention to follow Chielo with Ezinma on her back to see Agbala, Chielo also chides her: "How dare you, woman, to go before the mighty Agbala of your own accord? Beware, woman, lest he strikes you in his anger. Bring me my daughter" (86). In her possessed chants was an ethereal force, which transformed the human Chielo into a supernatural being. The narrative voice states: "Ekwefi recoiled, because there was no humanity there. It was not the same Chielo who sat with her in the market and sometimes bought bean cakes for Ezinma, whom she called her daughter. It was a different woman – the priestess of Agbala, the Oracle of the Hills and Caves (…) Chielo was not a woman that night" (91).

Clearly, Ekwefi, like all Umuofia community members for that matter, recognize and sanction this special gift accorded Chielo by the gods. At moments like this, Chielo becomes herself the spirit of Agbala, the Oracle of the Hills and Vales. The spirit of possession takes over her being, transforming her into a medium through which the worlds of the living and the dead interact. Through her performance of rituals as interpreter or medium, the priestess is able to bring messages from the world of the living dead and ancestors to the community of the living. Her powers and privilege are extensive, guiding communication between the living and the dead.

Nonetheless, one can still say that Ezeani, the priest of Ani, has an edge over Chielo in showing how the supernatural and the gods regulate the political life of the community. It is Ezeani who enforces the laws about peace and harmony during the Peace Week in Umuofia, whereas Chielo exerts leadership ability mainly over the womenfolk in her community. To wit, Okonkwo commits abomination against Mother Earth, by beating his wife. But, Chielo is not the one who punishes Okonkwo for his transgression, it is Ezeani: "Before it was dusk, Ezeani, who was the priest of the earth goddess, Ani, called on Okonkwo in his *obi*. Okonkwo brought out a kola nut and placed it before the priest: 'Take away your kola nut. I shall not eat in the house of a man who has no respect for our gods and ancestors'" (26). Three times, Ezeani brings down his short staff of office on the floor to emphasize his points, namely, that the laws of the land may not be transgressed with impunity. Clearly, in carrying out his duties, Ezeani demonstrates his commitment to the preservation of the communal life, through respect of the laws and mores, respect to the gods of the land, especially Mother Earth. It is difficult to say that Chielo might have been bold to speak to a man in that fashion, given the times and beyond the women's sphere of influence.

Conclusion

Chielo demonstrates female privilege and power in *Things Fall Apart*, and by extension, in the Igbo traditional world. Through the execution of the Igbo concept of duality, confided to Chielo and Ezeani, *Things Fall Apart* demonstrates the Igbo principle of duality for completeness and fullness. There appears to be no inherent inequality of privilege and power based on gender in the Igbo world as seen through the lens of Umuofia, although there might exist a difference in the nature of tasks and the intensity with which they are performed.

Notes

1. The female principle that is of interest to us in *Things Fall Apart* is a force to be reckoned with, not only in religious rituals but also in community government. Clearly the Igbo world foundation on the concept of duality-- *ife kwulu ife ozo akwudebe ya* (when something stands something else stands beside it)—is evident in the existence of a male agent for the earth goddess, Ani, without whose benevolence the community perishes, and a female agent for the greatest of all gods of justice and fairness, Agbala, the Oracle of the Hills and Vales. Hence the characters of Chielo and Ezeani demonstrate the dual concept of balance with regard to harmony and peace. They represent its religious and political arms, which regulate the essence of the Igbo person as a complex being of dual existence, who is at once a creature with a life-force that makes her or him part of the cosmos and also part of the living dead of the community.

    The Igbo notion of personhood takes shape from this assertion, as a being with four aspects: *chi* or inner god, which is a small part of the Supreme Being responsible for destiny; *eke*, which is a part of the living dead and/or ancestors that makes a person part of *umunna* or the extended family, and finally one's individual *self*. Hence, with life-force, chi, eke, and self, the Igbo person has a deep bond that goes beyond the community of the living. That explains why communal life for the Igbo is a constant struggle and effort to maintain equilibrium between one's four aspects of personhood. At every point, communal life is presented as the living above in relation to the dead below.

In matters of religion, the Igbo person's belief is monotheistic, because belief is in one Supreme Being, the creator, referred to constantly in *Things Fall Apart* as *Chukwu, Olisa, Chineke*, who is perhaps not the same as the Christian God, for the people do not consult him directly, but rather through his agents, such as interpreters, be they diviners or mediums. Second, the religion is also polytheistic, because the said Supreme Being sits at the apex of a pantheon. It is other smaller deities, priestesses and priests, ancestors, living dead, plants and other creatures that are really agents in the god's service. Third, the religion is also pantheistic, given that the other aforementioned deities in service to the Supreme Being are in fact the Supreme Being in multiple forms. One such being, according to *Things Fall Apart*, is Ani, the goddess of the earth, responsible for plenty to nurture the people, and who receives them when they die. Like children, they return to the mother at death. Needless to add that the worst wrong anyone could be guilty of in the Igbo community is *nso ani*, a wrong committed against Mother Earth. By the same token, the highest dishonor one could suffer is to be refused burial or abode with Mother Earth at death, for fear that she or he might taint the mother. Such a person is cast into the Evil Forest to be devoured by prowling beasts and left to rot on the surface of the earth. There are other deities: Ifejioku, the god of Yams and as such also God of plenty, note taken that yam is seen as a male crop and a king among crops in the Igbo worldview; Amadiora, the God of Thunder and Lightning, deemed to be male and ministers justice and retribution, just like the Greek god, Nemesis; the female Idemili, the river goddess, and female Ogwugwu, also a river goddess, and Agbala, the goddess of the Oracle of the Hills and Vales. All of these goddesses are also implicated in the provision of plenty, justice and fairness. It is the priestesses and priests who intercede for human beings before the Supreme Being and his agents, as diviners.

There are two kinds of diviners: the interpreters and the mediums. The interpreter can be an oracle, whom villagers take recourse to for knowledge about the past, present and future. As evident in *Things*

Fall Apart, the oracle can be reached through its priestess, who proclaims the will of Agbala. Interpreters employ sheer intellectual process to see relationships, because they live in the community and know what goes on there. Chika, a priestess of the oracle, tells Unoka off when he goes to the Oracle to complain that his harvest year after year does not give him good results. Of course, Chika knowing Unoka to be a lazy man, who enjoys making merry all year round, quickly puts two and two together and chides him:

> Hold your peace! You have offended neither the gods nor your fathers. And when a man is at peace with his gods and his ancestors, his harvest will be good or bad according to the strength of his arm. You, Unoka, are known in all the clan for the weakness of your machete and your hoe. When your neighbors go out with their ax to cut down virgin forests, you sow your yams on exhausted farms that take no labor to clear. They cross seven rivers to make their farms; you stay at home and offer sacrifices to a reluctant soil. Go home and work like a man (16).

Moreover, in ordinary times, the interpreter is an ordinary person until possessed. Chielo is an ordinary community member until possessed by the spirit of the goddess. Then she becomes a channel for the message from the living-dead and the ancestors to the living. Unlike the interpreters, the mediums are mere vehicles, the means of the transference of the oracle, and they do not touch the message they are given:

> No one had ever beheld Agbala, except his priestess. But no one who had ever crawled into his awful shrine had come out without the fear of its power. His priestess stood by the sacred fire which she built in the heart of the cave and proclaimed the will of the god. The fire did not burn with a flame. The glowing logs only served to light up vaguely the dark figure of the priestess (*Things Fall Apart* 15).

When people come to consult their dead ancestors at the oracle, Chielo is a mere channel for this relationship. People hear the oracle's voice through her. They see her form and this only vaguely over a dim flame, because the form of the messenger is not as important as the content of the message. Such is Chielo, when she carries off Ekwefi's only daughter, Ezinma, to visit Agbala, for example.

There are also the *egwugwu* or masquerades, masked mediums that are really spirits of the living dead and the ancestors, spirits who are believed to crawl out of ant holes to sit in justice over the living in the community. At once as judge, jury, litigants and witnesses, they may not be contradicted, because they represent the spirits of the ancestors and the living dead. Their idea of justice is not to alienate one party from the other through sanctions to the guilty, but rather to maintain peace and harmony in the community by bringing people together. Clearly, what is paramount is the control of human behavior through ritual expressions, such as the Igbo ritual of the New Yam festival, a rite of passage designed to transform the community, time, and individuals in several ways. The festival connotes that interval between the past and the New Year, but also a period of reversal or suspension of normal behavior. It is like the end of the world, after which the Igbo feels refreshed and morally fortified to begin anew, again.

2.   Then his tone changed to command: "You will bring to the shrine of Ani tomorrow one she-goat, one hen, a length of cloth and a hundred cowries" (27). And his word is final. No insult to the Earth Goddess shall be brooked. Before he gets up and leaves, however, Ezeani admonishes Okonkwo further:

> "Listen to me," he said when Okonkwo has spoken. "You are not a stranger in Umuofia. You know as well as I do that our forefathers ordained that before we plant any crops in the earth we should observe a week in which a man does not say a harsh word to his neighbor. We live in peace with our fellows to honor our great goddess of the earth without hose blessing our crops will not grow. You have committed a great evil" He brought down his staff on the floor. "Your wife was at fault, but even if you came into your obi and found her lover on top of her, you would still have committed a great evil to beat her." His staff came down again. "The evil you have done can ruin the whole clan. The earth goddess whom you have insulted may refuse to give us her increase, and we shall perish" (26-27).

Works Cited

Achebe, Chinua. *Things Fall Apart [and Related Readings]*. Evanston, Boston and Dallas: McDougall Littell Publishers, 1997.

_____. "The Role of the Writer in a New Nation", in *Nigeria Magazine*, No.81, June 1964.

Acholonu, Rose. "Outsiders or Insiders? Women in *Anthills of the Savannah*." In *Woman in the Academy*, eds. Seiyifa Koroye and Noel C. Anyadike. Ibadan: Heinemann, 1996. 311-321.

Azodo, Ada Uzoamaka. "Masculinity, Power and Language in Chinua Achebe's *Things Fall Apart*". In: *Emerging Perspectives on Chinua Achebe: Omenka the Master Artist: Critical Perspectives on Achebe's Fiction*. Trenton, NJ: Africa World Press, 2004. 49-65.

Bicknell, Catherine. "Achebe's Women: Mothers, Priestesses, and Young UrbanProfessionals." In: *Eagle on Iroko*. Edith Ihekweazu. Ed. Ibadan: Heinemann, 1996. 265-279.

Nnaemeka, Obioma. "Chinua Achebe: Women, Language and Border (Lines) Lands." In: *Eagle on Iroko*. Edith Khekweazu. Ed. Ibadan: Heinemann, 1996. 280-298.

Okereke, Grace. "Speech as an Index of Woman's Self-Concept in Chinua Achebe's Novels." In: *Eagle on Iroko*. Edith Ihekweazu. Ed. Ibadan: Heinemann, 1996. 298-311.

Traore, Ousseynou B. "The Narrative Grammar of *Things Fall Apart:* Gender and Structural Functions of the Mosquito Myth." In: *Eagle on Iroko*. Edith Ihekweazu. Ed. Ibadan: Heinemann, 1996. 323-345.

CHAPTER 4

CHILDREN OF THE HOME: EZINMA, BEAUTY TO BEHOLD

Blessing Diala-Ogamba

Things Fall Apart is one of the most exciting novels written by Chinua Achebe. In a quick study of this novel, one can conclude that Achebe relegates women to the background because he does not revere them as much as he does the men, especially Okonkwo, the protagonist. However, with careful reading of the text, one can begin to delineate the roles the women play in this novel as the backbone of the men. There are actually several reasons for the neglect of women in some traditional African societies. Rose Mezu is of the view that:

> Reasons for women's neglect and marginalization can obviously be located in a pre-colonial, patriarchal past where man ruled supreme in the manner of the Roman *paterfamilias*, where the woman was a possession as wife, an object of batter and exchange as a sister or daughter, to be defined only in terms of her relationship to the man and never as an autonomous entity. Power over her was total (33-34).

Even though, Umuofia is a patriarchal society, Achebe envisages the role of women here as much more than being a possession as seen in the way he portrays them. Achebe therefore makes sure that Okonkwo suffers indictment in his poor treatment of his wives in this novel. This becomes more obvious when one considers the role of the women as a labor force. Cindy Courville observes that:

> Unlike many other world areas, *labor* not *land* was the scarce factor of production in Africa. The extended family was the fundamental production and consumption unit, with women and children forming the economic sub-unit .... Women's productive and reproductive capacity made them a social and economic resource which provided men with political leverage. African women were primarily responsible for the economic, social and political reproduction of the household; the bearing of and caring for children; the production, storage and preparation of food (33).

The above assertion by Courville highlights more of the importance of women in the family and the community at large. If women do not maintain the home, the children may turn out to be unruly. In view of this, Rose Acholonu advocates that feminism should be "positive and dynamic in its recognition of the symbiotic relationship between the genders as well as the appreciation of the women's potential for growth and development which has to be harnessed and fostered for the well-being of the family, and the society at large (9). This is the set up that Achebe wishes for Umuofia patriarchal society where the novel is set. Within this patriarchal society, Ezinma, Okonkwo's first daughter is also given prominence instead of the first son Nwoye, because of the qualities she possesses. Apart from the circumstances surrounding Ezinma's birth, she grows up to be a beautiful and charismatic young woman, dearly loved by her father, Okonkwo. Her strong, selfless, independent and masculine characteristics are what make Okonkwo revere her, and make him wish she were a boy.

Achebe in *Things Fall Apart* goes back to his tradition of portraying the culture and norms of his people before the invasion of the Europeans. He tries to prove that his people have a government, culture, rules and regulations guiding them. According to Chukwuma, "The idea of rehearsing the past is itself a cultural affirmation of a vibrant heritage and further a way of finding out, using Achebe's terms, 'where the rain started beating us'" (VII). On the other hand, Achebe in one of his essays in *Morning yet on Creation Day* also says that he writes,

> to help my society regain belief in itself and put away the complexes of years of denigration and self-abasement.... I would be quite satisfied if my novels especially the ones set in the past did no more than teach my readers that their past with all its imperfections ... was not one long night of savagery from which the first European acting on God's behalf delivered us (45).

Achebe therefore makes Okonkwo his protagonist in *Things Fall Apart*, portraying him exactly the way the traditional Igbo man is expected to look after his family. The man has to be strong and able to take care of his house hold; otherwise, he is relegated to the background by the members of the society, just like Unoka, Okonkwo's father. Having come from this culture where expectations are high for the males, Okonkwo raises his children to be strong. He expects the boys to do manly things like going to war and be capable, when they get married of protecting their families and to become respectable members in Umuofia society. He is therefore highly disappointed and frustrated, when his first son, Nwoye shows traces of becoming lazy just like Unoka.

Okonkwo has both male and female children, but Ezinma, his first daughter is the one he truly loves because she possesses the qualities Okonkwo is looking for in his first son, Nwoye. Okonkwo after noticing that Nwoye is turning to be lazy like Unoka, tries hard to stamp out this laziness from him, by abusing him verbally and physically when Nwoye makes the slightest mistake. Ironically, instead of improving his behavior to Okonkwo's liking, Nwoye's fear of his father takes him farther away from relating to him as much as Okonkwo would love. Nwoye prefers to stay in his mother's hut to listen to folktales, rather than his father's heroic tales about killings, wars, strength and show of masculinity. Ezinma on the other hand, relates to Okonkwo better, and quickly exhibits her independence in taking initiatives. She is everything that Nwoye is not, that is why Okonkwo dotes on her, and always wishes that she were a boy. He expresses this sentiment a number of times, but cannot really do anything about it other than to love her.

The coming of Ikemefuna into Okonkwo's household helps Nwoye emotionally. Both become very close and Nwoye is encouraged to spend time listening to Okonkwo's stories about wars. Ikemefuna transforms Nwoye as the later looks up to Ikemefuna as an elder brother. This transformation makes Okonkwo happy as he watches both of them.

> Okonkwo's son Nwoye who is two years younger, became quite inseparable from him because he seemed to know everything. He could fashion out flutes from bamboo stems and even from the elephant grass. He knew the names of all the birds and could set clever traps for the little bush rodents. And he knew which trees made the strongest bows (*TFA* 28).

Ikemefuna greatly influences Nwoye to Okonkwo's liking. Okonkwo even becomes very fond of Ikemefuna, but does not show it outwardly as he believes that it is a sign of weakness to show emotion openly (28). However, the killing of Ikemefuna turns Nwoye away from his father completely. Nwoye rejects everything that his father stands for. Once Okonkwo gets to Mbanta with his family during their exile, Nwoye seizes the opportunity to join the missionaries, to his father's disappointment. Okonkwo vehemently warns the rest of his sons:

> You have all seen the great abomination of your brother. Now he is no longer my son or your brother. I will only have a son who is a man, who will hold his head up among my people. If any one of you prefers to be a woman, let him follow Nwoye now while I am alive so that I can curse him. If you turn against me when I am dead I will visit you and break your neck (172).

Okonkwo does not like the disappointment he receives from Nwoye; on the other hand, Ezinma embodies the characteristic he desires in his sons. The writer explains that: "Okoknwo was very lucky in his daughters. He never stopped regretting that Ezinma was a girl. Of all his children, she alone understood his every mood.

A bond of sympathy had grown between them as the years had passed" (172). Agbasiere also observes the good qualities Ezinma exhibits and ties them to her relationship with her parents.

> Ezinma strikes a balance in reciprocating her parents' love. She is close to her mother and father. She is chatty and gives Ekwefi effective companionship. In fact, she takes liberties with her, calling her, unlike all other children, by her first name.... The relationship that crystallizes is not that of mother and child but rather that of companionship between adults and equals. Similarly, she has a deep understanding of her father. She is quick in understanding his every mood and keeps him good company (73).

Ezinma, being the only child of her mother, Ekwefi, also enjoys a good relationship with her. Ekwefi is Okonkwo's second wife, and has always been in love with Okonkwo. She runs away from her first husband to marry Okoknwo when he is able to pay her bride price. Ekwefi loses many of her children when they are young, and Ezinma becomes her only surviving daughter, and also "the center of her mother's world" (*TFA* 76). In view of this, Ezinma gets the attention an only child usually gets from her mother. She calls her mother by her name unlike children her age. Her relationship with her mother "was not only that of mother and child. There was something in it like the companionship of equals which was strengthened by such little conspiracies as eating eggs in the bedroom" (76-77). Ezinma has shown signs that she is determined to live, when suddenly she falls ill at night. Okonkwo rushes out that night to prepare herbs for her to drink. The medicine man, Okagbue is invited, and he is able to dig up Ezinma's "Iyi-uwa" (80), severing her bond with the world of the changelings. The fact that Ezinma is an only child does not have anything to do with Okonkwo's love for her, but he has shown with Ezinma's sickness that he is also emotional, but does not want to show it openly in order not to be regarded as a "woman" or be termed as being "weak".

Another incident that portrays Okonkwo as someone with human sympathy especially in relation to his children and particularly to Ezinma is seen in his reaction when Chielo comes to take

Ezinma to the Oracle of the Hills and Caves at night. Okonkwo comes out to plead with Chielo to leave Ezinma until morning before she takes her, but Chielo refuses and dares Okonkwo to stop her. She lashes out: "Does a man speak when a god speaks? Beware"(101)! Even though Chielo warns Okonkwo not to follow her, Okonkwo and Ekwefi meet each other by the cave waiting for Ezinma. This act portrays Ekwefi as a very strong and independent character and Okonkwo as a caring father regardless.

Ezinma is always assertive in her relationship with her mother and especially her father, thus bringing out her masculine tendencies. This presentation is a plausible image of what Okonkwo really wants and by extension, what he expects from Nwoye. Ezinma's assertiveness in a male dominated society prompts Okonkwo each time to wish that she "were a boy". In exhibiting this assertive characteristic, Okonkwo does not try to stop her because he realizes that it is a good trait to acquire. According to Chukwuma, "Feminism or womanism in Africa does not advocate a negative stance against the male or indeed a life without men nor does it negate the family. Rather it advocates a complementary relationship between the sexes where female individualism and character are given ample opportunity for life and expression"(ix). Okonkwo realizes that Ezinma's boldness as it were, will benefit her in raising her children and in her relationship with her future husband, and accommodates this characteristic as a positive trait.

Achebe in *Things Fall Apart*, does not really denigrate women rather he paints a picture of the status of women in his society. The abilities of the women to achieve are played down, but behind it all, we notice that the women are the brains behind the success of the men. Chielo is an ordinary woman but the priestess of a powerful oracle—Agbala whom no man, not even Okonkwo dares to challenge. Everybody knows his or her place when it comes to Chielo. According to Alagoa and Fombo, "a man normally obtained his birthright through the status of the mother ... In the religious sphere, the supreme being or God was a woman, a mother" (27). Achebe therefore recognizes and appreciates the important roles women play in the society in his portrayal of Chielo. In an interview with Rose Mezu, on how he views women in *Things Fall Apart*, Achebe says:

> ... Okonkwo was always violent with everyone. Both he and his society had weaknesses which included the female species, and the adoration of power. They paid terribly for these. Okonkwo paid a terrible price by being banished for ever in the evil forest, and so did the Igbo society by suffering defeat at the hands of an alien civilization (29).

Because of his belief in the strength of women, Achebe portrays Ezinma as reminiscent of all strong women before her, which is a trait that Okonkwo appreciates. The Umuofia society expects men to be strong forces to be reckoned with in the society. Okonkwo, unhappy with his son, Nwoye, however, turns his attention and love to Ezinma, his daughter who represents what he desires in life for his son.

Ezinma is a very insightful and opinionated young girl who knows the right time to intervene or speak with her father Okonkwo. After the killing of Ikemefuna, Okonkwo is not able to eat for two days. "He only drank palm-wine from morning till night, and his eyes were red and fierce like the eyes of a rat when it was caught by the tail and dashed against the floor" (*TFA* 63). Ezinma notices that Okonkwo is restless and uncomfortable by participating in the killing of Ikemefuna, but her father is not known to show emotions openly. Okonkwo invites Nwoye to sit with him in his hut, but Nwoye out of fear, slips out quietly once he notices his father sleeping. On the third day when Okonkwo eventually decides to eat, Ezinma takes his favorite meal prepared by Ekwefi to him and says, "You have not eaten for two days .... So you must finish this" (63). Ezinma waits for him to finish his food thus making Okonkwo reflect again: "She should have been a boy" (64). He further expresses to Obierika his best friend,

> I am worried about Nwoye. A bowl of pounded yams can throw him in a wrestling match. His two younger brothers are more promising. But I can tell you, Obierika, that my children do not resemble me. Where are the young suckers that will grow when the old banana tree dies? If Ezinma had been a boy I would have been happier. She has the right spirit" (66).

Okonkwo has been observing his daughter, Ezinma who is not afraid of him. She is also not afraid to confront or engage him in conversations. Ezinma understands that Ikemefuna has been killed and that Okonkwo can protect him, if he believes he has a choice. The fact that Okonkwo is unhappy and refuses to eat for two days gives her the impression that her father is not happy to participate in this killing; he is simply following the tradition. She notices Okonkwo's misery and decides to not only wait for him to finish his food, but encourages him to finish it. This action endears her more to Okonkwo. Ezinma does not have to ask him the details of what happened to Ikemefuna, since she already knows that he is not happy. Okonkwo being sensitive to Ezinma's actions keeps comparing her to Nwoye. Okonkwo worries about Nwoye's lack of masculinity and feels that Nwoye has "too much of his mother in him" (66). Jeyifo believes that Okonkwo "struggles against colonial conquest and a nascent imperialist domination, but with an aggressively masculinist personality and its deep alienations" (194). It is also important to note that Umuofia society is a deep-rooted patriarchal society where the men give orders and expect the women to obey, thus the subordination of women in the novel.

Ezinma does not manifest any type of feminine inferiority but is very outspoken and intelligent, and does not conceal her dislikes. Ekwefi takes Ezinma and Obiageli to harvest cassava while they are in Mbanta. Ezinma tells her mother, "I dislike cold water dropping on my back. We should have waited for the sun to rise and dry the leaves" (*TFA* 164). Some children her age may only grumble, and not have the courage to tell their mothers about their dislikes. Ezinma shows her intelligence when she expresses surprise that her mother lifts a hot pot from the fire with her bare hands. She asks her mother once, "is it true that when people are grown up, fire does not burn them.... But Nwoye's mother dropped her pot of hot soup the other day and it broke on the floor" (40). Her intelligence shows in her analysis of the situation before her mother answers telling her about Nwoye's mother. For her, if Nwoye's mother can drop her pot of soup, not all grown women can lift hot pots from the fire with bare hands.

Ezinma is sometimes called "Ezigbo" by her mum, which means "the good one" (41). Her name Ezinma, also means mean the good one, real beauty, therefore her name reflects her characteristics. She observes people very well and knows exactly when to interrupt. Ezinma takes food to Okonkwo on one occasion and goes to sit with Obiageli who has already brought her mother's food. Okonkwo shouts at her to sit like a woman, but that does not stop Ezinma from asking if she can bring her father's stool to the wrestling match for him.

Ezinma grows up to be a very beautiful girl, just like her mother. Even though beautiful, she "had her moments of depression when she would snap at everybody like an angry dog. These moods descended on her suddenly and for no apparent reason. But they were very rare and short-lived. As long as they lasted, she could bear no other person but her father" (173). Ezinma's attitude shows her strength of character just like her father, and determination like her mother. She and her father understand each other and have great bonds. Okonkwo tells Ezinma one evening, "There are good and prosperous people here, but I shall be happy if you marry in Umuofia when we return home.... Your half-sister, Obiageli, will not understand me .... But you can explain to her" (173). Okonkwo does not have to explain his reason for telling Ezinma to marry in Umuofia. These words are enough for Ezinma to understand her father's feelings, and the fact that he plans to get back to Umuofia in a grand style in order to regain his status. Okonkwo also trusts her enough to convince her sister Obiageli to do the same. The two girls wait until they get back to Umuofia before they get married. Okonkwo becomes very happy for the sacrifice Ezinma is making by putting her father first, and again, he wishes Ezinma were a boy:

> I wish she were a boy... She understood things so perfectly. Who else among his children could have read his thoughts so well? With two beautiful grown-up daughters his return to Umuofia would attract considerable attention. His future sons-in-law would be men of authority in the clan. The poor and unknown would not dare to come forth (173).

When Okonkwo and some elders of Umuofia are imprisoned, Ezinma breaks her twenty-eight day visit to her future husband's family and comes back home to find out what the Umuofia men are doing about bailing the elders. When they are released, Ezinma is at home to prepare food for her father, who eats silently just to please his daughter. Okonkwo is probably happy within himself that his daughter stands and will always stand by him.

A feminist reading of *Things Fall Apart* shows that Chinua Achebe subtley shows this tendency in order not to conflict his belief with the thinking of the patriarchal society he is portraying. In this way, he is able to relay exactly the way society views women at that particular time. Okonkwo's wives and mother are kept in the backstage in order to bring out Okonkwo's masculinity and prominence, and also show why he is overzealous. Okonkwo attributes strength and power to the men because he comes from a society "in which patriarchy intrudes oppressively into every sphere of existence. It is an androcentric world where the man is everything and the woman nothing. In domestic terms, women are quantified as part of men's acquisition ..." (Mezu 212). Ironically, Nwoye turns out to be the weaker personality while Ezinma becomes the pillar that Okonkwo wishes Nwoye to be. Okonkwo therefore has no choice other than to dote on his beautiful daughter, Ezinma. This goes to strengthen the fact that "mother (female) is really supreme" and that a woman's beauty is appreciated in physic as well as in character.

Works Cited

Achebe, Chinua. *Things Fall Apart*. New York: Anchor, 1994.

———. *Morning yet on Creation Day*. London: Heinemann, 1975.

Acholonu, Rose. In *Women in the Academy: Festschrift for Professor Helen Chukwuma*. Ed. Seiyifa Koroye and Noel C. Anyadike. Port Harcout: Pearl Publishers, 2004.

Agbasiere, Julie. "The Child-Victim in Chinua Achebe's *Things Fall Apart*" *Emerging Perspectives on Chinua Achebe*. Ed. Ernest Emenyonu. New Jersey: Africa World Press, 2004.

Alagoa, E.J. and A. Fombo. *A Chronicle of Grand Bonny*. Ibadan: University of Ibadan, 1972.

Chukwuma, Helen. Ed. *Feminism in African Literature*. Enugu: New Generation, 1994.

Cournville, Cindy. "Re-Examining Patriarchy as a Mode of Production: The Case of Zimbabwe" *Theorizing Black Feminism: The Visionary Pragmatism of Black Women*. London: Routeledge, 1993.

Jeyifo, Biodun. "Okonkwo and His Mother: *Things Fall Apart* and Issues of Gender in the Constitution of African Postcolonial Discourse" *Chinua Achebe's Things Fall Apart: A Case Book*. Ed. Isidore Okpewho. New York: Oxford U.P. 2003.

Mezu, Rose. *Chinua Achebe: The Man and His Works*. London: Adonis and Abbey, 2006.

_____. *A History of Africana Women's Literature*. Baltimore: Black Academy P. 2004.

PART II

CHAPTER 5

ALIENATED HISTORIES: MAPPING LANDSCAPES OF WOMEN'S PARTICIPATION AND AUTONOMY IN ACHEBE'S *THINGS FALL APART* AND *ANTHILLS OF THE SAVANNAH*

Anthonia C. Kalu

On July 15, 2009, Chansa Kabwela, "… news editor of *The Post* in Zambia was arrested for circulating photographs of a woman giving birth without medical aid outside the University Teaching Hospital."[1] Kabwela faced charges of "…circulating obscene materials with the intention to corrupt the morals of society."[2] Based on section 177 1(b) of the Penal code, the charges were brought against Ms. Kabwela by President Rupiah Banda of Zambia after she circulated the offending pictures to identified national leaders in an effort to raise awareness about the plight of the people during a strike by medical workers. Government officials—male and female—who saw the picture said that they were outraged and shocked. Rather than seeing that picture of the birthing mother's most private moment as a violation resulting from the failure of essential workers' responsibility toward the citizens, the pictures were seen as pornographic images. In November 2009, Ms. Kabwela was acquitted of the pornography charges following vocal outrage by journalists, women's groups and other interested parties in Zambia and around the world. Throughout the five-month period of her trial, Ms. Kabwela was publicly accused by many Zambian women and men, including Mrs. Zulu, a 19-year veteran police investigator who was quoted as saying, "We are all Zambians here. We all know this is not allowed in our culture."[3]

In traditional African practice, keeping men away from the birthing space as well as the birthing process largely had to do with the fact that in some instances men lacked knowledge of what to do and in other instances, the process in its traditional setting necessarily is the domain of women—whose participation is both normalized and structured. Clearly this is in contrast to modernity where most of the OB-GYNs are male with women having assistive roles in many countries. Thus, in contrast to tradition where the normalized process ensured that women understand pains that only women experience and therefore ensure that it is as collective as possible, in modernity, such pains are often individualized and at times open to collective public opprobrium as the trial of Chansa Kabwela on charges of pornography demonstrate. Ms. Kabwela's experience in Zambia is not unique; it is similar to what Africans, especially women in many contemporary African countries like Nigeria are experiencing on a daily basis whereby the miscuing of tradition and modernity result in unwarranted distress for citizens.

According to Clive Seale (1998), in any given society people share meanings constructed by society's members in their interactions with each other (29). They do this by transcending "...individual subjectivity to construct an *intersubjective* world" (31). By constructing "an intersubjective world… [in which] they *produce common sense*, and they do so quite ordinarily and routinely – and so are able to take it for granted" (31) (emphasis in original). As a result, they interpret the meaning of elements of their social and cultural life using information from a shared knowledge base. If people share common-sense, then they share a definition of the situation under discussion. Also, the sharing of common-sense means that sometimes that which is shared can be distorted. Thus, depending on the situation and the nature of the shared information, shared divergences of meaning emerge. The latter situation depends on self-presentation which affects or determines perceptions of individuals and cultures.

In the verbal arts, self-presentation is used deliberately to direct perception and inform self-knowledge of the individual or community. Consequently, and to a large extent, journalism and other narrative forms contribute to the maintenance of fluidity of cultural norms. Generally, such fluidity enables constructive change and the acknowledgement and incorporation of same in society. However, in contemporary Africa, and as a result of the prevalence of failed African leadership since independence, it is difficult to determine concurrence between information from traditional core sets of ideas and those that have emerged following the various efforts of African leaders to maintain their holds on the nation state and therefore the national psyche. This means that situations like the one Ms. Kabwela encountered above do not represent anomalies in cultural change or practice in the continent. Ms Kabwela's encounter would have been unheard of anywhere in Africa before the entrenchment of Africa's modernity and progress. The experiences of both Ms. Kabwela and her countrywoman whose story inspired her illuminate Africa's encounter with cultural self-negation despite immense wealth in natural resources.

Although and traditionally, African women kept men as well as women who were not directly involved away from the spaces where women give birth, it is difficult to understand which culture Mrs. Zulu and other Zambian public officials were referring to in the above reports. Frequently, encounters between tradition and modernity fall prey to multiple metaphors, analogies and/or intersubjective interpretations—that if care is not taken causes a society and the interpreters of its cultural practices to chase shadows rather than substance. In this essay, modernity is examined as a continuing part of a process; it is part of the changing nature of tradition and its adaptive capacities. Using specific references to women in selected works of Chinua Achebe, this essay examines the interplay between tradition and modernity in contemporary African life.

Initially, contemporary African literature focused on the explication of the intersubjective realities within and between various aspects of African life and culture. Basing their assumptions on the intersubjectivity between people when they agree on a given set of meanings or definition of a situation, early African writers began to carefully examine those agreements as well as their nature. However, since language is communal, it soon became obvious that intersubjectivity in the African's experience required agreement on a new and different level. For example, given that language deploys meaning in very specific ways, the problem of Africans' self-presentation in the colonizers' languages was evident from the beginning. Specifically, metaphors, analogies, proverbs, etc., are linguistic devices that help narrators (writers/researchers/analysts) to explore the richness, imagery and empathetic contexts of events, especially in a given cultural space. Miscuing any of these linguistics devices often results in the loss of meaning; especially where intersubjective devices and tools are deployed. Quite frequently, encounters between tradition and modernity – often wrongly explained as oppositional concepts – fall prey to multiple metaphors, analogies and/or intersubjective interpretations. In the example here about African women's traditional practice of keeping men away from spaces where women give birth, which in modernity we call hospitals, the problem that emerges is that of bifurcation of meaning. Without the formal structure introduced by the European colonizer, the African child whose birth is attended to by local women is already perceived as beginning life with a socio-cultural deficit in contemporary Africa because those women are not seen as 'trained' practitioners of their craft. And because of the status associated with hospitals as part of the European legacy to Africa, being brought into the world in a hospital is part of the privilege that helps to redefine intersubjectivity in contemporary African society. Thus as shown in the Zambian situation under discussion, it appears to make more sense for a contemporary African woman to give birth on a piece of plastic in a parking lot 'near ... hospital' than risk the certainty of a successful delivery assisted by a group of 'untrained' local women.

Rather than a dismissal of modernity, this work asserts that the emergence of different intersubjective interpretations in post-independent Africa has led to a situation where African women's lives and experiences are pushed to the periphery in the various efforts to present a modernized image of Africa and Africans. Although it has not always been played out to the extent witnessed in Zambia in the Kabwela case, that image has been in the making from the beginning of Africa's encounter with Europe whose need for differentiation during the colonial period led to the initiation of bifurcating categories such that Europe was perceived as a space of modernity and Africa as a traditional (more at primitive) space. In Africa, bifurcation occurs on two levels – among Africans, and between Africans and European cultures. Intersubjectively, these encounters are intense and frustrating for the African whose language use and competence in the post-independent environment requires clarity of outcomes. This work uses selected examples from Chinua Achebe's works to illustrate some of the elements that inform individual and communal efforts to understand how common-sense agreement in the traditional setting may be distorted as the development of modern images continue to influence Africans' self-presentations. The main problem with self-presentation is the tendency for individuals to appropriate prospects for group advancement as opportunities for self- promulgation.

For the purposes of this work, it is significant to understand that common-sense is not common. In other words, it is not the case that every individual in a given community knows the cultural fundamentals that its members agree on "...as common-sense, shared meanings constructed by people in their interactions with each other and used as an everyday resource to interpret the meaning of elements of [their] social and cultural life" (Seale, 327). On the contemporary African scene, this means that cultural shifts brought about by colonialism and the incursions of European orthodoxy affected shared meanings as individual and group memberships shifted to incorporate the mandates of the new dispensation. For example, while Achebe's introduction of the persistent problem of infant mortality in *Things Fall Apart* (1958) has yielded discussions about Igbo people's understanding of *ogbanje*, or the spirit child such discussions have yet to result in investments in medical research and development leading to interventions on behalf of children identified as ogbanje in contemporary Igbo culture and life. As a group, there are few efforts that engage Igbo women-as-mothers in ways that help them to

fully understand the different causes of infant mortality in contemporary Nigeria. This is important because in the traditional
setting, whether or not prescribed remedies were effective, traditional institutions found ways of engaging the woman-as-mother,
ensuring her participation in the process of alleviating some of her
pain and suffering resulting from this and other phenomena that
affected her well being. For full cultural recovery, and given global
advancements in health and medical research, the discussion about
the ogbanje should engage the psychological and physical health
of both mother and child. This could be achieved through sustained research that clarifies the connections between traditional
and contemporary thoughts on infant mortality on the continent.
This need to clarify is also important to understanding the roles of
traditional and contemporary healers. Achebe's narrative style in
Things Fall Apart provides an avenue to creating such understandings in the contemporary arenas.

Regarding the healers' roles for example, after Chielo takes
Ezinma, Okonkwo's favorite daughter to the Oracle of the Hills
and Caves, she returns her safely to her mother's hut in the early
hours of the morning. Although the reader follows her voice
through the night, Chielo is never fully visible except to the reader
who also knows Igbo culture; all other readers follow only her
silhouette through the dark night. That night is described as, "…
impenetrably dark…. The moon had been rising later and later
every night until now it was seen only at dawn…" (67). Chielo
arrives at Okonkwo's household just after the evening meal and
Ezinma and her mother are sharing a storytelling session. About
that night, Achebe's narrator says,

> A palm-oil lamp gave out yellowish light. Without it,
> it would have been impossible to eat; one would not
> have known where one's mouth was in the darkness
> of that night. There was an oil lamp in all four huts
> on Okonkwo's compound, and each hut seen from the
> others looked like a soft eye of yellow half-light set in
> the solid massiveness of night (67).

It is against this background that Chielo takes Ezinma into the
hills with Ekwefi following closely but unable to see '…beyond

her nose...' (73) in the utter darkness. Not only does Ekwefi frequently run into the weeds growing in the side of the path, but she trips and falls once. Representing Igbo (African) women at various stages of self-awareness, Chielo, Ekwefi and Ezinma are mostly seen as part of the heart of Africa's darkness because they were not made fully visible in early contemporary African writing. In modern societies, the above presentation about Chielo and her successful night's visit to the Oracle with Ezinma on her back, would be more familiar if the presentation were to be compared with the modern day "ambulance or other medical emergencies" in which emergency vehicles speed off with the sick while family members are left behind either to go to the hospital later or even if present in the hospital, are left behind closed doors— much like Ekwefi and Okonkwo's experiences at the mouth of the Oracle. Although comparisons between the ideas of hospitals, churches, doctors and priests could bear more and focused research and analyses here, that is not the focus of this work. However, since the bifurcation of intersubjectivities still prevail in most contemporary African countries, women continue to hold their own, persisting and insisting on full self-presentation. Images of the women's self-assertiveness are evident through short and crisp conversations between them. Their loss of voice in the public arena during this period is reflected in other ways. For example, the diversity of talents and expertise within Umuofia and between the people of Umuofia and the colonizers are obliquely referenced through Ekwefi's narrative about tortoise's efforts to represent all the birds at the feast in heaven.

However, whether one is examining Nwoye's mother's attempt to reassure Ekwefi as Chielo runs into the night with Ezinma, Chielo announcing that the Oracle wants to see Ezinma, or Chielo calling out a curse at Ekwefi who is following behind her in the dark night, individual portrayals of the women is scant because the narrator relies heavily on the people's common-sense knowledge about their land, tradition and shared language. Although the women's interactions with each other derive from common-sense agreements that use information from a common knowledge base, it is necessary to observe their conscious efforts to support one another within an intersubjective reality that seems to collude with the aggressive foreign language that threatens to suffocate theirs.

For example, even after she realized that Chielo was not going directly to the caves, Ekwefi continued to follow her through the dark night because she knows that wherever Chielo went, Ezinma would be with her. Following Chielo's voice, Ekwefi's feet find a grip in the familiar foot paths of Umuofia despite the alienating darkness. And, she continues in their mutual quest for Ezinma's health, knowing that "...[t]he moon must be preparing to rise, its sullenness over." Using her knowledge of and agreement with Umuofia's interpretation of the moon relative to their lived experiences, she is able to hold on to Chielo's occasional outbursts by relating the darkness to familiar understandings about husband/wife relationships, "When the moon rose later in the night, people said that it was refusing food, as a sullen husband refuses his wife's food when they have quarreled" (74). Countering Conrad's (1902) dark images of Africa, through the deployment of familiar African images, Achebe's portrayal of women facilitates re-entry into problematic physical and ideological terrains in this early exploration of the African woman's experiences in the novel. Although Ekwefi and Chielo are friends during the day, she is fully aware of Chielo's changed identity and magnified stature as a priestess as they traverse the expanses of Umuofia that have been darkened by night. On her part, Chielo is undeterred by the 'burden' (75) of the sick Ezinma on her back. Although Chielo knows that Ekwefi is following her, she says nothing directly to her throughout their journey. In contrast, Okonkwo does not participate in the women's unwavering confrontation of circumstances, adherence to rules, rituals and custom as they jog through the villages of Umuofia in the prescribed circuitous route that will deliver Ezinma to the Oracle of the Hills and Caves. Their determined search for a viable solution despite the odds works at the psychological level, enabling all the women to survive by sheer will.

The above encounter is framed by two seemingly unconnected events in the story: Okonkwo's love for Ekwefi manifested in their shared anxiety about Ezinma and his efforts to regain his self-confidence after killing Ikemefuna, the boy who called him, 'Father.' Both events delineate Igbo cultural anxiety about physical and emotional health and the traditional processes installed to ensure that individuals remain dynamic contributors to community life and engagement. Earlier in the story, that shared anxiety resulted in Okonkwo's invitation of the medicine-man Okagbue to find Ezinma's *iyi-uwa,* the visible representation of the pact she is said to have made with other spirit children and which, if not found by the living, would facilitate her return to them through death. Okonkwo springs into action as soon as Ekwefi wakes him up with the news of Ezinma's illness. He diagnoses her illness as *iba,* or malaria and goes into the nearby bushes to find the herbs to bring down the fever. Achebe's narrator says,

> Okonkwo returned from the bush carrying on his left shoulder a large bundle of grass and leaves, roots and barks of medicinal trees and shrubs. He went to Ekwe-fi's hut, put down his load and sat down.... Okonkwo *selected the best from his bundle, in their due proportion,* and cut them up. He put them in the pot *and Ekwefi poured in some water* (60) (*My emphasis*).

Throughout the novel, Okonkwo's prowess as a warrior, wrestler and political leader in Umuofia remain dominant. Frequently and in the various discussions about Achebe's works, Okonkwo's collaboration with his wives and his efforts to teach his children to become good citizens of Umuofia are lost in the initial efforts to reclaim the land from the colonizers. Eventually, Igbo (African) self-presentation engaged the need to measure up or surpass colonial legacies. This last involved the struggle to adjust to the new dispensation and resulted in self-presentations that sometimes negated ancestral common-sense agreements in the effort to formulate a contemporary homeland whose landscape could no longer yield the kind of footholds that the Ekwefis of Igbo land would be able to traverse on dark nights. Instead, adaptive strategies were developed by indigenous elites in the "modern spaces" for traditional power elites like Okonkwo. The struggle between African peoples and European cultural legacies necessitated refutations of traditional agreements about the maintenance of order in the traditional community.

In *Things Fall Apart* that order is evident in the practice of the careful record keeping among the people of Umuofia. For example, despite his poverty Okonkwo's father Unoka keeps records of his debts using chalk marks on the red earth wall of his *obi.* Also, toward the end of the novel, the narrator asserts, "It warmed Okonkwo's heart to see such strength of numbers" (142). Achebe's narrator uses this requirement for accurate records keeping to point to the obligation for balance in Igbo self-presentation to maintain narrative pace in the novel. Throughout the novel, a disruption of balance within the core frequently accompanies an imbalance in the order of Umuofia life. Although this search for balance is not always articulated as such, it is acknowledged in the arrangement of things in Umuofia life and existence. In *Things Fall Apart*, that arrangement is frequently predicated on the balance between male and female and is apparent in the carefully maintained relationships between men and women.

For example, one of the common-sense numbers in Igbo life is the number "four"[4]; there are four market days in the Igbo market week. On the night Ezinma is presented to the Oracle, the narrator calls attention to the oil lamps in "...all the four huts on Okonkwo's compound,'"and "Nwanyieke [who] lived four compounds away..." (67). In both cases, one of the compounds counted is Okonkwo's. As the novel ends, it becomes apparent that Okonkwo killed a total of four people – all male. Through his suicide on the day when he is happy about how the people of Umuofia are finally coming together in large numbers to protect themselves, Okonkwo fulfils Evil Forest's self-revelation to Uzowulu during the trial where he brings his in-laws before the clan for refusing to allow his wife to return to him, "I am Evil Forest. I kill a man on the day that his life is sweetest to him" (66). Within the intersubjective discourses of the novel, the unspoken revelation of Okonkwo's identity as "...the second *egwugwu* with the springy walk..." by "Okonkwo's wives, and perhaps other women as well..." (64) foreshadows Okonkwo's suicide. Unlike Ekwefi's inability to engage the human side of Chielo throughout the night of the visit to the Oracle, the women's implicit unmasking of Okonkwo as one of the egwugwu, metaphorically exposes him to the uninitiated, indicating Umuofia's inability to survive intact during this time of stress. As a prominent son of Umuofia, participation as an egwugwu reveals Okonkwo's status in the land; while his unmasking speaks to his inability to live up to his natural and ascribed roles in Umuofia. As an egwugwu, he stands next to *Ajofia*, or Evil Forest, the leading egwugwu of Umuofia. Okonkwo's earned role is that of the second egwugwu in Umuofia. However, Okonkwo always wants to be the first in all things and attempts to take on Ajofia's role when he kills the messenger. In so doing, he attacks the order of things in Umuofia; and, things fall apart as the clan implodes, reverting back to the unmediated idea of Ajofia from which the egwugwu, aided by other ancestral norms, are supposed to protect the people. Okonkwo's self-presentation, though viable in times of peace, is untenable during this time of stress when all rules must be closely followed to maintain security within the group.

Unlike Ekwefi who feels reassured when Okonkwo arrives at the entrance of the cave while she is waiting for Chielo and Ezinma, although Okonkwo's heart is warmed by the strength of numbers, he is not strengthened by it. When Ekwefi recognizes Okonkwo in the near darkness at the entrance to the Oracle, "Tears of gratitude filled her eyes. [And] she knew her daughter was safe" (76). Rather than attributing Ekwefi's gratitude as a woman's response, it makes sense to also see it as her understanding of Umuofia existence in ways that Okonkwo did not. This expanded interpretation is supported by the fact that when Chielo comes out of the cave with Ezinma, "...she did not as much as look[ed] at Okonkwo and or show[n] any surprise at finding them at the mouth of the cave..." (78). The women take for granted the fact that there is strength in numbers while Okonkwo tries to control outcomes despite strong indications of participation and approval by the people. This bifurcation of common-sense agreement between Okonkwo and the women becomes part of the new dispensation's self-presentation because Achebe's appropriation of the form of the novel is assumed to reflect an appropriation of European narrative norms in which the protagonist's actions and thoughts prevail over the community's.

In *No Longer at Ease* (1960), Obi Okonkwo, Okonkwo's grandson returns from England with a degree in English classics but lacks understanding about the common-sense agreements underlying both Igbo and English traditions. Despite the opportunities provided by his formal western education, he is unable to make a sound decision about how to proceed in the new dispensation. When he runs into financial trouble and begins to take bribes, he is arrested by the officials of the new dispensation in a physical and temporal location where people from his birth community cannot rescue him. Further, although he loves her, Obi Okonkwo cannot protect Clara, the woman he wants to marry because he has neither the language nor the social competence in either culture to claim her as his wife. Socially, then, it becomes possible to perceive Obi Okonkwo as an ogbanje. But unlike Ezinma, his iyi-uwa was buried in a European educational framework whose language most members of the Umuofia Improvement Union spoke with uncertainty or not at all. For him there is no Chielo to rescue him from the dark night of a transient illness into a life of promise supported by the goodwill of a benevolent community. Thus, although Ezinma Okonkwo eventually gets married and has children; her nephew, Obi Okonkwo becomes a victim of the bifurcated self resulting from his unspoken decision to uphold his father, Nwoye's literal interpretation of the Christian message when he discards his birth family to join the missionary arm of the colonial enterprise.

The bifurcated existence which seems the norm in the contemporary Igbo experience is an intensification of the agreement of those who, like Nwoye, decided to discard most aspects of Igbo tradition in the effort to validate themselves using undeveloped understandings of European cultural expressions in Africa. This last is different from European culture in Europe and is violent in many aspects. However, and in terms of language, the expression of European cultures in Africa is frequently characterized by emphasis on compassion, a hallmark of Christianity. Consequently, constructing contemporary African communities in the post-independence state has proved challenging because Africans began work on the contemporary community using the assumption of shared meanings despite the violent output of the colonial encounter.

In contemporary African literature as well as other areas of the African experience informed by socio-cultural interactions for the creation of a contemporary intersubjective existence, miscuing on the interpretive level became an avenue that ensured the mis-representation of the African woman. For example since the words for woman, female and feminine are frequently the same in Igbo, for example, it is difficult to engage in constructive analysis or interpretation of situations that contain those terms. Also, since the Igbo language does not differentiate gender, the words 'male' or 'female' are used as prefixes. However, the Igbo words for 'male' and 'female' are homonyms for 'man' and 'woman.' Consequently, in the above example of the efforts to alleviate the effects of Ezinma's ogbanje, it is easy to miss the fact that Okagbue digs for the iyi-uwa during the day while Chielo works toward the same end at night. Significantly, while Okagbue is watched by interested spectators as he digs for Ezinma's iyi-uwa, Chielo's efforts are associated with the night. While it is now possible, in today's technologically advanced spaces, to view physicians in surgery—fully masked, a privilege that was not possible even in traditional European spaces 60 years ago—it is still difficult, in many parts of the world including Africa to admit the fact of women's capacity to openly participate in the healing process. This is the case whether the healing issue in question is about health, human rights or the ending of wars around the world. For example, although in Igbo culture an individual who braves the dark is perceived as having emotional strength, it is more difficult in the novel written in English to reclaim Chielo from the darkness. This is because in most European discussions about Africa, the continent is equated with darkness and except for its rich natural resources is mostly perceived as evil. This part of the novel's plot asserts Chielo's roles both as a woman with access to the community's guiding principles and a healer. Telling her story in English makes it difficult to see the positive aspects of her role in an Umuofia whose role as a foil to Europe's dark Africa is already determined for it by the novel's language. In other words, notions of intersubjectivity become bifurcated as the idea of Umuofia develops in the novel. Simply put, from this new and foreign language an Umuofia (African) community emerges in which there exists no common meaning for the idea of evil. This bifurcation enables and reinforces the loss of the woman's significance in the culture during colonial intervention in Africa.

Subsequently, as African literature and African literary studies developed, it was easier to study the medicine man that works during the day than it was to engage the activities of the priestess who works at night. Although Chielo is as strong and reputable as Okagbue, she remains relegated to the background.

Sensitive to the miscuing that occurred as a result of the misreading of the Igbo woman's social position in the new order, Achebe addresses the problem in *Anthills of the Savannah* (1987). Beatrice Nwanyibuife Okoh has a degree in English from University of London's Queen Mary College. Not only does she ponder her relationship with the men but Achebe makes sure that readers do not miscue the importance of her role in his discussions about women and gender in African literature and Igbo life by ensuring that she addresses her relationship to the Chielo, the priestess character in *Things Fall Apart*, "As a matter of fact, I do sometimes feel like Chielo in the novel, the priestess and prophetess of the Hills and the Caves" (105). As an acknowledgement of the miscuing that enables the successes of the colonial era, Beatrice's character engages the woman's question and makes for a better understanding of this work's exploration of intersubjectivity. Using, Chris Oriko and Ikem Osodi, two writers who are characters in the novel, Achebe engages the nature of the bifurcation that occurs in Igbo life during this period. Ikem, the poet and editor of the National Gazette has access to the people and the ability to draw the reader into the depths of Igbo imagination and narrative vision. Continuing with his claims for the novelist as teacher, Achebe deploys Ikem's skills as a prose-poet in the unsigned insightful piece, "Pillar of Fire: A Hymn to the Sun" (28-30; 194). Just before Chris is shot to death on a roadside, he gives the only copy of the poem over to Emmanuel Obete, the President of the Student Union. Achebe's application of traditional Igbo narrative vision becomes evident on closer examination of the characters. Looking for a way forward for both African literature and Africans, Achebe creates a complex of characters that recognize that the current situation is not an accident but part of a historical trajectory which can be corrected if they work together using their combined expertise. As in the traditional narrative, Achebe's references are theoretical with some bordering on the mythical. For example, by using Beatrice Nwanyibuife to create a relationship between *Things Fall Apart* and *Anthills of the Savannah*, Achebe evokes an interpretive relationship between the two works, their characters and their roles in his overall narrative project. Regarding the question of women, *Things Fall Apart* mostly examines the female principle. However, in *Anthills of the Savannah*, he is openly engaged in responding to questions about his negligence of women and their affairs at the personal, public and national levels. Beatrice Nwanyibuife Okoh, graduates from University of London's Queen Mary's College with "first-class honours in English" (68) and is a Senior Assistant Secretary in the Ministry of Finance. She has been good friends with Ikem since her undergraduate days in England. And, Ikem, Chris and Sam, Kangan's President have been friends from their secondary school days in Lord Lugard College. Through Ikem, she meets Chris who wants to marry her. Thus, she becomes intimately involved in the relationship between the three men whose troubled friendship becomes a mirror of the nation's difficulties. Beatrice's interactions with the men and Elewa articulate existing agreements about common-sense not only among western educated Igbo but also people from other parts of Kangan. Using Ikem Osodi, the poet from Abazon, the area that continues to have problems with national affiliations, Achebe calls attention to how the problematic relationship between post-colonial Kangan might be resolved by the newly educated elite. For example, where traditionally, Ikemefuna's death may have had the appearance of signaling an end to him and his progeny, Achebe engages the question at the level of negotiated futures, the original intention of the exchange that resulted in Ikemefuna's three-year sojourn in Okonkwo's household. Thus, the negotiated relationships between Beatrice and the three men in *Anthills* ensures that her understanding of their intentions embedded in Chris Oriko's last words, "The Last Grin…" are translated and explained to Emmanuel Obete, the student who learns about dignity from Chris' last act of kindness. Unlike Ikemefuna in *Things Fall Apart* who is killed after he is given as part of the exchange negotiations for the woman killed by his people, Chris dies protecting the young woman, Adamma from the soldier. In the post-colonial interventions where the Christian story takes over the lives of Kangan citizens, the relationship between the names Chris and Emmanuel and the actual relationship between the characters become obvious on close examination of the phrase *uwa t'uwa*, "…world inside a world, inside a world without end…" (77) which Beatrice uses to examine the nature and structure of relationships that profoundly show the continuity of tradition in modernity. Achebe engages the discussion further when Emmanuel Obete wants to follow Chris.

Chris asks Emmanuel, "Do you people have a proverb about a man looking for something inside the bag of a man who is looking for something?" Emmanuel replies that "...they did have something that resembled it: about digging a new hole to get sand to fill an old one" (174). Eventually, Beatrice's discovery that some things, including people, which appear to be alone, are always part of a series of worlds within each other, without end.

Thus, in the end, Ikem Osodi's death does not foreclose a path to the future as the little group from different parts and life styles of Kangan convene in Beatrice's flat to give a name to Ikem's daughter. Following one of Achebe's narratives' logic from *Things Fall Apart* to *Anthills of the Savannah*, Amaechina: May-the-path-never-close... the beautiful path of Ikem... (206) is the ultimate aim of the negotiations for life between the people of Umuofia and Mbanta. However, in the new dispensation, the question seems to be about choice in the abstract. But, Achebe, the novelist and teacher asserts that Ikem Osodi also met a violent death by armed men who pick him up in his home at night after ransacking it. The question becomes: Does Ikem or Ikemefuna die a more honorable death? Is it easier for a nation to bear the loss of its son when he dies by the matchet or by the gun? Although both were part of the negotiation between Umuofia and its enemy about the murder of Udo's wife, why did Umuofia not kill the nameless virgin that was given to it at the same time as Ikemefuna? Would Udo have been able to marry another wife? These and other questions need to be asked about peace-keeping in traditional Igbo society and the policy issues and decisions that emerge should be compared with what efforts at maintaining civil society in contemporary Nigeria and other African countries. Of particular importance is the question of what contemporary African countries do about the loss of women's dignity and lives. Rather than national outrage (as with Umuofia when Udo's wife is murdered), most issues about African women are left to the ingenuity and kindness of individual men. It is left to the Chris Orikos, Ikem Osodis and Captain Medanis to protect and support the efforts of individual African women. Women like Beatrice Nwanyibuife Okoh are mostly seen as sexual objects by many national leaders.

As part of the post independence environment, Chansa Kabwela's experience is illuminating. President Rupiah Banda of Zambia sees her only as an obstacle to be cast aside; or, as Achebe's Nwanyibuife would say, she's a female soldier who must be corrected, with violence. About this aspect of the African girl-to-womanhood experience, Beatrice asserts:

> I didn't realize until much later that my mother bore me a huge grudge because I was a girl—her fifth in a row... and that when I was born she had so desperately prayed for a boy to give my father.... But I must mention that in addition to Beatrice they had given me another name at my baptism, Nwanyibuife—A female is also something....

Perhaps it was the *nwanyi*, the female half of it that I particularly resented. My father was so insistent on it. "Sit like a female!" or "Female soldier" which he called me as he lifted me off the ground with his left hand and gave me three stinging smacks on the bottom with his right the day I fell off the cashew tree (79-80).

Seen as an anomaly by both parents, the contemporary female child who attains success in the new dispensation whether by staying alive despite the odds of infant mortality or by gaining high academic honors is perceived as a challenge. Unlike what was the case for Ezinma Okonkwo, there is no maternal protection for Africa's contemporary female children against the wishes of a father who wishes she were a son. Also, she cannot be like Chielo who confidently sells her wares in her market stall during the day knowing that she is authorized to run through the clan's pathways at night seeking health and life for the community. Instead, like Elewa, she is sent into the night in a rickety taxi whose driver is paid a twenty-kobo tip to drive her home because Ikem does not want to wake up next to her or any other woman, the following morning. Having labeled her a prostitute, he chooses to give her the option of not acting like one. Knowing that he can rely on Elewa to be there whenever he needs her, Ikem treats her as though she has another life to spare; and that that spare life belongs to him. Chris treats Beatrice the same way when he asks her to attend the party at the president's house while keeping all options open. Although the three men's friendship is deteriorating, they deliberately try to run the country on the basis of forgotten boyhood dreams while pretending that the women will survive the aftermath of their failed leadership. Eventually, Elewa and Beatrice live up to Ikem's (and Chris') expectations when they bring their small community together and pledge to keep the shinning path of Ikem open for posterity. In the end, what remains uncertain is whether Kangan will survive. In Kangan, Sam's decisions during his presidency are hampered by the fact that his ambition since boyhood is to do what he is told by his teachers. Unlike in *Things Fall Apart* where the leaders work from norms that are understood across enemy lines, the new leaders in *Anthills of the Savannah* have no guiding framework that sustains friendships let alone the lives of whole communities through time.

According to Achebe's narrators, the problem is not whether or not the women will protect Africa's posterity but that by ignoring and obstructing women's efforts to restore harmony in the community, Africa's leaders are slowly killing off those things which were missed by colonization and the colonizers. In this, their leadership represents both inept governance as well as a grotesque and failed effort at the erasure of tradition in modernity.

Finally, the weapon of choice is no longer just the knife, which as Obierika says, was "...put on the things that held us together and we have fallen apart." (125) As the recent case of Zambia shows, it is no longer the fact that Africa's leaders only kill other men whom they perceive as obstacles. By rejecting the idea that women can and should act as successful advocates for other women, men and the various communities, African leaders are embarked on killing Africa's future.

Notes

1. BBC News, December 9, 2009.
2. International Women's Media Foundation, November 27, 2009.
3. BBC News.
1. The numbers 'three' and 'seven' are more evident in rituals and symbols.

Works Cited

Achebe, Chinua. *Anthills of the Savannah*. New York: Anchor Books. 1987.

_____. *No Longer at Ease*. Oxford: Heinemann Educational Books.1960.

_____. *Things Fall Apart*. Oxford: Heinemann Educational Books. (1958). With an Introduction by Simon Gikandi and Don C. Ohadike (1996).

BBC News, "Surreal drama of Zambia 'porn' trial," http://news.bbc.co.uk/2/hi/programmes/from_our_own_correspondent/8358936.stm accessed December 9, 2009.

Conrad, Joseph. *Heart of Darkness*. Penguin Books: New York; London, UK. (1902).

International Women's Media Foundation. http://www.iwmf.org/article.aspx?id=1011&c=pastletter accessed November 27, 2009.

Seale, Clive. Editor. *Researching Society and Culture*. London; Thousand Oaks, California: Sage Publications (1998).

CHAPTER 6

LOVE AND MOTHERHOOD IN CHINUA ACHEBE'S NOVELS

Helen Chukwuma

"Life on the planet is born of woman."

— Adrienne Rich

The above quote situates woman as mother in the scheme of things on planet Earth. Bringing it home to Chinua Achebe's cultural space, I cite part of a poem by Phanuel Akubueze Egejuru:

Ife bu Omumu	Something is Reproduction
Ife bu Ozuzu	Something is Completion
Ife bu Nne	Something is Mother
Gini bu Nne?	What is Mother?
Nne bu ndu	Mother is Life
Nne bu Ozuzu	Mother is Rearing
Nne bu Nchedo	Mother is Protection
Nne bu Ihunanya	Mother is Love
Nne bu Chi	Mother is Spirit, personal god
ChiNne KA!	MOTHER's CHI IS SUPREME!

This paper shows that Achebe espouses his deep understanding of motherhood in his first two novels: *Things Fall Apart* (1958) and *Arrow of God* (1979) and raises the same question addressed by

Egejuru which is if mothers are so revered why does their status in society not correspond accordingly. This is seen in the ambivalence of female wifehood and motherhood. The female aspect seems to be the overriding principle that underscores women's status. The female, that being inferior to the male is the same one who becomes wife and then mother. She is mother, an elevated status to her children, their peers and age-groups, but this same woman is somebody's wife. The contention therefore is that though motherhood elevates a woman's status in society, her femalism continues to define and limit her.

In traditional Igbo ethos, motherhood is the quintessential honor and crown of the married woman. Motherhood becomes a duty, an obligation and a vocation demanded of every wife. This is the expectation of the husband, in-laws and the wife's natal family as well. This is an expectation and yearning the wife herself embraces. In a gendered structural society as the Igbo, womanhood and wifehood are equated with motherhood. In this regard therefore, in the traditional Igbo world as portrayed in Achebe's early novels, infertility in a woman is the tragedy of female absence or at best female malfunction. They had been denied the essential beingness and function of womanhood.

It is important at this early part of this essay to point the role of patriarchy and maleness in this context. Woman is there for and at the pleasure of men. Husband is supreme, is the head of the family and his responsibility is to maintain the family's name and uphold and ensure family continuity through male offspring. He plays his own part by marrying, bringing into his home a wife who with him will make that possible. The husband is relentless until he has a male offspring. This way he can depart this world in peace because he has perpetuated himself. This divine mission is ingrained in every Igbo adolescent male as he charts his way through life. The enormity of this responsibility and the desperation therefore of unfulfilled men is brought out by Elechi Amadi in the character of Madume in *The Concubine* (1966). Madume tried to procure a male offspring by his ambition to marry the beautiful widow Ihuoma. He died in his bid. Buchi Emecheta in *Joys of Motherhood* (1979) narrated how Amatokwu, Nnu-ego's first husband ruthlessly manhandled her and cast her off in favour of his newly acquired wife who bore him a son. Nnu-ego was childless. This therefore is the tragic and unwholesome situation that awaits a wife whom motherhood eludes, further, motherhood of sons.

It is from this background that we will appreciate love and motherhood in Achebe's fiction. We shall examine the significance of motherhood and mother-love in an overtly masculine society. The Igbo word for mother is 'Nne.' Motherhood is a term that encompasses the biological signification as well as a nurturing custodianship, thus the term 'Nne-ora' mother of all – The first wife in a polygamous household is "nne anyi" – our mother, as different from mother terminologies which are accompanied by the name of the fist offspring e.g. Nne Nwoye. Such specificity is an identifying tool for mothers.

My analysis here is informed by the tenets of African feminism which extol and so accommodate motherhood. And here reference must be made to Catherine Acholonu's *Motherism* a text in which she posits that motherism is the Afro centric alternative to feminism and nurture and alongside of it is concern for the environment. This culture of motherhood runs counter to the second wave feminism of the West which sees this as "a key source of women's oppression" (Erica Burman, 350) in that it does not allow for women's choice in the matter. For indeed, it remains a presumption that all "women can, will and want to be mothers."This may be true as some women cannot be mothers biologically (biological malfunction or lack of husband compatibility, etc.) and even at the present time, some women may not want to give birth but will nurture a child of adoption or of surrogate mother. These are interpolations of the modern era, however in Achebe's space then in *Things Fall Apart* and now, motherhood has a prime place in society.

Achebe's presentation of motherhood in his novels is one key point of consonance between him and African female novelists as Flora Nwapa and Buchi Emecheta. However, Emecheta was to branch out to interrogate the joys of motherhood and underscore the great irony of motherhood which in the person of the protagonist of *Joys of Motherhood* Nnuego, after much scorn, humiliation and suffering she later was the mother of many sons and daughters and though this brought her joy, fulfillment and social acclaim, motherhood was to be her doom in the end.

The prevalent image of the mother in African literature is the sacrificial mother, the one who gives her blood at birth and who gives all to her children in training and nurture. Emecheta captures this in Nnuego's musings in *Joys of Motherhood* after the birth of her twin daughters, she felt subdued and mused about motherhood:

> What have I gained from all this? Yes, I have many children, but what do I have to feed them on? On my life. I have to work myself to the bone to look after them, I have to give them my all. And if I am lucky enough to die in peace, I even have to give them my soul. They will worship my dead spirit to provide for them. It will be hailed as a good spirit as long as there are plenty of yams and children in the family, but if a young wife does not conceive, or there is a famine, my dead spirit will be blamed. When will I be free? (186-187).

The answer is 'Never,' so motherhood is forever. The basic question therefore is with all the constraints of motherhood, why is it an endearing pervasive ambition and dream of Igbo wives and other African women by extension. These are time-revered patriarchal tenets set in society. But still, existentially there is no other way of keeping the planet alive.

If women cease to give life, human kind will cease to exist. (except maybe by cloning). Motherhood therefore presents itself as a biological and humanistic imperative and transcends the individual. Men goad the women on by celebrating birth and motherhood. The Igbo have elaborate rituals of feasting, song and dance at the new birth. Motherhood is celebrated and women seize the moment to enact favours and make copious demands on husbands especially at the birth of sons. Motherhood in Achebe's space is both a natural and social duty and expectation. The power of a woman therefore is the power of procreation.

Chinweizu in his book *The Anatomy of Female Power* lists the five pillars of female power and sets the womb or mother-power as the greatest. He exclaims:

O womb, your power is great! You are the biological foundation, the tap-root of female power. As the goal net into which a man must shoot if he is to procreate, you are the part of a woman for which he will pay almost any price. And because you are priceless to him, you hold untold power over him, like a fabulous gold seam which rules a prospector's life (19).

From the above discussion, it is apparent that Achebe used the prevalent aspects of motherhood in his fiction. Ekwefi, Okonkwo's second wife, Achebe tells the reader "had suffered a good deal in her life. She had borne ten children and nine of them had died in infancy, usually before the age of three...The birth of her children, which should be a woman's crowning glory, became for Ekwefi mere physical agony devoid of promise" (77).

In Ekwefi's infant mortality, Achebe painted a grim picture of her to the extent that the loss of her infant children turned her into a disconsolate unfulfilled wife until the advent of her daughter Ezinma. Ezinma was sickly as a child but because she survived the onslaught of the "Ogbanje" spiritual cult, she was spoiled and pampered by her mother and dearly loved by Okonkwo her father.

Achebe's account of Ezinma's mandatory night journey to the Oracle of the Groves in the company of the Oracle's priestess Chielo showed up tellingly the limitless sacrifice a mother is willing to make for her only child. Ekwefi dared the priestess and her god and followed suit as the priestess whisked off Ezinma through the darkness and eeriness of the night. Okonkwo too, seeing his wife's courage and foolhardiness armed himself with his amulets and machete and followed wife – mother, priestess and their daughter. Ekwefi's life revolved on Ezinma and that was so with the other wives and their children.

Achebe portrayed another aspect of womanhood seen in the nurture the mothers provided for their children. Achebe showed the bonding among the wives especially in the care of their children. Child care was not the sole responsibility of its mother but a shared responsibility by all, men and women alike. An Igbo saying encapsulates it thus "Nwa bu nwa ora," a child belongs to all. This is reflected in the name of 'Nworah' – child of all, "Obiora," the wishes of all. This bonding among the wives is seen at the incident of Ojiugo, Okonkwo's third wife who went to plait her hair at her friend's and overstayed denying Okonkwo of his lunch. The following dialogue is indicative of the bonding of the wives and the common responsibility of child care.

"Where is Ojiugo," he asked his second wife…."She has gone to plait her hair." Okonkwo bit his lips as anger welled up within him…."Where are her children? Did she take them?" he asked with unusual coolness and restraint. "They are here," answered his first wife Nwoye's mother. Okonkwo bent down and looked into her hut. Ojiugo's children were eating with the children of the first wife. "Did she ask you to feed them before she went?" "Yes," lied Nwoye's mother trying to minimize Ojiugo's thoughtfulness. Okonkwo knew she was not speaking the truth. He walked back to his 'obi' to await Ojiugo's return (29).

The wives cover up for each other but more importantly, the children are their common responsibility.

It is in Okonkwo's forced exile that Chinweizu's statement, "O womb, your power is great," is best demonstrated. In Igboland, the children of the daughters of the home are much respected and enjoy a high status in their mother's hometown. An Igbo adage articulates this. "Oso chua gi na ebe nna gi, igba ga na ikunne gi…. When things go rough in your father's house and you are chased out, you have to recourse to your mother's home." That was precisely what Okonkwo did. When he and his family were cast out of Umuofia and exiled for seven years, his last and only resort was his mother's hometown Mbanta. Achebe narrates that as Uchendu, Okonkwo's maternal uncle saw him and his weary household of three wives and several children, "he guessed what has happened, and asked no questions" (129).

The significance of Igbo names will serve to elucidate and give credence to the power of motherhood. Egejuru's poem cited earlier recounts

> What is Mother?
> Mother is Life
> Mother is Protection
> Mother is Love
> Mother is chi (personal spirit or god)
> Mother's spirit is supreme.

Igbo girls' names range from Nneka – mother is supreme, 'Nne-buchi' Mother is chi. These names when given in full, bare a better elucidation of their great import. Nneka – literally means mother is greater....than chi. Nnekachi. The one says Mother is chi the other that Mother is greater than chi. Egejuru engages this question:

> "How then is mother equal and greater than chi?....
> the procreative power of woman bestows in her the
> power of chi, the creator. How is mother greater than
> chi? The answer is clearly provided in *Things Fall Apart*.
> When Okonkwo is abandoned by his Chi and is exiled
> by his people, he flees to his motherland where from
> the land of the spirits, his mother offers him protection
> and makes him prosper again. Thus the greatness of
> motherhood lies in its permanence and reliability. It is
> the only force that is steadfast in its love and coopera-
> tiveness" (13).

Nnekachi, because when your chi fails you, your mother picks you up, props you until you find your footing again. This is also part of the Igbo cultural ethos, thus when one in desperate need receives aid, the aid-giver is eulogized as the 'chi' in that situation. Mothers are perpetual givers to their children, their Chi when all else fails.

Motherhood is power and status especially mother of sons in a heavily patriarchal society as the Igbo. I had argued elsewhere that motherhood through birth songs offers woman a forum of "celebra-tion and cheer rehearsing female fulfillment in procreation. Further, they afford the women free expression and psychic release from the inhibitions of socio-cultural norms and expectations in this all female world, female individualism surfaces and inner motives and aspirations are bared same as misgivings and discontent hitherto bottled up in the guise of conformity and harmony" (23).

Motherhood is both" a site for strength and a site for struggle with women" (Burman, 352). The strength lies in the status of mother and the anchor it provides in a husband's house. This is more so as the wives had little or no economic means and relied on their husbands for up-keep. Thus motherhood gives a woman entitle-ment because she has fulfilled herself dispatched her responsibil-ity .Husband's gratification lies in presenting the newly delivered mother and mother-in-law with gifts, marked with celebration. Achebe records in *Things Fall Apart*, that when Okonkwo's first wife bore him three sons in succession, he "slaughtered a goat for her as was the custom."(79) and there was feasting and music. In all these, the women remain bearers of the fruit which in the final analysis do not belong to them. Mention must be made here of Ugoye in *Arrow of God* who stood helplessly by while her husband Ezeulu "sacrificed" her son Oduche to the white man's religion. She is his mother but had no say in the matter as Ezeulu repeatedly pointed out to her. So inhibiting are the customs and norms of patriarchy. The children belong to the father who controls them and enforces his will on them.

Oduche's mother, Ugoye, tried to reason with her husband but he was impatient with her. "How does it concern you what I do with my son? You say you do not want Oduche to follow strange ways. Do you not know that in a great man's household, there must be people who follow all kinds of strange ways?" (46). It was indeed very strange that Oduche imprisoned the town's sacred python in a box intending to suffocate it to death. When the deed was discovered, Ezeulu exclaimed "Today, I shall kill the boy with my own hand" (45). Then Oduche became Ugoye's son and it was the mother's protection only that shielded him from harm. Anosi advised, "Won't you find where your son is and tell him not to return home today" (45)? Ugoye sent her son to her kinsman (mother's home) for protection reminiscent of the succour Okonkwo received from his mother's hometown.

Ezeulu, in an ironic twist, desires to see his son Oduche again, and asked Ugoye where her son was. "Is he my son now?" she asked petulantly. Such selective motherhood with an overbearing husband further underscores the couple's limitations of femalism. As with the sons, so the daughters. Okonkwo without any consultation with his wife impressed on his adolescent daughters to delay their marriage till they rejoined their kith and kin in Umuaro where they will be courted by the rich and powerful in the land in order to boost their father's image. In the Igbo traditional household, female identity is ensconced in the husband/father's will.

In this clutter of female voicelessness, does the mother continue to be the outsider? No. her relief comes from her children especially her sons who when grown tend to situate their mothers firmly in the domiciliary schema. Nwoye the Christian convert left home and his father's displeasure to join the church. Achebe added "He would return later to his mother and his brothers and sisters and convert them to the new faith" (152).

The spiritual element in woman as mother is the source of her power in the subliminal realm. Mazrui writes of the "dual fertility" (161) of woman in procreation and fertility of the soil. She is not just woman but mother, earth mother whom the Igbo recognize as the goddess Ani/Ala. She gives fertility and nurture. Mother contextually is thought of as the climax, the zenith of events and incidents. Even the strong man of Iraq Saddam Husein referred to the American invasion of his country as "the mother of all wars" and it turned out to be for him. Thus Achebe narrates that when Ezeulu danced out during the festival of the Pumpkin Leaves, he was regaled in his most foreboding attire of Ulu Chief Priest and "on his right hand he carried "Nne Ofo" the mother of all staffs of authority in Umuaro" (*Arrow of God*, 71).

This link with maternity and divinity and the highest symbol of conscience and finality is seen in the spirit world. As usual, concepts and practices are ridden with contradictions of sorts. Women are restricted from participating in male masking and cannot even approach near a performing masquerade but must view it from a safe distance. Yet, when an egwu-gwu masquerade is desecrated, it was "the mother of the spirits who walked the length and breadth of the clan weeping for her murdered son" (Egejuru, 14). Ezeulu is the chief priest of Ulu, and Chielo is the priestess of the Oracle of the groves and hills. Two of them are esteemed in their roles but in normal life, while Ezeulu continues in his ambience of awe and respectability, Chielo becomes an ordinary woman stripped of all power and authority that attends her priestess state.

Mother is supreme because in her hands, as a potter at the wheel, she moulds the children of the clan and points them to the future. The men are in the outside world to conquer while the women, the mothers are home-bound to build. The anomaly is that these home builders (character moulders), and by extension nation builders, are relegated to the background, cast on the periphery of their achievement. This is embedded in her being female.

Motherhood as divinity which informs matrilineal societies, the rationale being motherhood is an undisputed fact but fatherhood can be. It is therefore only your mother who can tell you who your father is. E. J. Alagoa records that among the Ijo of Niger Delta, "God is not merely creator but procreator. The divine power to bring life into being is understood in the light of the function of women to replenish the earth. Accordingly, among many Central Delta and Western Delta Ijaw, God was simply Woyengi, Our Mother" (35). Motherhood separates a woman from being a mere sex object; it gives the instrumentality as a procreator.

Some parts of Igboland are matrilineal as Nnobi (Amadiume, 1987) same as the Fante in Cape Coast Ghana, and among the Akans which houses the beautiful proverb Mother is Gold. Okonkwo himself in *Things Fall Apart* attests to matriliny, "The world is large said Okonkwo." I have even heard that in some tribes a man's children belong to his wife and her family" (74). Why should the Okonkwos of this world discountenance their wives and mothers of their children and render them voiceless and ineffective in matters that concern the life and future of their children? The answer lies between dependency and muscular brute force. Normative values dictate subservience of the female especially in the home environment. Man is master and you and your children belong to him. Even the financial and material gains of the wife belong to the husband and can be disposed at will. The other aspect is the use of brute force to cow and bend to submission an untoward wife and indeed any female. Okonkwo constantly beat his wives and there was none to stop him. He paid the penalty for such excesses during the week of peace, but then he had the satisfaction that he had done it anyway.

Okonkwo's world and society have faded away into the horizons of history. Achebe, the master artist that he is has continued to upgrade his narrative reflecting the pulse of the times. His other novels leading to the *Anthills of the Savannah* (1981) show the female characters slowly reclaiming their self-worth. Clara in *No Longer at Ease*, did not succumb to letting motherhood only define her. Beatrice in Anthills, created her own identity as a person, educated, knowledgeable and accomplished. She did not clamor for marriage and motherhood in order to win social acclaim. The society accepted her in her own terms and respected her for who she is. Elewa had a baby for Chris because she chose to; she was not under any compulsion to prove her fecundity.

In today's world, motherhood remains a choice, though it is still desirable and still expected of brides. The noblesse and sanctity of motherhood are real and will remain so, a mother's work is eternal, even in death "your mother is there to protect you" (*Things Fall Apart*, 134). A mother's love and care is unquantifiable for as Okonkwo said while giving a big feast for his mother's people for hosting him and his family seven years "A child cannot pay for its mother's milk" (166). Also, "you cannot suppress the maternal bond because the Earth is Mother in Igbo cosmology and all humans belong to her. She nurtures and sustains them and at death, all life returns to Mother Earth" (Chukwuma, 2007).

Works Cited

Achebe, Chinua. *Things Fall Apart*. New York: Anchor Books, 1994.

_____. *Arrow of God*. New York: Anchor Books, 1974.

Acholonu, Catherine, Obianuju. *Motherism*. Owerri, Nigeria: Afa Publications, 1995.

Alagoa, E. J. "God is Mother: A Historical Review of Women in the Development of Niger Delta Communities," Nkparom Ejituwu and Amakievi Gabriel, eds. *Women in Nigerian History: The Rivers and Bayelsa State Experience*. Port Harcourt, Nigeria: Onyoma Publishers, 2002. 35-44.

Amadiume, Ifi. *Afrikan Matriarchal Foundations, The Igbo Case*. London: Karmak House, 1987.

Burman, Erica. "Motherhood," *Encyclopedia of Feminist Theories*. Ed. Lorraine Code. London and New York: Anchor Books, 1994.

Chinweizu. *Anatomy of Female Power*. Lagos, Nigeria: Pero Press, 1990.

Chukwuma, Helen. "Feminism and Femininity in Igbo Birth Songs," *Feminism in African Literature*, ed. Helen Chukwuma. Port Harcourt, Nigeria: Pearl Publishers, 2003.

_____. "Literary Strategies in Feministic Writing: Flora Nwapa's *Cassova Song* and Phannel Egejuru's *The Seed Yams Have Been Eaten*," *Nigerian Literature in English: Emerging Critical Perspectives*. Port Harcourt, Nigeria: 2007. 135-149.

Egejuru, Phanuel and Katrak, Ketu, eds. *Nwanyibu: Womanbeing and African Literature*. Trenton, NJ: Africa World Press, 1997.

Ejituwu, Nkparom C. and Amakievi O. I. Gabriel eds. *Women in Nigerian History: The Rivers and Bayelsa State Experience.* Port Harcourt, Nigeria: Onyoma Publications, 2002. 35-44.

Eko, Ebele et al. *Flora Nwapa: Critical Perspectives.* Calabar, Nigeria: University of Calabar Press, 1997.

Emecheta, Buchi. *The Joys of Motherhood.* New York: George Braziller, 1979.

Laremont, Ricardo Rens and Tracia Leacock Seghatolislami eds. *Africanity Redefined. Collected Essays of Ali A. Mazrui, Vol. 1.* Trenton, NJ: Africa World Press, 2002.

Lewis, Jan Johnson. "Adrienne Rich Quotes," *About Women's History.* http://womenshistory.about.com/cs/quotes/qu_adriennerich.htm. 2/23/2010.

Nwahunanya, Chinyere. *Tragedy in the Anglophone West African Novel.* Nigeria: Springfield Publishers, 2003.

CHAPTER 7

METAMORPHOSING FEMALE CHARACTERS IN SELECT ACHEBE'S NOVELS: WOMEN AS SIGNPOSTS

Angela M. Fubara

Gender is encased in every aspect of human life beginning from the home to religion, education, commerce/business and politics. These elements of life cannot be divorced from literary creativity. Intrinsically woven in Achebe's works is a compendium of social issues including gender which nestle on historicity, politics and governance stemming from the publication of *Things Fall Apart* (TFA) in 1958. The polarity of strength and weakness is the concrete mark of gender which characterizes the masculine society of TFA and *Arrow of God* (AOG).

This catalytic classic TFA, set in the tradition-based Igbo society awoke the sensibilities of later African literary writers. Achebe's creative energy has attracted readers from various fields of study with outpouring accolade: "a pace-setter, a talented writer and a genuine artist" (Ngara, 113-4). Achebe is equally classed as the metaphoric "Eagle on the Iroko". Iroko is a tree none can climb more than once in the Igbo proverbial index. Representing the iroko is the field of African Literature and eagle Chinua Achebe, who has literarily climbed and soared above the Iroko several times (Rose Mezu 210). Achebe in this earth-breaking classic recreates the primordial Igbo society depicted as a tradition-based uncompromising patriarchy.

Women are caged, possessed and are the leitmotifs of wives, yam barns and titles. These are the basic achievements a man of worth has to acquire to be recognized. Women are voiceless. A non achiever or a failure is regarded as a woman epitomized by Okonkwo's father, Unoka who is called "Agbala", depicting an effeminate figure who had neither titles nor barns of yam. Osugo in that same category is disgraced out of a meeting by Okonkwo, the achiever, who tells Osugo scornfully and derogatorily that "This meeting is for men" (11). Yam stands for manliness. It is a very labor-intensive crop which requires energy to cultivate. He who could feed his household from year to year with yams is regarded as a great man (23). Lesser crops like cocoyam with less regard are cultivated by women.

When a reader opens the pages of Achebe's works which are not tradition- based, s/he is quick to observe some changes in the lives of Achebe's female characters which this work semantically delineates as metamorphosing. Metamorphosing (metamorphosis used as a verbal, in present participle) connotes a continuing change. Metamorphosis simply means transfiguration, transformation and transmutation, a word used in the study of the life cycle of many insects, amphibians and fish in which the fertilized eggs, transmit to larvae, then to caterpillar. In the case of insect, the caterpillar transmutes to imago. The imago is the final stage in the life cycle of the insect when it becomes a sexually mature adult. At the imago stage the insect flies away from its cocoon. Signposts are indicative marks with meanings which nudge for attention. Focusing on the polarity between masculinity and femininity, this work hinges on Achebe's female figures and his progressive characterization of them which shows his changing attitudes in the select novels. Attempts would be made to delineate women as signposts in a changing society.

Woman Foreshadow

The masculinist society thus surveyed gives a glimpse of the pathetic female existence in Achebe's tradition-based novels. Women suffer various forms of abuse in the home such as wife-beating, which is a norm in the society of that time. Added to this brutality is the obnoxious lopsided emphasis on virginity before marriage. In the two Achebe's tradition-based novels TFA and AOG the issue of virginity receives full andro-cultural treatment. A female child must be a virgin before marriage but not the male. Obierika boasts to his in-laws that his virginal daughter Akueke will bear "you many sons like the mother of our town" (TFA 117). Amikwu Uchendu's son (Uchendu is Okonkwo's uncle) is marrying a new wife in Mbanta. Uchendu's elder daughter, Ndidi questions Amikwu's bride, "How many men have you lain with since my brother first expressed his desire to marry you? "None" is the bride's answer. To prove her truthfulness the bride must swear "on the staff of my fathers" says Uchendu. The hen's head (hen is gender motif) is thereafter cut off and the blood is allowed to pour on "the ancestral staff." Amikwu is not questioned. This depicts inequality of gender morality in this society. The woman remains the man's property whose pristine virtue must be intact never the man's.

Pitted against valour and violence is the female peacefulness. The polarity of masculinity and peaceful femininity appears to attract violence against women. "Do what you are told woman" is always the weighty force of the masculinist. This must be obeyed with absolute subservience. Okonkwo, the centre of Umuofia community, the embodiment of societal values holds firm the acute rod of the masculinist. He does not only beat his wife but also batters his household whom he "rules with heavy hands" (9). He beats his wife Ojiugo even during the Week of Peace (21). His feat of anger and severe masculinity is further demonstrated when he gives another of his wife, Ekwefi " a sound beating and left her and her only daughter weeping" (27).

It is not surprising that Achebe's female characters remain passive stunted and undeveloped. Men symbolize power and control and women weakness and subservience. However in the midst of this rigid patriarchy there stands a very powerful female figure, Chielo, a mother who is supreme. The significance of motherhood in the Igbo ethos as encapsulated in the given name "Nneka" is explained by Achebe through his mouth-piece Uchendu, Okonkwo's uncle:

A man belongs to his father's land when

things are good and sweet. But when there is sorrow
and bitterness he finds refuge in his
Motherland... And that is why we say
mother is supreme (94).

This assumed importance of the woman which wears a cloak of cynicism is seen as a socially contrived strategy to keep the woman powerless and subordinate. The woman who really stands tall in this primordial masculinist society is the Chielo, the Oracle of Hills and Caves. Chielo is positioned even at this primordial setting as supreme indeed. She is a woman not there for ridicule. Her activities demonstrate that woman has the capacity to soar over man. She is divinely empowered and can save life from powerful spirits that stifle life and hope of the future. (symbolized by Ezinma).

Chielo is spiritually endowed with power that makes men tremble and bow. At the subline level she can shout and reprimand any man including the powerful Okonkwo. It is evidently glaring that at the apex of this traditional society is the woman, Chielo who is dreaded and revered. Cloaked in the subliminal mantle of divinity she serves, Chielo wields power over men. She can scream and pronounce curses on Okonkwo "beware of exchanging words with Agbala (Chielo).Does a man speak when God speaks? (95). Chielo as a woman and a spirit is respected and feared by Umuofia. Although women are cocooned (apart from Chielo who is positioned both in the physical and spiritual) a woman can also defy the man to attain some goal. Achebe recalls the plight of Ekwefi in a flashback while she and her husband Okonkwo await Chielo and her sick daughter Ezinma near the Cave. The flashback informs on Ekwefi's first marriage to Anene, which lasted for two years, after which she could no longer bear him:

> And she ran away to Okonkwo...She was going to
> the stream to fetch water. Okonkwo's house was on
> the way to the stream. She went in and knocked at
> the door and he came out...he just carried her to the
> bed... (76).

Okonkwo was her first love; the love of her youth but he had no money to marry her then. Leaving the man she did not love had been her desire and dream and when she finally takes a leap to attain her goal no one could stop her not even her hitherto unfulfilling husband, Anene.

Achebe uses these women characters in his early novels to foreshadow the women "made of sterner stuff" (Julius Caesar 119). As Achebe's creative energy increases, his women characters change accordingly. When we step into the political pre-independence Nigerian environment in *No Longer at Ease*, we meet Clara who is contrasted with an undeveloped female character, Obi's mother. In what appears to be an allegorical depiction of the strength of woman, Obi tells us that there was dedicated to one of the great gods of Aninta (where his father was a catechist), a great he-goat. This goat became a menace with its unhealthy droppings and constant harassment of eating up their crops in the neighborhood. No one dared touch the goat including Obi's father, elders and the priest because they were afraid. A day came when the he-goat entered Obi's mother's kitchen and ate up her yams. "She took a sharp machete and heaved off the beast's head" defying the angry threats of the village elders (150). This is Achebe's woman in a metamorphosing environment and indeed, this is a woman when the woman in her is determined.

Clara is used to depict the emanating political pre-independence Nigeria in *No Longer at Ease*. She is presented as a beautiful, assertive young professional nurse, endowed with self-esteem, poise and financial independence. With these accomplishments she is figuratively viewed as the emanating political Nigeria in *No Longer at Ease* that is full of hope. This is however crippled by ethnicity (as depicted by the Osu Caste system) and corruption (as seen from Obi, her fiancé) which has dismembered the nation Nigeria. Obi and Clara are in love and are determined to marry but because of Osu caste system in Igbo land (which still exists till today) they are forbidden to marry. Obi's father admonishes him with these words:

> Osu is like leprosy in the mind of our people. I beg you
> my son, do not bring the mark of shame and of leprosy
> into your family. If you do, your children and your
> children's children unto third and fourth generations
> will curse your memory. It is not for myself I speak; my

105

days are few. You will bring sorrow on your head and
the heads of your children (121).

At this point of their relationship Clara is already pregnant and
since she and Obi cannot marry because of the ethnic-based Osu
system, the feotus is aborted. Clara's abortion of the feotus is a
pointer that cannot be overlooked. It demonstrates destruction
of Nigeria by ethnicity and corrupt educated Nigerians who hold
the reins of governance. At the imago stage Clara is unable to fly
out from the cocoon just like Nigeria that is unable to stand as
a nation. Her feotus is smashed by the doctor's scalpel and she
vanishes into nowhere.

Achebe uses Clara to foreshadow Nigeria's nascent democracy,
full of corruption and ethnicity which is smashed at its embryonic
stage by military coup thus predicted in *A Man of the People* by
Achebe and manifested in the real world of Nigeria, 1966.

Imago Emerges

In Achebe's fifth main novel, *Anthills of Savannah*, the woman
metamorphoses into imago and out of cocoon. She is now a recognizable figure that is seen and heard. The country designated as
Kangan in Anthills... is under military dictatorship. Beatrice is
introduced as a well- achieved woman with first class honours in
English from Queen Mary University London. She is the Beatrice
Okoh, the one "who beat the English to their game". She is introduced by the military dictator, His Excellency, as "the most brilliant daughter of this country". She is the Senior Assistant Secretary in the Ministry of Finance. She is so accomplished, financially
autonomous, intelligent and knowledgeable that she is able to
burrow into situations, give critical analysis and provide solutions.
She sees herself as the priestess whose powers soar above men
not just in the spirit but in the actual physical even under severe
autocratic, totalitarian, military regime. Hear her below:

> As a matter of fact I do sometimes feel like Chielo
> in the novel, the priestess and prophetess of Hills and
> Cave (114).

She has the independent voice to challenge the dictator and acting as a captain brings her will to bear upon his actions. She functions as a reliable narrator whose voice challenges that of the dictator. Beatrice is an epitome of modern African career woman who meets the men on her terms and as her ilk (Chielo) soars above them. Her boy friend, Chris recognizes the mettle she is made of with these words:

> Beatrice is perfect embodiment of my ideal woman beautiful without being glamorous peaceful but very very strong. I love her and woulsd go at whatever pace she dictates (*Anthills*...58).

Early in the novel she reads the signs accurately and forecasts a lot of trouble for Chris and Ikem from the heinous, destructive military dictator whom she depicts as what Ayi Kwei Armah calls, black predators and destroyers *in Two Thousand Seasons* She is designated as one of the novel's moral centres. The insincerity of His Excellency and his cohorts are all seen through the eyes of Beatrice. She is the perfect example of who the African woman can be and what she can achieve like #, Dr. Ngozi Okonjo-Iweala, former Managing Director of World Bank and currently Minister of Finance in Nigeria; Professor Dora Akunyili, former Minister of Informaton, Nigeria and many other professionals in various fields and numerous female professors in Africa and indeed world wide. Beatrice rejects the chauvinist cant that every woman needs a man to make life complete:

> I was determined from the very beginning
> to put my career first and if need be last.
> That every woman needs a man to complete
> her is a piece of male chauvinistic bullshit
> I had completely rejected before
> I knew there was anything like Women Lib. You
> often hear our people say: But that is
> something picked up in England, Absolute
> Rubbish! There was enough chauvinism
> in my father's house to last me seven
> reincarnations (80-81).

Elewa is depicted as half-illiterate sales girl in a shop owned by an Indian. She is living with her mother in the slums of Bassa (184). In spite of her disadvantaged position she radiates with warmth, attraction and confidence. With these very positive qualities of courage, devotion and integrity, the highly educated elite of Achebe's moral voice, Ikem, chooses her as a wife. Elewa is seen as object of veneration by Beatrice.

In her analytical mind she diagnoses why Ikem singles Elewa out from

> The millions just as unlucky as herself,
> There are something in her, that her
> luckless draw could not remove, that
> thing that draws Ikem to her and for
> that she must be given credit (184).

In depicting Elewa's character, Achebe suggests that women whether educated or not have the capacity for positive change. Elewa is carrying what Beatrice calls "a living speck of him (Ikem) within her, a child of new luminosity". Beatrice at the naming ceremony gives the child a metaphoric name as she makes this pronouncement; "we have our own version of hope that springs eternal. We shall call this child Amaechina: may the path never close" (222).

In the traditional society as Beatrice pointed out, the father named the child but here is the reversal. The woman names the child.

Conclusion

In studying Achebe's women, this work has used few of his female figures as signposts in their metamorphosing process and that of the nation Nigeria. The tradition-based novels portray the woman pathetically down-trodden, voiceless and powerless. She is a property possessed, beaten and battered without question. The man is her lord "Nnamukwu" as is called in Igbo. Achebe ingeniously uses the device of foreshadowing to give a picture of who the woman is and what she can be. Depicted as very powerful in the spirit she metamorphosos to a liberated financially autonomous figure in the physical. Each stage of the woman's changing status becomes a pointer to the changes of the political history of Nigeria. The hope smashed by the abortion of Clara's baby and her disappearance marks the termination of the nation's new political independence by ethnicity, corruption and the consequent military coup. At this stage the woman as well as the nation is still handicapped. Clara's impediment to complete success and fulfillment is not finance. At the fringes of Nigeria independence she has become financially autonomous such that she is able to give enormous sums of money to her financially battered fiancé, Obi. It is ethnicity, corruption and mismanagement of resources that crippled the nation and put the masses in abject poverty. The nation continues to crawl like the metamorphosing caterpillar.

Anthills... portrays Beatrice as the imago, the metaphoric full blown insect that emerges from the cocoon. The reference of Beatrice as the captain suggests leadership position women should occupy. In the same context we see her functioning as a real leader who is sensitive to the needs of the people. Women should be included in governance and because of their special skills and qualities can exert a moderating influence. Ngara's incisive commentary draws this home that:

> *Anthills*... re-examines....fundamental issues
> relating to political leadership, the place of
> women in society, the role of the artist and the
> whole question of revolution and social change (128).

The change is already apparent. Women have metamorphosed into a recognizable voice. Even the half-illiterate woman, Elewa has the undaunted strength among the elitist and through her offspring the new dawn of hope arrives: Amaechina.

Using the woman as signposts in each of Achebe's novelistic world suggests that the redemption of this nation (indeed all nations especially in Africa), nestles on the shoulders of women. The woman must therefore be assertive, forceful, educated, and financially autonomous; a rounded personality equipped to occupy leadership positions to effect the redemption of the nations. The cocoon is broken for the way forward. Ellen Johnson Sirleaf the redemptive first female president in Africa has set the pace. Her rulership in Liberia has brought sanity, peace, order and progress into that country. The imago is in motion. Whether the woman is Ekwefi or Elewa, she can take a leap and be at the apex.

Works Cited

Achebe, Chinua. *Things Fall Apart*. London: Heinemann, 1958.

_____. *No Longer at Ease*. London: Heinemann, 1960.

_____. *A Man of the People*. London: Heinemann, 1966.

_____. *Arrow of God*. London: Heinemann, 1964.

_____. *Anthills of the Savannah*. London: Heinemann, 1988.

Armah, Ayi Kwei. *Two Thousand Seasons*. London: Heinemann, 1973.

Mezu, Ure. *Chinua Achebe, The Man and His Works*. London: Adonis and Abbey, 2006.

Ngara, Emmanuel. "Achebe as Artist: The Place and Significance of *Anthills of the Savannah*" In *Chinua Achebe: A Celebration*. Eds. Kirsten Peterson and Anna Rutherfield. London: Heinemann, 1990.

Ojinmah, Umelo. *Chinua Achebe, New Critical Perspective*. London: Spectrum Books, 1991.

Opara, Chioma. *Beyond the Marginal Land*. Port Harcourt: Bellpot, 1999.

Palmer, Eustace. *Of War and Women, Oppression and Optimism*. Eritrea: African World Press, 2008.

Salamone, Frank. "The Depiction of Maculinity in Classic Nigerian Literature" in *JALA* Vol. 1 No. 1 2007.

Shakespeare, William. *Julius Caesar*. Ed. Temple Michael. London-Evans, 1996.

Yankson, Kofi. *Chinua Achebe's Novels: Sociolinguistic Perspective*. Oruowulu – Obosi. Pacific, 1990.

CHAPTER 8

REVALORIZING WOMEN'S AGENCY: MOTHERHOOD IN *ANTHILLS OF THE SAVANNAH*

Caroline Mbonu

The original oppression of Women was based on crude denigration. She caused man to fall ... our ancestors, without the benefit of hearing about the Old Testament, made the very same story differing only in local color ... The New Testament required a more enlightened, more refined, more loving even, strategy – ostensibly, that is. Therefore, the idea came to man to turn his spouse into the very Mother of God, to pick her up from right under his foot where she'd been since Creation and carry her reverently to a nice, corner pedestal. Up there, her feet completely off the ground she will be just as irrelevant to the practical decisions of running the world as she was in the bad old days. The only difference is that now man will suffer no guilt feelings; he can sit back and congratulate himself on his generosity and gentlemanliness.

Achebe: 1987, 97-98

Introduction

In rethinking women's roles in Africa, Chinua Achebe approaches the issue from both the African and biblical traditions. He argues for the deconstructing of chauvinism masked in irrelevant and uncritical glorification of a woman in the New Testament and in modern Africa. Achebe's use of biblical images in addressing contemporary issues in Africa remains significant. His usage points to the fact that the Bible, the most influential book in the West, has been appropriated by Africans in a new way. The Botswana biblical scholar, Musa Dube, suggests that Africans' admission that they now have the Bible implies that this text is no longer just a Western book (20). Evidence within the biblical text itself, however, suggests that Africa has had the Bible in some fashion long before it became a Western book. One cannot ignore the influence of this text in the contemporary African socio-cultural context as the Achebe quote rightly suggests. We must, however, take into consideration that the Bible represents a product of human culture with its ideologies, worldviews and orientation, perspectives, values and disvalues.

The above quote reveals a dominant notion of women resulting from centuries of androcentric scholarship. A male-centered scholarship, for the most part, provides the lens and language with which regular Christians appropriate the Biblical text. Undoubtedly, this form of representation often tends to diminish female qualities by idealizing her role as that which accompanies men in a subordinate capacity. Such reading also suggests women's insignificance in the scheme of things, "irrelevant to the practical decisions of running the world" (Achebe: 1987, 98). Moreover, literalism and fundamentalism in biblical interpretation continue to be the arena of male prejudice. Fundamentalism presents a growing concern in many African Christian communities because it embraces powerful rhetorical instruments of patriarchy. Fundamentalism, which represents radicalism in its primitivism, insists that it reproduces what it perceives as biblical-era beliefs and practices (Marty, 19-29). It is not infrequent that we hear preachers (mostly male) insisting that the Bible says, for example, women should do this or that. A fundamentalist approach to a biblical interpretation discounts the fact that biblical truths cannot be pre-packaged. It fails to recognize that truth must be found in actual interaction between a text and a context in the actual historical circumstances. Biblical interpretation is only a part of the story as Achebe notes. Our ancestors also have their fair share of blame for women's subjugation. Achebe suggests that "our ancestors, without the benefit of hearing about the Old Testament, made the very same story differing only in local color." Thus, if the morality of an act is determined by its life-giving potential, one may ask what the morality of women subjugation represents for Africa, past and present. I posit that a redemptive reading of those biblical stories can re-image the local colors that tend to give women and motherhood the wrong hue. An engaged reading of biblical and cultural texts can produce the brilliant colors of motherhood.

The concept of motherhood remains problematic. Motherhood means different things to different people. Although the full semantic range of both the literal and metaphorical meaning of motherhood cannot be achieved in this essay, I show motherhood to constitute service. Motherhood is about servanthood; a servant always on duty, always thinking about how to build up the family, the community and bring beauty to life. For from the experience of service as mothers, women move to the experience of community, burst the confining limits of their domestic tasks and discover themselves as creators of history. In this way, motherhood valorizes and can become liberative. In other words, motherhood reveals actions or events that unburden, lift up, or promote the humanity of persons, individuals and collective groups. Set out in three sections. First, I discuss motherhood from the Igbo tradition through the lens of the *mgbala/usoekwu*, or hearth. The biblical tradition which Achebe generously employs in the above quoted passage forms the basis of the discussion in the second section. I discuss reversals in the third section. Drawing from the characters of Beatrice Nwanyibuife and Elewa, I paint a portrait of a new motherhood.

Motherhood in Igbo Tradition through the Lens of the Mgbala/Usoekwu (Hearth)

The *mgbala/usoekwu*, in Igbo tradition provides the conceptual framework from which to engage the notion of motherhood in the culture. In Igbo life, the *mgbala* is not merely a fireplace; it is the soul of the household. This soul of the house represents the female domain. While the male is the indisputable head of the Igbo household, the female heads the hearth. There can be no household without a hearth. That is to say, men control the public sphere; women control the private-sphere, an arrangement that reinforces the binary principle: *ihe di abuo abuo*, "things exist in pairs" (Amadiume: 19). This kind of relationship checks unintended outcome of power within the homestead and particularly assures the rights of women and children.

At marriage, a woman undergoes a ceremony of *ikpube ekwu* that is, erecting a hearth or *usoekwu/mgbala*. Spatially, the *mgbala* includes a living room, bedrooms, kitchen, and a backyard. The kitchen space includes the circumscribed fireplace, the *ekwu* or *agbata-ekwu*. The *agbata-ekwu* constitutes another reality, a sacred space, by virtue of the meals prepared therein (Mbonu: 252-253). Within the *mgbala*, the female passion, compassion, and imagination coalesce in the very art of birthing, sustaining, and preserving life. In other words, in the *mgbala*, life is born and hope nurtured and celebrated; dignity protected and secured. Here, the mother and offspring engage in quality times of togetherness that foster intimacy and respect.

The head of the *mgbala* holds political, economic, and moral sway over every member of the hearth. The Nigerian scholar, Chinwiezu, insists that the matriarch authority in the nest (*mgbala*) is exercised not only over the children but over the husband as well for by this power, the woman distributes the resources, commodities and opportunities for her domain (109).

The spiritual aspect of motherhood is secured in the ritual space the Igbo tradition accords the *mgbala*. A young woman, at marriage, moves to her marital home with symbols of her family/ancestral deities, the *Chi*. Usually, these symbols pass from mother to daughter. She installs an altar of the *Chi* in her bedroom. In so doing, the entire environment and the whole time is occupied by religious meaning, so that at any moment the mother feels secure enough to act in a meaningful and religious consciousness. This practice of taking the symbols of one's natal deities is in contradistinction to the Greco-Roman world from which Christianity received its cultural definition. The Greco-Roman culture denies competence to the woman to worship her clan deities in her marital home (Cheikh Anta Diop: 112).

The Senegalese historian, anthropologist, physicist, and politician, Cheikh Anta Diop, clearly stated that the particularity of

African cultures based on matriarchy enables women to carry their clan deities to their places of marriage (112). I attest to this practice having witnessed firsthand the enshrined icons of the *Chi* in my grandmother, Nwaonu. Grandmother Nwaonu would speak of the *Chi* in these terms: *Chi nnem*, meaning, the *Chi* of my foremothers.

Religiously, the mother of the *mgbala* represents its cultic priest. She must pray and offer sacrifices for the wellbeing of her family. Together with her hearth, she offers prayers and sacrifices to *Chukwu* and to the ancestors. In their daily existence, they are officiants and practitioners of *mgbala* praxis. In today's language, we can designate this mother as priest of the house church. Curiously, the mother does not need delegation from her husband to exercise training and authority over the affairs of the hearth.

The practice of taking into marriage symbols of one's natal divinities is not peculiar to the Igbo. Such was the practice in ancient Israel, among the Canaanites, and their neighbors. Solomon's wives, for example, brought their tribal gods to Israel (1 Kgs 11). In the book that bears her name, Ruth, the Moabite daughter in-law of Naomi, pledges to abandon her ancestry deity to demonstrate her total commitment to Naomi. "Do not ask me to abandon or forsake you! … your people shall be my people, and your God my God" (Ruth 1:16-17). The American biblical scholar, Carol Myers argues that in terms of day-to-day experience of most people in ancient Israel, the household religious practices; especially of women were more prominent (11).

Women's religious practice in the hearth may not be unconnected with the rhythm of life which is tied to fertility. Fertility represents renewal and redemption. Regrettably in many African societies, some consider female fertility the quintessence of motherhood. Of course, the reproduction of offspring is essential to support the population. Offspring is critical in providing care, particularly for aging adults. In this context, infertility is a constant threat to the durability of the family. But that fertility is critical to the continuation and survival of the household and the community at large remains unquestionable. Fertility, however, is not synonymous with motherhood. Fertility not only of women but men as well must be secured and protected by the very agents from whom life is born, the mother. Thus motherhood cannot be divorced from religious practices. In essence, motherhood is tied to the everyday religious life of the *mgbala*.

In effect, within the *usoekwu/mgbala*, the child learns essential human abilities to engage the world. The child learns the mother-tongue. Mother-tongue in my use stands for a metaphor of cultural embodiment. Moreover, the freight that the designation mother-tongue carries reveals a web of relationships that exists between the mother and child on one hand, and the child and society on the other hand.

The centrality of the hearth highlights the significance of motherhood. Its implication in society as a whole resonated with the saying from William Ross Wallace's poem (1865) titled "What Rules the World: The Hand That Rocks the Cradle Is the Hand That Rules the World." In essence Wallace's insight highlights the fact that in the hearth, the child is socialized into the ethics and spirituality that shapes a child's imagination about how to understand herself or himself as well as how to experience life and death, success and failure, love and betrayal. Wallace's insight unearths to some degree the import of the hearth and leaves to the imagination to establish the *de facto* head of the household. In bemoaning the growing decadence of contemporary time, Wallace's insights raise a question: what became of the hand that rocks the cradle? The question also calls attention to the continued subjugation of women. Perhaps the decades of being absentees of history have taken its toll on society. Excluding women and the influence they bring to the conversation from full participation in social processes deprives humanity of the full synergy of human potential.

Achebe summaries the enormous influence of the head of the *usoekwu* on a child's life in the Igbo expression, *nneka*: (nne = mother; ka = greatest or supreme), meaning, mother is greatest or supreme. The author bemoans the tradition that reverences a mother with such high honor, yet, continues to disrespect and subdue her.

Meanwhile our ancestors out here, unaware of the New Testament, were working out independently a parallel subterfuge of their own. Nneka, they said. Mother is supreme. Let us keep her in reserve until the ultimate crisis arrives and waist is broken and hung over the fire, and the palm bears its fruits at the tail of its leaf. Then, as the world crashes around Man's ears, Woman in her supremacy will descend and sweep the shards together (*Anthills*, 98).

Even with exalted titles and honors, the author suggests, women have continued to be objects never subjects of history. But viewing the designation *Nneka* form the prism of *mgbala* offers an interpretation that conveys the full import of its meaning. This sense of *Nneka* draws attention to materials that can be retrievable and re-appropriated. In his classic novel, *Things Fall Apart*, Achebe employs the term *Nneka* in a way that interprets his quote in *Anthills*.

In *Things Fall Apart*, Okonkwo, the most powerful man in Umuofia of his time, inadvertently commits manslaughter. As tradition demands, he must go on exile from the land of Umuofia, for a seven-year period. The purpose of exile is to purify *Ala*, the Earth goddess, for the innocent bloodshed. Naturally, as the world crashes around him, Okonkwo fled to his maternal home, Mbanta. He seeks comfort in his mother's hearth. His maternal uncle, Uchendu, received him and his family with great generosity. But this aspiring lord of Umuofia took his banishment from his fatherland acrimoniously. In a dialogue steeped in irony, Achebe introduced the centrality of the mother in Igbo life.

On the second day of Okonkwo's exile, Uchendu assembles his sons and daughters to receive his troubled nephew. In the conversation that ensued, Uchendu addressed Okonkwo thus: Can you tell me, Okonkwo, why it is that one of the commonest names we give our children is *Nneka*, or "Mother is Supreme?" Uchendu proposes a response to his question since neither Okonkwo nor his cousins could offer any. Although a child belongs to the fatherland when things are good and life is sweet, Uchendu stated, but when there is sorrow and bitterness he finds refuge in his motherland." I posit that Achebe's introduction of the role of motherland, at this point of the narrative sharply contrasts and demystifies the aura of maleness or masculinity that Okonkwo spent his entire life building and protecting in his fatherland (Achebe:1994: 129-135). Thus, *Nneka* can also function as framework for motherhood.

A critical study of motherhood in Igbo life cannot be separated from the larger traditional Igbo religious expressions. A close reading of some figurines, statuettes, and paintings in the *Mbari*, particularly the character of *mgbekenwaekere*, the archetypal mother, clearly suggests the role of motherhood in the land. It also signifies that motherhood is a life-long enterprise.

I return to the issue of literal and metaphoric motherhood. Many understand motherhood in the literal sense, meaning—a biological reality. Viewing motherhood as a biological reality has its positives but it can be exclusive. The disproportionate emphasis placed on motherhood in the biological sense can prove limiting and oppressive to women who cannot be biological mothers. Women, who genetically are incapable of having children of their own, remain excluded from the "glories" motherhood confers. In the words of the Nigerian scholar, Oyeronke Olajubu, "For one, the inability to become a mother could begin a traumatic process of alienation and frustration for the Yoruba woman. She is perceived as a dead end through whom the ancestral line cannot continue and this could translate to ridicule in the society" (17). Olajubu shows the unconstructive implications the privileging of biological motherhood can have on woman. Women more than men, are likely to suffer indignity as a result of their inability to beget biological children. The humiliation and mortification they undergo constitutes life-denying condition, a situation that is completely antithetical to the rich metaphor that motherhood represents.

On the other hand, a metaphorical reading of motherhood is inclusive and can be liberating. Metaphorical motherhood can be defined as mother without child. Suffice to say that images of metaphorical motherhood abound in the Scripture. Fourth Ezra, a Jewish apocalypse written near the end of the first century C.E., for example, employs mother earth as a conceptual framework. In Igbo tradition, *ala*, the earth goddess is represented as mother. Do these ideas not resonate with the time-tested parlance of motherland? Thus motherhood in this broader sense is within the reach of everyone, women as well as men. In his first letter to the Thessalonians, the apostle Paul represents himself in a gynomorphic image. Paul compares himself to a mother, who nurses his children: "Rather we were gentle among you, as a nursing mother cares for her children. With such affection for you, we were determined to share with you not only the gospel of God, but our very selves as well (I Thess 2:7b-8)." Thus motherhood can be a universal image that expresses service. Service can be expressed in a regeneration of life through nurturing. One must also take notice of another category of motherhood, the Desert Mothers, *ammas*, of early Christianity and the contemporary Reverend Mothers of monasteries and convents.

Motherhood in the Biblical Tradition

In *Anthills*, Achebe confronts his reader, the Bible, and women. He employs Ikem's excurses to illustrate the role the Bible plays in the cultural imagination of women. Ikem likens women's lesser status in Igbo society to the Christian perception of Eve in the Old Testament, where man forcefully places a woman under his feet. He goes on to state that inferiorization of women in the New Testament is less dramatic but of like effect. Such perception of women represents the consequence of centuries of androcentric biblical reading. Because women believe these readings to be true shows that they have always been consumers of male theological reflection. Women have so much internalized these beliefs that they have no voice even in issues that are of concern to them as female human beings. This way of reading the sacred text has repressive implications.

Like Achebe, Olajubu's questions the liberating role of the motherhood of God in Christianity. She states that "The practice of Mariology, which exalts the position of Mary the mother of Jesus but fails to give credence to women's role in the leadership cadre of the Church, is full of paradox" (51). The reading of motherhood in the New Testament by both Achebe and Olajubu brings the reader to confront the impact biblical religion has on gender discourse in Africa as a whole. As Christianity develops, we see that motherhood did not confer recognition on women. From the first book of the Bible, Genesis, Hagar was driven away from her home regardless of the fact that she was the mother of Abraham's first-born son, Ishmael.

Thankfully, the Pontifical Biblical Commission in its 1993, Interpretation of the Bible in the Church, challenged women to unearth the feminine face of the sacred text, "Femininity helps to unmask and correct commonly accepted interpretations that were tendentious and sought to justify the male domination of women (Béchard, 272). Thus we can unmask the concept that "came to man to turn his spouse into the very Mother of God, to pick her up from right under his foot where she'd been since Creation and carry her reverently to a nice, corner pedestal."

Let me state that there is no point in trying to clear the vast and dense forest of biblical scholarship in order to address the issue. The space for my discussion in this forest is located in Luke 1:26-38. My choice of this Lukan passage corroborates Achebe's idea: "man to turn his spouse into the very Mother of God." This Lukan passage speaks of the Mary of Nazareth becoming the Mother of God.

There is no denying that certain interpretations employ the image of Mary in the New Testament to foster women's subordination as *Anthills* clearly states. The symbolism of Mary, the Mother of God, so intricately woven into the tapestry of Roman Catholic religious imagination evokes a variety of rich significance. Foremost, a critical evaluation of the song of Mary, *Magnificat* (Luke 1:46-55), for example, reveals that Mary should not be "on a pedestal," removed from the life of women, and society of every age. The English Anglican clergyman, Paul Avis, opines that the image of Mary remains more relevant in Catholicism than in Protestantism.

Avis contends that in Catholicism, Mary and the Church belong to the heavenly realm and the sacramental ministry, with its washing and feeding, counterbalancing the dominating male symbols of God (20). That is to say, practical service of people represents the essence of the Motherhood of Mary of Nazareth. Avis further argues that in Protestantism, Mary and the Church remain cut down to the human level – weak, mortal, fallible – and the ministry is conceived in terms of the male activity of preaching the word (20). This notion of Mary supports Achebe's ideas of the mother being carried "reverently to a nice, corner pedestal." The Anglican Marian tradition coheres in some ways with that of the Presbyterian. The American Presbyterian, Judy Siker, asserts that with the exception of a brief appearance every December, Mary has remained virtually absent from Protestant life and faith. This way of looking at the Mother of God in the New Testament supports the quote from *Anthills* at the beginning of this essay. But that does not say that the full potential of the image of the

Mother of God has been appropriated for women's advancement in Catholicism. To follow in Achebe's theology, Mary's attitude in the Lukan passage represents to "follow" and to "serve," – theological words for discipleship.

The immediate context of Mary becoming the Mother of God makes abundantly clear that the role of a servant remains central to her new status. On receiving her commission, Mary went with haste to serve, for three months, in the home of Elizabeth and Zachariah (Luke 1:39ff). Experience shows that Mariology is more about devotional and theological themes than women's empowerment. Had Mariology been about women empowerment, Mary's motherhood would have assuaged the quandary surrounding gender roles at least in the Church life. However, the Lukan passage under study persistently makes clear that motherhood, as Mary of Nazareth embraces it, can be a liberating concept if viewed in terms of service, relationality, and mutuality. The experience here is that deep bonding with life, which confers a special capacity for solidarity in the struggle for transformation. The mothers of *Anthills*, Beatrice Nwanyibuife and Elewa model such solidarity in their service of each other.

In addition, the American theologian, Elisabeth Schüsler Fiorenza, aptly states that biological motherhood is not enjoined on women. Rather, women like men, are called to faithful service in discipleship (146). Fiorenza insists that the truly 'great' are those who become servants of the community (148). Mary the mother of God as a symbol of womanhood in Christianity, models for people of faith a way of being related to the world, to serve, a primary function in the hearth, *mgbala*.

There is a close parallel of the hearth, *mgbala*, and the biblical "mother's house" in ancient Israel. The biblical mother's house constitutes that space where a child acquires a sense of self and belonging. In Genesis, for example, young Rebecca when confronted at the well with the prospects of marriage, ran off to her mother's household, to tell about her encounter with the servant of Abraham (Gen 24:28). After losing their husbands, Naomi entreated her daughters-in-law, Ruth and Orphah, to return home to their mothers' house so that they can regain the energy with which to begin life anew: "Go back," she said to them, "each of you, to your mother's house!" (Ruth 1:8). In the Song of Songs, the female protagonist would have no respite until she had brought her lover to her mother's house, "I would lead you, bring you in to the home of my mother" (Song of Songs 8:2). These encounters reveal the rich symbolism of the mother and her activities in hearth.

The sense of a mother's house is not only of female interest. In the First Book of Samuel, King Saul employs the term in berating his son, Jonathan, the crown prince. King Saul disapproved of the friendship between his son and David. Jonathan's association with David was a dishonor to the house of his mother, Saul stated: "Son of a rebellious woman, do I not know that, to your own shame and to the disclosure of your mother's shame, you are the companion of Jesse's son?" (1 Sam 20:30-31). These examples show that in the mother's house a child gains the self-understanding, the support, and the ability to engage the world. Indeed, the example of Jesus' upbringing in Mary's hearth in Nazareth grounds our example of motherhood and the impact of the *mgbala* in society.

The Lukan infancy narrative tells us that Jesus grew up in the hearth of a village Jewish maiden, Mary of Nazareth. Like the mother hen who gathers her brood, it was Mary who chided Jesus for wandering away for three days. Having found him, she took him back to her hearth in Nazareth. In Mary's hearth, Jesus grew into an enviable manhood, advancing in wisdom, and age. Jesus is called a Nazarene, truly a child of his mother.

In his mother's hearth Jesus began to learn the God-human encounter. Jesus' sense of servanthood developed in part from lessons learned from his mother's hearth, "Thy will be done," (Luke 22:42) echoing his mother's "Be it done unto me according to thy word" in the passage of the annunciation. From Mary's hearth, therefore, emerged that nucleus of life that the New Testament portrays: that is, a proper response to God's generous gift of love centered on a positive response to the word. This response cannot be separated from service of others.

The Reversal:
A Contemporary Perceptive of Motherhood

Achebe creates rich complex mother figures at the end of *Anthills*. Achebe combines African religious and the Christian traditions on the one hand and traditional culture and modernity on the other to create a reversal that parallels the *Magnificat*. He delicately piths patriarchy against matriarchy. While the former, represented by the mighty and powerful rulers of the Old Kangan, Sam, Chris, and Ikem, were thrown down; the later, characterized by the lowly, Beatrice Nwanyibuife and Elewa, are lifted up. A reversal meant the bad old days for women are over. Women have been lifted from the ash heap, and their feet planted firmly on the ground. They have become ubiquitous, no longer tucked away in a corner or placed under anyone's foot. Women have become active participants in and co-creators of history. They can now determine the future of their new society.

Like many women (Esther, Abigail) in the Hebrew Scripture who come into their own after men create crises they cannot resolve themselves, Beatrice Nwanyibuife and Elewa rose to the occasion. Male unbridled power and fierce pursuit of self-interest had tremendous cost to the community as a whole. Even after the destruction, the women found the means by which to re-engender the community. Beatrice Nwanyibuife became the mother of the remnant.

In the last chapter of *Anthills*, Achebe draws from a wealth of resources to create a scene that is steeped in paradox and irony. He blends a variety of insights from the sacred and secular to create a new motherhood. A motherhood that is both metaphorical as well as literal. Beatrice Nwanyibuife, a western trained civil servant representing the former and Elewa a semi-lettered sales girl representing the latter. The author assigns both mothers redemption roles and concretizes the role in the symbolic Amaechina, May-the-path-never-close. Amaechina, a girl-child born to Elewa and posthumously to Ikem, became the symbol of new motherhood. Another way to represent the significance of Amaechina is expressing it as a metaphor of existence. To say to an Igbo, *ama nne gi chie kwa*, may-your-mother's-path-be-desolate, represent a curse par excellence, it is tantamount to annihilation of the family.

Two women, Beatrice Nwanyibuife and Elewa, rose from the ashes of near annihilation. They fanned into flame the ember that was left from the ashes of the old Kangan and made a bon-fire, as it were, for the remnant that survived the destruction. Ashes, flames, bon-fire, these symbols of life are synonymous with the *mgbala*. In the confines of Beatrice's *mgbala*, she and Elewa, two mothers of a kind, with passion and compassion, nurtured hope, birth and celebrate life in Amaechina. Both women earned the name *Nneka* on both counts. They were servants in the true sense of the word and they descended in their supremacy and swept the shards together when crisis arrived and the "world crashes around Man's ears." Although the author compares the Christian ethos that elevated woman to the status of the Mother of God and the Igbo reverence of the woman as signified by the nomenclature *Nneka* or mother is supreme as simply another expression of the same stereotypical oppression (Muoneke, 150), he masterfully reverses this thought with the end of the narrative. He allowed the designation *Nneka* to speak for itself in the character of the two mothers, Beatrice Nwanyibuife and Elewa.

All through the narrative, Beatrice Nwanyibuife, proves herself a true servant. In the story, she showed the heart of a servant at all times. She never stopped thinking and caring for the good of the different characters in the story. As a civil servant, and friend of Sam, the head of Kanga State, Beatrice Nwanyibuife closes in to deliver him from selling out and falling prey a foreigner journalist. Her action at the Presidential retreat house is reminiscent of the English Margaret Green description of participants of *Ogu Umunwanyi* (Women's War). Green likens them to the Amazons, "powerful grandmothers hold sway over tribes of apparently unprotesting males" (Green, 139).

Of much curiosity is the character of Beatrice Nwanyibuife. Although deprived of the knowledge of her culture, she exhibits an acute sense of being, which makes her aware of the depth of resource she possesses. Like many western educated Africans,

> Beatrice Nwanyibuife did not know the traditions and legends of her people because they played but little part in her upbringing. She was born into a world apart. Was baptized, and sent to schools which made much about the English and the Jews and the Hindu and practically everybody else but hardly put in a word for her forebears and the divinities with whom they had evolved. So she came to barely knowing who she was.

> Barely, we say though, because she did carry a vague
> sense more acute at certain critical moments than
> others of being two different persons (*Anthills* 105).

Achebe seems to write into the character of his protagonist, some of his own experience. A son of a missionary father school teacher, who also is western, trained. Growing up, the author also seems to know very little about his own native traditions. But coming on to his own, he brought together, in a refined dignity, the best of two worlds.

Anthills challenges the contemporary African women to creatively bring together the old and the new world. Women must wed the imaginative fertile world of their foremothers and their rich Christian heritage in a renewed sense of self-becoming. The rich world of the *mgbala* and a westernized world of education and the Christian tradition must come together. Bringing together consists not of adaptation. Adaptation would not provide the proper integration because adaptation produces more or less a hybrid. A hybrid can hardly reproduce. Rather what is at stake is appropriation. Appropriation implies the practice of making one's own that which genuinely belongs to another. Cultural tourists, for example, do so all the time. They go to another culture, and partake of their ceremonies, foods, and customs and then appropriate it to enhance theirs. In this way, their culture becomes richer, finer and more beautiful. In so doing, *Anthills* can do for African women what Augustine of Hippo did for his time. In the fourth century, Augustine profoundly transformed both Christian and Greaco-Roman thought and practice by bringing biblical faith into dialogue with Stoic and Neo-Platonist thought. Achebe follows a similar path. He brings African tradition into dialogue with biblical tradition in the character of Beatrice Nwanyibuife. Thus, he renews the female narrative and invites women to continue the conversation.

Conclusion

It is no infrequent that the story of women's victim-hood fills the pages of our news papers. These stories are narratives of abuses and other social anomalies perpetrated against women. Rarely do we read stories of women's valor – even in ordinary events of life. *Anthills of the Savannah* revised that tide. Achebe tells the good news from a woman's perspective. The author's concern for redemption of a people is fully taken up in the story. *Anthills* retrieves and reconstructs motherhood. It makes motherhood contemporaneous. In a very subtly manner, Achebe captures the complexity of motherhood in the characters of Beatrice Nwanyi-buife and Elewa. He weaves an old understanding of motherhood with a new meaning of motherhood in contemporary society to create a new understanding of the term. He thus challenges women to do the same offering them a new metaphor in the name of the new born girl-child: Amaechina.

Notes

1. Ghanaian Mercy Amba Oduyoye writes, "Among the Igbo of Nigeria, to be creative is to turn the power of evil, sin and suffering into the power of love. When things are not going well in the community, in order to restore harmony and mutuality of existence, artists fashion a model of a whole community and all that they have in a house (*Mbari*), and the house and its artifacts are left as a sacrifice, which will renew the community (Oduyoye, 14).

Works Cited

Achebe, Chinua. *Things Fall Apart.* New York: Anchor Books, 1994.

_____. *Anthills of the Savannah.* Nigeria: Heinemann Educational Book, 1987

Amadiume, Ifi. "Igbo and Africa Religious Perspectives on Religious Conscience and the Global Economy," in *Subverting Greed: Religious Perspectives on the Global Economy*, eds Paul F. Knitter and Chandra Muzaffa Maryknoll, New York: Orbis Books, 2002.

Avis, Paul. *Eros and the Sacred.* Harrisburg, PA: Morehouse Publishing, 1989.

Béchard, Dean P., ed. "Pontifical Biblical Commission, Document on the Interpretation of the Bible in the Church, September 21, 1993." In *The Scripture Documents: An Anthology of Official Catholic Teaching.* Collegeville, MN: The Liturgical Press, 2001.

Chinweizu. *The Anatomy of Female Power: A Masculinist Dissection of Matriarchy.* Lagos, Nigeria: Pero Press, 1990.

Diop, Cheikh Anta. *Civilization or Barbariam: An Authentic Anthropology*, trans by Yaa-Lengi Meema Ngemi, eds Harold J. Salemson and Marjolijn de Jager. New York: Lawrence Hill Books, 1991.

Dube, Musa W. *Postcolonial Feminist Interpretation of the Bible.* St. Louis MO: Chalice Press, 2000.

Fiorenza, Elisabeth Schüsler. *In Memory of Her: A Feminist Theological Reconstruction of Christian Origins. Tenth Anniversary Edition.* New York: Crossroad Publishing, 2000.

Green, Margaret M. *Ibo Village Affairs.* New York: Frederick A. Praeger, 1964.

Marty, Martin E. "Fundamentalism as a Social Phenomenon," in *Review and Expositor* 79, no. 1 (1982), 19-29.

Mbonu, Caroline. *A Redemptive Reading of the Doulē in Luke 1:26-38: Towards a Liberative Process for Women in Igbo Society* (Ph.D. Diss., Graduate Theological Union, Berkeley, California, 2009).

Muoneke, Romanus Okey. *Art, Rebellion and Redemption: A Reading of the Novels of Chinua Achebe.* New York: Peter Lang, 1994.

Meyers, Carol, ed. *Women in Scripture: A Dictionary of Named and Unnamed Women in the Hebrew Bible, The Apocryphal/Deuterocanonical Books, and the New Testament.* New York: Houghton Mifflin Company, 2000.

Oduyoye, Mercy Amba. *Beads and Strands: Reflections of an African Woman on Christianity in Africa.* Maryknoll, NY: Orbis Books, 2004.

Olajubu, Oyeronke. *Women in the Yoruba Religious Sphere* (Albany, New York: State University of New York, 2003).

Siker, Judy Yates. "Blessed One: Protestant Perspective on Mary." *Review of Biblical Literature*, 6 (2004): 559-562.

CHAPTER 9

POWER PLAY AND GENDERED SPACES IN CHINUA ACHEBE'S *ANTHILLS OF THE SAVANNAH*: A CULTURAL MATERIALIST READING

Uzoechi Nwagbara

Since the publication of Chinua Achebe's first three novels – known as The African Trilogy, *Things Fall Apart, No Longer At Ease* and *Arrow of God*, he has used his artistic works to delineate the watersheds in Nigeria's nationhood. While this set of novels dramatises the dynamics of colonial invasion and culture conflict – the "Huntington's disease of our time" (Zizek 2008:119), his fourth novel, *A Man of the People*, engages the disillusionment resulting from political independence in Nigeria. Within the gamut of engagement, his fifth novel, *Anthills of the Savannah*, extends the frontiers of this interdiction – by incorporating the feminist question in the leadership formation of Nigeria as well as praetorian *modus operandi* for governance. Achebe's preoccupation with feminist aesthetics in the novel distils a synthesis of his vision and artistic predilection towards envisioning a solution for "the trouble with Nigeria", to use his famous locution. This study interrogates how the issues of power play and gender are played out in the novel. Power relations in *Anthills of the Savannah* in order to take cognisance of gender equality and empowerment, feminism couched in cultural materialist aesthetics is central. Cultural materialism espouses discourse of unbounded relativism as well as women empowerment following oppressive and gender-blind nature of patriarchy and materialism. This kind of investigation is essential in understanding the nature of power relations in postcolonial Nigerian leadership formation.

Introduction

The setting of *Anthills of the Savannah* is Kangan, an imaginary country in West Africa, where Sam, a Sandhurst-trained military officer – also known as His Excellency, has taken the rein of power by coup d'état. There is a distancing of authorial voice via the use of varied narrative channels, multiple point-of-views; while at the same instance, Achebe orchestrates his social vision for postcolonial Nigeria, which is in the throes of massive pillage and misguided leadership. The national tragedy – considered as the gist of this fictive work is principally relayed by three friends: Ikem, Chris and Beatrice. The intricate postcolonial malaise is captured here by Beatrice:

> For weeks and months after I had definitely taken on the challenge of bringing together as many broken pieces of this tragic history as I could lay my hands on I still could not find a way to begin. Anything I tried to put down sounded wrong – either too abrupt, too indelicate or too obvious – to my middle ear (82).

The above intractable tension in the polity occasioned by bungling military junta and socio-economic dissonance, are what *The Anthills of the Savannah* prefigures. The political crises in the novel escalate to counter coup d'états, power game, political assassination, feminist agitation and other integers of unwholesome state of affairs. However, in conspectus, the political turmoil in the novel basically stems from class struggle and power play, which are arguably fuelled by cultural materialist imperatives. The primal exchange between Sam, His Excellency and Chris Oriko, the Commissioner for information is a presage of power play and class war, which are fully developed as the novel progresses:

You are wasting everybody's time, Mr. Commissioner
for information. I will not go to Abazon. Finish!
Kabisa! Any other business?
　　'As Your Excellency wishes. But...'
　　'But me no buts, Mr. Oriko! The matter is closed,
I said. How many times, for God's sake, am I expected
to repeat it?
Why do *you* find it so difficult to swallow my ruling.
On anything?
　　'I am sorry, Your Excellency. But I have no dif-
ficulty swallowing *and* digesting your rulings' (1).

From the above speech act, Chris eventually pretends not to have
conceded victory to Sam – but he ultimately subscribes to His
Excellency's (Sam's) directives, as subsequently seen in the novel.
The portraiture of Sam depicts him as a military dictator and
inept leader, who relies on brute force, hegemony and violence to
consolidate his leadership and power base. Also, he considers the
state machinery as a private estate – that ought to be used for
the institutionalisation of mediocrity, private interest and above all
materialist pursuits. The atmosphere in the novel invokes political
buccaneering and crude use of force characteristic of the Third
Reich. Hitler, the *Fuehrer* consolidated his power base by enforc-
ing loyalty and subordination via clobbering his apparatchiks to
submission in order to ensure perpetuity and clout. Hitler's propa-
ganda minister, Joseph Goebbles, who is known for dissemination
of half-truths, cants and warped ideas, parallels Prof. Okon in the
novel; while the portrayal of Johnson Ossai, Sam's hatchet man
and the belligerent Director of the State Research Council (14) in
the novel, mirrors Heinrich Himmler, the Nazi chief of Gestapo
(Secret Police). Sam (His Excellency) and his foot soldiers – his
henchmen – constitute the cabal that tramples the nation under
foot. Wole Soyinka in his *Season of Anomy* sees this clique that
furthers violence, class attrition and materialist hegemony as "alli-
ance of the purse and the gun" (134). But in contradistinction to
the world-view of these power-profiteers, are Ikem Osodi, Chris
Oriko and Beatrice Nwanyibuife. These characters are depicted
by Achebe as sheer foil to His Excellency's persona as well as his
coteries'. We shall return to them presently.

It is against this social slough – redolent with power play, cultural materialism and praetorian landscape that Achebe's artistic perspicacity is heightened to underscore his major concern in the novel: military dictatorship, unabated materialism and patriarchal hegemony in postcolonial Nigeria. In congruence with this position, Chidi Maduka as cited in Udumukwu, insightfully paints the same picture:

> Thus, Achebe deftly opens the novel with an apt dramatisation of the power game which is a major concern of the work. Sam is a power seeker who ruthlessly silences opposition in order to show that he constitutes a formidable power base capable of resisting the assault of political opponents (Udumukwu 2007:68).

In addition, Nwachukwu-Agbada's statement regarding *Anthills of the Savannah* appositely re-echoes this reality. For him, "the novel is a study of power in an African state, and shows how original ideals are swept aside by the concept of power personalisation" (92). Consequently, in one of the well-known first statements ever written, Karl Marx and Friedrich Engels began their classic, *The Communist Manifesto* (1884) thus: "The history of all hitherto existing society, is the history of class struggles" (1992: 3). The overriding motif of this seminal masterwork was to unearth the subdued history of class struggle and the insidiousness of capitalist mechanism. It is also in this same light that Mary Wollstonecraft's *A Vindication of the Rights of Woman* (1792) and Simone de Beauvoir's *The Second Sex* (1949) as well as other works that adumbrate the negation of patriarchal ethos, the overarching structures of man's world and the gender-blind, oppressive mechanisms of power relations are written.

Taking a cue from the aforesaid, it could be gleaned *a priori* that the key issues in postcolonial Nigeria are power struggle and unabated frontier materialism. In tandem with this assertion Ojinmah has lucidly noted that

> In Achebe's view, the main problem in contemporary Nigerian Society as well as in many independent African societies, is the lack of restraint in wielding

power, added to an unbridled scramble for materialism, which in most cases result in the destruction of
democratic principles (1991: vii).

The cultural materialist resource and source for oppression of
women is in power struggle and ideology. And central to power
struggle is the cultural scaffold at work in a particular social space.
In their provocative work, *Conflict across Cultures*, LeBaron and
Pillay, have indicated that "Culture and conflict constantly shape
and reshape each other in an evolving interactive process" (2006:7).
The corollary of the interface between culture and class struggle
is how to acquire power for the dominance as well as possible
oppression of other classes in a given society. Of note, in this study,
there are basically two classes or worlds: the man's world and the
woman's world. This Manichean nature of power relations finds
testimony in fierce, unabated power play in gendered social space.
The attempts to curb the political, social, cultural and economic
scrapes engendered by patriarchal arrangement and to liberate
women from this mould of practice have given rise to feminist
ideology and aesthetics in Nigeria and the world over. It is within
this rubric that *Anthills of the Savannah* is significant. In apprehending the essence of this study, it is appropriate to know that
ideology is imperative in deconstructing the edifice of patriarchal
framework that supports the oppression of women. In this regard,
Udumukwu adroitly describes the historicity of feminist deconstruction of patriarchy: "...feminism... is animated by a desire to
reconstruct history in order to reconstitute the woman as subjects.
This implies that the woman is presented or re-presented not as a
mere object of history, put at the margin" (2007b:7). Moreover, the
feminist deconstructionist movement implies a set of strategies,
which resonate with feminist power play to alter the calculus of
power relations in postcolonial Nigeria. Thus, Helen Chukwuma's
terse statement is pertinent here – this project is "to strategically
transform gender relations in Nigeria" (Udumukwu 2007a:135).

In enervating Negritudinal, patriarchal system – an attempt
Rose Mezu calls "the will to change" (1994: 217), it is needful to
underscore that this is not merely a historical assignment: it is
largely ideological. This is because the relationship between literature and ideology spans the continuum of history. Literature and

ideology are in a soulful, interleaved relationship. Thus, "Literature espouses ideology and is mobilised in the internecine ideological struggles that [re]constitutes and [re]defines society in its [re] engineering processes" (James 2006:411). And in turn, ideology mediates literature – and it is markedly inhered in its architecture. Both are essentially interlocked in a kind of dialectical interface. This is what defines power formations in every conceivable class, space or struggle. Louis Althusser describes ideology as *interpellation*, which is integral in the processual rites of the formation of subjectivity in the intricate ideological representation, and the giving of roles to ideological categories. It is also considered as "the systematic analysis of ideas and sensations, of their generation, combination and consequences" (Thompson 1992: 29). It is therefore that which determines the nature, pattern and consequences of power relations in a social milieu. This is in the main the debate which informs the Marxist architectural metaphor of base and superstructure.

The base is the economic (materialist) structure, the main foundation with the forces of productions on which the superstructural edifice and as its apparatuses of aesthetics (literature), philosophy, religion, law, politics and customs, among others rest. The superstructure utilises these elements which it is constitutive of to further its ideological hegemony over the proletarian class or to advance its thesis of ruler-subject dichotomy. Thus, ideology is a moderating instrument for the legitimisation of economic domination, state violence, hierarchised social space and above all sexual discrimination, which Zizek specifically referred to in his latest work, *Violence: Six Sideways Reflection*, as "ideological violence" (9). In ensuring the inevitability of ideological supremacy, the class at the hierarchy uses "coercion and hegemony" (Dirks 1994: 4). This is the case in *Anthills of the Savannah*, where the protagonist, Sam (His Excellency) and his coteries rely heavily on brute force and hegemonic control to perpetuate their regime as well as demand obedience from the people.

Therefore, this study's emphasis on ideology is because it is used by the powerful class as emblem for the commodification of class relation as well as oppression. Thus, Gramsci's advancement of cultural hegemony has so much in common with the theoretical framework of this discourse, which is predicated on cultural materialism.

In this regard therefore, the feminist cultural materialist aesthetics is informed and sustained by the dialectics of countering and challenging the materialist (economic) philosophy and hiatus created by class dichotomy, which patriarchy promotes. This is the colour of feminism Jennifer Wicke offers definition here:

> A feminism that insists on examining the material conditions under which social arrangements, including those of gender hierarchy, develop ... materialist feminism avoids seeing this (gender hierarchy) as the effect of a single ... patriarchy and instead gauges the web of social and psychic relations that make up a material, historical moment (1994:751).

The materialist facet of feminist aesthetics is one of the fulcrums of this study: it is the main reason for social stratification as well as gender complex that percolates the trajectory of history. As history records, the seeming anthropocentric, peremptory logic of colonialism, was in the main ground on the anvil of capitalist (materialist) expansion of Europe (Lenin 1951: 99-100) and kneaded on the dough of cultural attrition. To this end, feminist aesthetics from the cultural materialist perspective, contends that power instead of being freely given or appropriated by a group, ought to be negotiated through economic interaction (Mills 2007: 49). Accordingly, Chidi Amuta has argued that

> [...] society manifest itself in terms of definite classes, groups and formations in the process of the production and reproduction of the means and ends for their sustenance. Therefore, literary values are not very literary but derive from the class configuration of social totality (1986:39).

Following from the above, the deep-seated systemic oppression of humanity – particularly the women, as patriarchy espouses is largely a function of materialism, which Marxist ideology sees as the base that sustains the superstructure. In addition, in her *Women Questions: Essays for a Materialist Feminism*, Lise Vogel widens the ballpark of (cultural) materialist feminism, she asserts that it "sought to replace the socialist tradition's theorising about the woman question with a materialist understanding of women's oppression" (1995: xi). Therefore, this approach considers the "construction of a materialist analysis of culture informed by and responsive to the concerns of women…" (Landry and MacLean 1993: ix-x) Achebe's aesthetic preoccupation in *Anthills of the Savannah* is steeped in the philosophy of redeeming women from the postcolonial Nigerian trammels. Similarly, in *Achebe: New Perspectives*, Umelo Ojinmah contends that "Achebe believes that the time is now for the new nations of Africa to invoke the female principle…" (103); an ideological invocation is principally part of answering complex feminist question. This artistic sensibility in the novel crystallises in the characterisation of Beatrice, a major character in the novel. She exemplifies Achebe's commitment to giving meaning to womanhood as against what traditional values and arrangement offered. Through Beatrice's actions in the novel, it is understandable by extrapolation that she renounces the fact that women are restricted to mere mother-type role in the society (Bicknell 1990:276). She is remarkably Achebe's first central female character in the novel. Beatrice Nwanyibuife is an independent woman. Her characterisation smacks of the balance that Okonkwo (in *Things Fall Apart*) and other female characters lack in Achebe's earlier works. Achebe's aesthetic and ideological contributions to the whole arsenal of debates to rid our world of gender chauvinism – and to make it freer and more humane find accommodation in *Anthills of the Savannah*. Apart from the leadership question, political upheaval and anti-people culture in Kangan – an imaginary Nigerian state, the feminist question is very central to the artistic philosophy underpinning the craft of this novel. Feminist rhetoric explains and addresses the historically oppressed position of women in our society. The human society is *ab initio* patriarchal, which is organised around male dominance. Feminist theorists and writers, which include Achebe, have provoked debates through which women, the "other" sex, to use Beauvior's term, seek to challenge their oppression, marginalisation and dominance by their male counterparts. Gendered space creates a world in which power play flourishes – it is the opium of the ideology behind gendered society. Fundamental to this study is power play; its understanding is crucial in this investigation.

Power play is the process and system whereby strategic manoeuvre, usually adopted in political, ideological struggle, diplomacy and power struggle, based on the use or threatened use of power as a conduit for coercion and acquiescence. It aggregates a set of strategies that employs aggression and coercive approach to enforce obedience or compliance in a given social space. Central to power game is the appropriation of the paraphernalia of authority and the state apparatuses, which make the chicanery employed by the political class in power relations, look constitutional and normative.

Theoretical Clarifications

Cultural materialism is the theoretical framework upon which this study is built. Attempts to negate the contradictions posed by gendered society as well as patriarchal sanctioned power relations in our world, is steeped in cultural resistance dialectics. This is so because culture is at the heart of the concept of gender identity and power play. As a theory, cultural materialism was first introduced by the American anthropologist, Martin Harrris in his seminal work, *The Rise of Anthropological Theory* (1968). But the thesis was refurbished by the Welsh culture theorist and leftist, Raymond Williams, as he incorporated it into literary criticism. Williams' *Marxism and Literature* (1977) laid the foundation for this ground-breaking literary and cultural approach. Cultural materialism is an attempt to bring to bear on that aspect of social existence – culture – that was considered by classical criticism to be less materialist (and even political) in scope. Right from the genesis of his preoccupation with what delineates cultural materialism in "Culture and Society" (1958) up to the pivotal 1973 essay "Base and Superstructure in Marxist Cultural Theory", Williams was concerned with power, that is, with the problematic of determination (Juan 1999: 3). Therefore, in Williams's perspective, the provenance of power (play) is lodged in cultural materialism. Thus, for Williams, cultural materialism "is the analysis of all forms of signification, including quite centrally writing, within the actual means and conditions of their production" (1984: 210). Put simply, cultural materialism is the materialist exploration of culture; it is

ACHEBE'S WOMEN: IMAGISM AND POWER

a system through which social order is experienced, reproduced and communicated. In this light, cultural materialist philosophy argues that human existence and relations of power are a function of practical issues of earthly, material reality. In line with the concern of this study, cultural materialist examination is appropriate in apprehending as well as achieving our objective in this investigation, as we shall see presently.

There is a palpable narrative shift in Achebe's craft in *Anthills of the Savannah*. The paradigmatic shift in content and style reflects a literary commitment towards addressing the issues posed by women's thraldom in postcolonial Nigeria. Therefore, this shift in artistic presentation is a transition from gender disparity to equality, which is the hallmark of "...changing practical consciousness" (Williams 1997:54); and this is the mainstay of Raymond Williams' premise in his theory of cultural materialism. As a political novel, *Anthills of the Savannah* dramatises Nigeria's politics of female subjugation, which is gauged by the catatonic state of women's economic state and social immobility given the realities of oppressive, patriarchal practice and power play.

Theorising Power: Achebe's Women, Power and (Cultural) Materialism

In *Of Woman Born: Motherhood as Experience and Institution*, the American feminist, Adrienne Rich, argues persuasively about the nuances of African gender relations and power acquisition; she remarkably describes patriarchy as:

> The power of the fathers: a familial, social, ideological, and political system in which, by direct pressure – or through tradition, law, and language, customs, etiquette, education, and division of labour – men determine what parts women shall or shall not play, and the female is everywhere subsumed by the male (1977: 57-8).

On the heels of the above, the need for power acquisition in postcolonial Nigerian experience is precipitated by the material uncertainties of the times as well as the quest for domination, as indicated above. According to the Nigerian historian, Elizabeth Isichie in her book, *A History of the Igbo People*,

> Times of great uncertainty ... seem to encourage materialism. Men try to attain the psychological security which the social context of their time denies them by creating a little charmed island for themselves (1976:149).

A construal of Isichie's "psychological security" above finds resonance in power acquisition and power play, which Wole Soyinka in his *Reith Lectures* (2004), refers to as "... the ancestral adversary of human freedom" (9). Psychological security is necessary for both sexes in gender relations – it is crucial for women to attain some measure of material balance, which affords psychological security. This is also a major source of power acquisition by women. And in the context of Soyinka's statement above regarding power, women's attainment of psychological security through materialist fulfilment and pursuits will inform balance and power necessary for countering men's subjugation and marginalisation in gender relations. Hence, psychological security – a spin-off of cultural materialism, furtively allocates power to men, while the women are subjected to thraldom resulting from this paradoxical enemy of human (women) freedom.

Thus, in negating patriarchy, there is need to rethink power structure – by decentralising power across diverse social networks; this is the pivot of Foucauldian analysis of power. Thus for Foucault,

> Power is dispersed across complicated and heterogeneous social networks marked by ongoing struggle. Power is not something present at specific locations within those networks, but is instead always at issue in ongoing attempts to (re) produce effective social alignments, and conversely to avoid or erode their effects,often by producing various counter-alignments.
>
> (Gutting 1994: 112-113)

Power decentralisation that brings about "counter-alignment", to borrow Foucault's term, is the meat of feminist discourse. In Fanon's conceptualisation of power, this kind of counter-alignment resonates with "primary Manichaeism" (Fanon 1963: 39), an idea that makes a case for duality of powers or forces for "psycho-

affective equilibrium" (169), a penumbra of Isichiean "psychological security". Therefore, feminist discourse maintains that

> Women have the capacity to ... have social resources
> that often enable them to survive, whether in material
> terms or in terms of psychological support... (Lemke
> 2003: 65).

Furthermore, the *raison d'être* for challenging the patriarchal paradigm that consigned power at one locus: the men's world, galva-
nised this form of "narrative[s] of resistance" (Gikandi 1991:26),
which is amply demonstrated in the craft of *Anthills of the Savannah*. Accordingly, in his *The Novel and Change in Africa*, Onyemaechi Udumukwu argues unequivocally in the same light that

> [...] Chinua Achebe has not only adopted the appro-
> priate discursive strategies in *Anthills of the Savannah*
> in order to project the nature of the existing power
> structures in a post-colonial context but in addition,
> he adopts such discursive strategies in order to subvert
> the existing power structure (2006:196).

In such feminist discourse, as delineated above, "the focus is not
on uncovering the material and ideological specificities that constitute a group of women as 'powerless' in a particular context"
(Mohanty 1988: 200), but to demonstrate Achebe's preoccupation
with the burdens of traditional concept of power as it affects the
women as well as a burlesque of this stifling practice, which needs
subversion. Therefore,

> In the beginning power rampaged through the world,
> naked. So the Almighty, looking at his creation through
> the round undying eye of the sun, saw and pondered
> and finally decided to send his daughter, Idemili, to
> bear witness to the moral nature of authority by wrap-
> ping around Power's rude waist loincloth of peace and
> modesty (Achebe 1987: 102).

Also, Achebe has ideo-aesthetically crafted a vision of women that
ensconces motherhood as power. Thus, "*Nneka*, they said. Mother is

supreme" (98). For Achebe, this kind of power is acquired through enlightenment and self-discovery as well as reconstruction of the primeval notion of motherhood. This is fleshed out in a dialogue between Ikem and Beatrice, as Ikem comes to shocking awakening that women should be given due recognition in the society as against the roles traditional institutions offered. He reads out his rethink on women to Beatrice:

> The original oppression of women was based on crude denigration. She caused Man to fall. So she became a scapegoat. No, not a scapegoat which might be blameless but a culprit richly deserving of whatever suffering Man chose thereafter to heap on her... Well, that kind of candid chauvinism might be OK for the rugged state of the Old Testament. The New Testament required a more enlightened, more refined, more loving even, strategy – ostensibly, that is (97-98).

According to Francis Waffet, what the strategy highlighted above necessitates in the postcolonial era is largely about "the awakening of critical consciousness", which actually "leads the way to the expression of social discontents precisely because these discontents are real components of an oppressive situation" (in Freire 1972: 16). There is a rectilinear nexus between oppression of the masses in the postcolonial society and marginalisation, oppression and denigration of women in our gendered space: the former is the macrocosm of the latter. And to subvert this trend, identity consciousness is essential amongst the women folk. This will in the final analysis elicit change of gear in societal mobility of women – and the body politic. This is in sync with Ikem's opinion about negating the trammels sired on women by the "Old Testament" (98). According to Richard Taylor, the negation of patriarchal arrangement, which is enshrined in identity consciousness, should be viewed as thus:

> identity represents an evolving articulation of personal capacities, value identification and .... plans, ideals, expectations and opportunities (1986: 202).

In silhouetting Achebe's concept of women's power, it should be considered as "... the ability to take one's place in whatever discourse is essential to action..." (Heilbrun 1989:18) Consequently, in Achebe's vision, theorising power for women in the postcolonial Nigeria, has to do with disavowing any essentialist logic; there should be approaches and strategies that will relay the sinews of knowledge and experience as well as deconstructing the pristine view of women to depict strength (Udumukwu 2007b: 18). Also, such movement of liberation and re-creation of Nigerian (African) women, who are yoked by the pressures of traditional institutions, should entail a transition from the margin to the epicentre of affairs, rather than being "in the peripheral, tangential role of a passive victim of a masculine-based cultural universe" (Mezu1994:27-8). The women's transition from the margin to the epicentre of affairs, foregrounds placing them at the limelight. Beatrice sees this new reality thus:

> But the way I see it is that giving women today the same role which traditional society gave them of intervening only when everything else has failed is not enough, you know, like the women in the Sembene film who picked up the spears abandoned by their defeated mensfolk. It is not enough that women should be the court of last resort because the last resort is a damn sight too far and too late! (91-2).

The Pen and the Sword: Advancing Women's Power

Social responsible theory as understood in media practice is a framework that supports journalistic (artistic) writing that filters as well as advocates the place of the masses (the subaltern) in societal power play, which *prima facie* foregrounds the uplift of the political class. It galvanises as well as extends the story-line of the liberation of Achebe's women in *The Anthills of the Savannah*. It is an appropriate platform for women's movement from the traditional, patriarchal zero level to hero status. Through the nature of Achebe's craft in the novel, it is ostensible that with the media, women's fight for social justice and fairness will not be truncated on the morass of elite-salving patriarchy. Also, the media, as evident in the aesthetics of the novel, is a veritable instrument for the acquisition and consolidation of political power, particularly for the women, who are victims of gender complex and oppression. In addition, for the women (the masses) to achieve power, which is integral in bringing equitable order, the media has to hammer this on the anvil of ideology – by contributing in the shaping of a people's world-view, which is crucial in combating the ills of society. In the novel, the activities of Ikem Osodi, the editor of *National Gazette* and Chris Oriko, the Commissioner for information, all gear up for the reshaping of people's perspectives about the legitimacy of His Excellency's junta. Their efforts in this regard equally amounts to power play, hence, strategies for circumventing repression and female oppression are espoused via their journalistic enterprise. The Commissioner for information, Chris, uses his position to address the inhumanity and crude power-wielding in the novel without being cowed by the intimidations and brutalities of Sam, His Excellency. This is in the main ideological, which contributes in reconstituting the world-view of the people of Kangan. For Chidi Maduka, "There is no doubt that he (Chris) espouses values opposed to those of the government" (My parenthesis, 2007: 76). Also, the ideological penchant of Chris's finds counterpart in Ikem's. Ikem, the editor of the *National Gazette* "sees journalism as an instrument for social change" (77). Lumped together, their position in the novel finds ample detonation in resistance rhetoric as well as sheer "… struggle to reconstitute the language of the dominant power" (Udumukwu 2006: 222), in order to effect societal transformation and feminist rhetoric. Also, Achebe's aesthetic preoccupation in this instance shores up his commitment to use art to contribute to nation-building in Nigeria – and Africa by extension; this also dredges up the metonymic aphorism credited to Edward Bulder-Lytton, the English poet that "the pen is mightier than the sword". In the novel, the statement by the police Superintendent, who attended to Ikem as he visited the police station to pick up his vehicle particulars that were confiscated by the police constables on duty the previous Friday night at Bassa, re-echoes the efficacy of the pen to bring equitable social order. The Superintendent remarked: "Oh no. The pen is mightier than the sword. With one sentence of your sharp pen you can demolish anybody. Ha ha ha ha ha. I respect your pen…" (131).

The social role of a writer in the traditional societies as moulders of thought and teachers have been recanted in the postcolonial

Nigeria, where the crave for material benefit and power as well as trepidation resulting from possible onslaught by the powers that be, have detoured the traditional roles of writers as seen in the oral setting, where they were the mouthpieces of the people in the court of the powerful. There is an upturn of this traditional role in Achebe's reconstruction of the responsibility of the media in post-colonial Nigeria as seen in *Anthills of the Savannah*. Following this, for Achebe, social responsible journalism should be in the vanguard of efforts to point a flambeau towards "...where the rain began to beat us..." (1975:44). Achebe reckons that this integral, crucial task has been at the back-burner in view of the political power equation and power play at work in postcolonial Nigerian politics, where the media is uncritical of the system – and is rather power-seeking itself. According to the literary critic and poet, Wilfred Cartey in his *Whispers from a Continent: The Literature of Contemporary Black Africa*,

> Those who enter politics do so mainly out of self-interest; those who actively comment on the political scene, the journalists, are also clearly seeking their own interests in their manner of reporting political incidents. The mass of the people who are caught in the turbulence of politics are easily swayed and as easily erupt into violent action (1971: 160).

The concern raised in the above snippet about the vernal and power-seeking set of journalists in contemporary Nigeria (Africa) is parallel to the pressmen referred to in Achebe's political fiction, *A Man of the People*, where Chief Nanga, a prototype of modern Nigerian political heavyweight declares as thus:

> If you don't give them something now, tomorrow he will go and Write rubbish about me. They say it is the freedom to crucify thepress. But to me it is nothing short of freedom to crucify innocent men and assassinate their character... I don't say they should not criticise – after all no one is perfect except God – but they should criticise constructively (74).

There is a significant paradigm shift from the above portraiture of pressmen and writers – as seen in *Anthills of the Savannah*.

Although in both political novels by Achebe: *A Man of the People* and *Anthills of the Savannah*, there is a graphic distillation "of opportunistic politicians – both civilians and military – who appropriate state power and divert it to a lucrative means of acquiring material wealth" (Udumukwu 1998:23), but it is in the latter that the power of the media to contribute to power play is upturned. The emphasis here is the idea of communication – both artistic and journalistic in surpassing violence, power play and unbridled capitalism in efficacy.

Therefore, in *Anthills of the Savannah*, the well-known characterisation of the media as "the bastion of democracy" (Murphy 1976:11) is made bear. This is exemplified by the nature of the editorialising and reportage that the *National Gazette* undertakes through its political pragmatist and editor, Ikem Osodi. The texture of Ikem's editorials in this newspaper underpins his unswerving commitment to reform the Kangan nation that has been in chains from the authoritarian, military regime of Sam, and his toadies. Ikem's statement in view of the constricting perspectives of Chris, the commissioner for information, whom His Excellence used (initially) as a dyke to Ikem's journalistic activism, reinforces Achebe's idea about the power of the media:

> I wrote the editorial with so much passion that I found myself ending it with a verse to be sung ... As for my editorials, as long as I remain editor of the *Gazette* I shall not seek anybody's permission for what I write. I've told you that many times before (43-44).

Ikem's statement above illustrates what Alvin Gouldner calls "critical rationality". This concept entails when writers consider themselves as being imbued with heightened sense of power to change people's perception and ideological world-view about what the society has taken as its norms. In doing this, writers see themselves or are seen as ideological visionaries, who are centres of power – hence their journalistic mediation in the goings-on in the society helps to shape people's view about their world. This helps to negate the pressures of terror and marginalisation, which is central in apprehending women experience in postcolonial Nigeria (Amadi 1999:25). In *The Dialectic of Ideology and Technology*, Alvin

Gouldner sees this task by writers as an obligation to change their universe (1976: 71); this dovetails with Matthew Kukah's "advocacy journalism" (1999: 287). Thus, social responsible writing illuminates the path of feminist aesthetics – and helps in extirpating the dynamics of oppressive order in the militarised Kangan – a penumbra of postcolonial Nigeria. In the novel, Achebe's important illustration of the efficacy of Ikem's editorials in contributing to sensitising as well as agitating for the rights of the marginalised is expressed here:

> I had never met him before; I have never read what they say he writes because I do not know ABC. But I have heard of all the fight he fought for poor people in this land. I would not like to hear that he has given up the fight... (122).

Through Ikem's journalistic enterprise, the people developed faith in the power of the pen to effect change. So for the society to depend on writing and the media for change of leadership in Kangan, bear testimony to the power of the pen to propel good governance.

Feminist agitation, once considered a pawn in the power play of ideological conflict, came to have more relevance via the instrumentality of responsible media practice couched in the ideals of using the apparatus of news reporting to disseminate and correct warped ideologies that patriarchy has made normative in our world. In the novel, Achebe's ideo-esthetic predilection is elevated to underscore the fact that social criticism through responsible media is crucial in combating the ills of contemporary Nigerian nation. In advancing this philosophical preference, Achebe maintains that "unchained" writing is very crucial. In his 1966 article, entitled "The Black Writer's Burden", Achebe dredged up this clarity:

> We must seek the freedom to express our thought and feeling, even against ourselves, without the anxiety that what we say might be taken in evidence against our race (139).

The power game, brutality and militarised atmosphere evident in the novel are sheer simulacrum of the real conjunctures in the Nigerian society. On this strength, as Achebe warns in his statement above, writers should be the conscience of their age: they should say the truth – there should not be any need for sensationalism. And as writers do this our world will be free from gender captivity and power play. In the novel, the impacts of Ikem and Chris' writings exemplified in agitating women's (and the people's) rights against the tenets of patriarchy, ensconces the place of social responsible media practice in contributing to human freedom. Here, Walter Lippman's statement concerning the relevance of populist committed and social responsible media is pertinent: "there can be no liberty for a community which lacks the means by which to detect lies" (Guinness 2002:17).

The State, Violence and Women: Feminist Resistance Narrative

The history of Nigerian State since political independence has been shaped and sustained by violence. The colonial administrative mechanism and structure underpin this logic. The imperial conquest was itself a classical case of violence and militarism. This development has largely forged Nigeria's (Africa's) political power architectonics and capitalism. It is also in this light that Nwachukwu-Agbada reasons: "It is equally clear that part of the colonial success in Africa is traceable to the military might of the colonising power" (2007:85). As the colonialists left, they put in place a network of operation to further have a hold on the Nigerian nation as well as other African countries. This neo-colonial dominance theory is being advanced by the Nigerian political class in cahoots with the foreign compradors. In Kangan, the government in power is a military one, whose stock in trade is to use brute force and violence to sustain its structures. In addition, this regime came into existence through violence: coup d'état, even though it proclaimed at the beginning that it was going to be a corrective regime. The state in this instance is a sheer departure from the Weberian definition that considers it as a socio-political entity responsible for the enforcement of constitutional provisions. In the postcolonial state – as being foreshadowed in *Anthills of the Savannah*, the state has taken an unusual characteristic, which

147

finds accommodation in violence and power play. On top of this, the parthenogenesis of this metamorphosis by the state reaches its apogee in the materialist pursuit as well as class domination by the wielders of power or "soldiers-turned politicians" (Achebe 1987: 141). According to Adele Jinadu in his *Fanon: In Search of African Revolution*, "the state is viewed as the agent for the furtherance of class interests, a function necessitated by the exigencies of the productive relations between a class of exploiters and a class of the exploited" (1980:100). In view of this backcloth, most of the postcolonial states have been referred to as failed states or collapsed states. This inept and harrowing pattern is what Elewa's uncle addresses here in the novel:

> We have seen too much trouble in Kangan since the white man left because those who make plans make for themselves only and their family... I say, there is too much fighting in Kangan, too much killing. But fighting will not begin unless there is first a thrusting of fingers into eyes (228).

In furtherance of the reasons outlined in the above snippet, the postcolonial Nigeria is a theatre of horror and psychological violence, which are built on the scaffold of class attrition and capitalist oppression. And again, the women are the worst hit in this kind of status quo, in view of the realities of patriarchy. Part of these realities is what Achebe sees as disillusionment resulting from the mess that the emergent Nigerian political class has made of self-rule and political independence (Ojinmah 1991:107).

Coursing through this development, the Nigerian state has wielded a kind of monopoly of power and violence in order to accomplish its agenda of dominance and power. Since independence, Nigeria has had to contain with issues of leadership and nation-building. The reason for this despicable landscape is easily fathomable, given her national terrain: a theatre of brutality, marginalisation and a place of state-sanctioned violence. In the main, this unwholesome pattern draws its source from the cruel and harsh living conditions of the masses (Mayowa 2001:195). This has also elicited an asphyxiating form of struggle. In defining the terrain of this struggle, "which obviously extends the contest against capitalism not only to its economic foundation but to its cultural and ideological roots in everyday life" (Sachikonye 1995: 7-8), the state resorts to privatisation of violence and liberalisation of coercion. The nation of Kangan dramatises this as graphically illustrated by His Excellency's characterisation in the novel as well as his coteries. Ideally, in every modern state, there should be an organised system and a constitutional order, which ultimately constitute a lodestar for the smooth operation of a nation. But the absence of this order naturally impinges on the socio-economic harmony and political operation of the society. Predominantly, in *Anthills of the Savannah,* the mould of power relations between the military (political class) and the people (the women) mediates the ethos of public and private morality in a society that is oblivious of its past and rather seeks material rewards in its future.

In all of Achebe's works before *Anthills of the Savannah,* there is a palpable aesthetics of violence – beginning with Okonkwo's beating of Ojiugo to other crude and violent treatment of women in other works. But there is an overt change of gear in *Anthills of the Savannah* – where Achebe envisions an idea of women which ensconces respect for the women as well as recognition of their identity. Here, the women are perceived as subjects, not mere objects in the society. The meat of Achebe's feminist narrative in the novel is to foreground women subversion of man's ideals and institutionalised practices as well as educating the society about stopping violence meted to the women. Some of this violence is largely psychological – a belief handed down from generation to generation. A clear illustration of the subversion of this patriarchal arrangement and violence is Beatrice's giving of Elewa's baby-girl's name. Two things are relevant in this ceremony. One the baby was named Amaechina – a male name; and secondly the ceremony was performed by a woman: Beatrice. These two variables question the legitimacy of man's supremacy in the society – made possible by psychological violence and patriarchal ideology. Beatrice and Abdul's statements on this occasion find resonance in the psycho-logical negation of androgenic contradictions – which is a form of violence; a rebuttal to the time-worn violence meted to the "other" sex. She contends:

> What does a man know about a child anyway that he
> should presume to give it a name... Nothing except
> that his wife told him he is the father ... (222).

Power Play and "Nwanyibuife" Dialectics: Negating Androgynous Contradictions

Through history, there seems to be no substitute for the denigrated people and the invidious gendered world presented in Kangan – a simulacrum of Nigeria – except the alternative of what Theodor Adorno calls negation. In Adorno's thesis, art (literature) and ideology realise themselves quite full well not in what they demonstrate as positive, but in what is made bear through the decomposition and negation of what has been taken as the norm (Adorno 1974: 126-7). Therefore, the craft of "Nwanyibuife" is to undermine the primal, patriarchal world-view. This dovetails with Helen Chukwuma's idea about the essence of new women, which is enshrined in the philosophy of feminism. Thus, feminism "... seeks to give the woman a sense of self as a worthy, effectual and contributing human being..." (1994: xiii). There is a distillation of this during the naming ceremony of Elewa's baby-girl, Amaechina. Beatrice's actions in this event – by presiding over the ceremony and naming the child herself as well as the male-type name she gave to the girl, culminate in deconstructing the patriarchal paradigm; this sees the women as "ife" – something. It is against this background that

> Beatrice has decided on a sudden inspiration to hold
> a naming ceremony in her flat for Elewa's baby-girl.
> She did not intend a traditional ceremony... There was
> an Old Testament prophet who named his son The-
> remnant-shall-return. They must have lived in times
> like this. We have a different metaphor, though; we
> have our own version of hope that springs eternal. We
> shall call this child Amaechina: May-the-path-never-
> close. Ama for short (217-222).

The context of the above excerpt is two-pronged: first it points touch to de-genderisation of names, which obviates the trauma of male chauvinism and secondly, Beatrice's role in the event referred to above shows that social roles are man-made; they are *interpellated*, to use Althusser's term. These two events are what Udumukwu calls "double reversal" (2007a: 323). The mainstay of these developments is lodged in Achebe's artistic faithfulness to upturn feminist agitation – for a more social inclusive society. And Beatrice's political answer to the elders' question: "who gave her the name?", makes room for a democratic system, which is populist; she intoned: "All of us" (225). The aesthetic fervour of this statement is couched in feminist subterfuge to negate male domination. Herein lies the fact that negating androgynous contradictions amounts to "low-power distance", as enunciated by the Dutch organisational anthropologist, Geert Hofstede. In his power distance theory, power distance amounts to the degree of acceptance and deference of unequal power, which exists between people or classes (LaBaron and Pillay 2008:46). Low-power distance makes a case for democratic order. This is in the main, one of the cardinal tenets of feminism. In addition, apart from the equitable and gender-blind society that Achebe envisions in *Anthills of the Savannah*, there is also a recrudescence of women power and support, which are needed for society to gain balance and purpose. Chikwenye Ogunyemi's statement adds credence to this negation of machismo evident in Kangan. She asks: "is it any wonder that the country is in shambles when it has failed to solicit the help of its better half (women) ... for pacific pursuits, for the betterment of the country?" (1988: 60).

Morphologically, "Nwanyibuife" is constitutive of triadic entities (morphemes). By transliteration, "nwanyi" means "woman"; the second is "bu", meaning "is"; while the third morpheme is 'ife', and this means "something". Creatively, this word has aesthetic, linguistic, ideological and political undertones. It is largely a form of Achebe's response to some critics (and possibly) readers, who might have accused him of overt romanticisation or palpable feminisation of his female characters in his earlier works. Furthermore, this aesthetic, ideological characterisation crystallises in Beatrice, Achebe's symbol of contemporary womanhood. Her persona in the novel evokes sense of renewed and liberated womanhood – a departure from the marooned and exploited women of the old. Beatrice is more than a character in *Anthills of the Savannah*; she exemplifies the image of a new Nigeria – and a new world, where gender equality, human rights and socio-economic stability will hold sway. Herein lies the essence of her baptismal name: Nwanyi-buife – meaning "A female is also something" (87) in guaranteeing societal cohesion and development.

Part of the evils of Nigerian postcolonial society is the furtherance of the logic of social attrition and class war; these two variables are largely sustained by the gendered African (Nigerian) traditional set-up, which are a corollary of her cultural experience. And in *Anthills of the Savannah*, Achebe maintains that to surmount this social anomie, the feminist question needs to be part of the debates regarding arresting the malaise in Nigeria, so as to effect wholesome change in the polity. Following this, Udumukwu has argued that "Achebe's re-visioning especially in the positive image conferred on women marks a willingness to espouse change" (2007a: 311). What could be taken away from this instance is Achebe's artistic commitment to the politics of feminist narrative that advances the cause of women in Nigeria, and on the African continent. So, in power play discourse, the nature and texture of power women wielded as daughters and individuals in their biological homes have been remarkably radicalised in their remade social status as new women expressed in their wifely roles as well as in their activities in the larger society (Chukwuma 2007:135). Beatrice's poignant statement bears up this position:

> But the way I see it is that giving women today the same role which traditional society gave them of intervening only when everything else has failed is not enough, you know, like the women in the Sembene film who pick up the spears abandoned by their defeated menfolk. It is not enough that women should be the court of last resort because the last resort is a damn sight too far and too late! (91-2).

In the Hegelian construct, Nwanyibuife ideo-aesthetically amounts to "antithesis", which literally translates to negation of the "thesis" – that is the contradictions in the postcolonial Nigerian social space. And within the confines of this investigation, these contradictions manifest mainly in the gendered, patriarchal arrangement of the postcolonial Nigerian society. The interface of these two variables is a correlative of "synthesis" – which largely entails Achebe's progressive social vision of postcolonial Nigerian society. Accordingly, in his *Social Responsibility in the Nigerian Novel*, Udumukwu argues insightfully in this direction: "from a dialectical point of view these contradictions are materials that must be negated for society to evolve a new order" (1998:43).

Therefore, in adopting the Nwanyibuife schema, the essence is to assert the place of a new woman through feminist rhetoric against the pristine concept of womanhood as being weak, marooned, unrepresented and oppressed. Thus, in the Achebean sense, the Nwanyubuife aesthetics is lodged in feminist power play and negation battle waged in the socio-economic and politico-cultural turfs of the society, which is *prima facie* patriarchal and disempowering of women. Basically, societal realisation of women's inherent strength and true worth will shape the quest for women's recognition as well as liberate them from patriarchal, cultural materialist thraldom; it will equally galvanise a rethink of the contribution of the oppressed in the development of the Nigerian nation. It is on this strength that we come to terms with the import of this statement in the novel that "this world belongs to the people of the world not to any little caucus, no matter how talented" (232).

Conclusion

It is pertinent to restate at this point that the issues of power play and gendered universe as argued in this study are thereby inconceivable without the inscriptions and mediations of cultural materialist criticism. In enervating the social atrophy engendered by patriarchal tenets, it is essential to incorporate cultural materialist criticism, which shores up feminist rhetoric – and this is integral in occluding the pristine, traditional concept of women as culturally and economically disempowered. At the root of cultural materialist theory lies the arsenal to effect change in our world; a change necessitated by the political, social, ideological and economic subjugation of women, made possible by the logic of patriarchy as well as mercantalised power relations, which represses the masses.

Therefore, it is within the ballpark of cultural materialist study that it could be stated that the national discontents highlighted in the novel transcend the confines of fiction; they are reified in the lived world – as seen in the realities of postcolonial Nigeria. It is on this score that *Anthills of the Savannah* is a piece of fiction centred on power play in the gendered postcolonial Nigeria, where women have been kept at the zero level for a long time. Consequently, to move Nigeria forward, cultural materialist approach is crucial, as it will help to illuminate our vision and goal towards re-writing the dehistoricised account of the oppressed – the women, particularly in the cultural and socio-economic spheres. This is basically one of Chinua Achebe's artistic preoccupations in the novel. The patriarchal tendency to de-emphasise women's true worth and the historical damage done to their rights and power have been given expression in Sheila Rowbotham's *A Century of Women*: "Women's history has been part of a pervasive impulse ..." (1997:3). Besides, cultural materialist study will equally contribute in rescuing the postcolonial Nigeria from the rubbles of patriarchal pillage and purblind subjectivities. It is to this end that the title of this study: "Power Play and Gendered Space in *Anthills of the Savannah*: A Cultural Materialist Reading" is important in apprehending the political historiography as well as feminist aesthetics of postcolonial Nigeria.

Works Cited

Achebe, Chinua. *Anthills of the Savannah*. Ibadan: Heinemann, 1987.

_____. "The Writer's Burden". *Morning Yet on Creation Day*. London: Heinemann, 1975.

_____. *A Man of the People*. London: Heinemaan, 1966.

Adorno, Theodor. *Minima Moralia*. Trans. E.F.N. Jephcott. London: Veso, 1974.

Amadi, Fred. *Errors in Nigerian Journalism & Thought*. Owerri: Kosoko Press, 1999.

Amuta, Chidi. *Towards a Sociology of African Literature*. Oguta: Zim Pan, 1986.

Bicknell, Catherine. "Achebe's Women: Mothers, Priestesses, and Young Urban Professionals". *Challenging Hierarchies: Issues and Themes in Colonial and Post-Colonial African Literature, Society and Politics*. New York: Peter Lang Publishing, 5 (1998): 125-136.

Cartey, Wilfred. *Whispers from a Continent: the Literature of Contemporary Black Africa*. London: Heinemann, 1969.

Chukwuma, Helen. "Literary Strategies in Feministic Writing: Flora Nwapa's *Cassava Song and Rice Song* and Phanuel Egejuru's *The Seed Yams Have Been Eaten*". Ed. Onyemaechi Udumukwu. *Nigerian Literature in English: Emerging Critical Perspectives*. Port Harcourt: M & J Grand Orbit Communication, 2007.

_____. Ed. "The Identity of Self". *Feminism in African Literature: Essays on Criticism*. Port Harcourt: Pearl Publishers, (1994): xiii-xxvii.

Dirks, Nicholas. Ed. *Colonialism and Culture*. Ann Arbor: The Uni. of Michigan Press, 1992.

Fanon, Frantz. *The Wretched of the Earth*. Trans.

Friere, Paulo. *The Pedagogy of the Oppressed*. Middlesex: Penguin, 1972.

Gikandi, Simon. *Reading Chinua Achebe: Language and Ideology in Fiction*. London: James Curry, 1991.

Gouldner, Alvin. *The Dialectic of Ideology and Technology*. London: Macmillan Press, 1976.

Guinness, Os. *Time for Truth: Living Free in a World of Lies, Hype and Spin*. London: Baker Publishers, 2002.

Gutting, Gary. Ed. *The Cambridge Companion to Foucault*. 1ST ed. Cambridge: Cambridge Uni.Press, 1994.

Hofstede, Geert. *Culture's Consequences: International Differences in Work-Related Values*. California: Sage Publications, 1984.

Heilbrun, Carolyn. *Writing a Woman's Life*. London: Women's Press, 1989.

Isichie, Elizabeth. *A History of the Igbo People*. London: Macmillan Press, 1976.

James, Tsaaior. "Ideology and the African Literature". *An Encyclopaedia of the Arts*. 4.5 (2006): 411-421.

Jinadu, Adele. *Fanon: In Search of the African Revolution*. Enugu: Fourth Dimension Publisher, 1980.

Juan, San E. Raymond "Williams and the Idea of Cultural Revolution". *College Literature*. (Spring 1999): 1-18.

Kukah, H. M. *Democracy and Civil Society in Nigeria*. Ibadan: Spectrum, 1999.

Laudry, Donna and Gerald Maclean. *Materialist Feminism*. Oxford: Blackwell, 1993.

LeBaron, M and V. Pillay. *Conflict across Cultures*. Boston: International Press, 2006.

Lemke, Stefanie. "Empowered Women and the Need to Empower Men: Gender Relations and Food Security in Black South African Households". *Stud.Tribes Tribals*. 1. 1(2003): 59-67.

Lenin, V.I. *Imperialism, the Highest Stage of Capitalism*. Moscow: Foreign Languages Publishing House, 1951.

Maduka, Chidi. "Chinua Achebe and Military Dictatorship in Nigeria: A Study of *Anthills of the Savannah*". Ed. Onyemaechi Udumukwu. *Nigerian Literature in English: Emerging Critical Perspectives*. Port Harcourt: M & J Grand Orbit Communication, (2007): 64-80.

Marx, Karl and Engels, Fredrich. *The Communist Manifesto*. Oxford: Oxford University Press, 1992.

Mayowa, Anthony. "The State and Ethno-Communal Violence in Nigeria: The Case of Ife-Madokeke". *Africa Development*. xxvi. 1&2 (2001): 411-421.

Mezu, Rose Ure. Women *in Chains: An Abandonment in Love Relationships in the Fiction of Selected West African Writers*. Owerri: Black Academy, 1994.

Mills, Sarah. "Geography, Gender and Power". *Space, Knowledge and Power*. eds. Jeremy, W. C and Stuart E. Hampshire: Ashgate Publishing, 2007.

Mohanty, Chandra Talpade. "Under Western Eyes: Feminist Scholarship and Colonial Discourse". *Feminist Review*. 30 (Autumn 1988): 65-88.

Murphy, David. *The Silent Watchdog: The Press in Local Politics*. London: Constable, 1976.

Nwachukwu-Agbada, J.O.J. "Intervention without Salvation: the Military and Society in Nigerian Literature". Ed. Onyemaechi Udumukwu. *Nigerian Literature in English: Emerging Critical Perspectives*. Port Harcourt: M & J Grand Orbit Communication, (2007): 81-107.

Ogunyemi, Chikwenye. "Women and Nigerian Literature". *Perspectives on Nigerian Literature: 1700 to the Present*. Ed. Yemi, Ogunbiyi. Vol 1. Lagos: Guardian Books,1988.

Ojinmah, Umelo. *Chinua Achebe: New Perspectives*. Ibadan: Spectrum Books, 1991.

Rich, Adrienne. *Of Woman Born: Motherhood as Experience and Institution*. New York: Norton, 1976.

Soyinka, Wole. *Climate of Fear*. http://www.bbc.co.uk/radio4/reith2004/lecture2.

_____. *Season of Anomy*. London: Thomas Nelson, 1973; 1980.

Taylor, Richard. "Black Youth and Psychosocial Development: A Conceptual Framework". *The Black Family: Essays and Studies.* Ed. Robert Staples.California: Wordsworth, (1986): 201-210.

Thompson, John. *Ideology and Modern Culture.* Cambridge: Polity Press;Oxford : Basil Blackwell, 1992.

Sachikonye, Lloyd. Ed. *Democracy, Civil Society and the State: Social Movements in Southern Africa.* Harare: Sapes Books, 1995.

Udumukwu, Onyemaechi. *Signature of Women: The Dialectics of Action in African Women's Writing.* Owerri: Onii Publishing House, 2007.

_____. *Social Responsibility in the Nigerian Novel.* Port Harcourt: Sherbrooke Associates, 1998.

_____. *The Novel and Change in Africa.* Port Harcourt: University of Port Harcourt Press, 2006.

_____. Ed. "The Niger Bridge or Reconfiguring the Postcolonial Nation in Achebe's *Anthills of the Savannah*". *Nigerian Literature in English: Emerging Critical Perspectives.* Port Harcourt: M & J Grand Orbit Communications, (2007): 311-325.

Vogel, Lise. *Women Questions: Essays for a Materialist Feminist.* London: Routledge, 1995.

Williams, Raymond. *Marxism and Culture.* Oxford: Oxford Uni. Press, 1977.

_____. *Writing in Society.* New York: Verso, 1984.

Zizek, Slajov. *Violence: Six Sideways Reflections.* London: Profile Books, 2008.

CHAPTER 10

FEMINIST STANCE AND LANGUAGE: A FOCUS ON BEATRICE IN CHINUA ACHEBE'S *ANTHILLS OF THE SAVANNAH*

Margaret Fafa Nutsukpo

Anthills of the Savannah (1987), regarded by critics worldwide as Achebe's best work till date, was interpreted by many critics as Achebe's response to criticism of his traditionalist portrayal of women in his earlier works, and of his political views. Indeed, *Anthills of the Savannah* is a departure from Achebe's portraiture of women in *Things Fall Apart* (1956), *Arrow of God* (1964), *A Man of the People* (1966), and *No Longer at Ease* (1969).

Yakubu criticizes the above works for depicting women

> whose lives revolve around the home and family...
> [who are]... hardly seen involved in any productive
> work...[and who]...mostly serve as sexual and
> ego pawns for male protagonists (82-83).

Feminist critics have, over the years, challenged and criticized Achebe as being a sexist writer. It is therefore surprising that after a twenty-one-year hiatus, Achebe bursts out in a new song which heralds the new woman – intellectual, assertive, independent, vocal, and an active part of the human work force. The difference between Beatrice and Achebe's other women could not have been more significant and symbolic!

Although some critics refuse to recognize this new slant in Achebe's work as a shift in his position on women, it is evident that consciously or unconsciously, Achebe has created a radical feminist whose stance is clearly defined by her actions and by her language. It is this character, Beatrice, that this paper seeks to reveal, through a careful examination.

According to Gloria Chukukere,

> genuine African feminism addresses the issue of the legitimacy of the feminine as a subject matter of discourse. It, therefore, devotes conscious and unapologetic attention to the social, political and psychological presence of women in African Literature (101).

Achebe, in *Anthills of the Savannah*, indeed addresses the above issue through Beatrice.

Anthills of the Savannah, set in the fictional Kangan, revolves around three friends – Sam, Chris and Ikem – all intellectuals and key players in the government of Kangan, through whom Achebe demonstrates how the quest for power and self interest can lead to individual and communal destruction. For the first time, Achebe places a female character, Beatrice, in a central position in his novel to underscore the fact that a woman can be a source of inspiration, strength, and hope in the face of conflict and adversity, a role player in the developmental process, and an avenue through which the problems of a nation can be identified and resolved. Chris describes Beatrice as, "a good and tastefully produced book, easy on the eye. No pretentious distractions. Absolutely sound." (57-58).

Achebe presents the happenings in the novel mostly through the points-of-view of Ikem, Chris and Beatrice, and the third person omniscient narrator. This gives the reader an opportunity to make personal connections with these characters, not only through their actions, but also through their emotions, thoughts, words and experiences, and to make a personal judgement based on these.

Beatrice is portrayed as an intellectual who is incredibly intelligent, more so than many of her male peers. This is revealed during her fateful visit to the Presidential Retreat, when Sam, the President, introduces her to the American journalist as one of the "most brilliant daughters of the country, the only person in the service, male or female, with a first-class honours in English" (68). Beatrice is a beneficiary of Western education, having been educated at Queen Mary College, University of London, a similar educational system as that which had shaped Chris, Ikem and Sam. Educationally, Achebe thus places Beatrice on the same, if not higher, pedestal as the men.

Through Beatrice, the importance of education in the upliftment of women is highlighted, for her educational achievements create an opportunity for an excellent career in the Ministry of Finance as a Senior Assistant Secretary, and with this position comes individual and economic independence, as well as an avenue for Beatrice to venture into the socio-political world of Kangan.

Beatrice's independence and assertiveness as a woman are emphasized in the novel through her actions and her words. We catch a glimpse of this even in her childhood when she realized that her mother bore her a grudge because of her gender, and that she had been given the name, Nwanyibuife-a female is also something (which she had hated as a child and found totally demeaning as a woman)- to pacify both parents.

Beatrice's feminist perception of independence and selfhood embodies her lifestyle as an individual and a single woman. Her uninhibited love affair with Chris is evident of this fact. Not for her "the panic and stampede" into marriage at "the thought that time is passing..."(80), in order to meet the expectations of a society that dictates that in order to be regarded as complete, and recognized, a woman has to be married. Beatrice voices her views on this subject in the following words:

> That's when you hear all sorts of nonsense talk from girls: Better to marry a rascal than to grow a moustache in your father's compound; better marry Mr. Wrong in this world than wait for Mr. Right in heaven; all marriage is how-for-do; all men the same; and a whole baggage of foolishness like that (80).

Beatrice is obviously not against marriage and looks forward to a future union with Chris. However, for her, independence and selfhood open other avenues of choice, of which marriage is just a part.

Beatrice is free-spirited but highly sensitive and wary in the manner in which she handles her affair with Chris (unrestrained, yet private), which reveals that she is not sexually promiscuous.

Achufusi asserts that "when a woman is resourceful and self reliant, independent of the man financially, she can boldly exercise the right to choose between alternatives" (160). Beatrice's economic viability therefore equips her to make clear choices and decisions, and actualize them.

As a character, Beatrice is very perceptive, forthright and strong. She is the first to realize the implications of the gathering political storm in Kangan, and warn Chris and Nkem to iron out their differences and unite to save themselves and perhaps, Kangan:

> I see trouble building up for us. It will get to Nkem first. No joking, Chris. He will be a precursor to make straight the way. But after him it will be you. We are all in it, Ikem, you, me and even Him…you and Ikem must quickly patch up this ridiculous thing between you…(115).

The above warning comes on the heels of her enforced visit to the Presidential Retreat where she discovers that the reason for her invitation was to give Lou, the American journalist, a good impression of Kangan from the woman's angle, and to provide sexual gratification for the President, after a very cheap and public proposition. Beatrice rebels against this affront by leading the President on and humiliating him in front of his guests, with the following words:

> If I went to America today, to Washington DC. Would I, could I walk into the White House and take the American President hostage. And his Defence Chief and his Director of CIA? (74).

That the President and key members of his cabinet could demean the seat of the nation's power and render it so vulnerable before a foreigner through their conduct is totally unacceptable to Beatrice, and her response to this situation is drastic and radical. Beatrice also realizes, at this point, the danger looming in the horizon for Chris, Ikem, and herself, and for the nation of Kangan as a whole, for Sam's government was definitely not the government they had envisioned.

Despite her efforts, Chris and Ikem realize too late what she had been predicting, and later acknowledge: "BB said all that needed to be said when it might have been useful… But we were too busy with our private diversionary war" (135). The implications become even clearer when it dawns on Beatrice that the men had indeed failed, and the onus is now on women to decide what has to be done! This role becomes even more significant at the demise of Chris, Ikem and Sam, when the nature of Beatrice's incredible strength is revealed. Chris had earlier attested to this strength by observing that Beatrice is "peaceful but very strong. Very, very strong…" (58).

That the other characters gravitate to Beatrice after the death of Chris, Ikem and Sam is, therefore, no surprise. She is the one who must reveal the truth and carry on the vision as she does, by interpreting Chris's last words: "The last green bottle" (214), and urge others to uphold this truth:

> Chris was sending a message to beware. This world belongs to the people of this world, not to any little caucus, no matter how talented… (215).

It takes Beatrice's feminine insight to decode and acknowledge the truth in the above words as 'beautiful', and to urge the gathering of Abdul, Emmanuel, Elewa, Agatha and Adamma to pledge to uphold this truth, and to demand: "It had better be better than some pledges we have heard lately", a statement with which all the others concur in one voice: "Ise!" (215).

A rather radical aspect of Beatrice's feminist nature is her language.

According to Scot McLaughlin, "human communication surrounds us, defines our existence and supports our survival, describes our experiences and influences our understanding of the world around us." (2). Indeed language is power, and can therefore serve as an instrument of domination or liberation. Beatrice is a true feminist whose feminist idiolect enables her to explore her consciousness, assert her values, and express her opinions rather radically. Her language embodies her thoughts, feelings, words, experiences and actions, as well as her vision. This is what sets her miles apart from Achebe's traditional women who, according to Petersen, "are happy, harmonious members of the community, even when they are repeatedly barred from any say in the com-munal decision making process and constantly reviled in sayings and proverbs" (qtd. in Greenwald 1).

Andy Greenwald observes that Beatrice

> emerges as the true spirit and heart of the novel. Removed from the inner-workings of the men's government, she alone is able to observe the status of Kangan with a perspective more geared towards reality…(4).

Beatrice takes on all three political players in the following assessment:

> All three of you are incredibly conceited. The story of this country as far as you are concerned, is the story of the three of you (60).

Through these words, Beatrice strongly reminds Chris to put selfish interest aside, and focus on the collective need of the masses. She also ridicules and decries the inherent chauvinistic attitude of men towards women in the African society in her loaded response to Chris's observation as to what Ikem could possibly have to say to a young and illiterate Elewa:

> Ikem doesn't say much to any girl. He doesn't think they have enough brains (59).

For Grace Okereke, language is "gender-specific and, therefore creates a dichotomy between man and woman especially in tradi-tional patriarchal society" (qtd. in Nutsukpo 109). The language of Achebe's earlier female characters was therefore imbued with passivity and silence. In *The Madman*, Mgboye is portrayed as:

> a woman of peace who rarely demanded the respect
> due to her... she would suffer Udenkwo's provoking
> tongue sometimes for a whole day without offering a
> word in reply. And when she did reply at all her words
> were always few and her voice low. (*Girls at War* 4-5).

It is evident that Mgboye's pride is subsumed within the polygamous situation in the home, and the dictates of tradition and patriarchy, that a woman should be seen, not heard.

Beatrice breaks away from this docility. She is very vocal and opinionated, and, on occasion, her language is radical, a deliberate twist away from the cautious, decent and discreet, features that characterize the language of women. As such, Ikem expresses mock-outrage when she asks, in public, if Chris was one of those men who "pack their wife conveniently away to her mother and the village midwife as soon as she misses her period" (82).

Swear words are not avoided when Beatrice voices out issues she feels strongly and passionately about, or when disputing traditional values that subjugate women, and asserting her feminist stance:

> I was determined from the very beginning to put my
> career first and, if need be, last. That every woman needs
> a man to complete her is a piece of male chauvinist
> bullshit [emphasis mine] I had completely rejected
> before I knew there was anything like women's Lib
> (80-81).

On another occasion, Beatrice lets out her frustration at a system that denies women any active political role, and makes a case for their inclusion in national development:

> The way I see it, giving women today the same role
> which traditional society gave them of intervening
> only when everything else has failed is not enough...
> It is not enough that women should be the court of

last resort because the last resort is a damn [emphasis mine] sight too far and too late! (84).

Traditionalists expect women, like children, to speak only when spoken to. However, Beatrice never hesitates to ask for the right to be heard when the occasion demands it, as is evident in an argument with Chris:

> "Please don't interrupt... I go off forty miles to this weird party."
> "BB, you never told me it was to Abichi."
> "Please, let me finish..."

Another instance is when Beatrice ceremonially names Elewa's baby, by giving the girl-child a boy's name – Amaechina (may- the- path- never- close) and in the following words, justifies her action:

> What does a man know about a child anyway that he should presume to give it a name...(206).

Abdul's ready and witty response to these words ridicules the high premium placed on the traditional role of the man in the naming ceremony ritual: "*Nothing except that his wife told him he is the father*"(206).

Through the singular act of initiating the naming ceremony, and naming the child (a role traditionally reserved for men), Beatrice does not only subvert tradition, but also reveals how adept she would be at the helm of affairs. Although she denies being ambitious, she would have been a better President than any of the other characters. This is evident in the way she inspires Agatha, the housegirl; Elewa, the market woman; Abdul, the soldier; Emmanuel, the student activist; Braimoh, the cab driver; and Adamma, the student. She would have done a better job at uniting people from different strata of the society, initiating and carrying out reforms, bearing in mind how important it is for every individual – man or woman – to be ready to play an active part in the reformation of society. She would be strong, focused and dedicated; a president that would be perceptive and sensitive to the needs of the people and the nation.

Indeed, through Beatrice's actions and language, Achebe demonstrates that, for Africa to come into its own, each individual should be recognized, and allowed to play a part in the developmental process. Beatrice represents change – the new feminist-conscious woman, who must rise up, break her silence and declare her stance by carving a niche for herself through the roles she plays in the society.

Achebe imbues Beatrice with a strong, feminist stance which manifests through her actions and language, gives greater impact to the experiences she portrays, and reveals an honest recognition of her feelings, ideas, opinions and values, and, thus, renders them more "implicit and authentic to the reader, and the language more personal and assertive" (Nutsukpo 110).

Beatrice is a true reflection of the feminist-conscious contemporary African woman who is ready and geared to play any role in the African society, including that of President! Through Achebe's Beatrice, Maria Rilke's vision of the future of feminism, literature and society can be distinctly visualized:

> The great renewal of the world perhaps consists in this, that man and maid, freed from all false feeling and aversion, will seek each other not as [adversaries] but as brother and sister, [and] as neighbours, and will come together as human-beings [for their own benefit]. (qtd. in Greer 115).

Works Cited

Achebe, Chinua. *Anthills of the Savannah*. Britain: William Heinemann Ltd., 1987.

———. *Girls at War and Other Stories*. London: Heinemann Educational Books, 1972.

Achufusi, G. I. "Female Individuality and Assertiveness in the Novels of Ifeoma Okoye." *Feminisn in African Literature*. Ed. Helen Chukwuma. Enugu: New Generation, 1994.159-175.

Chukukere, Gloria, C. "Feminist Consciousness and the Realistic Impulse in the Writing of Grace Ogot." *Feminism in African Literature*. 100-114.

Greenwald, Andy. "Postcolonial Feminism in *Anthills of the Savannah*." *African Postcolonial Literature in English in the Postcolonial Web*. 21

March 2002. http://www.postcolonialweb.org/achebe/greenwalds.
html.

Greer, Germaine. *The Female Eunuch*. London: Grafton, 1981.

McLaughlin, Scott. *Introduction to language Development*. Canada:
Thompson Delmar Learning, 2005.

Nutsukpo, Fafa Margaret. "*Feminist Consciousness in the Novels of Nawal
el Saadawi and Ifeoma Okoye: A Comparative Study.*" Diss. U of
PortHarcourt, 1998.

Yakubu, Anthonia M. "The Valuation of Women's Work in Nigerian
Literature." *Woman in the Academy: Festschrift for Professor Helen
Chukwuma*. Ed. Seiyifa Koroye and Noel Anyadike. PortHarcourt:
Pearl Publishers, 2004. 75-95.

CHAPTER 11

THE POWER TO NAME: THE NEW IMAGE OF AFRICAN WOMANHOOD IN ACHEBE'S *ANTHILLS OF THE SAVANNAH*

Irene Salami-Agunloye

Preamble

Chinua Achebe's *Anthills of the Savannah* was part of the new political novels by many African literary writers in the seventies and eighties which dealt with neocolonial realities, manifesting intense displeasure with the political system. The novel can be regarded as a social criticism, an expression of Achebe's disenchantment with the country, and an attempt to articulate the nature and extent of the political disaster. It is set in an imaginary African state of Kangan, most likely Nigeria. *Anthills of the Savannah* reflects the agony of the people in the face of military tyranny.

By creating three major characters who are members of the country's political cabinet and information organ, Achebe projects his work as a political commentary. The vivid contrast between the ruler and the ruled that characterized Kangan Republic, leads to the political tragedy in the novel.

Many feminists have often criticized Chinua Achebe for the suppressed agency, subservient, peripheral and marginal roles women played in his previous novels, especially *Things Fall Apart* where women are given nominal roles. The women are voiceless and play insignificant role in the society, portraying them from a perspective that is male and limiting. They remained in the margin and are seen in the shadow of the men as wives or mothers, daughters, stepmothers and grandmothers, roles which are traditionally assigned to them by the patriarchal society, and are completely dependent on the men for survival. With the exception of Chielo, the priestess, the other women play trivial roles. From these works one can easily perceive men's world and men's voices. The male characters make very uncomplimentary comments about the female characters. Critics have often commented that these earlier works are a reinforcement of stereotypical male chauvinistic impressions about African womanhood (Banyiwa-Horne: 1986) some have also described him as a phallic writer, in various instances. Chikwenye Okonjo-Ogunyemi (60-61) frowns at Achebe's definition of women, Eustace Palmer (38) observes that woman "has had to take second place to numerous other concerns", Nnolim (59) finds an "appalling image of the Nigerian woman (helpless, dependent, brutalized, disparaged, who are either prostitutes or concubines or good time girls), in the works of Achebe, Cyprian Ekwensi and Elechi Amadi. Similarly, Florence Stratton (6) laments Achebe's women, who are always down on their knees before their men folk, and they are regularly making exits from all spaces in which power, economic or otherwise, is exercised. The status of women in Umuofia she observes is very low: "He had a large barn full of yams and he had three wives". She also points out the systematic exclusion of women from the political, the economic, the judicial, and even the discoursal life of the community. This is apparent not only in the composition of the governing council of elders, the *ndichie*, but also in the membership of the powerful *egwugwu* cult, which is, in both cases all male (25). Reiterating the same sentiment, Kerz Okafor (142) states that Achebe's women are mere echoes and voices and [that] they are unquestionably acquiescent to the status quo'. According to Chinyere Nwagbara, (345) women in Achebe's previous works are essentially objects, and causative agents, they are there to draw attention to their men's heroic ethos.

Adding her voice, Ezeigbo (53) faults Achebe as one of the novelists who 'formerly relegated women's experience to the background'. Although I agree that these statements are true and the instances they have cited are very obvious, as we see the sub-servient status so completely inscribed in these women's psyche that they accept their situation without questioning it, but like Sophie Ogwude (32) have observed Achebe's character portrai-ture, remain authentic within the specific periods in our history in which they are situated. Achebe presents to us a slice of reality of the period under discussion. What we see in these works is a rep-resentation of the early twentieth century rural Igbo community. One may question why Achebe in his status as a master story teller did not use his skill and creative license to create an ideal society where there is better gender power relations. We must not forget that Achebe's main preoccupation in *Things Fall Apart* is first and foremost a response to colonial writers like Joyce Cary, Conrad, and others. However, in an attempt to 'restore dignity to African past', to subvert and dismantle the racial codes of this authorita-tive colonial text by contextualizing it in an alternative discourse, and to evade romanticizing the African past, Achebe valorizes a section of the sexual allegory and masculinizes the Igbo culture (Stratton: 37).

No matter in what way we see it, the creative shift we see in *Anthills* shows Achebe is a socially committed writer who is sensi-tive to the socio-political changes in modern society. This ability to align with the tide of times when necessary, has distinguished him as one of the leading literary giants of our time.

After *Things Fall Apart*, Achebe, gradually, began to move his women to the centre. Our attention is drawn to characters like Clara in *No Longer at Ease*, who is unperturbed by her social status as an outcast, in *A Man of the People* we see women been used as political campaigners, which is a level of participation. As the women move to the urban spaces, we begin to see improved visibility.

By the time Achebe wrote *Anthills of the Savannah*, we see a woman with great strength of character who stands out tall in her society even among men. His work in *Anthills of the Savannah* has been commended to give expression to the aspirations and prob-lems of African women, challenging the hegemony of other male authors. In the book Achebe subverts and dismantles the radical male codes. This has made many critics to believe that Achebe's earlier works and pronouncement come under scrutiny in *Anthills of the Savannah* (Stratton: 164). *Anthills* challenges Achebe's earlier works as he attempts to revise earlier images of women. It is apparent that he interrogates *Things Fall Apart*, critiquing the heavy dose of masculinity in the novel.

This chapter explores Achebe's attempt at empowering his women in *Anthills of the Savannah*. It investigates the reconstruction of womanhood, and the central claim is that Achebe in his reconstruction is involved in a radical dismantling of the masculine gender codes which had denied women visibility in his earlier literary works. In deconstructing these codes, he challenges patriarchal language and representations, thereby undermining the dominant phallocentric paradigm.

By introducing Chris and Ikem as central characters who are members of the elite governing clique, the ruling cabinet, Achebe presents his work as political a commentary. He projects Ikem as the voice of the people. With the situation he portrays in Kangan, Achebe views contemporary Nigerian society as vested in corruption and indiscipline and as such in *Anthills,* he responds to social realities and expectations, realizing the potential and relevance in contemporary African society. To relate his story, he relies on witnesses which prove very successful. However, there are times when one can perceive authorial commentary leaping out of the pages.

The New Image of African Womanhood

Traditionally, the gender division of roles, a patriarchal construction, emphasizes masculinity, valor, and patriarchy and relegates women to the background, a position where she has minimal visibility. For a long time in Africa, male writers dominated the literary scene, and as such they create characters from their own perspective. The female characters they construct are sometimes manipulated to manifest their circumscribed role. Although colonialism has grossly influenced Nigerian literature, it cannot be denied that patriarchy has played a major role in the shaping of Nigerian literary production. In assessing Nigerian post-colonial literary texts by men, one is confronted with the glaring influence of patriarchal social structure.

The ideology that men are naturally superior to women permeates these writings. It is assumed that power is gendered as masculine, and this has affected a broad conception of what constitute greatness, distinction in and significance in aesthetic constructions. These masculine values have typically placed men at the centre of power and marginalized the essential qualities of female power [Amin: 15]. Often the sexuality of female characters is given so much prominence at the expense of other attributes and potentials as if they have no other role outside their sexual roles, as they are often cast in sex moulds. Women are appendages and these characters usually help elevate the images of male protagonist who are the central characters, commanding the attention of the women to him in every sense of the world. In an authorial voice, Achebe (90) voices out through Ikem that "...women are, of course the biggest single group of oppressed people in the world..."

The traditional image of women in male written literature evokes ideas of docility, victimhood. These male authors characterize society as strictly patriarchal and excessively masculinist. The vivid portrayal of women as voiceless, images that serve to rationalize and therefore perpetuate inequality between sexes; and the romanticization and idealization of motherhood, is a means of masking women's subordination in the society. As a result Lloyd Brown (3) concludes earlier that African literature is a literature of men, created to endorse men's control (3) of power. Commenting on this Naana Banyiwa-Horne asserts that these "male images of African womanhood lack psychological growth in such portraitures which seems to suggest that they are largely male fantasies of womanhood" (120). In many proverbs, folktales and legends, women are portrayed as destructive figures that hatch and execute evil. They are portrayed as been very seductive and corrupt. The evil image of women is always the root cause of all evil perpetuated by men, as if men are incapable of any evil. Politically minded women are usually seen as dangerous, promiscuous and not to be trusted. Women are usually portrayed as bad, malicious, jealous, envious, ruthlessly exterminating rivals and enemies, often through the use of witchcraft, 'juju' or poison. They are manipulative, deceitful and not to be trusted. They are seen playing roles such as mothers, daughters, step-daughters, lonely women, old woman, divorcees and spinsters. There is a portrayal of women who are in constant war with other women reinforcing the popular 'Pull Her Down' phrase. Women are perceived as commodities of trade and as symbols of exchange, who are valued for their ability to reproduce babies and produce wealth. These female characters are portrayed in men's literary works as stereotypes used to reinforce, usually, negative ideas which support the patriarchal system, they are seldom rounded or realistic characters.

Also in many contemporary texts, 'phallocentric' views attempt to subordinate women to men; hence according to Mabel Evwierhoma (10), believers in woman-centered ideologies demand strongly positive female characters and a re-reading of texts from the female perspective. In an attempt to situate herself in the male dominated literary space and to debunk these stereotypes, Nigerian women writers, have resolved to rewrite these negative portrayal in texts written by men. They are beginning to interrogate, critically analyze the patriarchal canon and the male hegemony. In doing this they are constructing new identities for the female characters or heroines who are employed as the writer's mouth piece to buttress her feminist view point and engage in a criticism of the social order, [Tobrise: 11] as well as stressing and affirming their existence through metaphors and 'home groomed images' of power and revolt against the male domination.

Unlike Achebe's earlier plays where male heroism and excessive display of masculinism take centre stage, in *Anthills of the Savannah*, Achebe grants women agency, empowering them as strong and vibrant characters. The novel is inscribed in the general frame of feminist discourse. He creates heroines with masculine qualities, bringing them from the margin to the centre. Achebe takes a stand against marginalization and commoditization of women. *Anthills of the Savannah* represents a shift in contemporary literature "men writers portray engagement with women writers in dialogue on gender. It also portrays a shift in Achebe's works as we now see a transformation of the status of women from that of object to subject" (Stratton: 159). As Julie Agbasiere (361) asserts, "in Anthills Achebe paints a picture of dignified womanhood". His frequent authorial statements indicate his new commitment to giving women a better image. In an interview where he laments women oppression, Achebe suggests that Beatrice, his heroine, represents the ideal womanhood in the role she performs as the harbinger of the new social order (Stratton: 159). In order to deconstruct the traditional, he reverses stereotypes, we find some women showing signs of masculine traits and some men also appear to have 'supposed' feminine traits. While we see that the men are quarrelsome, they gossip, backbite, compete for attention, the women are confident, fearless, 'usurp' power. Here, Achebe dares to question this male domination, and break the hegemony of male perception and evaluation of the merits and virtues of female power, thereby validating it. As he writes this novel, his outlook and stance towards women take a more positive outlook. The full potentials and capabilities of women begin to dawn on him. In this novel he makes a 'U' turn, moving away from seeing women as victims, this novel, women resist male dominance, they rather wish to be in charge and control of their lives; they are independent, self confident no matter their social status. In comparing male and female leadership style, Achebe shows male leadership style as "detached, brutal and based on producing fear" (Amin: 27) while female leadership is democratic and just. As Achebe, attempts to counter the myth of the 'traditional woman', he subverts the constructing of womanhood by appropriating African feminist theories in the African literary context. By so doing, he constructs a female identity that is open to change. He creates strong female protagonist, but does not out rightly discredit the male as subjects in any way, however he privileges the female as subjects. He changes the subservient and passive woman in the male text to assertive and confident woman who is bold and holds her own. Women are, in other words not conceptualised as the Other but as self defining, putting female subjectivity in process.

Also, in order to erase the traditional images of women such as self-sacrificing wives who sacrifice their comfort and sometimes lives, for the sake of their children or husband, perpetuated by male writers, Achebe overturns this popular image in favor of a feminist approach, in which he portrays BB as a powerful woman who swiftly steps into the shoes of men, picking up the mantle of leadership to continue with the crusade of liberating her people from the stronghold of bad governance. In challenging the predominant male views on women, he defies tradition. Overturning his earlier portraiture of women, he also challenges the conventional and popular views of women in literature. Like Ikem, Achebe turns around to recreate the African woman. This leads to a big shift from Achebe's women set in stereotypical mould of traditional life to empowered women who take control of their lives and who decide their own destinies.

There is no clear cut hero in *Anthills of the Savanah*, Achebe adopts collective heroism, one of which is Beatrice, a woman, and this is much unlike Achebe. By this attempt he tries to reinvent the female role, by placing BB centre-stage and he endows her with noble character, depicting her as superior to men intellectually. He projects her as a female national subject. Through her, Achebe challenges the marginalization of women in modern society, crafting her as a woman with high moral and intellectual strength, to transform society, a society dominated by men (Umunnakwe: 341), he creates an 'exceptional woman', with strength of character, an admirable women, who stands out as a role model and a quintessentially independent woman who would not allow herself to be exploited by men. Economically, she is independent, politically she is active and civically she is competent. The power to foretell the future which BB possesses in the novel challenges the traditional view of women who are normally portrayed as irrational beings. This remarkable character; qualifies her to become a life force to her group by virtue of her deep compassion. Portrayed as a democratic role model, she brings together different groups of people with different backgrounds, thereby transcending the prevailing political machinations. Beatrice exudes superior intellect, she is beautiful, and with such impeccable credentials Achebe rewrites the African woman (Nwagbara: 348). Nadine Gordimer describes BB as "one of the most extra ordinary, attractive and moving women characters in any contemporary novel" (in Nwabueze 8-9). Also shows the new African woman as depicted by Beatrice as not gullible, cannot easily be moved, she is able to resist the president's love advances and she refuses to be controlled by him. She interacts with him, unlike his earlier novels where women were denied access to the top. In rewriting the African woman, Achebe cuts across class, by bringing Beatrice, a woman of high repute, to mingle with Elewa, a near illiterate sales girl. He advocates for a collapse of gender and class barriers, which he depicts with Ikem's relationship with Elewa, this relationship elevates semi-illiterate, urban rural girl, Elewa.

In *Anthills of the Savannah*, Achebe seems to be saying that the society misses out when women's voices are silenced, when they are repressed, when women like BB, with great potentials, are excluded from governance by the 'power hungry' patriarchal maniacs. He criticizes society for denying women like BB the opportunity to lead; and succeeds in instigating many provocative ideas and in challenging traditional views regarding women's place in politics and in the society. In BB, Achebe seek to equal the rights of women with those of men and to remedy whatever mansculinist views that had been expressed by other writers that have sought to relegate the women to the rear of literary portraiture. Creating this type of character can be corrective as well as affirmative, in as much as it seeks to correct female marginalization and affirm the individuality of female character in text and reality (Evwierhoma: 51).

By casting Beatrice as one of the leading characters in the novel, Achebe is indirectly against tokenism, where women are mere figure heads who are dependent on their men, he also discredit male politician's assumption that female politicians and those in power are wayward. Ultimately the women he creates are not dependent on male relationship for protection and economic survival. Beatrice lives with her house help, Elewa lives with her mother. Both of them are gainfully employed.

Motherhood: The Right to Make a Choice

In African tradition, only motherhood can confirm a woman's identity. Marriage and fertility defines womanhood. Motherhood gives cultural legitimacy to female power; and it is so ingrained in the psyche of women that they see no other sense of fulfillment than being a mother, (Nfah-Abenyi: 39) as women are socialized to accept the roles cut out for them as procreators of society.

On the contrary, a man depends on his power over others, starting with the woman and her children (Rich: 1976). Although motherhood is regarded as supreme, the crowning glory of a woman, African motherhood does not in any way imply supremacy over anyone but rather reaffirms her subordination in the patriarchal structure, for Marriage and Motherhood domesticate women.

Motherhood is an institution, and the institution is under male control and as such male authorities interpret it. The centrality of motherhood in African culture has its root in patriarchy. It is such an exalted position in traditional African societies that there is no worse misfortune for a woman than being childless, for pregnancy legitimizes marriage. The "barren" African woman is called names, undergoes numerous humiliating rites, all to advert the society's perception of her as incomplete. Women are not valued for themselves, but for their ability to 'breed' and procreate for the purpose of continuing the linage or generation. They are not valued for who they are, but for what they can produce, if the product is a male child, they 'will have higher premium.' For most African people, motherhood is symbolic of creativity and continuity (Christian: 214) and sons are always preferred to daughters.

Motherhood is central to the themes of the works of many African writers, both male and female. In African literature, motherhood has been the most consistent framework of identity for women, according to Nfah Abenyi (39), "this is probably because motherhood is so closely linked to understanding African women's lives and identities within their sociocultural contexts." Projecting the character of African women, these writers have ultimately shaped women by certain limited and limiting idealism that assumes that marriage and motherhood per se are unequalled routes to female fulfillment. On one hand the idealized image of the African woman in the male literature is that of mother, while the more "realistic" image of woman is that of woman who is manipulative in her sexuality (Christian: 218).

Male writers have also projected images of women who use their power as mothers to manipulate their sons to secure positions of power. The African portrait of perceiving a woman as closer to mother is a patriarchal construct. Brown has called on counter images, and for writers to construct portraits closer to life, realistic portraits of mother.

Achebe in *Anthills* challenges the prevailing notion/definition of women in society especially in relation to motherhood and sexuality. He creates a space in *Anthills* with in which feminists can interrogate motherhood. In this novel he confronts motherhood as never before, challenging the prevailing views of motherhood held by our society. He presents his views of experience of motherhood in contrast to the previous views. By affirming the experience of motherhood as a very valuable one, he protests the view by society that compels every woman to be a mother. He agrees that the name Nneka (mother is supreme) though it flatters women, however "these are cynical strategies for keeping women subordinate and powerless" (Palmer: 213). The honored mother is the same person who is regarded as a second class citizen. She exerts no supremacy over anyone apart from her children and her fellow women. Her life is that of constant sacrifice, service and submission to the patriarchal system.

BB's delay in getting married and the subsequent delay in becoming a mother can only be understood within the context of sexual politics which bearing children is inscribed and valued in the traditional Igbo society of Nigeria, and the various societies in Africa as a whole. For BB, every woman should be allowed to make her choice about childbearing. BB's reluctance in stepping into the role of motherhood is a form of resistance to male domination. She refuses to find fulfillment in the traditional mode of ideal womanhood.

In *Anthills*, Achebe gives us a glimpse of the traditional African motherhood institution as depicted by BB's mother who is battered and brutalized for several 'offenses' among which is 'her inability' to produce a male child. As a mother, bearing only female children brings her sorrow and anguish instead of the joy other mothers who have male children exhibit. Consequently she transfers this frustration to her daughter BB, because she is one daughter too many. Not producing sons restrains her from expressing the joy of motherhood. She probably feels that her chi has failed her for not giving her a son. She is ignorant of the fact that it takes a man and a woman to determine the sex of a child, and the determining chromosome for a male child is produced by the man. So, battered and subdued she remains silent, venting her anger and frustration on BB, her daughter. Having grown up in this environment, BB is not in a hurry to become a mother.

Emenyonu (in Agbasiere: 364), in querying Achebe's construction of BB as a woman fulfilled in her singlehood has asked if this implies that Achebe is excluding educated women from motherhood. Here Achebe is only saying that women should be allowed to make their choice as regards when, how and if they want to become mothers, rather than the society compelling them to marry and become mothers. That is why Rich has argued for motherhood to be an experience of choice for women, not an institution.

Singlehood with Honor and Dignity

In African society being a wife defines womanhood and femininity, being a wife can be very challenging, for subtlely, marriage is meant to subdue women. It is not uncommon for one to hear a phrase like 'she does not behave like one under the control of a husband', "she does not have a head". This implies that a married woman should be calm, gentle, patient, subdued, exhibits self control etc. Wives are socialized to be submissive, patient, enduring, gentle, meek, long suffering, develop the ability to suppress her feelings; these are the virtues of a virtuous woman. Ama Ata Aidoo has condemned marital practices that have enslaved and exploited women 'through history and among all people' (in Nfah: 58). In her novel *The Promised Land,* Grace Ogot (1996) wrote that 'marriage is an imprisonment', for a woman. In her play, *Two Women in Conversation,* Flora Nwapa (1994) labels marriage as female enslavement, saying that 'marriage as a modern institution should be abolished from the face of the earth'. In Tess Onwueme's *Tell it to Women,* Ruth calls marriage 'an unforgivable insult to women', and she proceeds to say that 'she sees no reason why any educated woman with her head still sitting on her shoulder should give it a thought" (p.87). Ruth's words here is in agreement with Grace Ogot's earlier expression of marriage being an imprisonment. This low status of women as subservient probably has discouraged many women like BB from not hurrying into marriage. In many African societies, single women have poor reputation, as marriage is regarded as the ultimate status for any woman, society has no pity or respect for single women; many are compelled to marry because of this patriarchal conception of singlehood, so for such women their freedom in many aspects of life is curtailed. In traditional African society, women are discouraged from acquiring higher education as women with higher education are said to make bad wives. Education is seen as unnecessary for women as it is thought to distract them from their gendered roles of wives and mothers. Moreover, higher education is always associated with men as it is deemed fit to meet their needs. BB subverts this ideology by surpassing even the men, emerging with a first class honours degree in English. She refuses to confine and to define herself only in terms of wifehood and its accompanying domestic chores like her mum. She decides to enter into her mother's world. By pursuing her career as a high ranking officer, and delaying her marriage to Chris, she redefines what is seen in her society as a naturalized women's place (Nfah-Abbenyi: 63). Being educated gives BB the confidence she needs to maneuver her way through the world of men. Education according to Helen Chukwuma (xvii) makes women question the status quo that oppresses them. With education, women become conscientized enough to see through the oppressive lenses and thereafter come to a full realization of how firmly rooted patriarchy is in the society. In her novel *Changes*, Aidoo depicts the patriarchal impression of seeing higher education for a woman as an unfortunate postponement of her self-fulfillment (51), any successful career outside the home is seen as naturally for men and a few 'ugly' women (51). In *More Than Dancing*, Salami echoes the society's belief that women are not socially acceptable if they are not under the 'protection' of a man. Like other authors, she represents in the play, Nigerian marriage as being structured around men's authority over women. She problematizes here, a marital mode that demands of women to lay down their careers or ambition so that they do not constitute a threat in any way to their husbands. This is also vividly portrayed in her other play, *Sweet Revenge* where Aisosa had to resign her job as a consultant gynecologist to enable her husband travel abroad for further studies, while she remains home to take care of the children. Later in these two plays we see the author redefining marriage on equal lines.

Achebe's novel conveys discontent about the poor status of single women in our society and stage a revolt against it by constructing the character of BB, who refuses to be enslaved and silenced by tradition in a marriage. She dismantles a tradition that endorses the silencing and subjugation of women, subverting their powerlessness. She refuses to be intimidated by men, unlike her mother who quietly accepts her fate, scared of confronting the patriarchal system she finds herself in. The confidence she exhibits even though she is single, is instrumental in the shaping of her subjectivity as articulated in the novel. By remaining single she is able to embark on a radical dismantling of the patriarchal social structures in Igbo naming tradition. To redeem single women's image, in *Anthills*, Achebe reworks the status of women through BB to grant her agency, making her an intelligent woman, indomitable, and unsurpassed by the men. The cultural construct, that marriage is the surest guarantee of security and honorable for women is questioned in *Anthills of the Savannah*. She says confidently that, "I was determined from the very beginning to put my career first and, if need be, last. That every woman wants a man to complete her is a piece of male chauvinist bullshit I had completely rejected before I knew there was anything like women's lib" (80-81). Here BB places her career over and above marriage, for as she says, that is what gives a woman prestige and not marriage. BB's statement subverts the patriarchal notion of female singlehood. She shuns the cultural constraints which regulate women's lives. She claims to derive fulfillment from her singlehood and refuses to be cast into a sexual mode prescribed by her society. In BB, Achebe constructs a heroine who questions society's rejection of single women, through this; he undermines traditional practices that oppress women. BB though single bears her singlehood with dignity and honour, staying unmarried did not in any way seem to agitate her; rather she is single and content. For her, as she says above, the most important thing for a woman is to be empowered, that is empowerment derived from educational background, empowerment derived from economic sufficiency and empowerment derived from upward mobility in ones career. BB confidently asserts her freedom as a single woman who cannot be intimidated by anyone. She is determined to challenge the perception of single women in her society, she refuses to allow the society to map out her status, honour and dignity, a status which is controlled by a blatantly discriminating cultural script (Nfah-Abbenyi: 45). She sees marriage as a patriarchal institution, and therefore can be limiting for women. By refusing to find fulfillment in marriage, BB challenges societal chains that bind women. For any woman Achebe advocates that career development is of utmost importance. Marriage is not the ultimate in a woman's life. In BB's voice,

Achebe interrogates gendered views about marriage and the myth of female singlehood and powerlessness.

In this novel, Achebe is saying that every woman should be left to decide whether she wants to marry or not. Living in a society where marriage is paramount for every woman, it is surprising that neither BB's father nor mother nor sisters persuaded her to get married. Achebe's silence about this is deliberate; it implies that people should learn to respect the choice of lifestyle by others.

Sisterhood: A Time for Bonding

In *Anthills of the Savannah*, Achebe foregrounds sisterhood, portraying women as good collaborators. Here he deconstructs the "the traditional woman" mode, creating a new feminine image and granting her agency. He portrays female solidarity in face of threatening circumstances. By bringing women together in spite of their social background, he demystifies the much talked about myth that women can never unite. This collective action and sisterhood solidarity becomes a major empowering tool that Achebe uses to assist the women to access and acquire power in the traditional arena. The death of Ikem and Chris becomes a spring board for the women to unite, and BB becomes the moving force behind the women's unity and vision. By bringing in Elewa, and making peace with Agatha she initiates female bonding and strengthens the unity and commitment within the group.

As Elewa moves in to stay with BB, their relationship strengthens. This relationship provides a space for both to explore the pleasure of true friendship between women. Before the death of Ikem and Chris, BB and Elewa were not particularly very close friends, BB at the same time never looked down on her, when occasion demands, they interacted very well, and she showed concern, for instance, she asked after her mother when she was sick. Shortly before Ikem's death, when he was suspended, their bond becomes stronger. When Elewa wanted an explanation of the meaning of suspension, she did not turn to Ikem with whom she was speaking, rather she turned to BB, " I beg my sister wetin be suspension?" (138). This respect and acknowledgement of BB's better insight made BB in response to call her 'my sister'. Elewa is confident that BB will have the patience to explain the word to her in such a way that it will be plain enough for her to understand. Speaking to Elewa in such a simplified manner relaxes her and she also calls BB 'my sister' too. This change, of calling sister instead of friend, is what Achebe uses to highlight women's solidarity and strength which stimulates Elewa's growing self-awareness. This turn around brings about the sisterhood bonding. Here Achebe delves even more emphatically into what many believe is the bane of women's crisis, that is lack of trust for one another and the refusal to appreciate one another's gifts or talents. Achebe subverts this by making Elewa show her preference for and appreciation of BB's intelligence. Elewa from henceforth looked up to BB for direction and support. When offered the baby for her to name, she passes on the privilege to BB, saying "na you go name am" (206). Here we see the women showing commitment for each other's plight. By coming together to plan to support BB as she initiates the naming ceremony, Achebe is simply saying that for women to be fully integrated into the traditional system, a greater solidarity among women is needed. For him the time of women's struggles being played out in private spaces is over, rather he encourages collective action and portrays that it is only by sisterhood and bonding that women can assert themselves in a patriarchal society. By coming together the women are able to dismantle the many structures that undermine their ascension to leadership position. By doing this Achebe set the women up to resist patriarchy. With BB's assertion, "What does a man know about a child anyway that he should presume to give it a name..." (206), everyone present both male and female agree that gender is no barrier to affirmation of agency. The discussion that ensues after this shows that breaking the back bone of patriarchy will require all the women, and men bringing fresh perspectives to the table.

When BB is going through a very critical moment, Elewa and Agatha stand by her encouraging her as best as they can. On one of such occasions, Agatha says prophetically, "Madam make you no worry at all," "Whether they look from here to Jericho, them no go find am. By God's power" (172). In response Elewa in solidarity shouts "Amin," "Na so we talk." This is an indication of the strong bond that has developed between the three of them. The word 'we' here becomes very relevant as we see a turning point in the relationship between the three of them. At this stage, there is a collapse of all barriers, class, ethnic and religion. Here, Achebe seems to imply that for a successful inclusion of women in public affairs, women have to come together whether, literate or illiterate, educated or not, regardless of ethnic bias. This is the situation in Salami's *More Than Dancing* (2003) where women from all works of life, religion, ethnicity, and educational background came together for a common purpose – to support a female presidential candidate, Nona. Because of this great support and mobilization of women, she won the presidential race in spite of the intrigues masterminded by the men. Likewise we see Aina and Adama show solidarity during the naming ceremony. Aina, Braimoh's wife had willingly vacated her bed and nearly sent her children to a neighbor's house just so that BB can have some privacy with Chris. She is so committed to the cause that she does not allow religion to restrict her participation, as she joins joyfully in singing and dancing to the Christian choruses. Adama like others abandons her parents and finds refuge in BB's home, supporting and serving as best as she can.

Male Leaders and Female Power

In Africa, power is constructed as masculine and firmly entrenched in the male domain, Chinua Achebe in *Anthills of the Savannah*, attempts to subvert and deconstruct this. Literary critics have commended him for privileging women in this book. His vibrant portrayal of women and creativity as displayed in this novel shows a very impressive representation of the new African woman. Here Achebe advocates for power shift from the men to the women, showing how the men have failed in their attempts to rule the people. He shows how the women are excluded from the cabinet of Kangan and power hierarchy. The executive cabinet of Kangan is made up of only men. The government is masculinized, resulting in a government suffused with strong male ethos in which women did not command any power. In *Anthills*, Achebe shows vividly the evil of military dictatorship and their recklessness in managing power. This was a common feature of many African countries at the time, Nigeria inclusive. In the cabinet of Kangan, all the ministers who are men feel threatened by the president's authoritarianism. They are sycophants and have to constantly massage his ego to remain in favor with him. Like zombies, they follow slavishly, laughing at his very dry jokes, backstabbing their colleagues to remain acceptable and relevant in the government. At the least provocation he shouts at them (commissioners/ministers), they feel honored and privileged to do his bidding. None of them, apart from Chris dare challenge his authority or disagree with him; all they do is smile or listen when he is talking, no one dares contribute. They are never consulted when important decisions are taken. They are power-less when the president keeps them under house arrest for no just reason. Showing no resistance, they forget that there is power in numbers; and allow themselves to be subdued and manipulated by one single individual who is exercising his blotted power. His train-ing did not prepare him for politics; rather his military training was on "aloofness from politics and public affairs" (11). He is said to have no leadership qualities, Chris confirms when he says, "His Excellency came to power without any preparation for political leadership" (11). Conscious of the fact that he is running an illegal government, and that he has no constitutional right to power, he lacks the confident to rule the people passionately. As Palmer asserts "as a professional soldier, he does not have much experience of politics or state craft" (204). He is paranoid, hunted by fears of plot, conspiracies, revolts, etc, as a result, he encourages discord, intrigues and rivalries among ministers. To hide his deficiencies, he resorts to acting out roles and temperaments displaying his lack of sincerity and genuineness. Corrupted by power, he refuses to heed the voice of reason, rather seeks for ways to eliminate those who out rightly oppose him.

To further prove his maleness and political prowess, he resorts to surrounding himself with a harem of women, including BB in one instance. This probably could be his way of defining his defeat over his friend Chris; by showing he has control over his girlfriend. He uses his maleness and power as a potent weapon of power and control. Here, Achebe captures most profoundly, the way society uses women to entertain African leaders. As we peep 'behind the scene', Achebe exposes the president for who he is, he perpetuates falsehood, insincerity, cynicism and lack of concern for his people's wellbeing. Apart from Chris, the other male leaders are as crooked as the president. Their concern is for them to remain in power at all cost. They are concerned about themselves and not the future of their nation.

Although Bernice Carroll's (in Njoku: 333) definition of power means control, dominance, and influence, however, recently, power has come to mean ability, energy, and strength. If this is the case we can confidently say that women in *Anthills* possess power in various degrees. In this regard I will attempt to explore the sites of women's power within the context of their daily lives. Rebbeca Wilcox (121), discussing Mariama Ba's works, delineates two models of female empowerment, the woman who empowers herself at the expense of other women contrasted with the woman who empowers herself by working, however subtly, to empower all women. Chimalum Nwankwo (155) puts it succinctly, in commending Sembene and Ngugi, that as writers, they are aware in their works that a campaign for social justice is meaningful only when all disadvantaged people in human society receive undiscriminating attention. This is exactly what Achebe does in *Anthills*. For Achebe reformation can only come through a reformed political order which recognizes the African woman as a major player and the de-emphasizing of male dominance in the political affairs (54). Unlike many Africans of his time, Achebe does not put much confidence on the coalition of the masses (peasant and workers) and students, as the machinery for the transformation of their society, but rather on women and the next generation represented by Elewa's baby.

In Africa, women are socialized to be subordinate to men, timid, gentle, etc while the men are groomed to be aggressive, bold and authoritative. Male superiority and female inferiority is ingrained in the psyche of the African woman right from childhood. Whenever there is a resistance to this set up, especially when women refuse to maintain the status quo but to move into the male space to share power with them, conflict erupts and the power structure is destabilized. Achebe deconstructs this power structure by creating an empowered character like BB who moves to and fro in the power hierarchy. He lends his voice to his female characters in order to empower them. He moves away from the usual practice of many writers of his time who endow women with so much beauty and seductive body. BB is not particularly a beauty queen, she is independent, confident and fulfilled in her own world. Achebe describes BB as "a perfect embodiment of my ideal woman, beautiful without being glamorous. Peaceful but very strong. Very, very strong" (58). For him the ideal African woman whether beautiful or not, must be strong, very, very strong and assertive. Thematically and stylistically, Achebe has come to prove through BB that the new African woman can no longer be perceived as marginal to the empowerment process of Africa. By creating BB, he, deconstructs his earlier creations, using her to mobilize others against the repressive forces in the society. Portraying BB as a subject of feminist and national aspiration, the author constructs an alternative form of subjectivity. Although Achebe projects a society where mainly the men have a voice and participate in the political arena, however he empowers BB above all, by this he is saying that for women to successfully participate meaningfully in politics, public affairs and lead the people, education is a very vital tool. He clearly illustrates that women's marginalization is deeply rooted in their lack of education which culminate in lack of political power. In countering this, he endows BB with education, making her push the boundaries of her gender roles; he empowers her to confront men in whatever situation. Educated women have confidence, boldness, not easily intimidated by men, and as Helen Chukwuma (xvii) says, 'education makes women question the status quo that oppress them'. Chris and Ikem have high regard for BB, she influences Ikem to make a turn around as regards his impression of women. From Chris' impression " Ikem doesn't say much to any girl. He doesn't think they have enough brain (59). This chauvinistic male perception slowly gives way to a more realistic perception, even though he didn't live long enough to fully manifest this new change of thought. In trying to sensitize Ikem on the important role of women in society, BB engages him in dialogue; she deconstructs his outdated notion of women which she feels must change. She exhibits the spirit of nationalism in many situations in the text; she attacks Mad Medico for his criticism of the president and deliberately humiliates herself by flirting with president to bring him to his senses. Chris had told her before she left that she should yield to any demand from the president, BB is sensible enough to disregard this advice. If she had given in to the president, it would have robbed her of her agency and reduce her to an object of exchange and manipulation. As the president tries to control BB, it becomes obvious that she is not a woman that can be easily subdued, by this action, she affirms her social status. She refuses to use her bottom power to reconcile the three friends. Rather she resorts to her smart mental and psychological personality.

Though not a member of the cabinet, she seems to have better understanding of the political intrigues and manipulation better than Ikem and Chris. With great insight she predicts the fall of Ikem, Sam and Chris. She prophesies saying, "...I see trouble building up for us. It will get to Ikem first...He will be the precursor to make straight the way. But after him it will be you. We are all in it..." (105). It is important to note that she does not exempt herself from the group in this prophesy, though physically she is not affected, she is the one who is left behind to bear the emotional burden of their deaths, and the one who is to sustain the group and carry on with the fight. This prediction actually is fulfilled before the end of novel.

BB interacts with the men, the three main characters and even more; she is at the vanguard of social transformation, mobilizing opposition to the corrupt Kangan government. As a leader who is sensitive to the needs of her followers, she supports them meeting them at the point of their needs. She refuses to be intimidated by the president or any man in the society. In spite of a childhood that threatened her liberty, selfhood, she grew up determined to resist her oppressors with a determination not to relinquish the means by which she is able to reassert herself and her power as a woman. She asserts her individuality, resolving to control her own life rather than be intimidated by the fact that she is a girl, instead of the expected boy. She refuses to be intimidated and enslaved by tradition, rejecting to become an instrument in some else's scheme; rather she is relaxed with herself in the company of others and is economically and socially well adjusted, devoid of complexes. She exacts her power through a variety of roles and action; explore sites of women's power available to her within the difficult context that life presents her. Refusing to be the object of men's gaze, she did not allow tradition in any way to stifle her individuality or define her identity as a woman, but rather, she depicts her self-actualization in a way that challenges other women. She cuts a niche for herself, with her own standard and action based on the principle of truth (Njoku: 334).

As the trio departs from the scene, BB is left to rebuild the new Kangan. Her style of governance differs a great deal from male style of governance, which empowers only a small caucus. She pulls together everyone irrespective of tribe, religion, gender or status. As she steps into the vacuum created by Chris and Ikem's exit, she claims constructive power, which affirms her positive role in the group and frees her from the constraint demanded by patriarchal tradition. The exit of the three friends, from the stage, brings BB, Elewa and Agatha into their narrative space, BB been the major source of inspiration to all. Her house becomes the rallying point for the struggle (Agukwe: 355) and a place where they all meet to strategize. BB tries to keep the group together; she reconciles their differences, like in the case of Emmanuel and Major Medani. She mends fences and gives direction, allowing all to participate, even the house help. She brings together different gender, different religions, different tribes, different class etc. Achebe is saying here that the new Africa needs to harness the peaceful nature of women to bring about political unity in Africa. Without her political savvy, it is doubtful if the group would have remained or even come together. She rejects the invitation sent by the new president for Chris' funeral because she sees no difference between the new and old president. As she mobilizes for the naming, BB keeps alive the opposition group. By naming the child, Achebe ascribes to her the role of a leader, head, and father. In naming the baby, Beatrice reclaims her agency.

In Beatrice, Achebe shows how a woman can claim constructive power, which later affirms her positive roles in the lives Elewa and Agatha, freeing them from the constraints put on them by the patriarchal system. In her "autobiography" as she defines herself with her own words, she performs an act of self definition and self analysis.

In reconstructing the new image for the African women Achebe employs the use of mythology. By so doing he suggests women be positioned as leaders for effective transformation of Africa. By using Idemili, one of the old Igbo deities, to depict good leadership, Achebe implies that leaders should be morally upright, modest and pursue after peace instead of displaying pride and arrogance, corruption and brutality (Palmer: 213). Achebe sees the Nneka myth as inappropriate for the modern African woman. He creates his own myth enthroning BB as "new leader in a society where men have failed to redeem the people (Agbasiere: 362).

In *Anthills* Achebe shows confidence and a strong belief in the redemptive power of women. He endows the women with greater power than in any of his novels. The two prominent female characters are empowered in their right, while BB is educated, employed, self confident; Elewa is also employed, in a serious relationship with a man far above her social status. She is confident in herself and not easily intimidated by anyone, not even Ikem whom she loves. She is quick to recognize a gender issue when she criticizes Mad Medico's action of sending a woman to Sam as a "belly warmer" after his illness, saying, "But woman done suffer for this world-o", even BB was too interested in the discussion that she did not notice this. Elewa's street sense becomes an assert as she enters a new phase of life with the death of Ikem, the father of her child. It is significant that Achebe gives Ikem a girl not a boy child. The baby is a representation of the new womanhood, as women will be very powerful for the continuation and development of Nigeria. A girl will keep Ikem's torch burning.

BB shows without any restraint that she has power over her sexuality. She controls the relationship between herself and Chris, and Chris is willing to move at her pace as he says, "Beatrice is a perfect embodiment of my ideal woman, beautiful without being glamorous. Peaceful but very strong. Very, very strong. I love her and will go at whatever pace she dictates" (58). In fact BB dictates the pace of the relationship, her realm of power extends to their love making moments. She invites him to "come in" as the built up ecstasy gets out of control. From there she takes charge, leading him by the hand; as he slips, she pulls him up with great power and authority (104) and as Njoku (338) says, "she holds absolute power and Chris is like a child cradled in her arms and breast, her eyes watching anxiously over him".

Achebe in this novel emphasizes the essence of complimentarity of the sexes. He shows the masculine in BB, for the strength of character that BB displays is considered masculine; he also shows the feminist instinct in Chris and Ikem. At the naming ceremony, we see Emmanuel serve drinks and food along with Adama, a gender role usually ascribed to women. By doing this he advocates androgyny in agreement with Coleridge that great minds do tend towards androgynous (in Njoku: 336).

Unlike many African women feminist, BB boldly declares herself a feminist, not shaped through western influence and contact but through lived experiences. She succinctly puts it, "That everywoman wants a man to complete her is a piece of male chauvinist bullshit I had completely rejected before I knew there was anything like women's Lib. You often hear people say: But that is something you picked up in England. Absolute rubbish! There was enough male chauvinism in my father's house to last me seven reincarnations!" (80-81). Achebe seems to be saying to feminists here that female marginalization has always been with us, it was established in our society before the colonial era. Supporting this BB's stand for feminism and many women's disregard for it, Helen Chukwuma (xiii) says it is often seen as "a disorder, a deviation, an extremism associated with misguided, frustrated or disgruntled women" (Chukwuma: xiii). It is in line with this disrepute that Afolabi (35) has come out with three concepts of feminism: 'womb-man', 'we-men' and 'woe-men', all emphasizing the point that feminists are 'frustrated' and 'wayward' women. BB's intention is to undermine the negative notions that people have of feminism. She debunks the belief that feminism is elitist and exclusively practiced by urban and educated women. Helen Chukwuma (xvii) contends that African feminism is not elitist at all and not the exclusive preserve of the educated woman. African feminism is informed from African social realities.

With Elewa and Agatha, Achebe delineates a different kind of power. Elewa though semi -illiterate exhibits high intelligence and is very enlightened. She is very conscious of her right as a woman, as she objects to Ikem's decline to drive her home one night, she tells him off saying, "...I beg you, no make me vex... Imagine! Hmmm! But women done chop sand for dis world-o... Imagine! But na we de causam; na we own fault. If I no kuku bring my stupid nyarsh come dump for your bedroom you for de kick me about like I be football? I no blame you. At all!" (31). When Ikem pretends he is ignorant of what she means, in anger she replies, "How you go know? You no fit know". She scolds him,

"Imagine...to put a girl for taxi at midnight to go and jam with arm robbers in the road". Even when Ikem tries to tell her that there were no more robbers in Bassa, she replies sharply, "Why you no drive me home yourself if say arm robber done finish for Bassa. Make you go siddon" (32). She is not threatened in any way by the gap in their status. She asserts herself and does not allow her educational deficiency to intimidate her in her relationship with Ikem. Ikem too does not see this as a shortcoming. He is not ashamed of her, rather he is proud of her, she accompanies him to social gatherings, and he openly announces in public, his intention to marry her. Like BB she is confident in herself, assertive, "she radiates this warmth and attraction and self-respect..." (168), she easily submits to BB's leadership. Staying with Beatrice, Elewa adapts herself to her new situation, learning from and allowing herself to be mentored by BB. She is the first to accept the paradigm shift as BB names the baby.

Agatha also exhibits a different kind of power. Although critics have heavily criticized her for been hypocritical, Agatha only tries to excise power within her own space. Having lived with BB, she has learnt to exercise power like her boss, however, while BB is compassionate, Agatha is not, but later, when BB shows her extra love, she responds changing her attitude towards others. With the new bonding with BB and Agatha, the potentials in her begin to manifest. With a heart full of joy and love she burst into singing at the naming ceremony, bringing in other religion to rejoice with her.

Reconstructing Tradition: The Power to Name

In recent times many writers, both male and female are beginning to take a second look at some of our traditional practices, conscious of the fact that culture is dynamic, they are beginning to reconstruct them in such a way that they can fit into the realities of contemporary world. Helen Chukwuma (xix) has rightly observed concerning our cultural traditions, that the dynamics of change cannot be stopped, as change is inevitable. She advocates for a discarding of retrogressive and oppressive norms and practices against women. Literary writers have been advised to use the power of the pen and creativity to reconstruct our tradition positively (Salami-Agunloye). Achebe agreeing that our tradition is faulty says, "Exactly. So I think that our tradition is faulty there" (206), sets out to reconstruct it, implying that justice and fairness should prevail in executing our traditional practices.

Writers like Flora Nwapa, Buchi Emecheta, Tess Onwueme, Julie Okoh, Irene Salami-Agunloye etc, have challenged some of these traditional practices in their various societies through their literary works. Some of these negative practices erode the empowerment of women and relegate them to the margin. With these new voices, women are beginning to move from the margin to the centre.

Edewede represents in some way Julie Okoh's attempt to realize her own perspective that tradition must be used constructively and contemporaneously. In the play, she cleverly articulates in an authorial voice, using Edewede, that: "What is good is worth keeping, what is bad is worth throwing away" (39). Corroborating this Adetokunbo Pearce says, "It is the duty of every generation to use its cultural heritage for its own advantage" (Pearce: 73). For Edewede and the other market women, since circumcision did not in any way further the empowerment of women, it is only fit for the garbage bin of cultural practices and not to their advantage (Salami- Agunloye: 13). In *Idia, the Warrior Queen of Benin* (2008), Irene Salami-Agunloye also interrogates some cultural practices of the Binis of Edo state, Nigeria. Challenging the killing of the Queen Mother upon the ascension of the new king, Idia protests, "I stand to question our tradition… why must I, a woman, stand condemned to die simply because I am the mother of a reigning King? Is being the mother of a king a crime?" (4). With this, Idia constructs herself as an independent woman who defies cultural taboos and traditional definition of her role as a queen mother. Further, Idia also subverts tradition by going to war. For Idia, going to war allows her a space to redefine herself and to successfully break free of the stereotypes attached to women (Fifer: 125). Thus she breaks into the male domain of worriorship, successfully subverting the patriarchal norm in her society. Also lending her voice to this, Catherine Acholonu says,

> … Cultural healing can be effected in two ways: by grafting and by Transfusion Grafting is done by a process of cutting off of the diseased part or the bad cultural habits and replacing them with a new, more

> proactive behavioral pattern. But when a cultural trait
> is deeply embedded in the soul of a people the process
> to be employed is transfusion i.e. flushing out the
> unwanted behavioral pattern from the entire system
> and replacing it with… new idea, custom, or tradition,
> tested and proven. This is the terrain of the storyteller
> i.e. the Artist (Acholonu: 2002).

Acholonu's recommendation is a thought shared by this paper, the literary artist has a responsibility of repositioning the society, in such a way that societal cultures is used for the benefit of the people. Cora Kaplan observes that literary texts rely on the ideology and "reality" surrounding it (in Salami-Agunloye: 22).

Achebe's vision in *Anthills* is not to destroy tradition, but to invigorate it with new thinking and to stimulate people to become active agents of change. The women must become actors promoting change. His vision for the future of Kangan society is a space for innovative change and dynamic transformation. To stimulate change, he reverses roles and responsibilities in the novel without the men putting up any resistance. He unravels complex, subtle biases and discrimination against women in Kangan patriarchal society as perpetuated by some of these traditions. Achebe also questions the male right to name a child and the relegation of women to an on-looker at the naming ceremony. He dismantles gender discriminatory practices that are ingrained in the system. In making a very formidable case for women, Achebe legitimizes a women's role as both the one who conceives and brings forth to life, therefore the rightful person to name the child. Here Achebe shows sympathy for women, and appreciates their labor in child bearing; he challenges traditional gender relationship by questioning women's subordinate role at naming ceremonies. Patriarchal tradition is disregarded here, and justice prevails. BB names the baby and thereby assumes a prerogative which is entirely male (Njoku: 335).

Achebe like many other African writers, particularly women, employs tradition to explore, expose and reflect on the injustice women encounter in patriarchal societies. He succinctly portrays in *Anthills of the Savannah* how tradition and cultures exploit women in traditional system by denying them the power to name their children. In Africa, names are very significant; the life or destiny of a child is said to be tailored in line with the type of name the child bears. Some names are prophetic; prophesying into the life of the child like Elewa and Ikem's baby who is named Amaechina, may your path never close, while others are expression of feelings at the birth of the child. The power to name resides with the most senior male member of the family. However, women are free to give their own names, but the child is never called by these names, at best it can become the middle name. The power to name connotes phallic power for the Igbo identity. This is a symbol of power which is reserved exclusively for the men, in this novel we see Achebe reconstructing the naming ceremony as a place of power, creating space and making it available for women. Ideally, the mother should be the one to name the child, since this will create a space for her to express her experiences. In this instance, Achebe positions BB to challenge the system by initiating the naming ceremony and going ahead to name the child. By making his heroine confronts tradition head long, Achebe creates a new brand of woman who confronts without reservation, male hegemony, condemning tradition. BB's decision to name the child is a direct challenge of the African traditional system which is powered by patriarchy. Here she seems to be protesting against the subjugation of African women by the patriarchal tradition. The decision to name the child becomes the subversive moment of redefining her marginal position as Other. BB by this action she flouts patriarchal authority, refusing to walk the path laid out by tradition, she represents in this novel, the next generation woman who hunger and thirst after gender equity and equality in public affairs. Here Achebe, is implying that the new African woman must be determined to assert herself and posses power, as Chukwukere says of Ogot, define her own freedom and pursue it relentlessly (Chukukere, 102).

Bride price is essential and it legitimatizes any marital relationship. It is only when it is paid that the extended family recognizes the existence of any relationship, otherwise such a relationship is declared illicit. Regardless of the non-payment of bride price by Ikem for Elewa, Elewa's uncle overlooks tradition and accepts the new change. Here Achebe jettisons tradition as Elewa's uncle welcomes the new trend, accepts the child and upholds the ceremony performed by BB. Traditional convention is subverted here.

In advocating for a mythic revision, Achebe supports his portrayal of women in *Anthills* with positive mythic representations that shows that traditional society has myths that depict women in very active and substantial roles. By playing these roles, moderator, counselor, Achebe compares BB to Idemili, the mythic figure (Njoku: 362).

Conclusion

Acebe's positive representation of women and critical analysis of our political situation is one the hallmarks of his literary success in *Anthills of the Savannah*. In it, we see Achebe taking his craftsmanship in storytelling to a level, where he employs the use of humor, myth, feminization of his literary vision (Okoye: 341). He emphasizes the need for social change in the status of women. He advocates for a change from tradition as this propagates patriarchy and subjugation of women. In reversing this trend, Achebe resorts to presenting the African woman with a new image, eliminating the old one from the pages of his literature. As he does this, he restores dignity to womanhood in African literature. In the process, his creative expressions are channeled towards crafting positive images. No doubt with the writing of *Anthills*, Achebe has earned a place in the African literary history as he has with his classic *Things Fall Apart*. He has been able to redefine the Nigerian literary tradition through this book. In it, he has been able to uncover gaps and silences, expose biases and prejudices, by initiating dialogue on gender, and have been able to set in motion, change in the African Literature. This novel has not only challenged the hegemony of male literatures but also the representation of African women in literature.

Here, Achebe seems to be saying that the best access to women's total emancipation or liberation from harmful cultural practice is through education. For him, empowering women educationally is the key to assertiveness and self-actualization. In this novel Achebe redirect our attention from powerful men who dominate their world to powerful women who exercise strong influence in their world bringing a balance to female portraiture in literary works.

As the story concludes BB becomes the rallying point, the unifying factor, the leader of the new or renewed Kangan who is the one saddled with the task of appeasing an embittered history. The sharp contrast between the undemocratic beginning and democratic conclusion is worthy of note, it reemphasizes Achebe's advocacy for female inclusion in governance as is also advocated by Ogundipe-Leslie in STIWANISM.

As the novel concludes, we see patriarchy dethroned, leaving the stage for a liberal system, where everyone is 'something.'

Works Cited

Achebe, Chinua. *Anthills of the Savannah*, New York, Doubleday Publ, 1987.

_____. *Things Fall Apart*, London, Heinemann Educational Books, 1986.

_____. *No Longer At Ease*, London, Heinemann Educational Books, 1960.

_____, *Arrow of God*, London, Heinemann Educational Books, 1964.

Agbasiere, Julie, "Feminist Assertion in Chinua Achebe's Novels: A Study of *Things Fall Apart* and *Anthills of the Savannah*", in Eme- nyonu, Enerst, *Emerging Perspective on Chinua Achebe*, Trenton, Africa World Press, 2004.

Agukwe, E., "Achebe and the African Womanhood: *Anthills of the Savan- nah*", in in Emenyonu, Ernest, *Emerging Perspective on Chinua Achebe*, Trenton, Africa World Press, 2004.

Amin, Dina, "Challenging the Master" in Banham, Martin. *African Theatre Women*, Oxford, James Currey Ltd, 2002.

Banyiwa-Horne, Naana, African Womanhood: The Contrasting Per- spectives of Flora Nwapa's Efuru and Elechi Amadi's *The Concubine* in Davies, Carole, *Ngambika: Studies of Women in African Literature*, Trenton, Africa World Press, 1986.

Brown, Lloyd, *Women Writer In Black Africa*, London, Greenwood Press.

Christian, Barbara, *Black Feminist Criticism*, New York, Pergamon Press, 1986.

Chukwuma, Helen, *Feminism in African Literature*, Enugu, New Gen- eration, 1994.

Cousin, Helen, 'Submit or Kill Yourself...Your Two Choices' in New Women's *Writing in African Literature* ed. Emenyonu, E., Africa World Press, Trenton, 2004.

Emenyonu, Ernest Ed., New Women's Writing in African Literature, Africa World Press, Trenton, 2004.

Eziegbo, Akachi, "The Dynamics of African Womanhood in Feminism" in African Literature, Enugu, New Generation, 1994.

Evwierhoma, M., *Female Power and Dramatic Creativity*, Caltop Publ., Ibadan, 2003.

Fifer, Stacy, "Building Alternative Communities: Race and Female Sexual Agency in Calixthe Beyala's Amours sauvages in Azodo and Eke's *Gender & Sexuality in African Literature and Film*, Trenton, Africa World Press, 2009.

Nfah-Abbenyi, *Gender in Women's Writing*, Indiana University Press, Bloomington, 1997.

Nnaemeka, Obioma, *The Politics of Mothering*, Routledge, New York, 1997.

Nnolim, Charles, "House Divided Against itself" in Chukwuma, Helen's *Feminism in African Literature*, Enugu, New Generation, 1994.

Nwagbara, Chinyere, "A Woman is Always Something: A Re-reading of Achebe's *Anthills of the Savannah*" in Emenyonu, Enerst, *Emerging Perspective on Chinua Achebe*, Trenton, Africa World Press, 2004.

Njoku, Theresa, "Male Politics and Female Power in Chinua Achebe's *Anthills of the Savannah*" in Emenyonu, Enerst, *Emerging Perspective on Chinua Achebe*, Trenton, Africa World Press, 2004.

Nwankwo, Chimalum, "The Feminist Impulse and Social Realism in Ama Ata Aidoo's *No Sweetness Here* and *Our Sister Killjoy*" in Davies, Carole, *Ngambika: Studies of Women in African Literature*, Trenton, Africa World Press, 1986.

Ogundipe-Leslie, M., *Recreating Ourselves. African Woman and Critical Transformations*. Africa World Press, Trenton, 1994.

Ogunyemi, Chkwenye, *Africa Woman Palava* Chicago Press, Chicago, 1994.

Ogwude, Sophie, "Achebe on the Woman Question" in Emenyonu, Enerst, *Emerging Perspective on Chinua Achebe*, Trenton, Africa World Press, 2004.

Okafor, Kerz, "Ngugi's Women: Positive Aspects of Social Regeneration" in *Feminism in African Literature*, Enugu, New Generation, 1994.

Okoh, Julie, *Edewede*, Totan Publ. Owerri, 2000.

Onwueme, Tess. *Reign of Wazobia*, Heinemann, Ibadan, 1988.

_____, *Tell To Women*, Heinemann Educational Books, Ibadan, 1995.

Palmer, Eustace, *Of War and Women, Oppression and Optimism,* Trenton, Africa World Press, 2008.

Pearse, Adetokunbo, "The Didactic Essence of Efua Sutherland's Plays" in Jones *Women in African Literature Today,* Trenton, Africa World Press, 1987.

Rich, Adrienne, *Of Women Born* Norton & Co, Toronto, 1976.

Salami, Irene, *More Than Dancing*, Saniez Publ., Jos, 2003.

_____, *Sweet Revenge*, Africa World Press, Trenton, 2008.

Salami-Agunloye, Irene, Idia, *The Warrior Queen of Benin*, Saniez Publ., Jos, 2008.

_____, "Cultural Practices and the African Women, as Portrayed in some Selected Dramatic Texts" in Irene Salami-Agunloye *Women, Theatre and Politics,* Jos, Saniez Publ. Jos, 2007.

Stratton, Florence, *African Literature and the Politics of Gender,* London: Routledge, 1994.

Umunnakwe, Ngozi, "The Changing Female Image in Achebe's Novels" in Emenyonu, Enerst, *Emerging Perspective on Chinua Achebe,* Trenton, Africa World Press, 2004.

Wilcox, Rebecca, "Women and Power" in Mariama Ba's Novels In Azodo, Ada *Emerging Perspectives on Mariama Ba,* Trenton, Africa World Press, 2003.

CHAPTER 12

VIOLENCE AGAINST ACHEBE'S WOMEN: OKONKWO AND "THE GUN THAT NEVER SHOT"

Onyemaechi Udumukwu

In Achebe's classical novel *Things Fall Apart* the main character, Okonkwo, is acknowledged to embody a sense of identity and dignity. Both identity and dignity become indices of power. But in spite of the enormity of the power that Okonkwo wields, we see an implicit failure to establish quality interpersonal relationship with members of the opposite sex. The absence of solidarity is replaced by incidents of violence against the women in his life. This paper will investigate the forms of violence against women in Achebe's narrative especially *Things Fall Apart, No Longer At Ease* and *Anthills of the Savannah*. The paper argues that incidents of violence against Achebe's women are a mark of the intention to interfere with their personal freedom. In terms of practical analysis we will adopt three Igbo words and their implicit semantic values in order to explore forms of violence against women.

I. In the fourth and fifth chapters of Achebe's *Things Fall Apart*, we are presented with two separate incidents of violence against two female characters. The female characters are Ojiugo, Okonkwo's third wife, and Ekwefi, his second wife. Earlier, in chapter three (pp. 12-18), we are told of another pattern of violence against a set of female characters identified as the "nine wives" of an elder and "a wealthy man in Okonkwo's village" (13) called Nwakibie. The intersection between Okonkwo and his wives and the complementary relationship between Nwakibie and his nine wives point to a substantial reality within which violence against Achebe's women can be apprehended. This substantial reality is the lack of interpersonal relationship with the other or an absence of empathy for our fellows. Although Ekwefi and Ojiugo are fictional representations of the vision of violence in Achebe's early fiction and the position of women in his early narrative, the relationship between these female characters and their husbands reveal a paradox in their milieu. As Charles Larson has argued Umuofia as a leitmotif of Igbo society is achievement oriented or acephalous. In this regard, Larson shows, "a man could not inherit title and rank from his family, but, rather, had to achieve these by his own abilities" (Larson, 31-32). The paradox then is that a society that encourages achievement at the same time perceives a half of its population, women and their acquisition, as a mark of success. Thus Nwakibie is introduced as "a wealthy man ... who had three huge barns, nine wives, and thirty children" (13). Observe the order in this listing. The wives are given secondary place after the huge barns. And as we will see later in this paper, even though violence is abhorred in traditional Igbo cosmology it nevertheless features prominently in the concretization of Okonkwo as a figure of dignity especially in relation to his ability to control the women. From the foregoing explanation, therefore, "Achebe's women" do not refer to the writer's interpersonal relationships in real life.

Beyond these characters is the palpable fact that traditional society itself was bound to violence. Apart from the account of abandoned twins and the account on the death of Ikemefuna, the *othering* of women, their "castration" not essentially in an Oedipal sense, but their inferiorization in patriarchal society which emphasizes that they are not only different from the men but that they are inferior. As Diane Hamer has argued the injury that translates as femininity is concretized under a process of brainwashing or castration in which the girl child is circumscribed within the "Law of the Father". She asserts: "in so far as the girl ascribes possession of the phallus first to her father and then to all men, and regards herself, her mother, and all other women as lacking it, she has accepted the Oedipal law" (Hamer, 138). In relation to Achebe\s women then, this primary level of violence to which the woman was circumscribed was intensified with a more pernicious order of violence unleashed on traditional society generally by colonialism.

The second half of our title, viz.: "Okonkwo and the Gun that never shot", also conveys an implicit paradox. On the one hand it conveys the relationship between Okonkwo and the female characters in *Things Fall Apart*. As Hilary Seymour has noted, this is a relationship that is defined by a "*de facto* social apartheid based on sex" (Seymour, 3). Seymour's characterization of this relationship manifests in the context of her account of what she calls "textual silences" in the African novel. The "gun" is a sign of power. By the standard of Umuofia, that power is domiciled in Okonkwo. But Okonkwo's failed gun in Ekwefi's sarcastic remark is not about the literal gun. Rather it is a reference to the failure of Okonkwo's power in solidarity with the woman. On another level, the subtitle underscores a tragicomic pattern in the African experience. This is especially when we recall that characters, their characterization, and other formal strategies in a work serve to represent an implicit significance. As Pierre Macherey has underscored the meaning of a work "is in the relation between the implicit and explicit ... And what is important in the work is what it does not say" (Macherey, 87). Thus, while we cannot ignore the obvious pain emanating as colonialism put the knife in the fabric of African experience, the condition of women especially in the "domestic mode of production" made them casualties of self-afflicted wounds.

Besides, the subtitle of this chapter equally encapsulates a fundamental point in the rereading of Achebe's women. Part of the full text reads thus: "the wife who has just been beaten murmured something about guns that never shot" (TFA, 28). We can note the following:

1. It is just a "murmur" yet it carries much import and resonance
2. Also we see the juxtaposition of two contrastive verbs, "murmur", suggesting silence and discreteness, and "shot" suggesting loudness, noise and brashness.

3. We note, as well, the woman's murmur becomes a provocation because the utterance qualifies as what W.J.T. Mitchell has called "verbal imagery". As verbal imagery, the woman's murmur resonates because it "deflects attention away from [its] literal subject [the gun]" (Mitchell, 21). This deflection of attention away from the gun is earlier anticipated in the narrator's telling. Earlier then we are told: "He had an old rusty gun made by a clever blacksmith... But although Okonkwo was a great man whose prowess was universally acknowledged, he was not a hunter. In fact he had not killed a rat with his gun" (TFA, 27).

4. We can note the choice of words that prepares the ground for the woman's onslaught. The gun is old and rusty though made by a clever workman. In other words, in spite of the ingenuity of the craftsman, the gun has become invalid and therefore powerless.

When viewed together, the woman by deflecting attention away from the gun takes us back to its owner. We should recall that the context is that of her beating. In this regard she seems to be affirming that though you may have beaten me because you are man; I know really that you are ruled by weakness. It is this reference that triggers the gun's loud report. Again Okonkwo's lack of skill suffices as the woman is quite unhurt. Consequently, Ekwefi's use of verbal imagery in her murmur becomes a powerful strategy of survival for Achebe' women.

Yet, there is still another dimension to the whole incident. Ekwefi as the second wife occupies a special place in Okonkwo's heart. It is with her that Okonkwo expresses acts of romantic love. In the course of the action we are referred to an incident in their earlier days. In that incident we witness Okonkwo's passion for this woman as " he just carried her into her bedroom and in the darkness began to feel around her waist for the loose end of her cloth" (76). Is Ekwefi's verbal image of the "limp" gun an icon of an aging Okonkwo whose sexual prowess has waned? Can this be the reason her mere murmur has provoked such an instant reaction? Apart from underscoring the fear that dominated his life did she equally touch on something none of the other wives dare mention? Apart from these other wives Ekwefi as a sexually active woman would have known that the man of the house seems to be a patient with possible erectile dysfunction. Can this be the "old rusty gun" that cannot even shoot a "rat" anymore?

This explanation on the title of this paper will bring us to our main concern. The female characters in Achebe's earlier novels, *Things Fall Apart* and *No Longer At Ease* are victims of a double yoke. The first yoke is traditional system of patriarchy that undermines the women's rights. The second yoke is the nationalist discourse of which these novels themselves project. Ultimately, these double yokes are indices to the pattern of violence against the African woman. But beyond this, and contrary to the earlier feminist reading of these earlier novels by Achebe, it will be seen that these women are not mere objects. They adopt strategies of their own in order to interrogate the status quo of patriarchy. We have already illustrated this in the case of Ekwefi.

Our central concern will be accomplished by considering the nature of violence from different theoretical traditions including, Judeo-Christian tradition, Buddhist tradition, contemporary anti-colonial discourse as represented in the work of Frantz Fanon. We will then, see the manifestation of violence in Igbo world view as encapsulated in three Igbo words, namely: *mmegbu, mkpagbu,* and *mmehie*. The three Igbo words have a common root in *"mme"*, to do, to act or doing, suggesting that their significance is directed outward to another that is not the subject who is the source of the doing. Apart from this common root they semantically imply a lack of empathy to that other person who constitutes the destination of the doing. *Mmegbu* can be translated to mean a relationship with that other person, the object of action, in such a way as to cheat, to inferiorize, and to stigmatize her. *Mkpagbu* conveys a sense of oppression, denial of access, constriction, castration especially in the sense of enervating the object with the intent to deny her a voice and place her at a disadvantage. In a broad sense both *mmegbu* and *mkpagbu* underwrites the type of relationship that exists in traditional Igbo society between the *osu* and the freeborn. We will recall Achebe's attack on this relationship in *No Longer At Ease*. As Obi Okonkwo sits before his father pondering over the rejection of Clara as a potential spouse, he wonders thus: "What made an *osu* different from other men and women? Nothing but the ignorance of their forefathers. Why should they, who had seen the light of the Gospel, remain in that ignorance?"(*No Longer At Ease*, 152). From this we gather that the basis for this absence of empathy is the "ignorance of the forefathers". *Mmehie* refers to sin generally speaking. But the use of the term refers to that possible sin against our fellows in such a way as to hinder interpersonal relationship.

These three words will serve as veritable signs and will point us to the pattern of violence against women in Achebe's novels. In order to achieve our overall aim, the analysis that will follow will be driven by a marriage of formalist concerns with issues of both ideological and historical considerations. In other words, as even the title suggests, characters and their characterization and representation will form a central concerns in our reading; at the same time these characters will be read as figurations of underlying ideological and historical forces at work in the context of the novels. In other words, a basic assumption that underwrites this work is that characters shadow a more substantial world. And in the real sense it is difficult to establish a boundary between these characters and their underlying world. In this regard, for example, Ekwefi's sarcastic remark in our title can be read as a woman's bitter attack at male attempt at self-reification. It is this dimension that propels Okonkwo's incensed reaction to a seemingly innocent remark.

II. In a primary sense the linguistic cognates of violence (Latin: *violentus* or *vis* – to violate – connoting to infringe, to transgress, disturb desecrate and profane.) are: savagery, turbulent, vicious, intense or severe force. It includes also injurious treatment or inordinate vehemence of expression, or feeling, and a distortion or misrepresentation of facts. It is the exercise of physical force so as to inflict injuries on or cause damage to persons or property. In addition, it implies a treatment or usage that tends to forcibly interfere with personal freedom. This definition, though significant is not final. But it underscores the two dimensions implicit in a violent action. These are the physical manifestation and the driving intention of violence. Instances of violence against women are animated by the intention to interfere with their personal freedom.

As Francois Lionnet has noted in his study on the "geographies of pain", violence against women "perpetuates their invisibility and dehumanization (Lionnet, 206). He recalls the specific practices of *de jure* and *de facto* polygamy and related forms of sexual slavery as constitution of the structures of violence against women (207). Whether we view violence as an abstraction or as an instrument of misogyny, the more significant purview is not the question: what is violence? Its main concern is to resolve the question what is the root of violence?

Since, violence is common to all societies; it is not enough to know what it is. Rather it is fundamental to apprehend its causes, its roots. In this connection we see a common thread in the scriptural evidence on the forms of violence in Judeo-Christian, Buddhist and traditional Igbo world view. The Bible especially the New Testament shows that the Judeo-Christian tradition disavows violence. This is because it privileges a view of society that is rooted in compassion for and solidarity with our fellows. This is translated as Love for our neighbour; a love that is unconditional and expresses true solidarity with the other irrespective of gender, race or faith. This is conveyed in the parable of the Good Samaritan and in St Paul's letter to the Corinthian Church. In chapter 10: 24 Paul told the Church at Corinth that, "Nobody should seek his own good, but the good of others" Among its attributes is a de-emphasis on self, that is, "it is not self-seeking". Equally as Jeffery D. Long has underscored, the Buddhist tradition recognizes that violence can only thrive where there is erosion of solidarity with others and the reification of self (Long, 156-157). Long also shows that the Buddhist concept of violence is derived from the Sankrit word *himsa* meaning "kill, strike, or injure". *Himsa* therefore refers to a desire to kill, strike, or injure (Long, 158). In Buddhist tradition violence is basically perverse and by definition is to be eliminated. Its opposite is *karun* i.e. compassion which is the elimination of suffering. Ultimately, then, violence from the view of these two traditions is a manifestation of the absence of love and a propensity for self-reification.

There don't seem to be a central term in Igbo that, conveys the equivalence of violence. Rather, Igbo words like, *mmegbu*, *mkpagbu*, and *mmehie* convey the absence of love for the other and a propensity for self-reification. Apparently, therefore, the Igbo abhor violence. This is rooted in the notion of duality which as Achebe has underscored is central in Igbo thought. This is implicit in the assertion: "wherever something stands, something else will stand beside it. Nothing is absolute" (*Morning Yet...* 94). Clement Okafor has identified this duality in Igbo cosmology as the "phenomenology of pairing" (Okafor, 70). Its import "is that nothing can exist by itself ..." This is another way of discouraging a possible reification of self or absolutism. Implicit in this phenomenology of pairing, Okafor notes, is the "Igbo concern or the maintenance of balance" (70). The significance of this for us is that violence cannot thrive in an atmosphere of balance. This is because for balance to exist there must be a sense of equality in interpersonal relationship. The individuals involved must see themselves as equals. What one sees in the relationship between male and female characters in *Things Fall Apart* is a negation of this principle of balance.

Our concern with the concept of chi is predicated on the light it can shed on the notion of duality and the possibility of improved interpersonal relations. But as Christopher Nwodo has explained, even though the notion of duality involves the "ultimate explanation of the totality of Igbo universe" its reference to duality is in relation to the "sense of the other" (Nwodo, 243-245). He shows in addition that "the world in which [the Igbo] lives has its double and counterpart in the realm of spirits" (Nwodo, 245). In spite of possible metaphysical truth implicit in the concept of chi, we believe that such metaphysics must acquire significance in the light of the need for balance in human relations. In this regard ideological and even metaphysical concerns are not mere abstractions as such, nor are they indices for the existence of conditions of false consciousness. Man creates subjective conditions and secures such conditions with appropriate forms of abstractions. In the case of Achebe's women and the violence against them, possible abstractions can be constructed in order to secure these women as objects of the dominant "ideological state apparatuses".

In spite of its abhorrence in Igbo thought, it is significant to note that violence continues to be a fact of life among the Igbo. It is not a secret that the three words, *mmegbu*, *mkpagbu* and *mmehie*, even in spite of Christian Missionary activities and evangelization, continue to permeate experience. *No Longer At Ease* narrates the case and its effect on the social life of an upcoming professional, Clara. As we have noted earlier, Clara's dilemma is both a case of *mmegbu* and *mkpagbu* in traditional Igbo society. And even though it is not directly related to our concern here, it is important to note that in the postcolonial context the Nigerian film industry, *Nollywood*, is teeming with instances of *mmegbu*, *mkpagbu* and *mmehie* in Igbo society. This later manifestation of this phenomenon is common in issues of widowhood practice.

Mmegbu and *mkpagbu* convey the sense of exclusion. They express violence because they are animated by both the absence of love and the imposition of self-reification. In *Things Fall Apart* they are instrumental in the exclusion of the woman. This will be illustrated with the account on Anasi. The account on Anasi is embedded in Nwakibie's story. This account opens thus:

> There was a wealthy man in Okonkwo's village who had three huge barns, nine wives and thirty children. His name was Nwakibie and he had taken the highest but one title which a man could take in the clan (14).

It closes thus:

> Nwakibie cleaned his throat. It pleases me to see a young man like you [Okonkwo] these days when our youth have gone so soft. . . I can trust you. I know it as I look at you. . . . I shall give you twice four hundred yams (16).

The important issue in this story is not simply its significance in the presentation of the subject of identity. The crucial issue is the relationship between the story's taxonomic aspects including characters and objects. In terms of characters we see Nwakibie, Okonkwo, two elderly neighbours, Nwakibie's two grown-up sons, Anasi, and the other eight wives. The objects include: a pot of palm wine, a cock, kola nuts, drinking horns. In terms of character, the principal agent here is Nwakibie-the wealthy man, who has three barns, nine wives and 30 children. The other characters relate to him in terms of his possessions, what he has, and in terms of his male neighbours who, by their presence testify to the man's possession.

The taxonomic reference in this account is used to intensify an axiological value. In other words the relationship between Nwakibie, the main agent, and the others is indicative of an underlying opposition in this narrative between male and female i.e. *oke* and *nne* in Igbo. This is not an opposition generated on the basis of sex. It is an opposition defined in terms of ideological value of the subject and the subjected.

In this regard, Anasi and the other wives are hailed in order to be interpellated into the dominant subject position. We are told:

> When everyone had drank two or three horns, Nwakibie sent for his wives. . . Is Anasi not in? He asked them. They said she was coming. Anasi was the first wife and others could not drink before her and so they stood waiting (14).

First there was the gathering of the men in Nwakibie's *obi*. And when they had assuaged their thirst the women are hailed into the ideological state apparatus. This is done not for the stake of the women but to reinforce the authority of the men. At work here is not simply the issue of a social meeting and of refreshment in a traditional Igbo society. It is equally of how such social gathering serves as an instance of the exclusion of the women. Implicit in the account is the prevalent social relation of power in Umuofia. It is a relationship of the dominant and the dominated, the powerful and the powerless. Of Anasi we are told that she has "authority ... and the ruler of the women folk". But note that her authority comes not from her as such. In spite of her bearing she is still an object. Her object position is dramatized in the simple gesture of accepting a horn of palm wine from her husband. She: "then went down on one knee, drank a little and handed back the horn to the husband" (15). Note: "she walked up to her husband and accepted the horn from him. She then went on one knee, drank a little and handed back the horn. She rose, called him by his name and went back to her hut" (14-15). Compare Anasi's modesty with the wine, she "drank a little" with what happened earlier with the men. We are told of the men: "when everyone had drank two or three horns,

Nwakibie sent for his wives" (14). Apparently, therefore, Anasi and the other women are not invited to participate in the drinking session. Okonkwo's wine serves as the basis to put the wives on display. They are not there on their own merit. Hence Anasi quickly tasted the wine and handed it over to its own. The horn is the symbol of real male power. Her going down on one knee is a mark of her submission to that power.

The meal and the atmosphere may obscure the nature of violence of work here. The account on the female character serves as an interlude or moment of distraction from the main subject of Okonkwo's visit. The relationship between the male character and the female characters manifests as *mmegbu*. This is an index to the structural violence at work in Nwakibie's household and in Umuofia. It would have been otherwise if the female characters are placed on the same pedestal as their male counterparts. It is significant that an incident that signals the empowerment of Okonkwo is used to dramatize the "*de facto* social apartheid" in Umuofia.

Apart from the distinction between taxonomy and axiology and the differences they reinforce to the disadvantage of Achebe's female characters, there is another aspect in the narrative of this incident. We will highlight this aspect because, again, it is an expression of the subtle tool of violence against women. Note that at the beginning of this incident, we are told of the proverb: "let the kite perch and let the eagle perch too. If one says no to the other, let his wing break" (TFA, 14). Even though this proverb is used in this context of Okonkwo's empowerment, it reinforces the phenomenology of duality in Igbo cosmology. But what turns out in the course of the action is the negation of this duality on the basis of gender. In other words, this duality is honoured and perceived as honourable as long as it reinforces male authority. By contrast, this duality and the values it underwrites are subtly ignored in relation to the female gender.

In order to explain how this is actualized we will explore the narrative presentation in this particular incident on pages 13 to 16 of *Things Fall Apart*. We will recall Ferdinand de Saussure's categorization of the linguistic sign as constitutive of a "signifier" and a "signified" (i.e. a form and a meaning). For a narrative text such as *Things Fall Apart* the signifier is a "discourse" which is the mode of presentation while the signified is a "stay", that is, the action sequence.

In terms of the mode of presentation of this incident (i.e. its discourse) the account has not honoured its basic principle of duality with which it started. The world picture it represents is one that floats against tradition in order to project maleness. This manifests in simple linguistic preference used in the presentation. The account is presented through the third person point of view which is ultimately male. Forms of the third person masculine pronoun used include: "his", "he" and the plural form "them". In the early portion of the incident these forms are used about fourteen times. This is in addition to the use of neutral pronouns like "everybody" "it was this man", "everyone", and "the men". The repetition of these forms is semantic in motivation. The overall objective of this semantic motivation is to foreground a gender view that is ultimately phallogocentric in orientation. Phallogocentric from *phallus* (noun), adjective, *phallic*, from Greek *phallus* meaning penis. The orientation it conveys in the incident is not only about the sense of generative force, although this is implied as "Everybody agreed that Igwelo [one of Nwakibie's sons] should drink the dregs" (15). The explanation here is that "the thick dregs of palm-wine were supposed to be good for men who were going *into* their wives" (15). The phallogocentric orientation manifesting through the use of repetition which is designed to include the self-awareness of women and to contain their ability for self-expression. This is animated by what Elaine Showalter has described as "the cultural and historical forms that relegated women's experience to the second rank" (36).

This occlusion of the female in *Things Fall Apart* which is both an instance of *mmejo* and *mkpagbu* manifests in the mode of presentation of the account. Again the use of forms of the third person pronoun is significant. The mention of Nwakibie's first wife, Anasi, is followed by the use of pronouns like "them", "they" and "she". "She" is used three times. While "she" refers to Anasi the plural forms "them" and "they" are generalized references to the other female characters. Thus, while the male characters are presented with solidity, they speak and act. The female characters are amorphous, and elided. Their presence on the grounds of their summons seems to provide a hushed sensation, on interlude in the discussion of the men. Accordingly as the women disappear into the void of the inner compound the narrator returns to the narrative thus:

> The men continued their drinking and talking. Ogbuefi Idigo was talking about the palm-wine tapper, Obiako who suddenly gave up his trade (15).

The nuance of this portion of the narrative confirms that the women's presence rightly is a rude interruption on the men's discussion.

Again the question remains: how do Anasi and the other wives negotiate their domination. What strategies have they adopted for their survival in a world of violence against women? Even though the world of Nwakibie's household is a world created by men, the women are not mere objects trapped this world. A fundamental factor reported about these women is their spirit of independence. As we are introduced to Nwakibie's wives, for instance, we are equally informed that "some of them were not at home". This means that in spite of the great event of the gathering of the men, these women have their own engagements. There are indications that whatever tasks that kept them away are not initiated by the man.

Apart from this the appearance of Anasi exudes an atmosphere of authority. Of her appearance we are told: "there was authority in her bearing..."She is equally conscious of this authority. Though she lives in a man's world, her sense of independence is evident. This is because she appears at her own pleasure and with dignity. Even her sense of modesty which we have referred to earlier is itself an indirect affirmation of her independence.

Unlike Ekwefi's adoption of verbal imagery as a strategy of survival, Anasi and the other women in Nwakibie's household adopt a predominantly perceptual image in order to affirm their sense of independence. According to W.J.T. Mitchell, the major attributes of perceptual imagery is a stress on "appearance" and "sense data".(Mitchell, 10)the essence of this perceptual image is the projection through their behavior and action, a definite form of world picture of themselves. Observe, therefore, that appearance is an important factor in the presentation of Nwakibibie's wives.

In the fourth chapter, also, we are presented with the incident that centres on Okonkwo's beating of his wife Ojiugo. Ojiugo is Okonkwo's youngest and third wife. We are told that:

> Okonkwo was provoked to justifiable anger by his youngest who went to plait her hair at her friend's house and did not return early enough to cook the afternoon meal...
>
> He walked back to his obi to wait Ojiugo's return. And when she returned he beat her very heavily. In his anger he had forgotten that it was the Week of Peace... But Okonkwo was not the man to stop beating somebody half-way through, not even for fear of a goddess (TFA, 21).

On the surface, the account reflects another dimension of the pattern of domestic violence in Okonkwo's household. The form of violence here functions at two related plains as *mmehie* and also as *mkpagbu*. At the first level it amounts to a deliberate intention to harm and to inflict injury. Thus we are told that: "he beat her very heavily". In beating her Okonkwo assuages himself of his "justifiable anger". At the same time, in justifying himself, he desecrates the woman's body. Beyond the surface veneer of the violence merges the question of the interface between power and ideology and how these can underwrite the creation of powerlessness leading to the exclusion of the woman at the margin. The basis for exclusion is the tacit acceptance by all that the man is the subject and the powerful. He is projected as strong, full of masculine energy and as the one who can be provoked. Woman, by contrast, is the object, the powerless and, therefore, weak being who provokes the other. What we see in the fabric of this account will depend on our specific perspective. If we depend on the perspective that privileges the importance of the man from which the account is rendered, then we will react accordingly to the following phrases, viz.: "provoked to justifiable anger". "cook the afternoon mal, went to his obi to wait", in his anger he had forgotten" (22). In this regard Okonkwo is the subject who is provoked and due to that provocation, must not be in silence but must be strived into action. The woman here is not only the other, the object, but she is also endowed with an uncanny power to provoke and to be thoughtless. In other words, the beating is not deemed to inflict pain as such. On the contrary it is meant to subdue what Okonkwo believes is the uncanny lack of restraint in the woman which it seems has found expression in the Week of Peace. Incidentally, the "Week of Peace" is dedicated to the female deity in Umuofia, Ani. Even though Okonkwo is punished in the pronouncement of Ezeani, we are told that inwardly, he was repentant. But "he was not the man to go about telling his neighbours that he was sorry for beating his wife" (22). That Okonkwo beats his wife is regarded as *mmehie* at a secondary level because it is regarded as a desecration of the Week of Peace. Ezeani, the priest, is much perturbed with this spiritual dimension rather than the interpersonal angle of that incident of violence. In addition, the beating manifests as *mkpagbu* because Okonkwo's aim is to inflict injury in order to control.

Apart from the general acceptance of the man as powerful and as the subject, the process of marginalization and exclusion of the woman is executed through the ideological process of interpellation. The constitutive character of interpellation is that it "hails" concrete individuals as concrete subjects. Althusser has used the word "recruit" in order to further illuminate the essence of interpellation. In this regard, individuals are recruited or hailed by being transformed into subjects, i.e. subjects in the sense of subjected and not in the sense of agency (Althusser, 168).

Thus in the Okonkwo-Ojiugo dialectic we are told that: "After waiting in vain for the dish he went to her hut to see what she was doing". What greeted him in the woman's hut is her absence. This raises the charge against Ojiugo to the second degree. The first charge is that she "did not cook the afternoon meal". Secondly, she is absent from her hut. This warrants the hailing given by Okonkwo when he asks: "Where is Ojiugo?" But even before this question, the movement from the obi to the woman's hut constitutes a hailing as such. The obi having waited for the other to appear in its space goes to verify. That question is put to the second wife. The implication is that the second wife is recruited into the present case. When Okonkwo asks: "Where is Ojiugo" he actually summons the second wife to appear, to give account.

And typically, the woman responds by giving the information about how Ojiugo "has gone to plait her hair". Ojiugo's absence is described by the first wife as thoughtless. But even the response given by the second wife is equally thoughtless in the present circumstance. This is because the content of that response, "gone to plait her hair", ignites the ire of Okonkwo. Ojiugo's care about her makeup can be construed as indicative of the failure to respond to her hailing as subject. Hence Okonkwo "bit his lips as anger welled up within him". In the end Okonkwo walked back to his obi "to wait Ojiugo's return". The beating follows thereafter. What interests one and highlights the issue of marginality is that it is not only Ojiugo as an individual character who is hailed. In that hailing a chain of responses is instituted that connect all the wives to the "sin" of Ojiugo.

Nevertheless, that Okonkwo "bit his lips as anger welled within him" can be explained in another sense. Achebe does not directly tell us through his narrator the reason behind Okonkwo's gesture. This gesture anticipates the state of mind that will be expressed by his grandson, Obi Okonkwo in *No Longer At Ease*. In this instance as Obi waits for Clara in that other part of Lagos (or real Lagos) of "night soil men that smelled", "of little boy selling bean cakes under the lamp post", "of remains of dog" he reflects in that pensive mood, "I have tasted putrid flesh in the spoon". This expression conveys a note of disgust particularly when we see it in its Igbo transliteration as *"eligom nsi nonu"* The important issue is disgust at whom? Is it at Clara whom he has brought in this slum to make her clothes? Or is it disgust at the other characters in the incident, or at the setting? Obviously the object of Obi's disgust in this instance is the totality of the setting. But it also conveys a strand in his character, his pride, and wife, and the vision of himself, elite who lives in Ikoyi, waiting for a woman in this Lagos of putrefaction, where he literally drenches himself in the muck. It is this element of pride and a warped sense of self esteem that links Obi's expression of disgust with Okonkwo "biting his lips".

This inter-textual ink between Obi and Okonkwo may seem slight, but let us remember that the meaning of Ojiugo's name is literally "the eagle cola nut". It is said that this is a peculiar lobe in the cola nut seed that is highly valued. Frank Ugiomoh in his recent study on African aesthetic shows that the name Ojiugo conveys a sense of beauty that calls attention to itself. He argues that this sense of beauty is projected externally than inwardly. Again we will recall that Ojiugo is the youngest wife who is more preferred over the older ones. She is that "eagle lobe" in the cola nut and would have been called "*obi diya*", the husband's heart. We will recall a popular Igbo saying: "*aluta agboho atufue agadi* that is, when a man marries a younger wife he neglects the long standing wife of his youth".

The purpose of these examples is that it is not the woman that sets herself aside and designates herself as the "eagle lobe". It is the man that fetishizes the woman and yet subjects her as an object to be beaten or excluded. And this fetishism of the woman manifests as another instance of *mmegbu, mkpagbu* and *mmehie*. Note that in this interaction between Okonkwo and his wives we have under-scored the importance of interpellation. It enables the man to hail to the woman and bring her into his purview.

The instances of *mmegbu, mkpagbu* and *mmehie* are indices to understanding the broad effects of paternity on Achebe's narrative and by extension on literary discourse in Africa. Paternity refers to the father or the state of being a father, descent from a father, male parentage. But it is also used in relation to authorship or origin. The significance of paternity lies in its intersection with patriarchy. Patri-archy is about the domination of society of males. Anthropologists of the 19th century believed that a stage of matriarchy (domination by women) evolved into patriarchy. As men began to desire control of their children and property, they wrested political power from the women, instituted the reckoning of descent and inheritance through the male line. They also established "patrilocal" residence which allows the marked couple to live with the husband's father's kindred group and took over control of the children and women.

Derived from the Greek "rule of the father", the term patriar-chy describes authority and control exercised by men over women. Used by feminists to refer to what is perceived to be fundamental and universal state of male dominance. It is both a state of affairs and an ideology. As a state of affairs it conveys the condition in which men control social institutions to the disadvantage of women. As an ideology it is embodied in language and accepted as a given.

Interestingly, also, this brings us to the second part of our study. This is because Ekwefi's reference to the gun that never shot has relevance beyond her immediate relationship with her husband Okonkwo. The import of her statement lies in the link it establishes with the postcolonial context. In this regard, violence against women in the postcolonial context is a reflection of the lack of social responsibility and solicitude with the other. This is exemplified with Sam in *Anthills of the Savannah*. As the new leader in the postcolonial context Sam has not established the necessary ground for non-violence against women. On the contrary he epitomizes the instances of *mmegbu, mkpagbu* and *mmehie* against the woman.

The incidents of violence against women in *Anthills* ... will be understood in the overall context of the negation of independence. By negation of independence we mean "the failure of [leadership] to fulfil the goals of independence" (Udumukwu 1991, 472). This failure has precipitated a condition of violence that has placed the woman at great disadvantage. The more visible violence against women in *Anthills...* manifests in the opening incidents of the narrative. As the narrative begins in the account of the first person narrator and principal character Chris, we are introduced to the cabinet meeting of the military regime in Kangan. The more visible aspect of the meeting is not the domineering role of the military head of state, Sam. It is neither the sycophantic relationship between Sam and members of his cabinet nor Chris's scepticism. The obvious aspect of the meeting is the absence of the women of Kangan and the deliberate efforts to exclude them entirely from the discourse. Of the members of the cabinet, Chris says:

> I am not thinking so much about him [Sam] as about my colleagues, eleven intelligent, educated men who let this happen to them, who actually went out of their way to invite it, and who even at this hour have seen and learnt nothing, the cream of our society and the hope of the black race (*Anthills...*, 2).

Apart from Chris's ironic assessment of his colleagues we are not surprised that the constitution of the cabinet itself is a mere travesty. Observe that no concrete issue on social problems forms the agenda of the meeting. In fact there is even no agenda that has social relevance other than Sam's avowed commitment to be socially irresponsible. This is affirmed in his opening assertion "I will not go to Abazon" (1). As we recall Abazon is not just the region of the nation afflicted by drought. It also represents the deprived citizens of the nation. And so Sam's assertion critics agree is a reflection of lack of moral obligation and responsibility to society (Maduka, 74; Udumukwu (2007: 318)). This exclusion of women from this cabinet and in the scheme of things earlier in the novel constitutes instances of *mmegbu*, *mkpagbu* and *mmehie*.

This incidence of violence against women is graphically dramatized in the course of the private party at Abichi Lake Resort (pages 74-81). As the party begins Beatrice informs us that there "were ...eight men and seven women" (75). After a presentation of the men the narrative lens zooms on these women thus:

> The ladies were the most surprising. They were all overdressed or perhaps nobody had told them about the informality of the occasion; and none of them had much to say. ...Perhaps this drab group was chosen on pathetically incompetent advice to impress the American girl" (76).

The colourless set of ladies are in contrast with the men who are described as either as "excessively obsequious" or as "self-assured". And in the face of Sam's self imposed conviviality these set of ladies are said to be silent. Unlike the men, also, the ladies are "chosen" to be arrayed for the amusement of the American girl. Theses set of female characters and their presentation reminds us of the dilemma of the eight wives of Nwakibie in *Things Fall Apart* who are arrayed for the amusement of the male characters.

What propels this presentation and also serves to differentiate it from the earlier novel is that Beatrice constitutes the voice here. Her ironic perspective enables us to be detached from the events themselves. This unlike in the incident in Nwakibie's obi where the third person narrator adopts a *de facto* approach and encourages us to read the action as natural. Beatrice's detachment enables her to look beyond Sam's attempt to naturalize the intended violence against Beatrice herself. The climax arrives as she: "took him then boldly by the hand and led him to the balcony railings to the breathtaking view of the dark lake from the pinnacle of the hill" (81).

In Achebe's classical novel *Things Fall Apart* the main character, Okonkwo, is acknowledged to embody a sense of identity and dignity. Both identity and dignity become indices of power. But in spite of the enormity of the power that Okonkwo wields, we see an implicit failure to establish quality interpersonal relationship with members of the opposite sex. The absence of solidarity is replaced by incidents of violence against the women in his life. This paper has investigated the forms of violence against women in Achebe's narrative especially *Things Fall Apart, No Longer At Ease* and *Anthills of the Savannah*. The paper has argued that incidents of violence against Achebe's women are a mark of the intention to interfere with their personal freedom. In terms of practical analysis we have adopted three Igbo words and their implicit semantic values in order to explore forms of violence against women.

An important lesson begins to emerge from this rereading of Achebe's women especially in *Things Fall Apart*. Even though feminist critics have earlier denounced Achebe's first novel as an embodiment of a de facto social apartheid based on gender a theory of imagery rooted in ideology reveals that Achebe was not a mere spokesman for patriarchy. It is true that patriarchy has instituted male dominance. But the women are not mere objects as such. By their adroit use of language and presentation of themselves, Achebe's women recreate a world picture that is opposed to the status quo.

Works Cited

Achebe, Chinua. *Anthills of the Savannah*. Ibadan: Heinemann Educational Books, 1987.

_____."*Chi* in Igbo Cosmology". In *Morning Yet On Creation Day: Essays*. London: Heinemann Educational Books Ltd, 1975:93-103.

_____. *No Longer At Ease*. London: Heinemann Educational Books Ltd, 1962.

_____. *Things Fall Apart*. London: Heinemann Educational Books Ltd. 1958.

Althusser, Louis. "Ideology and Ideological State Apparatuses". In *Lenin and Philosophy and Other Essays*. New York: Monthly Review Press, 1971:127-186.

Harmar, Diana. "Significant Others: Lesbianism and Psychoanalytic Theory". *Feminist Review*. No. 34(1990): 134-151.

Larson, Charles R. *The Emergence of African Fiction*. London: The Macmillan Press Ltd, 1978.

Lionnet, Francoise. "Geographies of pain: Captive bodies and violent acts in fictions of Gayle Jones, Bessie head, and Myriam Warner-Vieyra". In *The Politics of (M)Othering: Womanhood, Identity, and Resistance in African Literature*. Ed. Obioma Nnaemeka. London: Routledge, 1997.

Long, Jeffery D. "Eliminating the Root of All Evil: Interdependence and the De-Reification of the Self". *Comparative Philosophy in Times of Terror*. Ed. Doug Allen. New York: Lexington Press, 2006.

Macherey, Pierre. *A Theory of Literary Production*. London: Routledge & Kegan Paul, 1978.

Maduka, Chidi. "Chinua Achebe and Military Dictatorship in Nigeria: A Study of *Anthills of the Savannah*". In *Nigerian Literature in English: Emerging Critical Perspectives*. Ed. Onyemaechi Udumukwu. Port Harcourt: M & J Grand Orbit Communications Ltd, 2007:64-80.

Mitchell, W.J.T. *Iconology: Image, Text, Ideology*. Chicago: The University of Chicago Press, 1987.

Nwodo, Christopher S. *Philosophical Perspective on Chinua Achebe*. Port Harcourt: University of Port Harcourt Press, 2004.

Okafor, Clement. "Igbo Cosmology and the Parameters of Individual Accomplishment in *Things Fall Apart*". In Chinua Achebe's *Things Fall Apart: A Casebook*. Ed. Isidore Okpewho. Oxford: Oxford University Press, 2003:67-81.

Seymour, Hilary. "Textual Silences: An Exploration of Patriarchy in *Things Fall Apart* and *God's Bits of Wood*". Unpublished paper presented at the Faculty of Humanities Seminar Series, March, 1984.

Showalter, Elaine. *A Literature of Their Own: British Women's Novelist From Bronte to Lessing*. Princeton, N.J.: Princeton University Press, 1977.

Udumukwu, Onyemaechi. "Achebe and the Negation of Independence". *Modern Fiction Studies*, vol.37, No.3 (1991) 471-491.

_____. "The Niger Bridge or Reconfiguring the Postcolonial Nation in Achebe's *Anthills of the Savannah*". In *Nigerian Literature in English: Emerging Critical Perspectives*. Port Harcourt: M&J Grand Orbit Communications Ltd, 2007:311-325.

CHAPTER 13

THE POWER OF NAMING: A CASE OF BEATRICE NWANYIBUIFE IN *ANTHILLS OF THE SAVANNAH*

Caroline Mbonu

> There was an Old Testament prophet who named his son 'The remnant-shall-return'. They must have lived in times like this. We have a different metaphor, though; we have our own version of hope that springs eternal. We shall call this child AMAECHINA: May-the-path-never-close (222).

Chinua Achebe insists in *Anthills of the Savannah*, that *nkolika*, "recalling-is-greatest" (124). I, therefore, begin this inquiry into the power of naming with recalling a story.

A tortoise fell into a pit. It was not an empty pit. The pit was a cesspool. After remaining in the pit for seven years (seven is the symbolic holy number), someone discovered that the tortoise had been missing and had been in this horrifying condition for a long time. As the rescue process was underway to get the tortoise from the cesspool, there was a slight delay. For the tortoise, however, the slight delay seemed like a thousand years. The yearning to be free again, to reclaim its imperiled dignity, impelled the poor tortoise to yell at the top of its lungs, from the depths, "Please get me out of here. I can no longer tolerate the stench in this pit!" Mind you, this was its seventh year of a humiliating existence. I must add, seven long years of uncommon fortitude.

Tortoise stories form perhaps the largest corpus of African-Igbo moral narratives. One can find a close parallel between the tortoise tale and the women's less than positive experience in general. That women are constructed, marginalized, deprived of certain rights, and ignored in certain circles remains a fact that stares humanity in the face and confronts gender relations. Like the proverbial tortoise, the situations in which women have lived for decades do not appear to penetrate their shell. In some way, hope of a newness has keep women's inner self intact. The tortoise attitude on the day of "liberation" suggests that the vexing conditions remained on the outside.

Most women like the tortoise, do not consider themselves to be permanently stained by the experience of exclusion and marginalization. But they do want a way out. Such a way involves securing their dignity which has been threatened by being absentees in history. This sense of dignity protects women from internalizing their untoward environment. Women know that no person or situation can take away dignity. Dignity is ingrained in selfhood. Just as in the tortoise tale, when the time came to assert the rights that protect its dignity it could no longer be silent, it yelled, "Please get me out of this pit." The sense of dignity impelled the tortoise to cry out. Women's uncommon fortitude had enabled them not to be indoctrinated by the situation in which the dominant voice in society, for the most part, has placed them. By maintaining its dignity in an extremely difficult situation, the tortoise affirmed that the sense of self resides within. The attempt to reach within informs the present narrative: The power of naming.

Introduction

The expression "what is in a name" falls flat on its face in most African and biblical cultures. Both cultures employ names metaphorically. A name is a story. It represents not merely a convenient collocation of sounds by which a person or an organization could be identified. Rather a name expresses something of the essence of that which was being named as Kenyan Anne Nasimiyu-Wasike puts it (48). Hence, to know someone's name means knowing something of the fundamental traits, nature, or destiny of the name-bearer. In this article, I will show how the Igbo employ names to construct the female. I retell, in a liberative manner, women's stories from Chinua Achebe's *Anthills of the Savannah* and two female Igbo/African names *Nwanyikwa* – ñwâɲyi ꞯa, meaning, "a female child again!" and *Ejinwanyiemenini* – I:dɜi: ñwâɲyi ɛmɛ ńinì?, meaning, "what can one do with a female?" By liberative, I mean actions or events that unburden, lift up, or promote the humanity of persons, individually and communally. In effect, this article is about deconstructing and reconstructing women's identity through name and naming.

My investigation shows that certain non-positive names employed to construct and silence women can be redemptive. A redemptive reading may indeed provide the key to reading a woman's role in society, a role which pejorative or inane names tend to obscure. In this way, the name as a story becomes critical to the gender discourse.

The present narrative engages the textual tradition and the living tradition of female names. Examining the tradition and the names of living women reveals the implication of name and naming. My experience as well as oral interviews of some women concerning their given names has revealed that not many contemporary women believe that debasing female names belong to the past. Women who think that debasing names are things of the past remain truly unaware of how much such a past influences contemporary relations. But unbecoming names are not totally of the past because what is rent asunder does not have the integrity to provide a complete vessel for its history. Inappropriate names, past or contemporary continue to support the ideology that foster women's subjugation in cultures that place significance on name designation. When someone has a name where integrity leaks every time they are called to identity awareness, how much agency can be expected? In a society where names are powerful symbols, words that act as markers, certain female names remain connected to structures that perpetuate women's subordination. For this same reason, the freight that the name designation carries cannot be underestimated.

While interrogating name texts that shrink women's horizons and hinder them from recognizing their full potential, my stance in this article seeks liberative insights from the Igbo historical past, symbols that always have been vehicles for redemptive honesty. Thus, I employ a hermeneutics of retrieval. The retrieval processes bring to the fore the fear and pain that individuals want so desperately to share, to own, but have lacked the means to, or rather, have not been permitted to do so. Retrieval of positive elements obfuscated by patriarchy, colonialism, sexism, androcentrism, and missionary proselytism remains integral to the present undertaking. I employ the term sexism to represent that which obscures the analysis of historical reality. The study of sexism in the historical discourse reveals the biases of patriarchal history. I use the term androcentrism in the sense the American biblical scholar, Elisabeth Schüsler Fiorenza, employs it to represent a world construction in language that legitimates patriarchy (162). Patriarchy represents the rule of the fathers. According to the Anglican English Priest, Paul Avis, the rule entails the systematic exclusion of women from the public sphere by legal, political and economic arrangements which operate to favor men (10).

Having introduced the discussion, the rest of the article divides into two major sections. Section one provides the ground for the significance of naming in an African-Igbo milieu by focusing on three subsections, storytelling, metaphor, and the significance of name and naming in sub-Sahara Africa. Section two concentrates on the subject of deconstruction and reconstruction of female names. I concern myself with retelling women's story and re-naming the girl-child. It employs the novel *Anthills of the Savannah* as well as personal experience and reflections from interview subjects. As a person of a Christian faith tradition, the stance I take in this narrative is that of the prophecy of Jeremiah 1:10 and Nehemiah 2:18. The prophetic tearing down and rebuilding describes the deconstruction and reconstruction I draw on in this narrative to facilitate the reimaging of women in contemporary African society. I find the oracle of Jeremiah an effective tool in interrogating the structures that diminish humanity of persons. Moreover, the idea of reconstruction in Nehemiah supports the rebuilding, which Jeremiah advocates. The Benin theologian, Valentin Dedji, would place the idea of reconstruction as the fourth phase of African theology (3). While employing the hermeneutics of reconstruction, a "hermeneutics of suspicion" will also enable the seeking out of social interests that shaped name texts that foster sexism, marginalization and other forms of oppression against women. Insights drawn from these analyses provide the tools with which to reconstruct debasing female names. I must state that I do not embrace in any fashion the Derrida notion of deconstruction or even the literary critic's appropriation of the term to define a methodology. Engaging and dismantling disenabling structures from their deepest foundation, therefore, requires critical retelling and interpretation.

Re-Telling the Story

The validity of a story lies in its power to proclaim a social reality, the American premier Old Testament theologian, Walter Brueggemann, insists (91). That is to say, stories announce a particular way of life, which raw facts thickly or thinly veil. In this sense, stories give women as well as men the paradigm for theological reflection. African women scholars, who are reflecting on theological issues, attempt to redeem non-liberative stories of women. The Ghanaian theologian, Mercy Amba Oduyoye, whose anthropologic-theological vision attempts to retell women's stories in her writings does so "not only to undermine the androcentric and patriarchal [mis]interpretation of the feminine modality of humanity, but also to retrieve in theological terms what it means to be truly human" (29). The retelling of women's stories aim at making sense out of their experience of chaos, institutionalized by centuries of domestication. Retelling women's stories attempts to call society back to its divine origins by fostering human dignity. Thus, the normative role of stories in the African oral corpus remains cathartic and therapeutic. These scholars critique of oppression focuses on instructional structures such as marriage, kinships, and other forms of gender relations. Engaging these macro issues has inspired other theological enterprises. This article, however, continues the women's story from a micro perspective. It engages those innocuous social issues that escape critical scrutiny, yet remain indispensible in social construction. These matters represent the building blocks or root metaphors utilized in the gender construction. One such matter is nothing else but name texts.

The constructions of certain given names practically essentialize the female. The American biblical scholar, Judy Siker, highlights the tension between essentialism and non-essentialism inherent in gender construction.

Essentialism suggests that there is one clear set of characteristics that all members of the group share across time. Non-essentialism, on the other hand, suggests that in addition to common characteristics, there are characteristics that not only differ but also change and change radically according to time and situation (111).

She further states that this "tension can be seen in theories contrasting biological and social constructionist approaches or contrasting the idea of identity as a fixed, trans-historical concept versus a fluid, contingent construct" (111). In Siker's view, and as I show, identity is not something uncovered so much as it is something constructed. Certain given female names in Igbo society constitute one such root metaphor employed in identity construction. As root metaphor, a name represents not merely a convenient collocation of sounds by which a person could be identified. Rather a name derives from the Igbo world-sense. Stories represent a basic form of communicating such life experiences and certain names encapsulate the reality of such knowledge.

Stories encapsulated in personal names represent cultural texts, whose textual qualities blend with other strands, to produce certain images of women that continue to prove non-liberative. I use text to include not only the traditional written word which affects humans and culture, but in addition to documents, symbols, visual arts, social systems, and the myths which maintain them.

The evocation of names as metaphors draws on imaginative reading of these cultural texts. Because the freight a name text carries includes a wide semantic range, the language of metaphor becomes a vehicle by which to access its approximate meaning. Thus, neither analytic speech nor the language of coercion can elicit effectively the deepest embodiment of a name. Paul Ricoeur's understanding of metaphor furnishes the critical tool as well as the lens with which to engage name texts.

Metaphor

Ricoeur defines a metaphor as a symbolic language (45). This language bears the characteristics of a poem in miniature, whose uniqueness resides in its figurative meaning. A symbol represents a semantic structure that can have a double-meaning. He further states that the figurative language of metaphor renders it unlike scientific works whose significance is to be taken literally. Ricoeur posits that a metaphor results from the tension between two terms in a metaphorical utterance. Typically, the tension between the two interpretations sustains a metaphor in existence. Thus a metaphor exists only through an interpretation.

Metaphorical interpretation presupposes a literal interpretation which self-destructs in a significant contradiction. It is this process of self-destruction or transformation which imposes a sort of twist on the words, an extension of meaning thanks to which we can make sense where a literal interpretation would be literally nonsensical. Hence a metaphor appears as a kind of riposte to a certain inconsistency in the metaphorical utterance literally interpreted (50).

The process of eliciting meaning makes obvious the sense of metaphor. In such usage, metaphor supplements inadequate human language. Because humans possess more ideas than they have words to express, they tend to stretch the signification of those words beyond their ordinary use.

As a rhetorical figure of speech, metaphors aim at making the probable more attractive. As work of discourse, a metaphor brings explicit and implicit meaning to light. Most especially, a metaphor represents the extension of the meaning of a name through deviation from the literal meaning of words (49). This claim of Igbo names as metaphors derives from the Igbo imagination of the universe. The Igbo live in a symbolic universe and tend to express their experience symbolically. Achebe puts it thus,

Since Igbo people did not construct a rigid and closely argued system of thought to explain the universe and the place of man in it, preferring the metaphor of myth and poetry, anyone seeking an insight into their world must seek it along their own way. Some of these ways are folk tales, proverbs, proper names, rituals, and festivals (67-68).

The symbolic understanding of names not only permits access into the Igbo world and life, it also illumines the role names play in social and identity construction. As a people of oral culture, myths form a greater part of the Igbo self-understanding and their perception of the world.

Myths represent a form of symbolic language that expresses the truths of human existence in a way that rational language cannot. By so doing, the language of myths obliterates any gap in a people's experience of the cosmos. Creation myths play significant roles in a people's understanding of themselves and their universe. The Tanzanian theologian Laurenti Magesa contends that more than all other myths, cosmogonic myths contain the primordial and pristine moral tradition of any given people (36, 43). Hence, myths provide a model of the relationship between the sexes and legitimize social institutions and practice in many African societies.

Names that signify ideological constructs share a family resemblance with myths, maxims, idioms, and proverbs on which the community hangs its mores. Myths serve to regulate the community consciousness. Some myths, though, represent structures that hinder women's full participation in life's processes. The task to uncover, recover and reconstruct these structures becomes evident in the community's quest for fullness of life, the flourishing of its members. Such activity involves a predictive position that can end the denial and the containment by the dominant male culture, a denial that deprives society of the synergy of human potentials. Thus, the prophet must at once evocatively confront enervating structures that weaken the community and establish invigorating and honest configurations that proclaim life. Retelling women's stories provide the foundation for honest assessment and evaluation of women's role in contemporary Africa. A cursory view on name and naming in sub-Sahara Africa highlights the import of a name as a critical tool in the construction of the female.

The Significance of Names in Sub-Sahara Africa

The African American womanist scholar, Alice Walker, once wrote, "How simple a thing it seems to me that to know ourselves as we are, we must know our mother's name." Walker's assertion of the import of name remains pertinent to a person's self-understanding. It is this quest for self-understanding that makes imperative a re-reading and a re-appropriation of the female given names in African/Igbo society.

Walker's forceful claim subtly directs attention to the influence of names on character and identity. In this regard, family names, given names as well as taken names provide a window into the self-understanding of a subject. Walker's insight unearths and calls for a closer examination of an Igbo tradition whereby a child is normally known by the name of her/his mother. That is to say, what the West considers a child's "surname" is the first name of the mother. For instance, Chinyere gives birth to a child named Uchechi, this child will be known as Uchechi *nwa* Chinyere, literally, Uchechi the child of Chinyere. One can argue that this was the case because of polygamous relationships. But when a kindred or an entire village is named after a female ancestor such as Umuogori (the children of Ogori), or Ndiebemgbeke (those from the house of Mgbeke) such designations suggest more than a convenience of polygamous identification. The practice of identifying children with their mother is very common among the Mexicans. Many Mexicans bear their mother's names as last names. Europeans were not settled on being second-named after their fathers until the recent centuries. People were named after their birthplace, for instance, Erasmus of Rotterdam, or profession, like Butcher, Cooper, Miller, Miner, Smith, Shepherd, and so on. Often their names changed when they were ennobled. If you were Celtic, you could take the name of any man who acknowledged you as his son, no issue of genetics. Furthermore, in Jewish tradition, although a child may bear the last name of the father, it is maternity that determines a child's Jewish heritage. To know one's mother's name, therefore, represents a metaphor of existence.

The import of the significance that a name bears on life cannot be ignored. A name is a story. Names constitute a kind of oral history. Achebe contends that the names of children in an Igbo family frequently tell of the family's hopes, fears, joys, and sorrows (69). Besides, a name becomes so important that it largely corresponds to the particular unique personality. Names are not only symbolic; they link the child to the ancestors and indicate the origin of one's personality. Hence, to know someone's name means knowing something of the fundamental traits, nature, or destiny of the name-bearer. It also means to have some exercise of power on them. In a similar vein, most biblical names have deeper meanings and can function as metaphor. A few examples would suffice. In Genesis 32:31, the one who struggles with Jacob refuses to reveal the name; perhaps to protect identity. The name of the One whom Moses encounters at the scene of the burning yields a whole religious and historical phenomenon. This One is called "The LORD … This is my name forever" (Exodus 3:15). Others include Samuel (1 Sam 1:20), Nabal, meaning the fool (1 Sam 25:25), and most striking are the names of the three children of the prophet Hosea and his wife Gomer: Jezreel, Lo-ruhama, and Lo-ammi (Hos 1: 3-8). The name Jezreel embodies the LORD's punishment on the house of Jehu for the bloodshed at Jezreel. Lo-ruhama meaning, "I no longer feel pity for the house of Israel." The last, Lo-ammi means, "For you are not my people." Hosea and Gomer did live during a turbulent period in Israel's history as evidenced in the names of their offspring.

In the New Testament, the name of Jesus (Luke 1:31-33) tells of a metaphor *par excellence*. Jesus' name appears to be synonymous with the person of Jesus both in his humanity and divinity. The New Testament writers generously underscored the unique personality that the name of Jesus conveys. In Luke 10:7, for example, on returning from their first mission, the seventy (two) disciples testify to their master that "even the demons are subject to us because of your name." In the Gospel of Mark, demons try to get a handle on Jesus' power by naming him, but he silenced them (Mk 3:11-12). Acts 3: 6 narrates the story of Peter and John healing the crippled beggar in the name of Jesus. The Apostle Paul insists that "at the name of Jesus every knee should bow" (Phil 2:10). Equating a name with a person is replete in the Hebrew Scriptures, particularly in the Psalms. Evidently, among the Semites as among the Igbo, names represent a metaphor of a person. Consequently, names have a sacred character and must be chosen and given with a grave caution.

For most Africans to call a person's name without a good reason dishonors her or him. An American longtime missionary in West Africa, Del Tarr observes that

Names of individuals are not used in greetings like:
'Hello, John, how are you today?' Names are simply not
used easily, even between friends. A name possesses an
aura and an essence of power related to 'life-force' (159).

Names appear to represent something mysterious, something felt
as being the actual person. In this sense, a name can carry an aura of
the sacred. Achebe represents this hallowedness of a name in *Anthills*. Of much significance are two female names in the narrative:
Nwanyibuife (ñwâɲyi bə ífɛ̀), meaning, a female is also something
and Amaechina (ámá ɛʃìnà), meaning, may-the-path-never-close.
These names represent the core arguments of this narrative.

This basic understanding of names renders it possible for the
many Igbo to appropriate the Judaeo-Christian law, which forbids
taking the name of God in vain. The Nigerian scholar, Oyeronke
Oyewumi, states that in Yorobaland, to call someone older by their
first name remains sacrilegious and an uncultured act (4-5). Frequently prefixes such as *daa* or *dede*, auntie or uncle function as a
hedge that secures the aura of the first name of an older person.
Examples include *daa Nwaobira*, auntie Mercy or *dede Amacha*.
Oftentimes the name of a child serves as the prefix in the name
of the parents such as mama *Uwanaghiakwa* or papa *Chinedu*. The
underscoring depths of significance in a name enable one to begin
to unravel its metaphoric connotation.

Given the freight a name carries in Igbo culture, naming a
child becomes a conscious, an intentional, and an attentive act.
A child unfairly named carries a life-long burden. In Genesis 35:
16-19, for example, dying Rachel names her second born son,
Ben-oni, meaning son of my affliction. Jacob aware of the gravity
of the meaning, which *Ben-oni* conjures, and the burden it evokes
quickly renames the infant, *Ben-ja-min*, meaning son of my right
hand. One may add that the child born to the widow of Phinehas
after Israel lost the Ark to the Philistines was named, Ichabod
"Gone is the glory from Israel" (I Sam 4: 19-22). Ichabod, indeed,
represents a religious and historical marker.

The burden an unfair name sustains bears on indignity and a
sense of loss. The Nigerian scholar, Chimalum Nwankwo, echoed
the Igbo attitude towards a derogatory name. Nwankwo states that
"In Igbo culture, to give or call one a name which one does not

like and accept is another ultimate insult" (338). The conclusion suggests that derogatory female names symbolize the ultimate disrespect and humanization for the female human being.

A pejoratively named person sinks into a kind of poverty, a poverty that extends beyond the physical. This kind of poverty strikes at the very essence of one's being as well as that of the society where the collective wellbeing derives from individual flourishing. Denigrating names negates individual creativity in the community. The Congolese (DRC) theologian, Bénézet Bujo's argues compellingly that the individual can enrich the community only when she/he is made a person by its individual members (93). When some members of the community markdown a child, a female child, with an improper name that child is effectively excluded from the collective wellbeing of the group.

If the purpose of existence consists in community and communion, what reading can render liberative, such pejorative female names as *Nwanyibuife* (ñwâɲyi bɘ ífɛ́), *Nwanyikwa* (ñwâɲyi qa), and *Ejinwanyiemenini* (I:dɔi: ñwâɲyi ɛmɛ́ ńinì?), which can be translated respectively as "a female is also something," "a female child again," and "what can one do with a female"? Each of these names represents a marker, which suggests ideologies of subordination and marginalization. The character of Beatrice Nwanyibuife in *Anthills of the Savannah* lends itself to the present conversation.

The choice of *Anthills* relates to the theme of redemption imaged subtly by the female characters in the novel. Pertinent issues in *Anthills* resonate with biblical and ethical themes that I grapple with in this research. Following Nehemiah's injunction, therefore, "Let us begin to rebuild."

Name and Naming: Deconstruction and Reconstruction

Anthills of the Savannah

Achebe locates the *Anthills* in the context of religion and culture, particularly that of Nigeria from which the Igbo ethos emerges. In *Anthills*, Achebe tells a story of three schoolmates and friends, Sam, Chris, and Ikem, who became major figures in a new regime in Kangan, a fictional nation of West Africa. The author addresses the course unbridled power often takes and demonstrates how the fierce pursuit of self-interest comes at a tremendous cost to the community as a whole. Consequently, the three friends paid the ultimate price because they forgot as, the Nigerian scholar, Romanus Muoneke, states that "this world belongs to the people of the world not to any little caucus, no matter how talented" (152).

Significantly, Achebe creates fully developed female characters in the novel and suggests that the women remain sources of moral strength, tradition, and hope in the face of violence and deception. Friendly to all three men, Beatrice Nwanyibuife, the chief protagonist, attempts to temper the strident masculinity of the Kangan society with the feminine principles of love, peace, and nurture. She attempts to rebuild and heal the society devastated by male aggression and abuse of power. In this story of death and devastation, Nwanyibuife broke the deadlock of the conflict situation. Becoming the leader of the remnant, she is a type of matriarch, and the progenitor of a new society.

Beatrice Nwanyibuife

In *Anthills*, Achebe grounds gender in the character of the female protagonist, Beatrice Nwanyibuife. I contend that Achebe represents the dual name, Beatrice Nwanyibuife, as a metaphoric text. As metaphor, the dual name can represent concomitantly the most debilitating and most invigorating trajectories of the life of a female in Igbo society. Metaphorically, the dual name represents several possibilities. At one level, the name contrasts Igbo tradition with Christianity and shows how one can redeem the other. While the name Beatrice represents Christianity, Nwanyibuife stands for the Igbo cultural context. At another level, the names seem to deal with the question of the restoration of women in a postcolonial context. The context of restoration integrates the Igbo past, present, and future. Achebe blends these epochs in the activities of the central female character, Beatrice Nwanyibuife, an unmarried and Western educated public servant. This character becomes a source of passion and inspiration in the narrative. She symbolizes the fundamental quality of the female, as the one who leads the community. Other African societies such as the Akan of Ghana celebrate women's leadership role in community. Oduyoye states that Akan proverbs reinforce women's leadership role by noting that most Akan migration stories place women at the center, with women leading the community to freedom and prosperity (8).

In this story, Beatrice Nwanyibuife is born into a Christian family. Her father Okoh is a Christian school teacher and her mother presumably is a homemaker. The family succumbs to patriarchal ethos that place less value on the girl-child by giving their fifth daughter the name Nwanyibuife – a female is also something. Later in life, the character of Beatrice Nwanyibuife reminiscences:

> I did not realize until much later that my mother bore me a huge grudge because I was a girl—her fifth in a row though one had died—and that when I was born she had so desperately prayed for a boy to give my father. This knowledge came to me by slow stages which I won't go into now. But I must mention that in addition to Beatrice they had given me another name at my baptism, Nwanyibuife – A female is also something. Can you beat that? Even as a child I disliked the name most intensely without being aware of its real meaning . . . it seemed fudged! (86-87).

Evidently, the giving of such a pejorative name in the context of baptism suggests an ironic situation. On face value, the name makes a judgment on the liberative teaching of the Gospel. The Apostle Paul writes: "For all of you who were baptized into Christ have clothed yourselves with Christ. There is neither Jew nor Greek, there is neither slave nor free person, there is not male and female; for all are one in Christ Jesus" (Gal 3:27-28). The undercurrent in the scenario, however, represents the imaginative field of patriarchy with all its epistemological assumptions and sociocultural exhibits of hegemony, placing the female as the "other," that which "is also something."

Even as a child, Nwanyibuife instinctively senses the burden her given name conveys. She disliked the name most intensely as a child even without understanding its full meaning. In an inchoate manner, she understood the name Nwanyibuife as a construction that suppresses her female embodiment. She rejects it because in her imagination, this given name under-represents the potential significance of who she is. She senses an alternative to what the name signifies. The denunciation of the name points to another possibility. This girl-child intuits that another world for the female remains a possibility because the world she presently inhabits does not represent a given. It represents a fraud, something "fudged", a distortion, a scheme designed to skew the veracity of the female.

Nwanyibuife's prophetic self was manifest even as a child, she listened and imagined differently. She entertained different realities in her "other world," *uwa-t-uwa* where deep calls on deep. Her *uwa-t-uwa*, meaning "world inside a world inside a world without end," became the root metaphor, the tap root that nourished her imagination of an alternative community where a female can be somebody and not mere something. In her thoughts, the name Nwanyibuife did not account for the dignity she possessed as a female. She instinctively recognizes the burden that the name signifies and summarily rejects it.

Regrettably, the naming of the protagonist Nwanyibuife empties the field of the possible action by God – Chukwunaenyenwa, God offers offspring. A name such as Nwanyibuife suggests that humans assume to run the world by their own idiom. Such assumption disregards the Igbo religious traditions that privileges the Providential order of existence. Thus, redemption of the female who "is also something" seems to lie in the Christian name Beatrice.

The juxtaposing of a Christian and an Igbo traditional name within the context of a baptism remains highly symbolic. Like most symbols, what the name does not say provides a clue to what it belies. Although in the narrative, Nwanyibuife functions figuratively in the place of its literal meaning, the name still raises a fundamental question about female identity. What does a female-child represent in the community? Without doubt, the circumstances surrounding this child's birth, "the fifth girl in a row," suggest an ambivalent response.

Literally, Nwanyibuife, "a female is also something," conjures up an alternative choice. Any person of Igbo origin hearing the name Nwanyibuife, would at once recognize its implication. The obvious meaning is that the naming family would rather have a male child in place of the female. That the family has one girl too many!

This passion for a male offspring represents a benchmark of patrilineal society. In a patrilineal society, the continuation of the family remains connected with a male progeny. Thus, the absence of sons represents the worst kind of misfortune that can befall a family. Obsession with a male progeny among the Igbo, however, may point to another direction. It reveals a deeper concern residing in the Igbo non-Christian past, the cult of the living-dead or the ancestors. Because the warp and woof of Igbo existence revolves around constant recall of the presence of their living-dead, a public function, that they reserved for their male. Although men generally perform ancestor rituals, it does not mean that women ancestors do not exist. The Nigerian scholar, Nkiru Nzegwu, argues for women's ritual acts and the female ancestral veneration in her discussion regarding the cult of the "Chi" (165,178). To maintain the traditional public function which men arrogate to themselves, it becomes imperative to have a male-child to fulfill the role. Similar circumstances exist even in societies considered matrilineal. The Nigerian Scholar, Amakievi Gabriel, observes the phenomenon among some Ijoid and Delta-Ediod communities in Nigeria. Gabriel states "In the matrilineal communities, descent is traced through the female line but the oldest male (not female) heads the lineage and performs political and religious functions on behalf of the lineage" (40).

In Igbo thoughts, the living-dead represent the concentration of life and vital energy necessary for the birth of all members of the lineage. A conscious as well as an unconscious awareness of the cult of the living-dead implicitly informs the Igbo attitude towards progeny. African foremost scholar of religion, John Mbiti, comments on the link between children and the living-dead as having roots in the African concept of personal immortality:

> This concept of personal immortality should help us to understand the religious significance of marriage in African societies. Unless a person has close relatives to remember him when he has physically died, then he is nobody and simply vanishes out of human existence like a flame when it is extinguished. It remains a duty, religious and ontological, for everyone to get married; and if a man has no children or only daughters, he

> finds another wife so that through her, children (or
> sons) may be born who would survive him and keep
> him (with the other living-dead of the family) in per-
> sonal immortality (25).

Without a family cult of the living-dead, the link between the living and living-dead ceases. Dead relatives remain eternally dead with no prospects for the afterlife. The cult sustains the tripartite notion of community, which consists of the living, the yet to be born, and the living-dead. An unbroken link, which is maintained by a male progeny, guarantees a participation in the fullness of life that goes beyond physical existence (141).

Even Beatrice Nwanyibuife's Christian family was not immune from this deep-seated cultural belief. Hence, Beatrice Nwanyibuife's mother bore her "a huge grudge," because her birth disappointed the family's hope for immortality. Accordingly, the name Nwanyibuife unequivocally registers the family's deepest disappointment. Nwanyibuife, deciphers the textual element of her given name as inimical to her *being*, and hence detests it as "fudged". This sense of rejection of that which "seemed fudged," is emblematic of the stand women must take against cultural norms they consider oppressive. Like a typical metaphor, the literal meaning of the dual names comprises two contradictory terms. While *Nwanyibuife* suggests a female's reduced status, the name Beatrice offers a more positive image.

The name Beatrice derives from the Latin name *Beatrix*, meaning she who makes people happy, the one who brings happiness to the group. Beatrice also means "voyager through blessed life." Metaphorically, the name Beatrice reveals that the female character symbolizes a light, happiness, and a blessing. Beatrice signifies a verity spoken of as "something" that renews the community.

Igbo tonal language offers the possibility of a subversive reading of the name *Nwanyibuife*. Dividing the name *Nwanyibuife* into three/four syllabi yields: (1) *Nwa-nyi*-(2) *bu*-(3) *ife*. While the first syllabus "*Nwa-nyi*" translates *female*, the second, "*bu*," represents the to-be verb, *is*. The shift occurs in the last syllable, *ife*. *Ife* can translate into *something*, as in the text or into *light*. Thus the reinterpreted meaning of *Nwanyibuife* can read "female-is-light." This redeemed interpretation of the name *Nwanyibuife* represents a deeper meaning of metaphor, which the dominant interpretation name-text hardly expresses. Possibly, the luminous qualities of the female remain concealed behind "something." Perchance the "also something" which conceals female luminous qualities, represents what Pope Benedict XVI terms "capability for self-knowledge." The Pope would describe that something as "not just something, but somebody [*Nwanyi*, a female], capable of self-possession, free self-giving, and entering into communion with others" (439).

The subverted or redeemed meaning of Nwanyibuife, "female is light," when yoked with Beatrice, "bringer of joy, the one who blesses," yields a fuller picture of the Igbo female identity: female, bringer of joyful light or a bearer of luminous blessings. This symbolism of joyful light is significant in interpreting the certain female biblical characters. Equally significant is the idea of remnant in *Anthills*. These themes closely parallel Matthew's presentation of Mary in his narrative of Jesus' genealogy. Latina theologians Ivone Gebara and María Clara Bingemer, highlight Mary's luminous joyful quality stating "The woman is the symbol of the faithful people [remnant], from whom the Messiah is born...the light-filled face of the people, God's faithfulness constantly reemerging from the ruins of destruction" (152) One can make a similar claim about all the women in Matthew's genealogy of Jesus. In the thick of a patriarchal account of Jesus genealogy, Matthew clearly demonstrates that God employs women's luminosity in saving God's people: Tamar, Rahab, Ruth, the wife of Uriah, and Mary (cf. Matt 1:2-16).

This subverted reading of the name Nwanyibuife, female is light, comes close to Dante's Beatrice. Muoneke, contends that the characters of Beatrice Nwanyibuife and Dante's Beatrice represent redemptive figures,

> In Dante's *Divine Comedy*, Beatrice signifies divine revelation. It is Beatrice who guides Dante through Earthly Paradise, whereby brotherly love and humility resign, to the celestial realm, where the dominant image is that of light. In the *Anthills*, Beatrice plays a similar role by fostering the new spirit of love and humility in micro-society. She guides the group through the dark tunnel of events to the light of understanding (152).

The theme of light in the names underscores the inherent quality of the female. In a progressive weaving manner, *Anthills* employs various strands of female characteristics to make the point. The name, Beatrice, *luminous*, in the interpreted context of Nwanyibuife, is highly suggestive of women's inherent quality.

Furthermore, the ability to interpret provides the key that unlocks and liberates texts inimical to women. The American scholar Vincent L. Wimbush forcefully states that the ability to interpret shows that one is fully human. The truly free individual represents one who seeks meaning through reading, "radical reading—open-ended readings about the self in the world, necessarily including the past readings that represent openness to other ways of knowing that expand the boundaries" (256). The character of Beatrice Nwanyibuife, evidently, radically read her double name, which she appropriated and embodied in her navigating the political terrain of Kangan. She demonstrated her role as the happy light shining on the remnant and the custodian of the community's core values: peace, love and justice.

This interpretation, therefore, yields an imaginative creativity. A creativity that coalesces with passion to produce that which women can appropriate for self-identification. Thus, the "light" emanating from *Beatrice* metaphorically shines on that which "seemed fudged," Nwanyibuife, exposing its true meaning, two brilliant lights adjacent to each other.

The Beatrice metaphor within the framework of *Anthills* continues to unravel when placed within the larger context of African women in modern history, particularly in the context of the Beatrice of the Congo. Achebe's Beatrice in *Anthills* is reminiscent of this historic Congolese seventeenth-century prophetess.

Kimpa Vita (c. 1682-1706): Beatrice of the Congo

The symbolic name, Beatrice, has a prized place in African's modern history. Born, Kimpa Vita (c. 1682-1706), this young woman of noble birth received the name Beatrice at baptism. According to Catherine Coquery-Vidrovitch, Dona Beatrice is one of the best-known women religious figures in modern Africa (47). Beatrice of the Congo rose to prominence when she felt the ruins of her country and called for the restoration of political order through religious regeneration. She formed an African Movement inspired by biblical teachings. Believing herself possessed by the spirit of St. Anthony of Padua, Beatrice named her group of followers, after the Saint, the Antonian. Seen as a mystic of renowned integrity, Beatrice's religio-political involvement drew strong support among peasants. In the climate of the day the Antonian Movement was declared a heretical sect and persecution ensued. At the instigation of the Italian Capuchin missionaries, Beatrice Kimpa Vita was condemned as a heretic. Both she and her infant son were burned at the stake as heretics in 1706 and her Movement disbanded. However, the spirit of the Movement continued to survive underground for more than two centuries. Graham Duncan and Ogbu U. Kalu, strongly suggest that a trace of Beatrice's vision rooted in African symbolism marks African Indigenous Churches (267). In some African Independent Churches women participate in the highest leadership and ministerial roles. A striking similarity appears between Kimpa Vita and Joan of Arc, a fifteenth century national heroine of France. Both were young, imaginative women who had great passion for their people. The active role of this Congolese light bearer in Church and society no longer can be ignored by mainline Christian churches. Her attempt at indigenizing the biblical teachings draws attention to materials that can be retrieved in the reconstruction of the image of women in Africa-Igbo society.

Beatrice Nwanyibuife and Amaechina

As a rhetorical figure, the name Beatrice Nwanyibuife represents other levels of interpretation. A victim of patriarchal subordination and one, who bore the burden of a name not her own, Nwanyibuife, did not play the victim. The oppressive milieu propelled her to prove that a female can indeed become somebody rather than be merely "also something." In the process, the character of Beatrice Nwanyibuife challenges patriarchal structures represented by the leadership of Sam, Chris, and Ikem as well as the "male chauvinism" she experienced in her father's house (88). In the end, Beatrice Nwanyibuife became that someone who offers Kangan hope; a new hope that ushers in a new reality.

This new reality is symbolized in the birth of a girl-child. Echoing an Old Testament prophet, Beatrice Nwanyibuife declares, "we have our own version of hope that springs eternal." *We shall call this child AMAECHINA: May-the-path-never-close* (222). Amaechina *(ámá ɛʃìnà)*, is a typical male name. By naming a girl-child born at the dawn of a new Kangan, Achebe institutes a new era for women in the society. Born to Elewa, a simple uneducated woman and a girlfriend of the slain Ikem, Amaechina, would become a symbol of continuity in the new society. Achebe makes a momentous assertion in his representation of the three significant female characters: Nwanyibuife, Elewa, and Amaechina as the cornerstone of the new society. He contrasts the female with the male. Significantly, the women replace the old society, which stood on three male characters: Sam, Chris, and Ikem. The latter brought death and destruction to the old Kangan. The former brought redemption. The girl-child crystallized the role of the female in the community, may-the-path-never-close. The question remains: How contemporary women can interpret and appropriate the metaphor: "may-the-path-never-close."

It seems to me that Achebe plugged in most of his female characters in *Anthills* from the pages of the Bible. A close parallel exists in the naming of Amaechina and Obed in the Book of Ruth. Two women, Ruth and Naomi "gave birth" to a male child, Obed. In a similar manner, Beatrice Nwanyibuife and Elewa, the girlfriend of fallen Ikem, "gave birth" to a female child, named Amaechina, a symbolic male name. In *Anthills*, the remnant of Kangan names a girl-child born to Elewa and posthumously to Ikem. The women (remnant) of a Bethlehem neighborhood name a son born to Naomi and Ruth. The American biblical scholar, Carol Myers, comments on the Ruth episode:

> That a group of women names the child is unusual, as is also the implication that both Ruth and Naomi are mothers of the infant. Usually mothers, but sometimes fathers, bestow names on newborns. Having two mothers and a whole group of female name-givers perhaps signifies Obed's role as progenitor of the future dynastic founder, who will belong to a whole nation.

Like Obed, Amaechina literally had two mothers: Elewa and Beatrice *Nwanyibuife*. By proposing the name Amaechina, a traditionally male name for a girl-child, the author puts the girl-child on equal footing with the male as progenitor. The metaphoric significance of Amaechina represents the desired future of Kangan. Generally, the privilege of naming a new born devolves on an elder who is usually a male. But this right became also the duty of a young female, Beatrice Nwanyibuife. She suggests a name and invites the group to name the child. The singular act of communal naming symbolically indicates the engagement of each member of the new society in reconstructing and recreating a community mirrored in the name, may-the-path-never-close. It suggests the flourishing together that guarantees the common good.

Specifically, the community's involvement in the naming reiterates the ethos that maintaining the common good is not the preserve of a single individual, a group of friends no matter how intelligent, or dependent on patriarchal structures. Upholding the common good, remains the right as well as the duty of the entire community, an act of solidarity, which the naming of Amaechina symbolizes.

The metaphor of Beatrice Nwanyibuife represents the new woman who challenges tradition in its incapacitating aspects. Although not a mother, and still unmarried, Beatrice *Nwanyibuife* possesses the power of naming and forges a future characterized by relationality and solidarity. Thus, this female character becomes a beacon of hope for the micro-society that survives Kanga's devastation. Reflections of two contemporary female names will substantiate and confirm the various ways the ideology of subordination remains entrenched in certain female names.

Reflection on Contemporary Female Names

Gender as a centerpiece remains a dominant factor in Igbo life. Nowhere more does gender as a focus create ambiguity, as in some traditional female names in Igbo society. There are extant female names which appear pejorative, undignified, inane, degrading, and unjust. Degrading female names represent a subtle form of silencing and as such have a potential for violence. A pejorative name minimizes the bearer's presence and creates a seemingly impenetrable crust to break through. The menacing aspect of unjust names remains the fact that those so named, even if conscious of its deeper meaning, often appear powerless to change the name. Their inability to act is because of massive cultural constructions designed to maintain the status quo. The powerlessness to act, however, does not suggest acquiesence. In *Anthills*, Nwanyibuife, even as a child, disliked her given "name most intensely" but she could not change it. She, however, retired into her *uwa-t-uwa* where she nurtured an imagination for later engagement with the situation. Examples of undignified names reveal how the Igbo society sustains the image of women as the "other": *Nwanyibuego/ Nwanyibuaku*, "a female is money/wealth"; *Ejinwanyiemenini*, "what can one do with a female /of what use is a female?" *Nwanyikwa*, "a female child again!" *Amandem*, "lineage of females!" These names, suggestive of objectification, inconsequentiality, and of ephemeral significance demand redemption.

On the contrary, the name given to the male-child is highly suggestive of sustainability, stability, and perpetuity. Interview subjects insist that generally women are given flattering or apologetic names. Flattery names such as *Nwanyinna*, "daddy's girl"; *Nwaobira/Obiagaeli*, "the one who has come to enjoy good fortunes"; *Nwaugo*, "the one as beautiful as an eagle," represent common examples. *Nwanyibuife, Nwanyikwa, Ejinwanyiemeni* represent the other end of the spectrum. The wide range of names indicates that the polemics employed to construct women range from subtle to severe. Besides some female praise names, particularly that of married women, equally can conceal language of subordination. Such include *Odozi aku*, "the one who takes care of possessions/wealth," or *Ori aku*, "the one who enjoys the wealth". Such praise names undermine the covenantal understanding of marriage, and places the female outside the covenant presenting her as a mere custodian in her matrimonial home. She represents but a steward to guard the accumulated possessions to keep a close watch on the income, to take charge of the household, biblical scholar Nigerian Teresa Okure confirms as much (50). By accepting the encomium, *odozi aku*, women implicate themselves in their own subjugation. In a personal conversation with Mercy Amba Oduyoye on October 3, 2007, she pointed out that name change in marriage represents the civil death of women. Such name change makes subordination under the law possible. Oduyoye further states that by law, couples may choose a new name. No law in the book authorizes adopting the name of the groom.

A reflection on the given names *Nwanyikwa* and *Ejinwanyie-menini* underscores the characterization of the female as the "other" and provides a quintessential example of construction by deconstruction. Engaging these names exposes the true identity of the female buried under a layer of false identity. Such engage-ment reveals what Siker insightfully articulates as "a depth identity behind a surface identity" (122).

Nwanyikwa

Nwanyikwa, Nwanwanyikwa, Nwanyiozokeekwa – a female child again! *Nwanwanyikwa*: The prefix, *nwa* – translates off-spring. *Nwanyi* therefore, means female offspring. The suffix, *-kwa* could translate "again," and in which case is synonymous with *ozo* or *ozokeekwa*. *-Kwa* can equally mean "also," "too" or "again."

The name Nwanyikwa literally means "another female child again?" Actually, *Nwanyikwa* represents an abridged form of either *Nwanyiozokwa*, or *Nwanyikeekwa*, or *Nwanyiozokeekwa*. The name which suggests a question is symbolic of the dominant cultures' attitude to women. That women allow themselves to bear the name or call each other by the name is something of a marvel.

The context of the name Nwanyikwa, "a female child again?" may seem like Nwanyibuife on the surface. But they are dissimilar. Unlike the latter, which translates "a female is also something," Nwanyikwa is just a female again! Indeed, it states loudly that a female is nothing. The suffice *-kwa* suggests so. The three letter word *-kwa* can create a lifelong frustration for the one so named. To begin with, the growing awareness of the emphasis *-kwa* attached to ones sex can proof enervating. In effect, the name expresses dissatisfaction and disaffection for the female human being. The full import of the name Nwanyikwa manifests when compared to a family of all male offspring.

A family that has a number of male children in a row would never give the next male child the name *Nwanwokokwa* "a male child again?" the opposite of Nwanwanyikwa. There can never be too many males in a family. To name a male child *Nwanwokokwa*, remains inconceivable in the Igbo imagination.

In actual fact, *Nwanyikwa* "another female child again?" does not represent a real name as previously stated. Rather *Nwanyikwa* depicts an *empty* name devoid of a personality. Empty naming does not exclude turning the girl-child into a faceless, voiceless, value-less human being because the very language of naming socializes. If a name corresponds to the unique personality of a child, naming a child *Nwanyikwa*, does not carry any aura of uniqueness. Such a name tends to symbolize "nonentity." Moreover, since a name sometimes corresponds to the identity of a person, a person given a pejorative name remains deprived of a model of self-identification. Thus a denial of identity translates into exclusion from participation in social processes.

The backdrop to such name as *Nwanyiozokeekwa* is connected to inheritance rights. Women generally do not have inheritance rights in a "thickly" patriarchal society. In fact, this assumption is codified in the name *Nwanyiegbuama*, a female cannot have an inheritance. Inheritance exists through the male line.

The modest value attached to a female child sometime corresponds to her social worth. Names such as *Nwanyibuego/Nwany-ibuaku*, "a female is wealth," embody female social significance. As rhetorical figure, *Nwanyibuego* represents an objectification of the female *par excellence*. In the market economy, the girl-child represents a source of wealth. At marriage, she attracts a bride-wealth. Bride-wealth can but not necessarily add value to her parent's economic status because the bride was not bartered.

When naming denies a girl-child a sense of self, it robs her of a model of positive self-identification. Her capability of perceiving the world becomes problematic. Consequently, this individual remains a nonentity. The nonentity status of the subject fosters inferiority and "otherness." Evidently, the subject remains excluded from defining her personal reality and that of the world in which she exists. She subsists outside the human community. Pejorative female names such as *Nwanyikwa* confirm androcentric linguistic and ideological systems of legitimization that sustain and contribute to women's silencing and invisibility. *Ejinwanyiemenini* "what can one do with a female?" represents another silencing name text.

Ejinwanyiemenini

Ejinwanyiemenini? Ejinwanwanyiemenini? Ejinwanyi? "what can one do with a female child?" *Ejinwanwanyiemenini*: broken down into syllables the name reads:

Eji – what; *nwa* – offspring; *nwanyi* – female; *emenini* – of what use?

The prefix *Eji-* and the suffix *-emenini* constitute a question. *Eji* and *-emenini* literally mean "Of what use is something?" In this case, it means "Of what use is a female child?" or "What can one do with a female?"

The name *Ejinwanyiemenini*, like *Nwanyibuife* and *Nwanyikwa* represents another construct of the female as "the other." In a world of limited resources, certain persons tend to construct an image of themselves largely by constructing who they are not, that "other." It does imply that in Igbo society, patriarchal sexism constructs the male identity by constructing women through names without any defined matrix. The women's struggle to re-construct the female identity, however, does not necessarily mean the construction or deconstructing of the male identity. Rather, a reconstruction of female identity employed in my narrative aims at deconstructing those constructions that silence women.

The name *Ejinwanyiemenini* reveals the systematic devaluation and repression of women not only in social structures but deeply embedded in ideological constructs. The name remains tied to female devaluation and exploitation. *Ejinwanyiemenini* is suggestive of female rejection. As in previous contexts, the birth of another female defers the family's hope of continuity and immortality. *Ejinwanyiemenini* implies that women have no purchase on the sphere of highest value and greatest worth, they cannot be an ancestor. Where *Nwanyibuife* expresses disappointment, *Ejinwanyiemenini* expresses an outright lament. In the former, the family accepts the girl-child as a "consolation," *also something*, whereas in the latter, the family *cannot find the use* for the child. Thus, the name, Ejinwanyiemenini implies a deep sense of grief, an epic-like drama, "of what use is this child?"

The name Ejinwanyiemenini plugs a hole on the Igbo notion of community. The Igbo who pride themselves as having a high sense of communion based on subsidiarity and solidarity can reject

248

"one female too many." The acclaimed sense of community rooted in Igbo notion of a *Chukwu* and *mmadu* (the Supreme Deity and the human person), stands betrayed when the community cannot find use for a girl-child. As a rhetorical function, the name Ejinwanyiemenini invites further information about women. It invites a story, women's story. It invites stories that rake up memories and fire up imagination of women's presence and activities in the Igbo society; such stories abound. The critical retelling of those stories reveals not just what women can do but what they have done. Indeed, in reviewing women's role in society, we may find out that the name Ejinwanyiemenini seem to function as a verb tool that protects the male ego in the perennial battle of the sexes.

The surfacing of depreciatory names such as Ejinwanyiemenini, raises a fundamental question concerning the composition of African communities. Do Africans still believe that women have no value, or that they are not counted? This intimation produces a crisis of identity in women. Such was the conflict the character of Beatrice Nwanyibuife confronted in her earlier years. In the protagonist, we see the struggle for identity. Like the proverbial tortoise, when the time to assert her identity came, she never faltered. Because a person's identity remains her most treasured possession, the struggle to claim and maintain it corresponds to the human craving for meaning. Beatrice Nwanyibuife gave meaning to her femininity in the name Amaechina. Dedji states that African social engineering has evolved a system in which individuals define themselves in terms of their relationship with others (67). Assuming such to be the case, a name as a means of self definition becomes a critical tool in social integration.

The idea of redemption or even a hermeneutics of reconstruction can create a rupture in the system that sustains the notion of the female as the "other," an idea that deprives her of fuller participation in society. The fissure in the system portends a horrific shake up of patriarchal society. The overhaul entails a massive deconstruction or rather remaking of "women," whom Simone de Beauvoir insightfully summed up as "Women and men are made, not born." Beauvoir's statement suggests that social positioning should not be determined by sex (301). Beauvoir's insight, "Women and men are made, not born," resonates with that of the Nigerian philosopher, Ifeanyi A. Menkiti. Menkiti posits that biological function alone does not confer personhood. A lived experience of the person determines their personhood (158). In our ongoing discussion, constructions "fudged" in the art of making women rings true in the name *Nwanyibuife*. The "making of women" constitutes a consolidation of control of those whose power to be depends on denial of being to others. But women must not abdicate their role: the ones who give birth to the offspring. As mothers who must nurture and rare the child they have a stake to naming that child. Women must realize that a single pejoratively-named female dehumanizes all females.

Re-Naming the Female-Child

In *Anthills*, Achebe provides the metaphoric lens through which to engage re-naming the female-child. He proposes the name *Amaechina*, may-the-path-never-close. Symbolically, a female girl functions always and in all respects as the "traffic" that keeps the path open. The name *Amaechina* in the context of the new Kangan reflects and reinforces an Akan proverb: Without women 'a lineage is finished. In effect, *Amaechina* announces a continuous flow, a renewal.

The designated name giver understands the dawn of a new beginning in Kangan. He seizes the moment and in addressing the new community states pithily:

> Do you know why I am laughing like this? I am laughing because in you young people our world has met its match. Yes! You have put the world where it should sit... My wife here was breaking her head looking for kolanuts, for alligator pepper, for honey and for bitterleaf... And while she is cracking her head you people gather in this whiteman house and give a girl a boy's name... This is how to handle the world (227).

The elder convincingly proclaims the inauguration of the future. He challenges contemporary female name-givers to take cognizance of the *signs of the times* and claim the possibility that the new world offers. Structurally, the name *Amaechina* constitutes a shift. The shift in this case represents a change from one way of thinking about women to another; something of a revolution, a transformation. The transformation in *Anthills* was driven by agents of change, specifically failed patriarchal hegemonic hold sustained by the three friends, Sam, Chris, and Ikem. The naming ceremony registers this shift, which can have potent social consequences for society. In a typical metaphoric logic, the name Amaechina responds to and subverts the name Nwanyibuife.

The birth and name of the newborn represent another "strange" phenomenon. Achebe remains unconventional in breaking with literary ethos that generally creates a male-child at the end of a tragic tale. In general prevalence the male continues the family line, hence the name, Amaechina. The author's exceptional creativity represents that opening through which women in contemporary Igbo society seek to make connection with the rich Igbo traditional past.

Naming the female-child in contemporary idiom admits another possibility. Modern female names that do not reflect women's self-understanding in current idiom risk implicating women in their own subjugation. The power of naming that Beatrice Nwanyibuife receives and exercises in *Anthills* supports the emerging new social order in which the female plays a key role. Such role challenges as well as call contemporary women to account in the redemption of their society. As bearers of offspring, women have the power to name. In naming, they have the power to influence for all time, root metaphor of social reconstruction. In so doing, reconstructing the identity of women in society always will involve multiple narratives grounded in contemporary history with a sense of the future.

Retelling stories, *Nkoli*, suggests that the primary mode by which the African communities reconstitute themselves represent telling and reinterpreting or deconstructing its narratives. Reconstituted name texts that represent a particular type of stories that women tell themselves can become the higher narratives. As the Nigerian poet and novelist, Ben Okri puts it; these narratives can assist the soul to fly up toward the greater light (126). Reading female names from these perspectives enriches a community's reflection on ancient memories and tradition. Schüsler Fiorenza echoes a similar thought in encouraging women's voice:

In every generation women have to challenge anew the patriarchal definition of reality, we have to speak "to re-invent the wheel" over and over again because patriarchy cannot tolerate the conscientization of the oppressed (172).

Reinventing the wheel suggests continuous reweaving, a constant retelling of women's positive actions in the community. The spinning wheel, where the threads for the stories emerge, is the very embodiment of women's life in their continual self-gift for the common good. Such retelling validates present actions of subjects and announces hope for the future.

In a similar manner, women must dream dreams and produce narratives that reflect their struggle of self-becoming for the present age. Such narratives of necessity will involve interrogating root metaphors, those primary tools employed to construct language and the concepts of existence. Moreover, humans cannot escape language because we experience, interpret and understand reality through it. Therefore, since language shapes reality, society must choose carefully language that recognizes as well as honors value. Such an approach can deal decisively with the choosing and giving of female names.

Conclusion

Naming remains a very powerful rhetorical tool in the construction of personal and social identities. Names as root metaphors have a kind of perennial power to evoke a response. Certain names generate new metaphors that cluster around and enrich them and draw vitality from them. The naming of the female-child served well in this regard. Such naming provided the semantic structures that have continued to sustain patriarchal sexism. Drawing from the oracle of Jeremiah 1:10, the women in Igbo society can begin to rebuild the Igbo semantic field in an attempt to reinterpret languages that tend to oppress and dehumanize women, and impoverishing society as a whole. Retelling liberative narratives that celebrate women's social and religious activities can provide a window into African traditional past. Such stories furnish the lens with which to engage the names that degrade women. Specifically, recalling narratives of women's positive contribution to society remains a form of resistance to repressive policies as well as call to the future. In so doing, metaphor and myth employed to silence and marginalize women begin to fall apart in the re-telling of these narratives. If to poison a nation means poisoning its narratives, it does imply that non-liberating stories, whether in elaborate tales or in name texts, have devastating consequences. Uncontaminated narratives, however, have the potential to transport to another world of infinite possibilities, the *uwa-tu-uwa*, where the imagination comes to life. Therefore, redemptive readings of texts that can be oppressive provide women in contemporary Africa the tool to construct positive models of self-identification.

Works Cited

Achebe, Chinua. *Anthills of the Savannah*. United Kingdom: William Heinemann, 1987; reprint, Ibadan, Nigeria: Heinemann 2003.

_____. "'Chi' in Igbo Cosmology," in *African Philosophy: An Anthology*, ed. Emmanuel Chukwudi Eze, 67 – 72. Oxford: Blackwell Publisher, 1998.

Avis, Paul. *Eros and the Sacred*. Harrisburg, PA: Morehouse Publishing, 1989.

Brueggemann, Walter. *The Word Militant: Preaching a Decentering Word*. Minneapolis: Fortress Press, 2007.

Bujo, Bénézet. *Foundations of an African Ethic: Beyond the Universal Claims of Western Morality*. Translated by Brian McNeil. New York: The Crossroad, 2000.

_____. *African Theology in Its Social Context*. Translated by John O'Donohue. Maryknoll, NY: Orbis Books, 1992.

Coquery-Vidrovitch, Catherine. *African Women: A Modern History*. Trans Beth Gillian Raps. Boulder, CO: Westview Press, 1997.

Dedji, Valentin. *Reconstruction & Renewal in African Christian Theology*. Nairobi, Kenya: Acton Publishers, 2003.

Duncan, Graham & Ogbu U. Kalu. "*Bakuzufu*: Revival Movements and Indigenous Appropriation in African Christianity." In *African Christianity: An African Story*. Edited by Ogbu U. Kalu, 245-270. Trenton, NJ: Africa World Press, 2007.

Fiorenza, Elisabeth Schüsler, ed. *The Power of Naming: A Concilium Reader in Feminist Liberation Theology*. Maryknoll, NY: Orbis Books, 1996.

Gabriel, Amakievi O. I. "The Dynamics of Culture and Feminism among the Izon and the Edo of the Niger Delta." In *Beyond the Marginal*

Land: Gender Perspective in African Writing, ed. Chioma Opara, 33-45. Port Harcourt, Nigeria: Belpot, 1999.

Gebara, Ivone and María Clara Bingemer. *"Mary."* In *Systematic Theology: Perspectives from Liberation Theology*. Edited by Jon Sobrino and Ignacio Ellacuría, 165-177. Maryknoll, NY: Orbis Books, 1996.

Ilogu, Edmund. *Christianity and Ibo Culture*. Leiden: E. J. Brill, 1974.

Magesa, Laurenti. *African Religion: The Moral Traditions of Abundant Life*. Maryknoll, NY: Orbis Books, 1997.

Mbiti, John S. Mbiti. *African Religions and Philosophy*, 2nd edition. London: Heinemann, 1990.

Menkiti, Ifeanyi A. "Person and Community in African Traditional Thought." In *African Philosophy: An Introduction*. Edited by Richard A. Wright, 157-168. Washington, D.C.: University Press of America, 1979.

Meyers, Carol, ed. *Women in Scripture: A Dictionary of Named and Unnamed Women in the Hebrew Bible, The Apocryphal/Deuterocanonical Books, and the New Testament*. New York: Houghton Mifflin Company, 2000.

Muoneke, Romanus Okey. *Art, Rebellion and Redemption: A Reading of the Novels of Chinua Achebe*. New York: Peter Lang, 1994.

Njoroge, Nyamburu J. "A New Way of Facilitating Leadership: Lessons from African Women Theologians." In *African Christianity: An African Story*. Edited by Ogbu U. Kalu, 389-407. Trenton, NJ: Africa World Press, 2007.

Nwankwo, Chimalum. "The Lake Goddess: The Roots of Nwapa's Word." In *Emerging Perspectives on Flora Nwapa: Critical and Theoretical Essays*. Edited by Marie Umeh, 335-352. Trenton, NJ: Africa World Press, 1998.

Nzegwu, Nkiru Uwechia. *Family Matters: Feminist Concepts in African Philosophy of Culture*. New York: State University of New York Press, 2006.

Oduyoye, Mercy Amba. *Introducing African Women's Theology*. Cleveland, OH: The Pilgrim Press, 2001.

_____. *Daughters of Anowa: African Women & Patriarchy*. Maryknoll, NY: Orbis Books, 1995.

Oduyoye, Mercy Amba and Musimbi, R.A. Kanyoro, eds. *The Will to Arise: Women, Tradition, and the Church in Africa*. Maryknoll, NY: Orbis Books, 2001.

Okri, Ben. *A Way of Being Free*, 2nd Impression. Great Britain: Phoenix, 2002.

Okure, Teresa. "Women in the Bible." In *With Passion and Compassion: Third World Women Doing Theology*. Edited by Virginia Fabella and Mercy Amba Oduyoye, 47- 59. Maryknoll, NY: Orbis Books, 1989.

Oyewumi, Oyeronke, ed. *African Gender Studies: A Reader*. New York: Palgrave Macmillan, 2005.

Pope Benedict XVI. "2007 World Day of Peace Message." *Origins* 36, no. 28 (Dec. 21, 2006): 439.

Ricoeur, Paul. *Interpretation Theory: Discourse and the Surplus of Meaning*. Fort Worth, TX: The Texas Christian University Press, 1976.

Siker, Judy Yates. "Unmasking the Enemy: Deconstructing the 'Other' in the Gospel of Matthew." *Perspective in Religious Studies*, 32 no. 2 (Summer 2005): 109-123.

Tarr, Del. *Double Image: Biblical Insights from African Parables*. New York: Paulist Press, 1994.

Walker, Alice Walker. *Mother's Garden*. Orlando, FL.: Harcourt Brace, 2003.

Wimbush, Vincent L. "Signifying on Scriptures." In *Feminist New Testament: Global and Future Perspectives*. Edited by Kathleen O'Brien Wicker, Althea Spencer Miller, and M. Musa W. Dube, 245-258. New York: Palgrave Macmillan, 2005.

PART III

CHAPTER 14

GIRLS AT WAR: ACHEBE'S SHORT STORIES
Patricia Emenyonu

Chinua Achebe's preeminence as a writer is based on the publication of the pioneering novel *Things Fall Apart* (1958) and his subsequent novels *No Longer at Ease* (1960), *Arrow of God* (1964), *A Man of the People* (1966) and *Anthills of the Savannah* (1987). These longer works of art have been the focus of virtually all of the critics' and readers' attention. His short stories by contrast have almost totally been ignored. For example, in Ernest N. Emenyonu's Volume I of *Emerging Perspectives on Chinua Achebe: Omenka the Master Artist: Critical Perspectives on Achebe's Fiction* (2004), thirty articles are devoted to analysis of his novels while only one examines his short stories. Even his children's books received more attention with four studies. It is equally true that attention to Okonkwo, Obi, and other male protagonists by critics to the virtual exclusion of any female character has projected Achebe as a writer with patriarchal blinders who has provided a male vision of the Igbo world without full recognition and respect for the strong females who history has shown led the Women's War of 1929 and who controlled trade routes and markets from England to Oguta and beyond. Achebe is a conscious artist and does not gloss over any essential element of his fiction. There is a balance between these essential elements including characters, narrative techniques, themes, artistic purpose, time and space. Women in Achebe's fiction are crafted to fit their historic time and space. No matter the odds against womanhood in peculiar circumstances, the essential female voice is never silenced. Even when Okonkwo beats his wives to satisfy his male chauvinist ego, Achebe does not deny them resilience, confidence and strength of mind. It is that resilience that could make them talk back when necessary; it is that confidence that could make Ekwefi follow Chielo, the Priestess, down to the shrine of the goddess in the middle of the night. And let's remember that it was the same Ekwefi who had the courage and presence of mind to walk away from her first marriage (possibly arranged, or imposed on her by her parents), and ignoring all possible sanctions, boldly move into Okonkwo's house to marry the man she loved. We need to look carefully into the subtleties of Achebe's female characters to appreciate their power and intrinsic vitality. Even little Ezinma whom Okonkwo yells at to "sit like a woman!" and "You are older than Obiageli but she has more sense," could still confidently ask her normally impenetrable father, "Can I bring your chair for you (to the super male sport, wrestling)?"

In *No Longer at Ease*, Obi, the dominant male character could humiliate Clara by abandoning her at a critical moment of need, but Achebe does not dissolve Clara into nothingness. Clara had her sense of dignity to turn her back on Obi when he returns without a tangible purpose to her hospital bed.

In *A Man of the People*, Chief Nanga could in his full manifestation of the arrogance of power, seduce Elsie and cheapen the female essence in her relationship with Odili, but in the same book, Eunice could pull the trigger at her fiance's murderer.

And in *Anthills of the Savannah*, Elewa, a complete illiterate, becomes an indispensable woman to the famous journalist, Ikem Osodi. And as Ernest Emenyonu points out in his article, "A Literary Reading of *Anthills of the Savanna* and Chinelo Achebe's *The Last Laugh and Other Stories* (1990), "in spite of her limitations educationally, Elewa has a surprising degree of confidence and absence of inferiority complex. She is not over-awed by the company of the sophisticated." What all this suggests is that a closer study is called for on Achebe's women not just focusing on their pre-conceived fragility and traditional silence, but an investigation of their inner strength of character and inward attributes.

Women may be silent, soft-spoken, or even out of sight, but that does not mean inactivity or incapacity.

However, the major focus of the present study is on women in Achebe's short stories where there is ample evidence to show that Achebe uses his short stories not only for crucial artistic purposes of experimentation, but also to show that despite all odds, the women in the stories are endowed with sufficient intrinsic powers to realize their desired feminine objectives as well as maintain their sense of female dignity. Through analysis of selected short stories, it will be evident that positive, dynamic women (contrary to popular generalizations) are there in Achebe's stories from the start.

Just as a painter will do a sketch for a larger painting he intends to create, so a writer may use a short story to examine a theme or character which may be expanded upon in a longer tableau. Achebe's first efforts at fiction featured in his University of Ibadan school days. In fact, the thirteen short stories contained in the collection *Girls at War and Other Stories* (1972) were written before and during the same period of time that his major novels were conceived and written. They, therefore, help to elucidate and project themes and issues Achebe takes on in his novels. For example, Bernth Lindfors (1982) has traced the short story "Marriage is a Private Affair" back to 1952 where it appeared in the *University Herald* as "The Old Order in Conflict with the New." The theme of love and marriage in modern Africa as featured in the short story was developed more fully in his novel *No Longer at Ease*.

These short stories also may be studied for their structure and craft. Charles Nnolim has identified the African short story as the most neglected genre in the African pantheon of creative works. Drawing attention to Achebe's "The Madman" in his 2004 article "The Short Story as Genre, with notes on Achebe's 'The Madman'", he describes the story as "near-perfection" in its construction and as advancing the short story genre by "moving away from the traditional folk tale." Thus Nnolim has begun the integration of this body of writing into the mainstream criticism it so deserves. Could he have anticipated the 2009 Oprah's Book Club selection of *Say You're One of Them*, a collection of short stories by a first time published Nigerian author, Uwem Akpan? Or did he remember that Karen King-Aribisala had won the Commonwealth Literature Award, Regional Prize (Africa) for Best First Book (1991) with her collection of short stories, *Our Wife and Other Stories*? Likewise, Sefi Atta also from Nigeria won the Commonwealth Literature Award, Regional Prize (Africa) for Best First Book in 2009 with her collection, *Lawless and Other Stories*, many of which had individually won awards between 2002 and 2006.

Such international recognition of the African short story propels the genre from the back burner, so to speak, to the front. It is appropriate and long overdue to study Achebe's short stories realizing their importance as a legitimate genre of literature and as an historic and personal testament of the thematic growth and development of Achebe as a writer. Using a selection of stories from the collection *Girls at War and Other Stories* (1972), this paper will examine critically, Achebe's craftsmanship in the short story genre to determine whether they reinforce or detract from Achebe's universal reputation as master story-teller or the prover-bial Igbo "owner of words." A central point in the study also is a close analysis of the female characters beyond the glib generaliza-tions of their inadequacies as the weaker gender.

The first story in the collection, "The Madman," is not directly about the war but could be interpreted as a metaphor for the Nige-rian-Biafran conflict. For who can say which side was the real mad man in that conflict? The Igbo (Biafrans) who were the victims of genocide and treated as aliens in their own country, were depicted as "mad" for daring to secede from the Nigerian union. But in pursuing the Biafrans, Nigeria often appeared to be in a mad chase after victory only to resume a unified country again, whole but scarred from that "chase." The "real" mad man of the story is simply identified as "he," while his counterpart, a man of high standing in Ogbu, is named Nwibe. Nwibe's firm control over his family as shown in the brief window into his daily life glimpsed early that fateful morning when, as was his practice, he stepped into the river to wash away the sweat and dirt from the farm, is reminiscent of Okonkwo in *Things Fall Apart*. The two wives, Mgboye, the senior, and Udenkwo, the junior, are quarrelling because the latter's little dog had gotten into the senior's soup pot. Instead of apologizing, Udenkwo turns on Mgboye to ask in her provocative way why she didn't cover the soup pot. Nwibe intervenes, demanding peace and quiet. Ironically and providentially he asks, "If Udenkwo is crazy must everybody else go crazy with her? Is one crazy woman not enough in my compound so early in the day?" (6).

Not to be chastised without a retort, Udenkwo sneers, "Thank you, great judge. Udenkwo is mad. Udenkwo is always mad" (7). But before she can finish, she is cut off by Nwibe. Thus the idea of the confusion of madness is introduced. This foreshadowing is an aspect of Achebe's craftsmanship that helps balance his tale and prepare the reader for the climax. When Nwibe enters the Eke day market stark naked in pursuit of the now clothed mad man who has evaporated into the throng of people in the market, it is the very same Udenkwo whose second wrapper is used to cover Nwibe's nakedness before he is led home now silent no doubt from the realization of his situation. His silence only confirmed his madness to the others, "One man whispered to another [as they led him home] that it was the worst kind of madness, deep and tongue-tied" (10).

This short story has a limited number of characters, but they are portrayed vividly so that we see and hear their voices just enough to lend credibility and depth to the plot and setting. Despite Nwibe's humiliation he never considers committing suicide like Okonkwo. And after two years he even contemplates taking the ozo title, but he is tarnished and the elders quickly "steer the conversation away to other matters" (12). But Udenkwo's role in the story cannot be ignored – her prophetic first mention of "madness" and her providing cover in the open market for the humiliated and exposed husband, Nwibe.

"Girls at War" in contrast to "The Madman" is a war story and although the narrator is masculine, the attention is on the young Gladys, a teenage student who left her school to join the Biafran militia and ended up in the Civil Defense. In the words of Reginald Nwankwo, the narrator,

> But after that encounter at the Awka check-point, he simply could not sneer at the girls again, nor at the talk of revolution for he had seen it in action in that young woman whose devotion had simply and without self-righteousness convicted him of gross levity" (103).

The irony of the story is that the narrator is the self-righteous observer. His family has been sent to the village for their safety and security. Meanwhile, he gives a lift and then hosts the beautiful Gladys at his official house in Owerri even escorting her to an extravagant party in the evening. "...we like to say it is because of air-raids [that our families are not around] but I can assure you there is more to it...we live the life of gay bachelors" (08).

In his eagerness to bed his "beauty queen" he dashes to his office that afternoon to make an appearance, but rushes eagerly home like a school boy to his lover. She has been busy in his kitchen working with his "house boy" to prepare lunch. She announces on his return that the larder was virtually bare. "You have nothing in your fridge" (109). To which Nwankwo replies that he is not like other "big men" she may know because he doesn't make money trading with the enemy or selling relief or swindling the government. He ends the conversation with, "I don't traffic in foreign exchange...We are fighting a war..." Their meal is interrupted by an air raid which sends them scurrying to a bunker in the back yard where the tension is broken when the air craft has flown over and the servant boys are discussing the interesting appearance of the planes if one could forget about their deadly mission.

Nwankwo continues to use Gladys for his own pleasure while condemning her actions and life style. While she dances with Captain Joe and the Lieutenant-Colonel at the "swinging" party that evening, he sits back and watches. In the car afterwards he explains, "I am sorry I didn't dance,...But I swore never to dance as long as this war lasts" (115). Gladys points out to him that he took her to the party which was given by his friends. After sleeping with Gladys, Nwankwo wakes up and continues to judge Gladys: "Gladys, he thought, was just a mirror reflecting a society that had gone completely rotten and maggoty at the centre. The mirror itself was intact..." (116).

While maintaining an emotional air of superiority, he is not entirely bereft of feelings. He had been touched and embarrassed by the sight of the "scarecrow crowd of rag tags and floating ribs" which bore witness to the special treatment he received at the WCC depot in Nkwerre. However, what his job entails and what his contribution to the war effort is we are never shown.

At every point in the story we see Nwankwo driving through the war in his chauffeur driven car. Not the kind of comfort and mobility we might expect in war-torn Biafran. Initially his route was between Enugu and Onitsha which is where he first encountered the girl, Gladys. He was stopped at a check point and by announcing his name and title –Ministry of Justice, ironically tried to bend the rules in order not to be inconvenienced by the delay that searching inevitably took. It was the young woman he had given a lift to who searched his trunk and pigeon-hole, identifying herself to him when the search was completed.

Two years later, he was on his way from Nkwerre to Owerri after loading cartons, bags, and tins of relief supplies for his family and sometimes remembering "when he got sizeable supplies" [emphasis mine] to give some to his driver and his wife and 6 children. As he passed a "very attractive girl by the roadside," he asked his driver to stop.

Roughly ignoring the other "dusty and exhausted" military and civilian pedestrians who swooped down hoping for a ride, he picked up the young woman shaking off an old woman who gripped his door handle as the car sped away. His self-indulgent gesture begins the actual story of the girl as seen through the detached and rational eyes of Nwankwo, the narrator.

Gladys in contrast to Nwankwo is always observant of the people and the situation around her. Although she has changed in outward appearance from the "girl in a breasty blue jersey, khaki jeans and canvas shoes with the new-style hair- plait" first encountered at the check point at Awka (101) to the beauty queen who flagged down a car heading to Owerri two years later wearing "a high-tinted wig and a very expensive skirt and low-cut blouse," (116) she is emotionally engaged in the war and has not changed internally. There is never a physical description of Nwankwo whose words and actions identify him as an intellectual and a manipulating civil servant.

Nwankwo plans his excursions as early as possible in the day believing that he will be safe before 8:30 am or after 6 o'clock. But war is never predictable. No one is ever safe. It is during one of the bombings that Gladys' vulnerability is most noticeable. She may be a tough survivor, but she fears the fighter planes admitting early in her encounter with Nwankwo that she had refused to work in Owerri since it was the center of the air attacks.

The first encounter turns out to be a false alarm, "What is that?' he asked the driver who had brought the car to an abrupt stop. There was no need for an answer. The small crowd ahead was looking upwards. The three scrambled out of the car and stumbled for the bush…" (101). But the sky was silent and everyone returns to their journeys. Her vulnerability is genuine.

Gladys still retains some aura of innocence and susceptibility. She refers to people by name. Her friend in Owerri is Augusta; her dancing partner is Captain Joe. We are never given the names of any person by Nwankwo. We know he has a wife and children, but they are anonymous. His driver is simply the driver. There is never any mention of any of his co-workers at the office. He even refers to Gladys as his "beauty queen" rather than use her real name. At the party when the Captain had escorted the drunk, white Red Cross worker outside and then returned, Gladys asks Nwankwo, "Do you know him?" Instead of answering her question, he speaks generally to the party, "The fellow was clearly drunk."

It is the last ride that is the turning point. Curious and suspicious that Gladys is being kept by some man, Nwankwo deceives himself into believing that he may be able to "rescue her." He begins by assembling half of the food he had received at the relief center the day before to give her, while imagining that he could equally arrange to have something delivered every two weeks thereafter. Gladys is in tears at his generosity which is entirely in character. But as they enter the car, they discover the battery is dead and it takes "at least half an hour of pushing it up and down the street…[before] the car spluttered to life" (118). It is now 8:30 am. For the first time ever Nwankwo screamed at the driver to stop for a disabled soldier who waved for a lift from the side of the road. Is Nwankwo growing sentimental or are we witnessing a transposition in the characters of Gladys and Nwankwo? Before they have gone far, as the car sped down a slope towards a bridge, the air raid shatters the sky and sends the occupants fleeing blindly into the bush. But through the tumult can be heard, "Please come and open for me!" (119). The one legged soldier has been left behind. And who will rescue him? Certainly not Nwankwo. It is Gladys who stops and turns back.

266

And so Achebe has created a fully human, caring woman [girl] in this story whose tragic death comes as a result of her selfless attempt to save the trapped and wounded soldier who was unable to get out of the car when the air raid came and the driver, Nwankwo and Gladys were fleeing for their lives. She seems to be Achebe's new African woman, socially relevant and committed to the communal cause. A character who is later developed into Beatrice in *Anthills of the Savannah*. She is feminine but formidable. We see her as a woman and as a soldier. When the occasion requires military discipline and power, this new African woman responds with courage and strength even to the point of martyrdom as in the case with Gladys.

In considering Achebe's female characters it is necessary to return to the short story "Marriage is a Private Affair" in order to examine his portrayal of Nene, the city girl. "In the cosmopolitan atmosphere of the city it had always seemed to her something of a joke that a person's tribe could determine whom he married" (23). And there lies the crux of the story, for Nnaemeka is Igbo and his self-selected fiance Nene is Ibibio. Having proposed marriage to Nene, it is now Nnaemeka's duty to write and relay to his father the good news. But before he could write, his father sends word that he has chosen a wife for him from the village – someone who though a dunce in school is a good Christian with proper home training. Nnaemeka goes home on leave and talks to his father who is very upset. After a brief argument the son says, "You will change your mind, Father, when you know Nene" (26). "I shall never see her," was the reply.

And true to his word he doesn't. When Nnaemeka sends him a copy of their wedding picture, he writes his son a letter:

> It amazes me that you could be so unfeeling as to send me your wedding picture... I decided to cut off your wife and send it back to you because I have nothing to do with her (27).

For eight years he would have nothing to do with Nnaemeka refusing his request to spend his leave in the village on at least three occasions. Ironically, in the village Nnaemeka's father is known to be "obstinately ahead of his more superstitious neighbors" (27).

But that obstinacy proves to be a powerful trait that keeps him from even allowing his son to visit him.

Meanwhile in Lagos, initial prejudice against Nene by Nnaemeka's countrymen and women is gradually dissolved by Nene's behavior and attitude of love and friendship. Just when the reader believes all hope of reconciliation is lost, Nene takes matters into her own hands and writes Okeke, Nnaemeka's father, a letter. The fact that much of the communication between the couple and the man's father has been in writing is an interesting twist. We imagine prejudice to be the result of ignorance and lack of education. Nnaemeka was raised a Christian by his father who is a Christian. He was sent to school to acquire the necessary education that gets him a salaried job in the city. He is able to visit home only when "on leave." Okeke himself uses the Bible to argue his points. For example, when Nnaemeka mentions that Nene is a teacher at a Girls' School in Lagos thinking that this would be a positive quality for a wife to have, his father retorts,

> ...no Christian woman should teach. St Paul in his letter to the Corinthians says that women should keep silence (25).

Okeke's kinsmen are also Christians. As they learn of Nnaemeka's decision to marry "a woman who spoke a different tongue," they can only commiserate with his father.

> 'What did Our Lord say?' asked another gentleman. 'Sons shall rise against their Fathers; it is there in the Holy Book' (26).

Achebe does not paint these village elders as ignorant pagans. They are 'gentlemen.' Their arguments are clothed in Biblical terms. So after eight years of protest, how can Okeke's heart be softened? It is Nene, the stigmatized female outsider, who finds the solution. She drafts a letter in which she pleads for the grandfather's permission for Nnaemeka to be allowed to bring their two sons on a visit to meet their grandfather.

...Our two sons from the day they learnt that they have a grandfather, have insisted on being taken to him. I find it impossible to tell them that you will not see them. I implore you to allow Nnaemeka to bring them home for a short time during his leave next month. I shall remain here in Lagos... (29).

In a dramatic backdrop of black clouds, rain, thunder and lightning which echo the old man's internal storm, Achebe quickly brings this short story to its joyful conclusion for the old man knew he could not shut his door to these innocent young boys. Achebe makes it easier by having these grandchildren males. But it is the wife who with her feminine intuition, "spoke the different" language, broke the eight-year long barrier of silence, and brought the ultimate reconciliation like a change of season.

In a typical Achebe manner, he first treats this theme as an inter-ethnic conflict [Igbo/Ibibio] in the short story before he ironically turns it into an intra-ethnic cultural conflict in the novel *No Longer at Ease* where he 'masks' a criticism of an age-long ancestral Igbo cultural taboo (the *Osu* caste system) in the veil of a love story. In the novel (an apparent off-shoot from the short story), he portrays the same type of father/son conflict over an adult son's right to marry a girl of his choice. Unlike the short story however, the encounter between father and son neither brings a resolution nor a happy ending. Here is the tumultuous encounter between Obi and his father as he comes home on leave to break the news of his plan to marry Clara, an *osu*:

> "You wrote to me some time ago about a girl you had seen. How does the matter stand now?"
> "That is the reason why I came. I want us to go and meet her people and start negotiations. I have no money now, but at least we can begin to talk." Obi had decided that it would be fatal to sound apologetic or hesitant.
> "Yes," said his father. "That is the best way." He thought a little and again said Yes, it was the best way. Then a new thought seemed to occur to him. "Do we know who this girl is and where she comes from?" Obi

269

hesitated just enough for his father to ask the question again in a different way. "What is her name?"

"She is the daughter of Okeke, a native of Mbaino."

"Which Okeke? I know about three. One is a retired teacher, but it would not be that one."

"That is the one," said Obi.

"Josiah Okeke?"

Obi said, yes, that was his name.

His father laughed. It was the kind of laughter one sometimes heard from a masked ancestral spirit. He would salute you by name and ask you if you knew who he was. You would reply with one hand humbly touching the ground that you did not, that he was beyond human knowledge. Then he might laugh as if through a throat of metal. And the meaning of that laughter was clear: "I did not really think you would know, you miserable human worm!"

Obi's father's laughter vanished as it had come – without warning, leaving no footprints.

"You cannot marry the girl," he said quite simply.

"Eh?"

"I said you cannot marry the girl."

"But why, Father?"

"Why? I shall tell you why. But first tell me this. Did you find out or try to find out anything about this girl?"

"Yes."

"What did you find out?"

"That they are *osu*."

"You mean to tell me that you knew, and you ask me why?"

"I don't think it matters. We are Christians." This had some effect, nothing startling though. Only a little pause and a slightly softer tone.

"We are Christians," he said. "But that is no reason to marry an *osu*."

"The Bible says that in Christ there are no bond or free."

"My son," said Okonkwo, "I understand what you say. But this thing is deeper than you think."

"What is *this thing*? Our fathers in their darkness and ignorance called an innocent man *osu*, a thing given to idols, and thereafter he became an outcast, and his children, and his children's children forever. But have we not seen the light of the Gospel?" Obi used the very words that his father might have used in talking to his heathen kinsmen.

There was a long silence. The lamp was now burning too brightly. Obi's father turned down the wick a little and then resumed his silence. After what seemed ages he said: "I know Josiah Okeke very well." He was looking steadily in front of him. His voice sounded tired. "I know him and I know his wife. He is a good man and a great Christian. But he is *osu*. Naaman, captain of the host of Syria, was a great man and honorable, he was also a mighty man of valor, but he was a leper." He paused so that this great and felicitous analogy might sink in with all its heavy and dreadful weight.

"*Osu* is like leprosy in the minds of our people. I beg of you, my son, not to bring the mark of shame and of leprosy into your family. If you do, your children and your children's children unto the third and fourth generations will curse your memory. It is not for myself I speak; my days are few. You will bring sorrow on your head and on the heads of your children. Who will marry your daughters? Whose daughters will your sons marry? Think of that, my son. We are Christians, but we cannot marry our own daughters."

"But all that is going to change. In ten years things will be quite different to what they are now."

The old man shook his head sadly but said no more (149-152).

Achebe, the artist, has taken the sketch, "Marriage is a Private Affair," and created a full blown novel, expanding on his themes and characterizations. This is true of "Girls at War" as well which had started to give insight into war situations and snap shots of military presence and its aura before its full blown depiction in *Anthills of the Savannah* (1987) two decades later. By examining the short stories we can appreciate the development of the writing craft of Achebe. We can see that even as he explores the intricacies of complex themes, he provides insight into the intrinsic vitalities of the female characters. It is clear that some of his short stories are trial grounds, a kind of gestation period for crucial themes, characters and narrative techniques before they are hatched at the fullness of time on the bigger canvass, the novel. All the important and significant elements in *No Longer at Ease* are as it were, the enlarged editions of their counterparts in the short story, "Marriage is a Private Affair". The fathers (parents) are enlightened and reside in the village while the sons reside in the city far away from the village. The two locations symbolize different perceptions of values and realities. Communication between father and son is by letter writing which signifies that the families are above the average families both in social awareness and exposure to the incoming new orientations. They provide, therefore, the proper environment to debate the essence and dynamics of social change. The sons somehow over simplify or even totally under-estimate the 'intellectual' resilience of their aging fathers. This is not a battle of wits between 'the ancient and the modern' where the latter easily wins. Achebe, true to his philosophy of duality in human affairs, is set to show us in an intriguing way, the two sides of an enigmatic issue. The winning side has only won a battle; the war is not over yet. The issues are too complex for cut and dried easy solutions as is now evident in the *osu* controversy in the Igbo culture which appears to have defied 'easy' solutions of a political nature for almost a century. The issue was not resolved in *Things Fall Apart*, and no less so in *No Longer at Ease*. The short story, "Marriage is a Private Affair," is a mundane variation of a deep- rooted socio-cultural dilemma. Nonetheless, unlike in the novel *No Longer at Ease,* the short story proffers a solution significantly evolved by a woman. As Helen Chukwuma has pointed out, "The short story deserves a key place in any consideration of contemporary African literature....For...it shows great originality, freshness and spontaneity, qualities often missing in the novels." (12) It is about time critics and scholars recognized the need to pay adequate critical attention to the short story genre in African Literature. Achebe's are a good place to start.

Works Cited

Achebe, Chinua. *Things Fall Apart*. London: Heinemann Publishers, 1958.
_____ *No Longer at Ease*. London: Heinemann Publishers, 1960.
_____ *Anthills of the Savannah*. London: Heinemann Publishers, 1987.

_____ *Girls at War and Other Stories*. London: Heinemann Publishers, 1972.

Chukwuma, Helen. "Two Decades of the Short Story in West Africa," in *WAACLALS (West African Association for Commonwealth Literature and Language Studies) Journal*, 1, Calabar, 1989.

Emenyonu, Ernest N. *Emerging Perspectives on Chinua Achebe: Omenka the Master Artist: Critical Perspectives on Achebe's Fiction*, Vol. 1, Trenton, NJ: Africa World Press, Inc., 2004.

_____. "A Literary Reading of Chinua Achebe's *Anthills of the Savannah* and Chinelo Achebe's *The Last Laugh and Other Stories*" in *Okike: An African Journal of New Writing*, No. 30, Nsukka, Nigeria, 1990.

Lindfors, Bernth. *Early Achebe*. Trenton, NJ: Africa World Press, Inc., 2009.

Nnolim, Charles. "The Short Story as Genre, with notes on Achebe's 'The Madman'" in E.N. Emenyonu (Ed.) *Emerging Perspectives on Chinua Achebe: Omenka The Master Artist: Critical Perspectives on Achebe' Fiction*, Vol. 1, Trenton, NJ: Africa World Press, Inc., 2004.

CHAPTER 15

THE PASSIVE ONES: CHINUA ACHEBE'S *ARROW OF GOD*

Chinyelu Ojukwu

Chinua Achebe, one of Africa's foremost novelists, in his second novel, *Arrow of God*, often described as the most ambitious of them all, delves into the intricate structure of the Igbo society in the pre-colonial period and their encounter with colonialism. In his attempt to acquaint the readers with the complexities of the situation, in the context of the conflicts in which the Igbo found themselves trapped in, with the coming of the colonialists, Achebe, inadvertently, extrapolates in this narrative the female situation in that society.

From the very beginning of this novel, we are given a hint by the young wife of Ezeulu, Ugoye, that all might not be well, with the awkward sitting of the moon. It is a woman who sees and feels the premonition of an approaching danger that much later engulfs the family. Ugoye's words foreshadow it: "Oho, I see it. Moon, may your face meeting mine bring good fortune. But how is it sitting? I don't like its posture... I think it sits awkwardly – like an evil moon" (2). Ugoye's proclamation subsequently seems to be the augury that portends the people's ruin.

Despite this prophetic declaration, the world around her still roars on, suffocating her incipient insight into the future that holds out precariously in front of them. On the contrary, Ezeulu's utterances on sighting the same moon, all point to the degradation of women in *Arrow of God*. First in his prayers after the appearance of the new moon and after his ceremonial eating of the fourth yam, he implores Ulu to "… let our wives bear male children" (6). There is no mention of female children anywhere in that solemn prayer. This is a signal that we are dealing with a patriarchal system where the woman might not have much liberty or opportunities to be heard.

Subsequently, while admonishing Obika who is frightened by an apparition as he rushes into the *'Obi'* shivering with terror, Ezeulu retorts, "hold yourself together. You are not a woman" (8). These utterances are quite in tune with a culture where women are seen to be weak and have always played passive roles, mostly as attendants to their husbands. They are those who receive instructions and orders on what to do and on what not to do. There is no basis for a heart-warming and mutual conversation between a husband and a wife. Mistakes are pointed out to the woman in threatening manners by the husband, as demonstrated by the communication between Ezeulu and his wife, Matefi. The woman proffers some explanation why supper is served late, "I went all the way to Nwangene to fetch water and…" Ezeulu interrupts, "if you like you may go to Nkisa. What I am saying is that if you want that madness of yours to be cured, bring my supper at this time another day…" (9).

We find such pronouncements all through the novel which remind us of Okonkwo's relationship with his wives in *Things Fall Apart*. One thus wonders why there seem not to be very warm relationships between the men and their wives in many of Achebe's early novels especially the ones depicting the world of the traditional Igbo society. Was he making categorical statements about these people? Or was it just a phase in the life of the people especially in the colonial period? Could it be attributed to the fact that probably at that period, emotions of love were more controlled and contained within the individuals than expressed in public? On the contrary, could it be that firmness and autocracy were viewed as marks or traits of manliness and strength?

Again, wife battery is demonstrated in the novel as Ibe beats up his wife, Akueke, to the point that her face all becomes swollen. Obika, Akueke's half-brother, is able to discipline Ibe as he binds the latter, hands and feet and, with the assistance of Ofoegbu, his friend, he deposits him under an 'Ukwa' tree in the compound of Ezeulu. Achebe, by this, effectively posits that within the strongly patriarchal system in the world of *Arrow of God,* actions are inadvertently fully counterbalanced by reactions which only to some extent address the female situation in the novel. It is obvious, though, that wife battery was not tolerated in that community.

However, one wonders whether Obika is able to come to the defence of Akueke because of their biological relationship as brother and sister. The woman situation is best assessed if there is no biological relationship between the man and the woman in question as in the cases of: husband and wife; male boss and female subordinate; male and female colleagues in schools, and in other establishments; business associates etc. That way, the man's attitude towards the woman can then be objectively assessed. Incidentally, in most cases, the chauvinistic instincts in the man manifest more in situations where there is no biological relationship between him and the woman, than in situations where the two are biologically connected.

The novel, in terms of contents, seems to be phallocentric as it generally explores the activities of men and their relationships with one another in the context of the cultural life of the society. Many wars are waged among various communities. The exploration of the female situation is tangentially attached to the entire structure. The women are thus subsumed in the political, social and cultural life of the community. They are simply not visible. This is in line with Chikwenye Ogunyemi's assertion on Nigerian Literature as cited by C.T. Maduka in his unpublished manuscript, "Feminism, Womanism and Motherism in African Literary Discourse" that:

> The Literature is phallic, dominated as it is by male writers and male critics who deal almost exclusively with male characters and male concerns, naturally aimed at a predominantly male audience. The male camaraderie has been insufferable for the few educated Nigerian Women (7).

The plot of *Arrow of God* centres more on the interaction between the white men (colonialists) and the natives. Achebe in the process, tries to capture the misconception by the colonialists of the cultural life of these people. They (colonialists) relate to the outside world their misinformed perception of Africa. For instance, it was obvious that Winterbottom could not get the full grasp of the details of the Okperi/Umuaro dispute. While the readers are given a vivid analysis of the dispute arising from Akukalia's misconduct and mishandling of the situation at Okperi, his mother's village, Winterbottom misinforms Mr. Clark on the issue.

By so doing, Achebe carefully demonstrates the issue of mis-interpretation, misinformation and misconception which have all been the hallmarks of the relationship between the early mission-aries and the Africans. This has been the bane of Africa until the publication of Achebe's *Things Fall Apart* and other African novels that reveal more details about the "dark continent." Captain Win-terbottom thus tells Mr Tony Clarke that, "this man from Umuaro having drunk his friend's palm wine reached for his *Ikenga* and split it in two" (37). It becomes funny to the reader who has fol-lowed the development of the story from the author's perspective and has seen how Akukalia and his two companions had rebuffed all courtesies of goodwill and how even kolanut, the symbol of peace, was also rejected by these emissaries. This brings to mind Achebe's own comments in *Home and Exile*, regarding the absolute power of a narrator or I would add, whoever pays the piper. "In the end I began to understand. There is such a thing as absolute power over narrative. Those who secure this privilege for themselves can arrange stories about others pretty much, and as, they like" (24).

Apart from clash of cultures, Achebe dwells more on the relationship between these Igbos and the British colonial admin-istrators. That is, we are made to witness the activities of the Lieutenant Governor, through the Resident and Senior District Officers down the hierarchy to Assistant District Officer. He also points out the fact that the British Colonial administration was instrumental to the proliferation of Chiefs and Kings among the Igbo who ab-initio never had any, by their system of governance. The narrative thus dwells largely on the activities of the male dominated government of the colonial administration and the appointment of paramount Chiefs to help stabilize their new and strange government as viewed by these Igbos. The Igbo women are thus not clearly depicted as being part of their people's conflictive encounter with colonialism in this novel. The situation here sharply and drastically contrasts with Akachi Ezeigbo's depiction of the Igbo world view in *The Last of the Strong Ones* where women participate actively in the socio-political life of the communities within the same period. Chinyelu Ojukwu observes that, "while Adimora-Ezeigbo recognizes the contributions of women in the anti-colonial struggle, Achebe's attention centres more on the efforts of the men in their attempt to rescue their people, tradition and land from being bastardized by colonialism" (5).

The plot of *Arrow of God* only occasionally reveals the women situation in the novel. The consistency with which contemptuous references are made to anything pertaining to women becomes a bit worrisome. For instance, Ezeulu in this narrative, is referred to as someone who usually does not react to women's hullaballoo: "The voices were getting louder and Ezeulu who normally took no interest in women's shouting began to strain his ear" (43). Further on, Ezeulu's intolerance of opposition especially from a woman is also apparent: " 'Shut your mouth', said Ezeulu, who did not want anybody, *least of all his own daughter*, to continue questioning his wisdom in sending one of his sons to join the new religion'" (My emphasis. 43). This again presents Ezeulu not only as a man who is intolerant of opposition but also as someone who has no regard for women generally, including his wives and daughters. This brings to mind Okonkwo's attitude to his wives in *Things Fall Apart* as he could beat up any of them for any trifle offence. He is thus dreaded by his entire family as depicted in these widely quoted lines, "Okonkwo ruled his household with a heavy hand. His wives especially the youngest, lived in perpetual fear of his fiery temper, and so did his little children" (9).

Later on in the same novel, we are also told how Okonkwo beats up his second wife for merely cutting a few leaves off the banana tree to wrap some food: "Without further argument Okonkwo gave her a sound beating and left her and her only daughter weeping. Neither of the other wives dared to interfere beyond an occasional and tentative, 'it is enough Okonkwo', pleaded from a reasonable distance" (27). The recurrent question that comes to mind is: Is Chinua Achebe's depiction of the family unit among the Igbo, in the pre-colonial period where the man remained more or less a demi-god in his *Obi*, and was revered as such especially by his wives who were seen but hardly heard, totally realistic? Was it really a society where the women were so suppressed that their opinions were never sought on important issues and they were never heard?

We are told in *Arrow of God* that Edogo who has a good reputation for carving facial masks for ancestral spirits, "could not do it in the home under the *profane gaze of women and children....*" (My emphasis. 51). The word 'profane' tells us that it is almost sacrilegious for women to see the making of these masks. One therefore believes that these restrictions and taboos in which the Igbo women of Achebe's novels were hedged during this period proclaim to the world that these were culturally subjugated, suppressed and oppressed women who despite their struggles remained largely unheard. This situation seems contrary to the position of women among the Yorubas of the western region of Nigeria, some of whom were members of some masquerade cults within the same period. A few women in this region even became Obas during this period. According to Akachi Ezeigbo, "In Yorubaland, where the monarchical system of government operated, female Obas in Ile-Ife, the Oyo Kingdom, Ondo and in other communities, were known to function effectively" (68).

It is also known that even in the Northern part of Nigeria, women participated very actively in the political life of the region. Again, in Ezeigbo's words, "The finest example was the magnificent Queen Amina of Zazzau, famous for her exploits in war and politics. She was a revered and beloved leader.... Other parts of the North, where strong female personages featured or wielded power in the pre-colonial political systems, were the Borno Empire, Tivland and Igalaland" (68).

More important, the Aba women's riot of 1929 was also recorded in Eastern Nigeria, Achebe's region. One therefore wonders why we could not see the fire of the Aba women's riot in Achebe's women. Chioma Opara also records similar women uprisings that occurred in other parts of Nigeria: "Of worthy significance is the Abeokuta women's protest against colonial taxation in 1949 as well as the Lagos women's protest against the introduction of water rate in 1909" (14).

The recurrent question that comes to mind is: Why are Achebe's female characters so passive and so contented being mere shadows trailing their men? Could Achebe have been possibly influenced by colonialism, having himself imbibed the colonial culture for approximately two decades before his first novel, *Things Fall Apart,* was born in 1958. *Arrow of God,* written in 1964 also tows the same line regarding the passivity of his female characters. Achebe could not have misrepresented the culture he witnessed in the 1950s and 1960s. This brings to mind Helen Chukwuma's often quoted statement in "Flora Nwapa Is Different" on the need to have a balanced portraiture of Nigerian womanhood in Nigerian literature: "the need to realize that the life of the Nigerian woman was not one of smiling and suffering shut away in the back rooms of her husband's Obi, waiting to be summoned at the will of her husband and generally peaceful when not wanted" (115).

Is it possible that Achebe must have therefore recalled the history of the precolonial period and embellished this narrative with characters he created from his experience of the colonial era when the role and status of women had drastically changed? According to Ezeigbo, "From what they used to be in the traditional precolonial society, they (women) plummeted to the subsequent political, cultural and economic powerlessness that was inflicted on them and has remained their lot even till this day. Nigerian women lost all political power and influence under British rule, and their position in the state and home became similar to that of women in Victorian Britain" (68-69).

Ezeigbo further laments that "Women's political organization, especially those in Igboland, became powerless and lost their judicial functions to the native courts which were set up in all the communities. Thus, the machinery which ensured that distribution of power was removed. And women became both politically and economically incapacited" (69). So by the time Achebe wrote his early novels, *Arrow of God* and *Things Fall Apart* women have left the political arena and are only found at homes or at festivals as well decorated objects in their beautiful regalia as demonstrated by the five wives of Nwaka in *Arrow of God.* The author captures the deliberate steps of these women during the festival of the Pumpkin Leaves as those of "an Ijele Mask lifting and lowering each foot with weighty ceremony" (68).

After the ceremony the women are again seen engaged in discussions on domestic issues. They are never seen discussing the bugging issues of the disintegration of their once united communities and the pressures and strains mounted on their culture and religion by the colonial government, personified by the presence of captain Winterbottom, Mr Wright and others. The question again is: Were the women so nonchalant about the presence of white foreigners in their midst that even Ezeulu's grown up daughters, Akueke and Adaeze who were married, and his wives, Matefi and Ugoye, could not ask their father and husband respectively, what the conflicts or problems have been between him (Ezeulu) and the white settlers? Is it possible that Igbo women at this period contributed little or nothing to the political struggle or the development of the political history of this region? Why were they not reflected in such magnificent works as Achebe's *Arrow of God* and *Things Fall Apart*?

Ezeulu's utterances in *Arrow of God* concerning the women are constantly negative and contemptuous. When Obika, his second son, drinks palmwine in excess and sleeps so deeply that he couldn't get up early enough in the morning, Ezeulu castigates him thus: "... A man who was roused in the morning by the women. Tufia! Spat the old priest. He could not contain his disgust" (79). One wonders how the women have become 'non-persons' and so relegated to the mud that even being roused from sleep by a woman is an anathema, a sacrilege and the man in question is made a laughing stock as he loses his respect.

Could this actually be a realistic picture of what was in the late 1920s and 1930s when women were reputed to have wielded so much power? Is it not possible that the Igbo society in the fifties (1950s) and sixties (1960s) had become so saturated with the influence of colonialism that Achebe writing at that time perceived the precolonial period through the lenses of the colonized world?

Molara Ogundipe-Leslie, according to Chioma Opara, has unequivocally asserted that:

> Colonialism has brought out the basic sexist tendencies in precapitalist Africa. It has calcified existing ones and introduced others. It has also thrown in new roles for women, which are creating conflicts since men are

> not yet able to adapt to them nor are they rid of all
> attitudes and expectations. The effect of colonization
> on the total continent has myriad forms (Opara. 13).

Again as Ezeulu advises his young son, Nwafor, about the lessons
of life and people's conduct, because of his disappointment with
his second son, Obika, he intones, "You see what has happened
to your brother. In a few days his bride will come and he will
no longer be called a child. When strangers see him they will no
longer ask 'Whose son is he?' but 'Who is he? Of his wife they
will no longer say 'Whose daughter?' but 'Whose wife?' Do you
understand me?" (93). This tells us that at every stage, a woman is
to be possessed by somebody. She has to be possessed by either a
father or by a husband. Hence she is perpetually owned by a man.
Nobody asks 'Who is she?' as is the case with the man but they
would rather ask 'Whose wife (is she)?"

In line with Achebe's presentation of women and his assignment of roles to them, we are not therefore surprised when 'jealous
Ojiugo' is caught gossiping about Oduche's adventure with the
royal python to Obika's new bride, Okuata, on their way to the
stream. As Ojiugo's words filter into the ears of Oduche who
incidentally is in their midst, he reacts by slapping Ojiugo to the
extent that it results in a fracas. From Achebe's account of the incident, it is obvious that Oduche has the upper hand, as he "replied
with even more fiery slaps and a final vicious blow with his knee
on Ojiugo's belly... But Ojiugo clung to her half brother crying:
'Kill me today. You must kill me. Do you hear me, Eater of python?
You must kill me" (127). We are finally told that "she bit one of
the people trying to hold her back and scratched another" (127).

The image that cuts across to us here is obviously one that
presents women as weak, sharp tongued and those who could
only resort to "biting" and "scratching" in a fight they would
only be thoroughly beaten. Achebe drives home his point when
he describes another female character, Ojinika, in the following
words: "Ojinika, a broad-looking woman who had an old quarrel
with Oyilidie. People said that in spite of Ojinika's tough appearance and the speed with which she flew into quarrels, her strength
was only in her mouth and a child of two could knock her down
with its breath" (128).

One would thus assert that in *Arrow of God*, just as in some of his early novels, Achebe's women seem to be puppets in the hands of the men who actually own, manipulate and put them to use as they (men) deem fit. The women's opinions are never sought. Even when assaulted, they cannot even fight back except 'bite' and 'scratch' their oppressors. Some of them, as presented by Achebe, are talkative and are so weak that they can easily be knocked down by the puff of breath of a two year old. What a woman! Again, in the world of *Arrow of God*, women are completely excluded from politics of the village. They have no influence on their husbands who are active participants in the politics and governance of their people.

The women are regarded with so much contempt that even after Obika returns from Okperi without Ezeulu who has been detained for refusing to respond to captain Winterbottom's call, he tells his people about Ezeulu's situation in Okperi. In anxiety, Ugoye asks a salient question about her husband, Ezeulu. " 'Who gives him food?' "(164). We are perplexed as Obika responds to the men instead of responding to Ugoye, who had posed the question: " 'You remember the son of Nwodika, who brought the white man's first messenger here,' Obika replied, though not to Ugoye but the men...'" (164).

To Obika, Ugoye, his father's young wife, is not worth being addressed in the presence of older and more important people like Akuebue and Anosi who are Ezeulu's friend and neighbour respectively. In other words, a woman could raise an important issue but should not expect to be given any explanations. The explanations must rather be addressed to the respectable men who would understand the situation better than the woman who had raised the issue. What immediately comes to mind is Helen Chukwuma's assertion in "Voices and Choices" on the female character in African fiction (mostly written by men): "In the home, she was not part of the decision making both as a daughter, wife and mother even when the decisions affected her directly. Docility and complete subsumation of will was demanded and enacted from her" (215). It is not therefore surprising when Ezeulu bares his mind to his friend Akuebue on his (Ezeulu's) recollections, as a small boy, of what his father had told him:

> In our custom, a man is not expected to go down on
> his knees and knock his forehead on the ground to his
> wife to ask her forgiveness or beg a favour. But, a wise
> man knows that between him and his wife there may
> arise the need for him to say to her **in secret**: 'I beg
> you.' When such a thing happens nobody else must
> know it, and that woman if she has any sense will never
> boast about it or even open her mouth and speak of
> it. **If she does it, the *earth on which the man brought
> himself low will destroy her entirely*** (My emphasis.
> 172-173).

Here, we are not told what happens to the man if the situation
were reversed. From the foregoing, the man may have need to say,
'I beg you' and it must be in secret. How importunate can any such
culture be. Simple logic dictates that any two intimate persons
should respect each other's privacy where the persons concerned
are responsible and mature. One wonders what makes it imperative on the woman alone to be honourable without which she is
condemned and completely destroyed by the earth, and the same
culture never makes any pronouncement on the male defaulter.
Ezeulu finally caps it all:

> That was what my father told his friend who held that
> a man was never wrong in his own house. I have never
> forgotten those words of my father's. My wife's cock
> belongs to me because the owner of a person is also
> owner of whatever that person has. But there are more
> ways than one of killing a dog (173).

Feminists have constantly protested against this 'ownership' syndrome
in the patriarchal society. As earlier stated in this paper, the woman
is always seen as someone else's property. That is, somebody's mother,
wife, or daughter. Therefore she is constantly under the control of
whoever owns her. In Gloria Chukukere's assertion: "Indeed no
matter the level of education, relations between the husband and wife
are based on an unequal power relation in which the woman expects
orders and gives in return, total obedience. The man's prerogative to
command his wife sometimes leads to physical abuse" (144). Again

the powerlessness and servile posture of the woman in *Arrow of God* brings to mind Zulu Sofola's contention that:

> The first level of damage was done when the female lines of authority and socio-political power were destroyed and completely eliminated by the foreign European/Arabian male centred systems of authority and governance. That was the first death blow to our psyche and the beginning of de-womanization of African womanhood... She became and remained only an extension of her husband, as was/is the case in the western world, and a mere shadow as in Arab culture. Consequently she developed an incurable dependence and inferiority complex.... Gradually, she grew to be irrelevant, ineffective, redundant, and dull, good only as an ornament, a wall flower-if allowed to be by her egocentric almighty husband (61).

The novel generally deals with the phallocentric concerns of a society threatened by the imminence of change. Achebe focuses his perceptive lenses on the patriarchal structure and organigram of the community. The power tussle between the Priest of Ulu in the person of Ezeulu and the Priest of Idemili in the person of Nwaka, becomes the point on which the people of Umuaro are torn apart. Ezeulu's detention in Okperi on Captain Winterbottom's instruction which is carried out by Mr Clarke, becomes the sore point on which Ezeulu bases his retaliatory attack not only on Nwaka but also on the entire people of Umuaro. He sees himself as the 'whip' with which the gods flogged Umuaro for not speaking up when his Chief Priest was unlawfully detained in Okperi for two months. Ezeulu asserts, "The gods sometimes use us as a whip" (208).

Ezeulu's refusal to name the date for the new yam feast causes great hardship for the people of Umuaro (both men and women) who would not harvest their yams if the ceremony had not been performed. Ezeulu too, could not name the date if the remaining sacred yams had not been eaten: "I need not speak in riddles. You all know what our custom is. I only call a new festival when there is only one yam left from the last. Today I have three yams and so I know that time has not come" (207). His subsequent statement puts a final seal on the hope and prayer of the delegates who have come to persuade him to eat the yams and announce the day of the festival. "You have spoken well. But what you ask me to do is not done. Those yams are not food and a man does not eat them because he is hungry. You are asking me to eat death" (207). We are, therefore, not surprised when Ezeulu comes out with the "announcement that his consultation with the deity had produced no result and that the six villages would be locked in the old year for two moons longer..." (210).

Achebe dwells also on other patriarchal issues of the clan such as the details of the carving of masks by Edogo and the different types of masquerades that attend certain occasions such as funerals, new yam festivals and others. *Ogbazulobodo, Udo, Otakaekpeli* and other masquerades are concepts that adorn the cultural life of the people in Achebe's *Arrow of God*.

One wonders whether the story would have ended differently if Achebe had allowed women to be more active in the cultural, sociological and political life of this community. Could Ezeulu have changed his mind on eating up the remaining tubers of yams and named the day of the harvest if he had listened to the voice of reason? That is, if he had softened up to the appeals of his wives, Matefi and Ugoye?. Couldn't these women have been able to persuade their 'loving husband' if they had been close enough?

The tragic end of the novel poses other questions such as: Could the clan/community have provided more succour and encouragement to Ezeulu, in the event of Obika's death if he had eaten the yams and named the day for the harvest? It appears that what gave the crack to Ezeulu's mind had been the circumstances and the mood of the clan before the tragedy occurred. Ezeulu could have borne it if it had come at any other time when there was no strife or tension occasioned by his stubborn refusal to name the Harvest Day in the Community. The entire clan would obviously have shared in bearing the weight of this burden. Ezeulu would not have felt a tinge of humiliation. He thus suffers alone: "It was not simply the blow of Obika's death, great though it was. Men had taken greater blows: that was what made a man a man... At any other time Ezeulu would have been more than a match to his grief. He would have been equal to any pain not compounded with humiliation" (229). Finally, Achebe concludes that, "Perhaps it was the constant, futile throbbing of these thoughts that finally left a crack in Ezeulu's mind" (229).

It is important to note that towards the end of the novel, there is no mention of Obika's new wife, Okuata, who is pregnant and we are not told how she receives the shock of her husband's death, especially when she had earlier cautioned Obika in these prophetic words: " 'Going out with this fever?' she asked. 'Obika have pity on yourself. The funeral is tomorrow. What is there they cannot do without you until morning?'"(224).

Could Achebe have forgotten this woman who carries Obika's baby just before his sudden descent into oblivion? Could Achebe not have cast a pathetic glance on this female character, knowing that the audience would have wished to know how she deals with the shocking news? Is Okuata not important enough to be mentioned even as preparations and arrangements for her husband's burial are being made, as clearly demonstrated in the novel? Not one word about her?

The novel basically is a detailed exploration of a sea of conflicts arising from man's relationship with fellow man and that with his gods. These conflicts also include the inner torments and strife that engage the minds of persons like Ezeulu, the Chief Priest of Ulu, regarding the concerns of the deity and the people of Umuaro as it relates to the clash of culture of these people with the alien culture and administration of the colonialists. All these conflicts centre on the man.

The only conflicts where women are involved are those that occasionally arise, touching on the petty jealousies, rivalries and tantrums among the wives of Ezeulu in their struggle to remain relevant in their husband's world. Thus the women and their actions remain delicately attached to the main issues in the novel. It thus presents a situation, albeit, society where, as earlier mentioned, women are only remembered when they have biological links to the men as their mothers, sisters and daughters or when they, as wives, tag along, like shadows of their men, incognito. Despite all of these observations on the profile and treatment of women in *Arrow of God*, the novel still remains largely an encyclopaedia of some sort on the culture of the Igbo people and their passionate struggle to rescue this culture from the strangulating influence of western norms, values and attitudes.

Works Cited

Achebe, Chinua. *Arrow of God.* London: Heinemann, 1964.

_____. *Things Fall Apart.* London: Heinemann, 1958.

_____. *Home and Exile.* New York: Anchor Books, 2001.

Achebe, Nwando. "Balancing Male and Female Principles: Teaching About Gender in Chinua Achebe's *Things Fall Apart.*" In *UFAHAMU: Journal of African Studies,* Vol. XXIX No. I, 2001-2002 (121-143).

Chukukere, Gloria. "An Appraisal of Feminism in the Socio-Political Development of Nigeria." In *Sisterhood, Feminisms and Power: From Africa to the Diaspora* Ed. Obioma Nnaemeka Trenton NJ: Africa World Press Inc. 1998 (132-148).

Chukwuma, Helen. "Flora Nwapa Is Different." In *Feminism in African Literature: Essays On Criticism* Ed. Helen Chukwuma. Enugu: New Generation Books, 1994 (115-130).

_____. "Voices and Choices: The Feminist Dilemma in Four African Novels." In *Feminism in African Literature: Essays on Criticism* Ed. Helen Chukwuma. Enugu: New Generation Books, 1994 (215-227).

Ezeigbo, Akachi. *Gender Issues in Nigeria: A Feminine Perspective* Lagos: Vista Books Ltd., 1996.

_____. *The Last of the Strong Ones* Lagos: Vista Books, 1996.

Maduka, C.T. "Feminism, Womanism and Motherism in African Literary Discourse" Unpublished Manuscript.

Ojukwu, Chinyelu. "Gender Complementarity in the Anti-Colonial Struggle: Akachi Adimora-Ezeigbo's *The Last of the Strong Ones.*" Paper presented at the 35th Annual African Literature Association Conference, Burlington, Vermont, USA. April 15-19, 2009.

Opara, Chioma. *Her Mother's Daughter: The African Writer As Woman.* Port Harcourt: University of Port Harcourt Press Ltd., 2004.

Sofola, Zulu. "Feminism and African Womanhood." In *Sisterhood, Feminisms and Power: From Africa to the Diaspora.* Ed. Obioma Nnaemeka. Trenton New Jersey: Africa World Press Inc. 1998 (51-64).

CHAPTER 16

MATRIARCHAL PREEMINENCE IN A PATRIARCHAL WORLD: WOMEN AS THE BACKBONE OF TRADITIONAL AFRICAN SOCIETY

Laura Miller

Theoretically considering the importance of the body's structure, the backbone is often under appreciated and unrecog-
nized for its strength, flexibility, and necessity; it keeps the body
erect supporting the body's carriage and frame. When other bones
of the body fracture, they can be mended; thus, new bone forms
to take the place of the frail, inadequate bone structure that once
existed. However, it is the backbone that is beyond repair. When
it is broken, it almost never heals because its precious density, with
all of its strength, is inimitable. As the human body is ill equipped
to reinstate or substitute anything in its place, the African woman
is reminiscent of the human backbone. Like this precious bone, the
African woman is an exceptional, irreplaceable being. As shown in
The Joys of Motherhood and *Things Fall Apart*, through her presence
the radiance of life is exuded; through her absence a permanent
void is impressed upon the hearts of those who will fail to know
the beauty of her soul.

As one author states, "For centuries, African women languished on the fringe of their universe—neglected, exploited, degenerated, and indeed made to feel like outsiders." (Ure Mezu 1). Like the backbone, the African woman's importance is often times not acknowledged until it is missed. However, two authors have displayed how the African woman has gradually risen from her oppression and is now considered too precious to be replaced and too highly valued to be ignored, for it is she who upholds the traditional values of African society. In *The Joys of Motherhood*, Buchi Emecheta, through her feminist voice of protest and commemoration, celebrates the role of African women in the substantiation of Traditional African, Nigerian society and the continuity of its principles. Unlike Emecheta, whether intuitively or not, Achebe's *Things Fall Apart* subtly applauds and acknowledges the African woman's uniqueness and exclusivity. Both authors uncover through their literary expositions how African women surpass the strength of men in medicinal healing for the soul. They are the true guardians and mouthpieces of African religion, and display the ability to govern their households and all other domestic affairs without the assistance, economically or emotionally, of their husbands or male counterparts; in brief, both texts explore the impossibility of ever duplicating an exact replica of strength, tenacity, and virtue: the African woman.

Achebe explores the significance of the woman's place and value as he describes her ability to surpass the efforts of most men in medicinal and curative efforts. He records through his omniscient narrator how Umuofia, a Nigerian village, is feared and respected by all surrounding villages in war efforts because they posses a secret weapon: an elderly woman. He records,

> Its [Umuofia] most potent-war medicine was as old
> as the clan itself. Nobody knew how old. But on one
> point there was general agreement-the active principle
> in that medicine had been an old woman with one leg.
> In fact, the medicine itself was called agadi-nwanyi, or
> old woman (Achebe 11).

It is here that Achebe gives power to the seemingly powerless woman and he subtly acknowledges the true anchor and backbone of this society. The elderly woman serves as a symbol in Achebe's text. The village of Umuofia recognizes their fallibility and ineffectiveness in war and every other venture without acknowledging and conceding that the woman is the core of their existence. The "agadi-nwanyi" (the old woman) is Umuofia's secret weapon because they recognize that their "potent-war weapon" lies in her wisdom which only ripens with her age; it is further significant that the woman introduced in the text is older because it denotes that the clan realizes that experience is also a necessary dynamic to defeating their enemies. The old woman discussed in the text only has one leg and can be seen "hopping about" which, instead of being recognized as a deficiency or encumbrance, actually signifies her strength; it is significant to know that like her one limb she can stand alone with unprecedented respect and verve doing the work of uninjured, strong, able bodied men (Achebe 12). Instead of being the one who must depend on the kindness, courtesy, and strength of others, the masses must depend on her.

Similarly in Achebe's text, there is another reference to the strength and significance of the African woman. Umuike, like Umuofia, recognizes the importance of allowing women to take center stage in their village in order for her strength and wisdom to guide them against hasty decisions and toward prosperity. As villagers discuss the wonderful, successful market in Umuike, Obierika steps forward to enlighten both the other villagers and the audience concerning the key to the market's success. Obierika states,

> It is the result of a great medicine. The people of Umuike wanted their market to grow and swallow up the markets of their neighbors. So they made a powerful medicine...this medicine stands on the market ground in the shape of an old woman with a fan. With this magic fan she beckons to market all the neighboring clans (Achebe 113).

There is no power in the medicine itself; rather, it is placed on top of the sculpted woman so that it may breathe in the strength and unsurpassed value that the woman has, which in turn, impresses the same prosperity upon the market. Hence, it is Umuike's desire for both the medicine and the market to possess the woman's comeliness, ascendancy, and incomparability. Without the statue, the medicine alone retains no power; it is only when it is allowed to take in the character and essence of a woman that it becomes potent beyond measure.

The religious reverence and admiration that women command is also evident in Achebe's text. Not surprisingly, it is again the women who are at the forefront and in command of traditional African society. In the time of generations past in Umuofia, the oracle communicates through a woman, Chika, and it is under her authority that religious deeds are carried out, halted, or reinvented. The text records,

> No one had ever beheld Agbala, except his priestess…
> His priestess stood by the sacred fire which she built
> in the heart of the cave and proclaimed the will of the
> god. The fire did not burn with a flame. The glowing
> logs only served to light up vaguely the dark figure of
> a priestess…She was…greatly feared (Achebe 16,17).

Although Chika is the priestess presenting the commands of another being, she is still in a position of authority and control. Chika, a woman, is the only living human being to ever behold the oracle; this is proof of matriarchal preeminence in African society. Why does the oracle choose to fill this position with a woman instead of a man in what is deemed a patriarchal society? Her quiet strength and denouncement of the need to be immortalized makes her the ideal spokesman; she will consider the village and its well being, even it means disregarding her pride and influence. Like the fire that glows in the oracle's cave, it is the woman's glowing warmth that must permeate the village to sustain its life and continuity. The fire does not burn for warmth itself; rather, its sole purpose is to emphasize and accentuate the priestess because she is representative of the need for the importance of a woman's role to be understood and appreciated.

Likewise, the audience is presented with yet another example of the preeminence of women in *Things Fall Apart*. Just as a woman is chosen to communicate to past generations in Umuofia, a woman is also chosen to be the spokesperson for the present generation in the village. Achebe's passage reads: "Chielo…was the priestess of Agbala, the Oracle of the Hills and the Caves. Anyone seeing Chielo in ordinary life would hardly believe she was the same person who prophesized when the spirit of Agbala was upon her" (Achebe 48, 49). Chielo did not need a spirit to come upon her. Her mysterious role as priestess does not overtake her normal behavior, but it is the norm. There is a parallel between her concealed greatness and the larger community's attitude. The woman's inconspicuous greatness is overlooked until the spectacular and unfathomable is needed or occurs. As one scholar details, "The... women respected in Umuofia are those like Chielo, the priestess of the Oracle of the Hills and Caves, who is removed from the pale of normalcy. Clothed in the mystic mantle of the divinity she serves, Chielo transforms from the ordinary" (Ure Mezu 1). The oracle's decision to choose a woman over a man speaks volumes about the African society. Men have only implied roles, roles in which they can often be seen and thus they appear to the naked eye to be in control. It is analogous to a theatrical production; the actors are fed their lines and may even possess the talent for engaging audiences, but it is the team of writers, producers, and directors responsible for creating a plausible, dramatic story line with several true to life acts and scenes. Meanwhile, the audience has little to no idea about the amount of effort it takes to decipher script after script to produce a wonderful work of art. Likewise, it is the woman who is behind the scenes directing and redirecting, editing and previewing making sure that all goes well in her household and in the general societal framework; she is the one who must decipher and make malleable the many rough edges in the drama of life. What the African society sees is the script that African males are following due to the encouragement from their wives. They never see the toil and anguish that African woman must suffer through.

Similarly, Emecheta explores the prominence and the need for women in African society though her exploration of the demands and seemingly menial rewards that motherhood offers. One scholar states, "All of Emecheta's novels expound upon 'the theme of female oppression... the archetypal African woman buried alive under the heavy yoke of traditional mores and customs'" (Ogunyemi qtd in Ure Mezu 3). In the novel, African women are not oppressed physically, but socially as men often attempt to intimidate them into keeping tradition. Initially, Emecheta discusses the woman's role in governing all household affairs in both the presence and absence of men. Nnu Ego, the protagonist and Cordelia, her friend discuss how the African men have been emasculated due to changes in the job market resulting from the colonization of Nigeria. They state,

> We women mind the home. Not our husbands. Their
> manhood has been taken away from them. The shame
> of it is that they don't know it. All they see is the money,
> shining white man's money...these our husbands are
> like slaves, don't you think? (Achebe 51).

The men in Lagos no longer view it necessary to maintain the traditional, masculine roles of farmers, warriors, wrestlers, and overseers of their families; they view their introduction into the world of the white man, undertaking however menial a task, at their arrival and introduction into manhood and urban society. They are stripped of their manhood because they are not courageous enough to resist the changes that distance them from their familial and ancestral responsibilities. Both Nnu Ego and Cordelia are accurate in their statements; the African men are unaware that they are losing their manhood because the money that the colonizers offer has clouded their judgment serving as a diversion to prevent the discovery of the colonizers' actual plan: the destruction of traditional African society. As one critic notes, "The Ibo women of Emecheta's novel find themselves...subjected to new forms of exploitation as they are asked to assume traditional duties and responsibilities under a newly imported economic system" (Derrickson 2). As the men are stripped of their manhood, the women must undertake yet another economic and social burden. They must in some way seek to give esteem back to their emasculated men, while overtaking the role of the men, and still fulfilling their own. Emecheta embeds an example in her text of the dangers of colonization in Lagos and how the women have an added burden. She writes,

> In Lagos, a wife...had to work. She provided the food
> from her husband's meager housekeeping money, but
> finding the money for clothes, for any kind of com-

forts, in some cases for the children's school fees, was
on her shoulders...They stopped being men long ago.
Now they are machines (Emecheta 52, 53).

In Lagos, women are required to make up for the deficiencies of
urban men. "... Many traditional African customs and mores are
worth preserving, most African feminists espouse womanism,
which Alice Walker defines as a philosophy that celebrates black
roots, the ideals of black life, while giving a balanced presentation of black womanhood ..." (Ure Mezu 4). It is on the woman's
shoulders to make home a comfort and safe haven for her family
and children even when the outside world is being sabotaged and
torn apart; she must be the glue which holds the center of Africa,
the family, together. Even men outside of the family in the larger
community of Lagos are made to recognize the woman's strength
and endurance. When Nnaife arrives home from war, even his
friends must acknowledge Nnu Ego's tenacity. The omniscient
narrator records, "Then Ubani shouted in joke, "'My friend, Nnu
Ego behaved very well during your absence, you know. She fought
the war here too in your family" (Achebe 183). Though Ubani
speaks in the form of a joke, his insight is far from humorous; it
is realistic. The war that raged inside of Nnu Ego's home formed
from her children being in constant want. She warred against her
own will and physical exhaustion to see that her children were fed,
clothed, and educated. Like the war Nnaife participates in, Nnu
Ego is triumphant and eventually wins; though she is stifled and
like Nnaife is captured and forced to participate in this war of want,
she tearfully, but faithfully undertakes the duties of a combatant
pressing forward to provide for her children under the most acute
circumstances. Similarly, in the courtroom scene Nnu Ego must
try to defend her husband and his "traditional" principles as he
attempts to take the life of a Yoruba man to defend his daughters
honor. Emecheta records, "Nnu Ego nodded, not knowing that
with that one nod, she had nailed the last nail in Nnaife's coffin. It
became clear that she was doing nearly all the providing and
that when Nnaife was away in the army for four years, she had only
received two allowances even though she then had five children
to look after" (Achebe 217). It is significant that this scene takes
place before a courtroom of observers; they are representative of

the entire collective body of patriarchal African society. It is before this body of observers that Nnu Ego serves as the silent spokesperson for the African woman. Before this crowd of observers on the witness stand, she exposes how Nnaife and other men are only physical deterrents attempting to distract attention from the enormity of the female role; it is finally clear to the African male that the woman is the moral fiber and the sole possessor of the mental and physical fortitude needed: their vertebral column of support. In fact one critic states that "... Emecheta's main thesis [is] that women have to struggle to succeed in an exploitative patriarchal society" (Prono 1). In this struggle the women finally win.

Emecheta provides yet another example of the role that women must play in carrying out tradition in a world surrounding them that is gradually progressing toward urbanization. As Nnu Ego ponders her present state the narrator records her thinking the following,

> She might not have any money to supplement her husband's income, but were they not in a white man's world where it was the duty of the father to provide for his family? In Ibuza, women made a contribution, but in urban Lagos, men had to be the sole providers; this new setting robbed the woman of her useful role...she had been trying to be traditional in a modern urban setting (Emecheta 81).

Nnu Ego in the aforementioned dialogue is demoralized by the fear that she will have nothing to contribute to her family in Lagos. Unknowingly, Nnu Ego actually does maintain her traditional values in a modern setting because she provides for her family when her husband refuses to provide. Nnaife, her husband, actually uses urbanization as an excuse to flaunt his "power." He attempts to lord over his family because he is thirsty for the power he has lost. He is contrasted with Nnu Ego has. She realizes that one can be traditional in an urban setting by refusing to compromise one's dignity by conforming to degrading tasks such as being a "man who washes women's underwear" (Achebe 49). Lagos is not urban at all; the demands are even greater on a woman in Lagos than in Ibuza. It is Nnu Ego who must arrive early in the morning at the market to ensure that she has the best place to sell; it is Nnu Ego who must scout for cigarettes to resale for a profit; it is Nnu Ego who must struggle with the decision to keep her young daughters from school because she can only afford to send her sons. Lagos is more stressful and more demanding than Abuja. Upon this realization, Nnu Ego begins to feel that she is a prisoner held in servitude by her desire for tradition and her love for her children. Emecheta records, "On her way back to their room, it occurred to Nnu Ego that she was a prisoner, imprisoned by her love for her children....It was not fair, she felt, the way men cleverly used a woman's sense of responsibility to actually enslave her." (Emecheta 137). Nnu Ego realizes that the men in Lagos actually use her sense of responsibility and duty to force her into the roles that they have predestined for her to follow; the men depend upon the virtue, love, and sense of duty that the woman has to keep her subdued and committed to her family even when the men remain uncommitted. What the men fail to realize is that the African woman, regardless of the ascending struggles that she must face, does not need to be cleverly pressed into her role as provider. Instead, she will undertake it cheerfully even though for her it will provide no cheer. The yam is a perfect example of the woman's role that must be undertaken. Nigerian women pound yam into meals for their families; like the yam, the woman is often trodden upon and compressed by a culture and society of people who under appreciate her. In the traditional Nigerian household, the mother trains her daughters to pound yam. She must prime and prepare her daughters to understand that although they are the sacrificial strongholds of society and their homes, they will often be undervalued.

Both Emecheta and Achebe successfully portray to their respective audiences the importance of the woman's role. Emecheta uses her feminist voice to celebrate the African woman and her quest in the substantiation of Traditional African, Nigerian society; Achebe applauds the African woman's exceptionality and distinctness. As The Center for Cultural Studies notes, the African community of women are, "mothers, healers, and writers centered in the image of co-wives with an absent husband" (Haraway). Nnu Ego ushers in a light of truth when she asks herself, "When will I be free? Never, not even in death. Until we can change all this, it is still a man's world, which women will always help to build" (Emechata 187). While Nnu Ego is downtrodden by the supposed domination of the men around her who build platforms for themselves off the bent backs of women, she can glory in the fact that the structural foundation of a building is more important than the building itself. If the structure fails or shifts, the entire building crumbles. Women are the foundational structure of African society upon which their children and husbands build. Both texts prove that the African woman has clothed herself with mold of invicibility; in turn, however, the mold has been broken so that no other will ever be precisely like her.

Works Cited

Achebe, Chinua. *Things Fall Apart*. Knopf Doubleday Publishing: 1994. Print.

Derrickson, Teresa. "Class, Culture, and the Colonial Context: the Status of Women in Buchi Emecheta's *The Joys of Motherhood*." *International Fiction Review*. Web. January 2002.

Emecheta, Buchi. *The Joys of Motherhood*. Oxford: Heinemann, 1994. Print.

Haraway, Donna. "Reading Buchi Emecheta: Contests for Women's Experience in Women's Studies." *Women: A Cultural Review* 1.3 (1990) 240-55. Web.

McLean, Patricia. "How Buchi Emecheta's *The Joys of Motherhood* Resists Feminist and Nationalist Readings." *Womanist Theory and Research*. Institute for African-American Studies. Web. Athens: Georgia, 2003.

Prono, Luca. "Buchi Emechetta." Oxford: Heinemann Educational Publishers, 2004. Web.

Ure Mezu, Rose. "Women in Achebe's World: The Absence of a Moderating Female Principle, Achebe's Progressive Vision of Women, Womanism, and Modern African Women." Baltimore: Morgan State University Press, 1995. Web.

CHAPTER 17

INDIVIDUALISM AND THE PULL OF TRADITION IN *THINGS FALL APART* AND *THE JOYS OF MOTHERHOOD*

Paula T. Wingard

Cross cultural reading serves a dual purpose. It exposes and interprets misreading and prejudices through self-reflective experience. With the case of Chinua Achebe's *Things Fall Apart* and Buchi Emecheta's *The Joys of Motherhood*, the western reader confronts cultural domination and dogmatism of the African culture. In other words, the African novel alleviates the tendencies to justify the misconception of African culture as seen in western media and literature. Examining these novels using postcolonial theory brings the significance of cultural identity and colonial rule to the attention of the reader, as he compares what he thinks of African culture and what he now knows of African culture. Postcolonial theory deals with otherness, the way dominant culture views non-dominant culture. The view of the non-dominant culture is usually skewed by physical and social differences, created by binary oppositions and the Colonizer's destiny to rule. As seen in both novels, the protagonists Okonkwo and Nnu Ego are stripped of their identity, their traditions, their culture and their way of life for their "betterment". In *Things Fall Apart* and *The Joys of Motherhood*, Achebe and Emecheta illustrate how one's inability to accept and adapt to change prevents self, community, and cultural progression.

In *Things Fall Apart*, the pull of tradition causes internal conflict within the protagonist Okonkwo. In Joko Sengova's "Native Identity and Alienation, Richard Wright's *Native Son* and Chinua Achebe's *Things Fall Apart*", he explains how Okonkwo's steadfastness in tradition blinds his rationality and ultimately leads to his demise. Furthermore, Sengova explains how Okonkwo's character represents resistance against colonial rule and Christianity:

> The hero of the novel, Okonkwo of Umuofia village, offers the central challenge to the new European politics and religion, since he champions traditional African Igbo customs and values.
>
> He lives within his community and runs his family exclusively on those precepts. Anything outside the axioms and accepted ways of his native traditions, especially its oracular precepts, is absolutely unacceptable to him.

Okonkwo's allegiance to his tradition is perhaps both brave and foolish. Brave, because he is willing to sacrifice everything, in order to sustain what he feels to be right. Foolish, because his bravery is inspired by fear of failure and weakness. Sengova notes that Okonkwo's "fear of falling prey to the things he views as undesirable in men constantly haunts him. Ironically, in order to avoid such a fall, he conducts himself through a channeled course of self-destruction and tragedy."

Within the novel, Achebe foreshadows Okonkwo's demise via fear of failure and weakness. Okonkwo is determined not to be like his father. It controls his life so much so, that it dictates how he raises his sons and how he treats his wives. The reader detects early in the novel that the only emotion Okonkwo is capable of expressing is anger. "Okonkwo never showed any emotion openly, unless it be the emotion of anger. To show emotion was a sign of weakness, the only thing worth demonstrating was strength" (Achebe 20).

Achebe also reveals how Okonkwo's internal conflict is tied to the already existing conflict within his village before colonization. Therefore, even the "rightfulness" of tradition is questioned. It is tradition for men of the Umuofia village to exert strength at all costs, to be warriors, and rulers of men. Many of the men in Okonkwo's village made it their goal to be great men of the council and leaders of the clan. One's lineage determined one's name and inheritance. However, Okonkwo's father was known as a "woman" weak and irresponsible. Early in Part One, Achebe notes Okonkwo's resentment and hate toward his father as his ultimate weakness. His impulsive behavior is seen in the following passage within the novel:

> Perhaps down in his heart Okonkwo was not a cruel man. But his whole life was dominated by fear, the fear of failure and weakness …It was not external but lay deep within himself. It was the fear of himself lest he should be found to resemble his father-- a playmate had told him that his father was agabala--another name for a woman--also a man who had taken no title. And so Okonkwo was ruled by one passion--to hate everything that his father Unoka had loved. One of those things was gentleness and another was idleness (9-10).

In all of Okonkwo's attempts to avoid failure and weakness, he inevitably walks into a trap, blinded by his stubborn self will and the pull of tradition.

Sengova notes that the thematic structure of Okonkwo's character in *Things Fall Apart* can be based upon three concepts: "Fear," "Flight," and "Fate." First, the ritualistic killing of Ikemefuna, surrendered to Umuofia by the neighboring village of Mbiano, in exchange for the murder of "a daughter of Umuofia." Secondly, the murder of Ezeudu, and thirdly, the murder of the white district commissioner's court messenger. Thus, Sengova asserts that "all three murders are thematically charged with motifs parallel with the three concepts: Fear, Flight and Fate." Perhaps Okonkwo is glued so much to his tradition, that he has no individuality. He has no identity separate from his clan, their principles, and their expectations. Although colonialism is bias as it seeks to assimilate and "cleanse" one's culture of ungodliness and bring forth "civilization," Okonkwo could have found other options than suicide, which ironically is dishonorable in his culture. His chances for over throwing the white man's rule were slim, but he could have found some sort of inner peace in adapting or adjusting to his new environment. As the biblical saying goes, one cannot put new wine in old wine skins. In Okonkwo's case, one cannot put old wine in new wine skins. Okonkwo tried to bring his tradition in a new environment.

Sengova insists that "Okonkwo's flight is supernaturally ordained by the putative spirituality of the earth goddess, Ani". The clan makes an effort to cleanse the land that Okonkwo has polluted with the blood of a clansman. "Once Okonkwo is pronounced an exile, his own "Fate" is sealed in the hands of the very tradition he fosters." This is seen in the novel when Okonkwo's possessions are destroyed and he is banished from the clan for seven years for murder:

> They set fire to his houses, demolished his red walls, killed his animals and destroyed his barn. It was the justice of the earth goddess, and they were merely her messengers. They had no hatred in their hearts against Okonkwo. His greatest friend, Obierika, was among them. They were merely cleansing the land whick Okonkwo had polluted with the blood of a clansman (87).

Okonkwo commits another sin against the earth goddess Ani, when he commits suicide and desecrates the land. One of the men in Okonkwo's village explains to the District Commissioner that "it is against our custom. It is an abomination for a man to take his own life. It is an offense against the Earth, and a man who commits it will not be buried by his clansmen. His body is evil, and only strangers may touch it" (Achebe147). Finally, the reader can identify that it wasn't so much colonization that causes Okonkwo's demise. It is, rather, his stubbornness and self-destruction via fear of failure and weakness. Also, the reader cannot negate the pull of tradition and its ability in stagnating self, community, and cultural progression within the novel. However, Achebe allows Okonkwo's dear friend Obierka to blame the District Commissioner (colonization) for Okonkwo's death: "That man was one of the greatest men in Umuofia. You drove him to kill himself; and now he will be buried like a dog..." (Achebe 147).

In *The Joys of Motherhood* Nnu Ego is just as self-destructive as Okonkwo. She literally sacrifices her well-being in pursuit of motherhood and cultural acceptance. In Salome C. Nnoromele's *Representing the African Woman*, she examines Nnu Ego's character and its relation to identity, tradition and motherhood:

> *The Joys of Motherhood* is simply the story of a woman who makes devastating choices and sacrifices her health and selfhood in the pursuit of failed traditions, capsulated in the idea of motherhood. I see Nnu Ego not as an object on which society heaps its "unfair" practices and demands, but as subject of her own actions, as an active determinant of her own destiny (183).

Like Okonkwo, Nnu Ego struggles to find balance between tradition and new environment. She also expects to put old wine in new skins. After her first marriage, she expects her second husband to not only accept her tradition but to conform to it as well. Although Nnu Ego environment changes, her obsession with self-actualization through motherhood does not change. Nnoromele explains Nnu Ego's struggle between her two worlds:

> It has been said that Nnu Ego's sense of disequilibrium is the result of the contrasts between two worlds in conflicts. The old world, represented by the village life in Ibuza, was one in which men romanced their wives, women supported their families through farming, family ties were strong and emotional, and financial support was abundant. The new world represented by life in Lagos is bewildering and tiring. There is no room for extended family support, no land to be owned or cultivated, and women have to enter the world of trade to find money (183).

Nnu Ego's character represents the pull of tradition in that Nnu Ego seeks self-fulfillment through motherhood, a traditional and cultural belief. "She had a singleness of purpose...wanting one thing at a time and wanting it badly (Emecheta 36). And the one thing Nnu Ego wanted "badly" was motherhood" (Nnoromele 183). Instead of adjusting to her new marriage and new environment, Nnu Ego is distracted by her obsession with motherhood. She is eventually coerced into learning a trade, and becoming a provider for her family but her new found motivation is short lived. "To survive in her world, Nnu Ego must acquire foresight, self-reliance, creativity, and flexibility to adapt to changing realities. These are the real tests for Nnu Ego, and she fails all of them as she clings to failed institutions and beliefs" (Nnoromele 184).

When comparing Nnu Ego and the other women in the novel, the reader must evaluate Nnu Ego's sense of self versus those of other women around her. "The women realize that a woman without her own economic power is not free, and they attempt to teach Nnu Ego that a mother who cannot provide for her own children, however doting she might be, is no mother at all" (Nnoromele 186-7). Nnoromele further notes on Nnu Ego's lack of consciousness and identity throughout the novel:

> Although Nnu Ego's consciousness and point of view dominate the novel, Emecheta provides the reader with other ways of seeing Nnu Ego by juxtaposing her ideology of self with those of other women around her, specifically her mother, Ona her co-wife, Adaku, and the collective voices of the community women. These women make choices different from Nnu Ego's. Like her, they grew up in the so-called patriarchal society. But unlike her, they have enough foresight and self-realization to know that life is much more than following traditions and doing what is expected of one (184).

Nnu Ego's demise was self-inflicting as seen clearly in comparison to those of other women within the novel. Nnu Ego seems even more different in comparison to her mother, Ona. Ona's desire for Nnu Ego was for her to master her own identity, independent of marriage or motherhood. According to Nnoromele, Nnu Ego is the direct opposite of Ona in her definition of womanhood:

> Ona's idea of womanhood runs counter to the general notion that African women equate womanhood or selfhood with motherhood. Ona wants Nnu Ego to be the master of her own fate, the subject of her actions rather than an object of other people's actions and decisions. This, to Ona, is what it means to be a woman, to be one's own self (185).

Along with the pull of tradition and the lack of identity, Nnu Ego is mentally unstable. "Failure to change with the times, to adapt psychologically, and to make tangible plans for the future is a form of madness" (Nnoromele 187). Perhaps, then, Okonkwo is also mad because he cannot adapt to his new environment. However, Okonkwo cannot adapt to his new environment because he refuses to. Nnu Ego, on the other hand simply cannot; it is not her stubborn will that prevents her but her somewhat unconscious obsession with motherhood. Within the novel, Nnu Ego's friend Ato tries to forewarn her concerning her reputation:

> You know what people will say…You know the beautiful daughter of Agdadi, the one his mistress had for him, the one who had a slave one as her chi, the one who tried to steal her mate's child, the one who tried to kill herself and failed on purpose so as to get sympathy--well, she is now completely mad (Emecheta 74).

Nnu Ego eventually dies, as her senses start to give way. She never finds the fulfillment she is searching for throughout the novel. Overwhelmed by circumstances, Nnu Ego "lays down by the roadside, thinking that she had arrived home. She died quietly there, with no child to hold her hand and no friend to talk to her (Emecheta 224).

As it relates to the ironic title of the novel, Emecheta proves through Nnu Ego's character that "there is no joy to life or motherhood for a woman who chooses to live an isolated, anachronistic life in a changing world. Having lived through such a life, Nnu Ego knows that motherhood does not always bring happiness and that, ultimately, women have the right to choose their own destiny. A woman must learn to be fulfilled in herself" (Nnoromele 188-9).

In conclusion, *Things Fall Apart* and *The Joys of Motherhood* illustrate how the inability to change and adapt prevents self, community, and cultural progression. Okonkwo and Nnu Ego could have lived a more fulfilling life had they sought self-actualization outside their culture and tradition. It is difficult to justify tradition when one's cultural practices are as destructive as the injustice inflicted by the colonizer. As seen in both characters, their destruction is self-inflicted and tragic. Nnu Ego and Okonkwo's fate make them tragic heroes as their visible strengths become a silhouette of their internal conflicts. These novels not only give insight to African culture and tradition, but they also show the effects of colonialism on non-westernized culture. Achebe and Emecheta do not seek to illustrate colonization as evil. However, both authors prove that one's identity cannot be tied to one's tradition or their changing environment. Instead, the search for identity should begin within ones' self.

Works Cited

Achebe, Chinua. *Things Fall Apart*. New York: Anchor Books, 1994.

Emecheta, Buchi. *The Joys of Motherhood*. Heinemann, 1994.

Nnoromele, Salome C. "Representing the African Woman: Subjectivity and Self in *The Joys of Motherhood*." Critique 00111619. 43.2 (2002): 178-191. Academic Search Premier. EBSCO. Jackson State U Lib. 29 Nov. 2008.

Sengova, Joko. "Native Identity and Alienation in Richard Wright's *Native Son* and Chinua Achebe's *Things Fall Apart*: A Cross-Cultural Analysis." *The Mississippi Quarterly* 50 (1997). 327-51. WILSON WEB. Jackson State U Lib. 29 Nov. 2008.

CHAPTER 18

PORTRAYAL OF WOMANHOOD IN ACHEBE'S *THINGS FALL APART* AND EZEIGBO'S *THE LAST OF THE STRONG ONES*

Blessing Diala-Ogamba

Chinua Achebe's *Things Fall Apart* is a novel that has withstood the test of time with its varied themes such as culture conflict, transliteration, and power consciousness. In this work, Achebe looks at women from the cultural perspective showing male chauvinism in a patriarchal society. His women are relegated to the background except in the case of Chielo the priestess of Agbala. Women's roles are restricted to domestic affairs and their opinions in the affairs of the society are not sought. This is a strategy to keep the position of the men intact as heads of households, but the Umuofia society does not believe in the maltreatment of women because women are regarded as weak. Ezeigbo on the other hand shows that women have always been recognized by their male counterparts at different levels in the traditional Igbo society as pointed out by Chukwuma, Adesina, Anderson and Zinsser, and other feminist critics and writers such as Sembene Ousmane and

Nuruddin Farah. For Ezeigbo, women contribute in meaningful ways in the affairs of the society just as men. Ezeigbo shows these different levels of recognition and contribution of women in the society in her work *The Last of the Strong Ones*. Both novels explore the different ways women are portrayed in Igbo society.

Women have not always been marginalized in most African societies as presented by some writers such as in Elechi Amadi's *The Concubine*, Ngugi Wa Thiongo's *Petals of Blood*, Flora Nwapa's *Efuru* and *Idu*, Buch Emecheta's *Second Class Citizen*. According to Diala-Ogamba, "several years ago women were respected in some parts of Africa especially in matrilineal societies. Some of these women have been politically and socially active in colonial and pre-colonial Africa" (285). Mary Kolawole traces the history of some of these powerful women who have been able to assert themselves from the Maghreb region in North Africa to Northern Nigeria revealing records of women rulers as early as 9th century (44-5). Achebe's *Things Fall Apart* is set between 1850 and 1900, the period just before the arrival of the missionaries in Umuofia. Okonkwo, the protagonist is introduced to us as a young wrestler. He later becomes a renowned warrior and a wealthy man who is also very influential in his society in Umuofia. He is one of the King makers revered by his people. Okonkwo comes from a very poor background with a father, Unoka, who is a musician, a debtor and a loafer. Not much is said about his mother probably because she dies when Okonkwo is at a young age. The only time Okonkwo remembers her is when he has sleepless nights after the killing of Ikemefuna. He reminisces on the stories she tells him about "the mosquito and the ear" which he brushes aside as women's stories. Jeyifo relates the position of mosquito in this story to "the male's neurotic fear of the female power as the nemesis of male impotence and life force" (185).

Achebe reinforces the lack of identity and invincibility accorded to women in Umuofia when Okonkwo's mother is portrayed nameless. This means that she has no identity in a man's world. Okonkwo's first wife is also nameless, but goes by his son's name, "Nwoye's mother". We should note that this is a patriarchal society where only the achievement of the men counts, therefore men like Unoka are regarded as worthless, or "efulefu", another name used to refer to "women" which means, weak. As worthless as Unoka is, he has a name. Since Okonkwo's father is a loafer, the burden of raising Okonkwo and his siblings falls on his mother. His mother being strong and quietly astute is able to raise a strong man like Okonkwo before she dies. According to Jeyifo, "the single, brief mention of Okonkwo's mother is extraordinarily suggestive both for reading Okonkwo's particular brand of misogyny and neurotic masculinist personality and for analyzing larger questions of the author's construction of male subjectivity and identity in the novel" (182). Not much is also said about his first wife, but she is there as a role model to the younger wives.

Ekwefi is Okonkwo's second wife who has the courage to leave her husband for Okonkwo who she truly loves, but the courage she exhibits in running away to Okonkwo is treated as a minor issue in the text.

> She had married Anene because Okonkwo was too poor then to marry. Two years after her marriage to Anene she could bear it no longer and she ran away to Okonkwo. It had been early in the morning. The moon was shinning. She was going to the stream to fetch water. Okonkwo's house was on the way to the stream. She went in and knocked at his door and he came out. Even in those days he was not a man of many words. He just carried her into his bed and in the darkness began to feel around her waist for the loose end of her cloth" (Achebe 109).

If Ekwefi does not possess strength of character and courage, she may not be able to run to Okonkwo. Her running away proves that she can be more independent if given the chance, and this is exactly what the patriarchal society is afraid of. Ojiugo, Okonkwo's third wife shows some signs of rebelliousness by going to plait her hair without first preparing meals for Okonkwo and her children. Her mind is first set on making herself beautiful for Obierika's daughter's wedding, because she may not have the time to make her hair the next day. Even though she lives in perpetual fear of her husband, it does not stop her from indulging herself.

Okonkwo attempts to shoot Ekwefi during the harvest season when people are supposed to be relaxing. Okonkwo being restless as usual tries to find fault with the person who cuts the banana leaves in his compound. By beating Ekwefi he breaks the law of the land and is made to pay a fine for it. Okonkwo commits another crime against the Earth goddess by beating Ojiugo his third wife for not preparing his evening meal before going to make her hair. This time is the "Week of Peace" when the law of the land forbids any form of violence. Because Okonkwo thinks that it is the duty of a wife to do the cooking, his impatience does not give room for any form consideration, thus the beating. In his heart, he wants to teach Ojiugo a lesson, but according to the law of his society, he is at fault and must pay for the crime.

Because the Umuofia society regards women as weak, they ultimately delegate crops like "cocoyam" as women's crops. To the men, the cocoyam is easy to plant, while "yam" is regarded as the "king of all crops" or men's crop. Umuofia is a society that reveres strong and influential men, warriors, brave men and title holders. There is no room for weak men in the society, no wonder Achebe's focus in this novel is on men and their achievements, the wars fought with the number of heads brought back to the village, the title holders and the number women taken as wives. Women and children are almost placed in the same category, except for Chielo, the priestess of Agbala.

Achebe's women in *Things Fall Apart* are generally relegated to the background; however, they are a force to be reckoned with. In view of the fact that their duties are house chores, having babies and cooking for their husbands, they are actually the foundation of Umuofia society as evidenced in the text. Achebe's women are not victimized or oppressed, but they are not given masculine roles to play. Achebe portrays the women in this text as emotionally and physically weak; he therefore assigns them feminine roles that mostly have to do with nurturing of children and husbands thereby exposing them as compassionate human beings. The women are portrayed as soft, but behind these cosmetic features are very strong-willed beings.

Later in the novel, we notice more that the community reveres women when a case of spousal abuse is brought to the leaders of

Umuofia, and the leader of the egwugwu known as the Evil Forest tells Uzowulu: "Go to your in-laws with a pot of wine and beg your wife to return to you. It is not bravery when a man fights with a woman" (93). To Mgbafor's brother, Odukwe, the Evil Forest says: "If your in-law brings wine to you, let your sister go with him" (93). With this instruction, the case is closed and no one goes against the authority of the egwugwu. When Okonkwo accidentally kills Ezeudo's son, he goes on exile to his maternal home because as his uncle reminds him, "mother is supreme". We notice that Okonkwo is depressed when he is on exile at Mbanta, his mother's land. His uncle, Uchendu, encourages Okonkwo to relax by explaining the importance of motherhood to him. He says:

> It's true that a child belongs to its father. But when a father beats his child, it seeks sympathy in its mother's hut. A man belongs to this fatherland when things are good and life is sweet. But when there is sorrow and bitterness he finds refuge in his motherland. Your mother is there to protect you. She is buried there. And that is why we say that mother is supreme. Is it right that you, Okonkwo, should bring to your mother a heavy face and refuse to be comforted? Be careful or you may displease the dead (Achebe 134).

With this admonition, Okonkwo tries to relax while making big plans for his return to Umuofia.

In another instance, Chielo, a widow with two children is the priestess of Agbala, the Oracle of the Hills and Caves. She is an ordinary woman when she is not possessed by the spirit of Agbala. She dares Okonkwo to follow her when she takes Ezinma to the shrine of Agbala without explaining the reason to Okonkwo and his family. Even when Okonkwo pleads with her to wait till morning because Ezinma his favorite daughter has been sick, she refuses to listen and swiftly lifts the girl from her bed. In her frenzy, she senses that people are following her and curses them. Okonkwo retreats a little bit, before following her again. At the shrine, Okonkwo is surprised to see that Ekwefi also follows them. Okonkwo at this time cannot challenge Chielo, because her position demonstrates the hierarchy and power she wields within the society.

Another power attributed to women is to Ani, the Earth goddess. Ani is the ruler of the earth. Okonkwo commits a number of crimes against the earth goddess and each time, he is punished for the crime. Most of the time, he commits these crimes out of fear and overzealousness such as in the killing of Ikemefuna. Ani is a deity of power and authority and is able to subdue a fierce man like Okonkwo. Okonkwo breaks the law of the land by attempting to shoot his second wife Ekwefi during the harvest season for plucking some banana leaves and making comments about guns that never shoot. He is made to pay some penalties to pacify the earth goddess. In the beating of Ojiugo during the Week of Peace, he is also made to pay some penalties to pacify the earth goddess. The killing of Ezeudu's son is another crime Okonkwo commits. Because the crime is inadvertent, it is regarded as a "female ochu", a female crime which does not carry heavy penalty. "It was a crime against earth goddess to kill a clansman, and a man who committed it must flee from the land. The crime was of two kinds, male and female. Okonkwo had committed the female, because it had been inadvertent. He could return to the clan after seven years" (Achebe 124). Ani, the earth goddess is revered in the society because without her, the harvest would be very scanty. Alagoa observes that "a man normally obtained his birthright through the status of the mother.... In the religious sphere, the supreme being or God was a woman, a mother" (27). Women are compassionate in a variety of ways and motherhood is extremely supreme and cannot be taken lightly.

In Ezeigbo's *The Last of the Strong Ones*, she portrays women differently, but positively. Her intention is to show that women have always been regarded highly in Igbo society, therefore her story revolves around bringing out the events where women play active roles to the benefit of the society. Theodora Ezeigbo explores the rich cultural heritage of Umuga community and the threat of change due to governmental set up. The people decide to fight the disruption and destabilization of their cultural norms. The type of change the community expects is portrayed through an authorial intrusion:

> Change by itself is not a threat. But what lay heavy on
> our soul was the nature of the change sweeping through

the land, like rain-bearing winds. Positive change is
creative and constructive; it is not seen as disruptive.
But the manner of change in Umuga was not positive.
For many moons, I meditated on the nature of change
in the lives of our people. My soul cried out against the
violation our tradition had suffered and would suffer
for a long time to come, if nothing was done to counter
the headlong rush to destruction (Ezeigbo 1).

The highest ruling body in Umuga community is the Obuofo and
its women's wing is the Oluada. The two groups make decisions in
the community. At one of their meetings, the women's group, the
Oluada:

> agreed to participate more intensely and vigorously
> in Obuofo and to continue to represent the women
> actively in the political body. Oluada resolved to
> support the removal of Okwara as warrant chief if he
> continued to obey Kosiri and disregard Obuofo and its
> reforms to improve Umuga as a whole. Oluada refused
> to cooperate with any power or anyone that planned to
> undermine the culture, the traditional judicial system
> and the economic well-being of Umuga (9).

The women leaders take unanimous decision in support of their
tradition instead of following the new culture being advanced by
the European invaders whom they call Kosiri.

The women also believe in building a home, family and
working together with the men to raise their children. The girls
are raised to marry early and parents feel uncomfortable when
their daughters do not get married when expected as seen in
Ejimnaka's case. Ejimnaka is a free thinker and very independent
as a young girl. She marries a very old man, Alagbogu with hope
that he will allow her do what she wants. She claims: "I did not
want to marry a young man ... I did not consider any of my young
suitors attractive or intelligent enough. In addition, I hated being
any man's appendage.... My independence meant everything to
me, indeed my life, and I guarded it fiercely" (Ezeigbo 21). When
she finds out that her husband is bent in clipping her wings, she
moves back to her parents' house. Her parents are not happy to

see her back because divorce amounts to bringing shame to the family especially when her reason is that, her husband "preferred to have me live in his own house to turn me round his little finger, I thought .... If I proved rebellious or peevish, it roused him to excitement and he renewed his effort to subdue me" (22-3). Ejimnaka sees Obiatu, a handsome young man who moves back to the village from the city and inquires about him. She sings a song about a palm wine tapper to attract his attention and it works. In a short while they get married. Both of them eventually become members of the Obuofo in Umuga. Ejimnaka is the leader of the women's wing. She weaves and decorates mats which she sells in the market. Another independent young woman is Aziagba, Ejimnaka's daughter. She chooses to stay at home to have male children for her parents since her mum does not have any male child.

Onyekozuru, another member of the Oluada like Ejimnaka, participates in the activities of the women. She reflects on how they organize the women against Egwuagu who "unjustly drove his wife away and threw her belongings out into the courtyard. We descended on him like a swarm of bees, with the full intent to sting sense into him. We turned ourselves into human litter, occupying every available space in his large ngwuru. A day later, he indicated his willingness to talk with his in-laws" (52). This incident shows that female bonding is highly valued in the society. We also see the same female bonding when Abazu shoots Onyekozuru. The women rally round and take a decision on how to react to the situation, before getting the information that Abazu commits suicide. Onyekozuru plays very good roles in the progress and peace of her village. Chieme is a female griot who chants at funerals and other ceremonious occasions for a living. Her husband sends her back to her parents because she is not able to have children for him. She is able to put all that behind her and focus on her trading business. Mezu observes that:

> because the African woman is operating from a milieu
> deeply steeped in sexist norms and mores and contend-
> ing with a plethora of problems which complicate her
> life and endanger her chances of a felicitous conjugal
> living...she suffers abandonment, she is aware of it and

her lament is no less heartfelt and traumatic than that
of her Western counterpart" (16).

Chibuka is another independent woman, who in spite of her husband's miserly attitude is able to maintain her own poultry farm
and help to raise her children. She decides to stay in the marriage putting up with her husband's neglect. As Egejuru observes
that a woman "accepts the temporary hardships and humiliation
of marriage to ensure the more ennobling and permanent state
of motherhood. Marriage is temporary even when a woman lives
out her life in marriage. Among the Igbo, a woman's obligation
to the man ends when she dies, but her obligation to her children continues" (16). This is a justification that Chibuka tolerates
the spousal abuse she receives from her husband because of her
children. Egejuru, here wonders why women still stay in marriage
even while they are being dehumanized. Chibuka can move out
of her husband's home to live on her own with her children, since
she is the one providing for them, but because the Oluada believes
in the marriage institution, Ezeigbo does not make her characters
leave their marital homes on their own. On the other hand, Chikwenye Ogunbiyi opines that:

> The double vision of woman as loving mother and
> hateful wife is a contradiction that women must sort
> out in the palaver. She must move from the back-
> ground or the outhouse, where traditional architecture
> confines her, to the front, in an effort to be herself
> in her right; the easiest route forward appears to be
> education, as educated women are among the most
> recognized in the country (19).

Ezeigbo uses the lives of these women to show case the fact that
traditional African women have not always been relegated to
the background. They have a voice when they have an organized
meeting like the Oluada and women leaders to speak for them.
They also have their individual family problems, but they do not
let these deter them from their various businesses and trades.
Ezeigbo makes the characters speak for themselves thus confirm-
ing Wayne Booth's belief that the house of fiction does not have

one window but "five million ways to tell a story each of them justified if it provides a centre for the work" (24). Ezeigbo uses this style of narrative to make the readers listen to the characters directly telling their own stories. It makes the stories plausible and takes the pressure away from the writer.

There is also a strong belief in the gods and ancestral spirits in Umuga tradition and the women consult the oracle when they are in need. The people believe in the protection of the gods in whatever they do and depend on the gods to solve their problems. Chime goes to consult Idemmiri and says: "Idemmiri, great mother, I have come to you for a solution. Why am I not like other women? Answer me, great goddess, wife of Nkwo, who defers to you in all things" (80). Chieme gets a reply through Onukwe, the priest of Idemmiri: "Daughter, Idemmiri said you should be yourself and live your life fully. That is her message to you" (80-81). When Chieme as a chanter has to perform at a funeral on behalf of her mentor she syas: "I called on Idemmiri, Isigwu and all our goddesses to help me. My performance was a huge success (82).

In African tradition, husbands are sometimes chosen for the daughters by their fathers without the consent of the girls concerned and polygamy is evident in African marriage. Onyekozuru is made to marry Umeozo who has a wife with grown up children. She tries to find out from her mother why the family makes her marry such an old man. Her mother reluctantly tells her that: "Umeozo had given my father a large piece of farm land, and he had cultivated it for years. Though we had enough food at home, my father was not well to-do. He had no real property, especially land and livestock. So, being an in-law of a man like Umeozo was very important" (39). In *Things Fall Apart*, Okonkwo and other title holders have more than one wife.

Male children are regarded as a form of insurance for the wife as she is entitled to the family property even at the death of her husband. Onyekozuru's children are given plots of land by their father "even while they were still little" (40), but it is different in Ejimnaka's case. According to her:

> Obiatu's people were unhappy that we had no male child, so they wanted him to marry another wife. Obiatu refused.... I was a mere spectator during that

family tussle. It was not my place to refuse to have a co-wife. My mother- in-law... held me responsible for her son's decision.... She called me an overly wicked and possessive woman. She began to act as if in mourning. Mourning the absence of a male child in the family. It was Aziagba who solved the problem.... She was willing to remain at home with us to produce male children for her father. After we had performed the nluikwa ceremony, she chose Okoroji as a mate (33).

In a family where there are only girls, one of them is made to stay back in her father's house and choose a male friend to her produce male children for the family. This is what Obiatu's daughter, Aziagba does to maintain the family name and lineage. Nobody bothers to think of what happens if the girl does not produce male children.

In both *Things Fall Apart* and *The Last of the Strong Ones*, a number of techniques are used to make the stories interesting. There is the use of traditional things such as songs, folktales, festivals and proverbs to spice the language of the adults. Songs are used for different purposes such as during marriages, funerals, wars, and other festivities. We see Chieme the chanter as she sings at a funeral praising the dead and his children who organized the funeral ceremony. In *Things Fall Apart*, the people sing war and heroic songs in praise of Okonkwo for winning the wrestling match. There are also songs and dance performances at weddings and other festivities. In both texts, proverbs are used freely by the elders to drive their point home. The proverbs also help to give a tone of finality in any issue raised, for example when Umuga people are looking for solution to the problem caused by the whites, the following proverb is used: "Our people say that it is the traveler who must make the return journey and not the owner of the land" (Ezeigbo 6). Unoka on the other hand tells Okoye "The sun will shine on those who stand before it shines on those that are sitting". This proverb tells Okoye that Unoka does not have money for him; therefore, he leaves without saying a word. Both writers also use transliteration to portray exactly what the speaker has in mind. "It is time we go to the head of our talk" and also, "Dawn has arrived and the day will not wait for anyone" Ezeigbo (6). Here Ezeigbo tries to portray the feelings of the people towards the incursion of the whites (Kosiri). Achebe on the other hand says: "Uzowulu's body, I salute you.... My hand has touched the ground" (93).

The portrayal of women in these texts is evident that women have not always been marginalized in African societies. It also confirms Adesina's view that women were not originally exploited and dehumanized as most writers portray in their works. Women have been leaders at various levels of human development and have also been at the vanguard of social justice and human development. This is exactly what we see in the women portrayed in Ezeigbo's *The Last of the Strong Ones*. Her women are very strong and vocal and see themselves on the same level as their male counterparts and there is mutual respect between the men and the women. Her female characters are fascinating and complex in a variety of ways. The women in *The Last of the Strong Ones* also believe in stable families and maintaining a strong family relationship. They believe in the institution of marriage, thus they are worried when their young girls do not get married when they expect them to as in Onyekozuru's case. They stay in marriage even when there is chaos or some kind of spousal abuse in their marital homes.

That women in these texts are protected to some extent in their societies does not mean that women have never been marginalized. Adesina points out that all over the world especially in Europe and Asia during the period of serfdom and feudalism, women "were no more than means of diversion and entertainment for the licentious rich who applaud their appearances in public out of sheer vanity and self-conceit. This did not signify any respect towards woman; she was important mainly because of the pleasure she brought to men" (132). Those days are over even in the countries where women are used for entertainment. Feminists are speaking out by exposing these negative attitudes and maltreatment of women in different areas. Helen Chukwuma for example opines that feminism means "a rejection of inferiority and a striving for recognition. It seeks to give the woman a sense of self as a worthy, effectual and contributing human being. Feminism is a reaction to such stereotypes of women which deny them a positive identity (ix). Ezeigbo's women have in various ways proven that they "effectual and contributing human beings" (ix). The writer makes us realize this from the point of view of the characters who tell their stories for the delectation of the readers. Anderson and Zinsser view feminism as "rejecting much, from basic cultural tenets to casual everyday behavior. Given ancient traditions which insist that women defer and subordinate themselves to men, given traditions which define women only by their relationships with men, given traditions which under-value women and take men as the standard, the only way for women to claim full humanity has been to reject those standards" (334). From Ezeigbo's portrayal of her female characters, they are not shown to be under-valued, but Achebe's women are shown to be subordinate to their men, thus they are not shown to hold such authority as seen in women in *The Last of the Strong Ones*. Apart from being vocal and assertive, Ezeigbo's female characters are also as nurturing and patient as Achebe's female characters.

In *Things Fall Apart*, even though women are not assigned important roles as the men, they are the brains behind the laws and norms of Umuofia society. Take Chielo for instance, she is an ordinary widow with two children, but she is the priestess of Agbala, a very important deity in Umuofia. No one dares Chielo when she is possessed, not even the powerful Okonkwo. She takes the sick Ezinma away in the middle of the night to the Oracle of the Hills and Caves and dares Okonkwo to follow her. Okonkwo is not able to plead his way to follow Chielo; he therefore follows her without giving her the opportunity to curse him. We are told that when Chielo is possessed, she becomes a completely different person.

All the crimes Okonkwo commits are against the Earth goddess, that is probably why things become difficult for him and he makes a lot of mistakes, one of which is by inadvertently shooting Ezeudu's son. Okonkwo is also penalized on the different occasions he commits crime against the Earth goddess. His insatiable greed for material wealth and show of strength, his lack of respect for Ani, the Earth goddess—a female, do not give him room to think; therefore, the crime continues without any show of remorse. These put together probably help to drive him to commit suicide, as he insists to fight alone.

Works Cited

Achebe, Chinua. *Things Fall Apart*. New York: Anchor, 1994.

Adesina, Bolaji. "Toward the Recognition of Woman's Dignity: An Islamic Approach" *Women in the Academy: Festschrift for Professor Helen Chukwuma*. Ed. Seyifa Koroye and Noel C. Anyadike. Port Harcourt: Pear, 2004.

Alagoa, E. A. and A. Fombo. *A Chronicle of Grand Bonny*. Ibadan: U of Ibadan P, 1972.

Amadi, Elechi. *The Concubine*. London: Heinemann, 1966.

Anderson, B.S. and Zinsser, J. A. *A History of their Own: Women in Europe from Prehistoric to the Present*. Vol 2. Harmondworth: Penguin, 1990.

Booth, Wayne. *The Rhetoric of Fiction*. Chicago: Chicago U. P., 1961.

Chukwuma, Helen. *Feminism in African Literature*. Enugu: New Generation, 1994.

Diala-Ogamba, Blessing. "The Non-Conformist Women in Nuruddin Farah's Blood of The Sun Trilogy". *A History of Africana Women's Literature*. Ed. Rose Mezu. Baltimore: Black Academy P. 2004.

Emecheta, Buchi. *Second Class Citizen*. Glasgow: Fontana, 1977.

Egejuru, Phanuel. and Ketu H. Katract. Eds. *Womanbeing and African Literature*. Trenton: Africa World P, 1977.

Ezeigbo, Theodora. *The Last of the Strong Ones*. Lagos: Vista, 1996.

Farah, Nuruddin. *Gifts*. New York: Penguin, 2000.

Jeyifo, Biodun. "Okonkwo and His Mother: *Things Fall Apart* and Issues of Gender in The Constitution of African Postcolonial Discourse" *Chinua Achebe's Things Fall Apart: A Case Book*. Ed. Isidore Okpewho. New York: Oxford U.P. 2003.

Kolawole, Mary. *Colonialism and African Consciousness*. New Jersey: Africa World Press, 1997.

Mezu, Rose. *Women in Chains: Abandonment in Love Relationships in the Fiction of Selected West African Writers*. Baltimore: Black Academy P, 1994.

Nwapa, Flora. *Efuru*. London: Heinemann, 1966.

_____. *Idu*. London: Heinemann, 1988.

Okonjo-Ogunyemi, Chikwenye. *AfricaWo/Man Palava: The Nigerian Novel by Women*. Chicago: The U of Chicago P. 1996.

Ousmane, Sembene. *Gods Bits of Wood*. Oxford: Heinemann, 1995.

Wa Thiongo, Ngugi. *Petals of Blood*. London: Heinemann, 1977.

CHAPTER 19

FROM THE MASTER CRAFTSMAN HIMSELF: INTERVIEWS AND CONVERSATIONS WITH CHINUA ACHEBE ON WOMEN'S PORTRAITURE IN HIS NOVELS

Christine Ohale

In a March 2008 interview granted to Bob Thompson of the *Washington Post*, Achebe explains that he is not entirely certain how his iconic book, *Things Fall Apart*, came into the world. Looking back on the book, Achebe tells Thompson, "It's a little mysterious in some ways; the book seized me, and almost wrote me. I'm not quite sure I wrote it … It was almost like my chi was making me into what I was to be." At this, Thompson quips: "What Chinua Achebe was to be, according to innumerable writers, scholars and admirers, was the father of modern African literature, a writer who would evoke the continent's true nature both for the world at large and for Africans themselves." Thompson's sentiment readily conjures up the rich legacy of Achebe's writing.

Achebe's writing is widely acclaimed as having restored a sense of pride to Africa. The 2007 Man Booker International

Prize which collectively honors everything Achebe has written thus far attests to this. Particularly in his two historical novels, *Things Fall Apart* and *Arrow of God*, Achebe depicts pre-colonial Igbo life in all of its complexity. Keith Booker posits that "*Things Fall Apart* is such an intricately crafted work of fiction that many critics have acknowledged its aesthetic merits, while noting the importance of its reminders that pre-colonial African societies were complex and sophisticated structures bearing little relationship to European myths of African savagery and primitivism" (66). Booker's assessment of *Things Fall Apart* resonates with legions of readers and commentators across the globe who concur with Booker that Achebe's first novel is a masterpiece of monumental proportions. Conscious of the enormous responsibilities that face him as a foremost African writer, Achebe treads carefully as he embarks on the arduous task of helping his "society regain belief in itself and put away the complexes of the years of denigration and self-abasement" (3). He subsequently proclaims: "I would be quite satisfied if my novels (especially the ones I set in the past) did no more than teach my readers that their past – with all its imperfections – was not one long night of savagery from which the first Europeans acting on God's behalf delivered them" (4). To this end, Achebe has delivered and has brought African literature to prominence and glory.

Indeed, all of Achebe's novels have been subjected to extensive reviews and all have enjoyed tremendous critical success but, nonetheless, the renowned author has been accused by feminist critics of doing a disservice to women, particularly in his early novels. In spite of the accolades of Achebe's literary achievements and his faithful recreation of pre-colonial Igbo society, Florence Stratton argues that "This claim loses a certain amount of credibility, however, when the treatment of female characters in the narrative is considered" (32).

Critics' Reactions to Achebe's Depiction of Women

Feminist critics have leveled innumerable accusations on Achebe for creating "back-house, timid, subservient, lack-lustre" (Chukwuma 2) female characters, particularly in his historical novels, thereby creating an apparent disparity between male and female characters. These critics have hoped for a more balanced representation of the African female in the novels. They question the consistent pattern in Achebe's first four novels – *Things Fall Apart, No Longer at Ease, Arrow of God* and *A Man of the People* – in which the heroes around whom the actions revolve are all male. Merun Nasser maintains that, "While Okonkwo in *Things Fall Apart*, Obi in *No Longer at Ease*, Ezeulu in *Arrow of God* and Odili in *A Man of the People* are celebrated as heroes, the women, on the other hand, are portrayed in an 'untraditional' role up to the point of total subservience to the males" (22). This disparity has caused feminists to wonder whether this is a deliberate omission on the part of Achebe or simply an oversight. They seem to be asking: Has Achebe not heard about the achievements, resilience and triumphs of Igbo women?

This uneasiness about Achebe's handling of the female character prompts Andrea Powell to state that "In his two historical novels, in fact, Achebe consistently side-lines the place of the postcolonial woman in order to focus on postcolonial manhood. Women's lives often serve as little more than fodder for the exploration of masculinity. And because Achebe does hold such a high-profile position in African studies, his gender-determined blind spots demand careful scrutiny" (167). Stratton dwells further on Achebe's lop-sided representation of male-female relations in his novels. She states:

> *Things Fall Apart* was written and published in the years immediately preceding Nigerian independence in 1960, a transitional period when political power was being transferred from the colonial masters to a Nigerian male elite. *Things Fall Apart* legitimizes this process whereby women were excluded from post-colonial politics and public affairs through its representation of pre-colonial Igbo society as governed entirely by men" (27).

She argues that Achebe does not attempt to restore 'dignity and self-respect' to African women (24); and goes further to state that Achebe does not always maintain "an objective stance on the issue of gender relations," but instead, aligns "himself with the sexist views of the male characters" (32). Stratton, however, admits that

"With the notable exception of Chielo, the powerful priestess of Agbala, Achebe's women are, indeed, 'down on one knee,' if not both, before their menfolk…"(25). She further acknowledges that the central divinity in *Things Fall Apart* is the Earth Goddess, a female deity, but hastens to add that the deity's values do not serve women's interests (28).

Rose Acholonu, joining the dissenting chorus, intones:

> In *Things Fall Apart*, we see Okonkwo playing his role as the traditional head of the family. He is a typical tyrant. He rules and directs his wives in the manner of a cattle herdsman. He roars like "the thunder" and administers physical blows to his wives at the slightest provocation. The wives live in awe of him.   Achebe, true to tradition and the precepts of Igbo custom, seems to condone this inhuman treatment of Okonkwo's wives" (39).

Rose Mezu, echoing the sentiments of preceding critics, asserts:

> Achebe's women are voiceless …. The world in *Things Fall Apart* is one in which patriarchy intrudes oppressively into every sphere of existence. It is an androcentric world where the man is everything and the woman is nothing. In domestic terms, women are quantified as part of men's acquisitions. As wives, women come in multiple numbers, sandwiched between yam barns and titles. These three – wives, yam barns, social titles – are the highest accolades for the successful farmer, warrior, and man of worth (2).

Contributing further to the argument, Nasser reaffirms that "The traditional role of the African woman has always been a complementary role and evidence of that fact has been widely supplied by social scientists" (21). She maintains that African male novelists, among whom Achebe is the most prominent, have failed to portray the complementary role of the African woman in society and, as a result, readers have "come away with the impression that the role of the African woman is barely above that of 'chattel'" (22).

Again, Powell argues that in *Things Fall Apart* and *Arrow of God*, Achebe "situates his female characters firmly in a masculine tradition that prevents them from moving into the positions of power, positions that women in Africa must occupy in order for their nations to serve their needs" (180). Mabel Segun agrees that in the early days of the development of African literature, male writers dominated the scene, and so their literature was replete with the projection of only the male perspective.

So far, the views of feminist critics have been presented as they blatantly voice their dissatisfaction with the status quo of male domination in the African novel. With this in mind, one can imagine their undisguised excitement about the debut of African women writers. They applaud the emergence of this new breed of writers and their efforts in charting a new course in the delineation of the African female character. Until their emergence, male characters loom large in all spheres of achievement in the African novel. Some of these female pioneers are Flora Nwapa, Buchi Emecheta, Nawal el Saadawi, Bessie Head, Ama Ata Aidoo, Ifeoma Okoye, Mabel Segun, Zaynab Alkali, and so on; the list continues to lengthen. Rose Acholonu writes: "These pathfinders … were empowered by liberal education and the acquisition of literary skills … to break the seals of silence and invisibility on the female protagonist by the early traditionalist male writers" (133). These writers who, for reasons their own, claim not to be feminists but "womanists," have undertaken to balance the tilt in characterization and correct the distortions by male writers in their writings (298). By pioneering a renaissance in women's writing, these writers have practically retrieved women from the back bench to the center stage, concretely establishing the evolution of the African female character from docility to assertiveness. These writers' timely intervention is a fitting tribute to "the ingenuity and resolve of African women who endure countless restrictions and limitations" (Ohale 131).

Feminists question the relegation of women to the back bench. They argue that "In every age and time there had been women who exhibited economic sense and resource management within and outside their homes even in the rural environment" (Chukwuma 16). Their contention is that African women have always had a legacy of achievement which dates back to antiquity. Chukwuma affirms that "African women have a rich tradition of women achievers in all spheres of human endeavor, including warfare and governance. It is left to our women writers to highlight these herstorical [sic] antecedents to spur women of our time to pick up the gauntlet" (51). Mabel Segun commends African female writers for altering the course of the female character and presenting "the ideology of woman – a person in her own right and not an appendix of a man, whose aspirations are human and legitimate and deserve to be respected and fostered" (298). Segun, nevertheless, cautions that female writers have not quite explored the full potential of African womanhood in their novels. This stems from her observation that:

> Female writers confine their writings almost exclusively to the domestic scene, thus giving the impression that patriarchal society is justified in excluding women from the public arena. Their themes centre [sic] mostly on love, marriage, motherhood, barrenness, marital infidelity and rape. There is thus the paradox of woman who claims equality with man but does not venture into the male preserve: politics (298).

Segun strongly urges female writers to strive to incorporate all areas of women's achievements in their novels. She further maintains that:

> There have been women activists such as those in the celebrated Aba Women's riots of 1937, who faced colonial guns to protest against what they considered an injustice – the erosion of their traditional powers in the township councils, although the immediate cause of the riots was a rumour [sic] about taxation. There was also Funmilayo Ransome-Kuti's grassroots mobilization of Egba women in Abeokuta against perceived victimization by a despotic ruler whom they succeeded in driving into exile. But the impression given in our literature is that such women have never existed in our society (298).

Segun reiterates that:

> The female writer "must combat the influence of the type of literature that encourages women to accept their subordination …. This involves raising the consciousness of women, motivating them to seek leadership roles in society and encouraging them to take their rightful place in the civil society which analysts say is a prerequisite for the success of the democratic process" (301).

Despite the dissatisfaction among feminist critics with respect to female characterization in Achebe's novels, some people are of the view that Achebe has been dealt an unfair hand in the arguments and that the gender debate constitutes a distraction from the core message of Achebe's fiction. The confusion, they believe, stems from an obvious misreading of the novels. Kenneth W. Harrow, for example, argues that Stratton's displeasure with Achebe's portraiture of women "reflects a warped reading of the novel" (177). He cites Stratton's most disturbing logic to be "the claim that a representation of inequality constitutes legitimization of it" (177). Harrow points out that:

> Achebe problematizes the patriarchal order repeatedly in the novel, ultimately blaming the fall of Umuofia on its masculinist rigidity, the failures of its governing bodies to adapt to new circumstances, and on a male-dominated authority that overreacted in its rejection of female qualities (177).

What Harrow calls legitimization of a 'representation of inequality' is evident in a number of essays in which Achebe is attacked but, for brevity, only two will be discussed. In her essay entitled "Women in Achebe's World," Rose Mezu states:

> Achebe's sexist attitude is unabashed and without apology. Unoka, Okonkwo's father, is considered an untitled man, connoting femininity (20). Coco-yam, of smaller size and lesser value than other yams, is regarded as female. Osugo has taken no title; and so,

in a gathering of his peers, Okonkwo unkindly tells him, "This meeting is for men" (28). Guilt-ridden after murdering Ikemefuna, his surrogate son, Okonkwo sternly reprimands himself not to "become like a shivering old woman" (72) – this he considers the worst insult.... Such excessive emphases on virility, sex-role stereotyping, gender discrimination, and violence create an imbalance, a resultant denigration of the female principle (2-3).

Nasser, in her turn, affirms that "Achebe's women look, sound, taste and feel subservient because Achebe, their creator-commentator, has not portrayed them with any kind of warmth or with the same sensitivity and passion as the male characters" (24). In these assertions both Mezu and Nasser imply that the plight of the woman in the novels is Achebe's doing.

Sophia Ogwude presents a different view from the views of feminist critics. She finds it ironic that "Although *Things Fall Apart* is maligned by feminists, there are very strong pointers to Achebe's feminist sympathies or leanings in the novel" (63). She further posits that "In the character of Ekwefi, the novelist depicts a woman who to all intents and purposes is a thorough feminist" (63). Ogwude recalls the circumstances of Ekwefi's initial encounter with Okonkwo in their early youth when he couldn't afford her and how she eventually abandons her husband to be with Okonkwo. She notes that "In that period of our history when prudery was often equated with acceptable female decorum, we find Achebe's Ekwefi jettisoning societal restrictions and expectations, and, even under what native wisdom would call questionable circumstances, she is able to forge a meaningful relationship with Okonkwo" (64). Ogwude provides reasons why she sees Ekwefi as a "thorough" feminist, reminding the reader that not only is Ekwefi Okonkwo's favorite wife and the only one with "the audacity to bang on his door" (Achebe 75), Okonkwo is sympathetic to her long-standing difficulties with motherhood. Ogwude maintains that:

Clearly, Ekwefi, the wife who has not borne Okonkwo a son, is unquestionably his favourite [sic]. Even the most casual reading of this novel reveals also that he favours [sic] his daughter, Ezinma, over his senior wife's first-born son, Nwoye. Again, the social function and status of Chielo, the priestess of Agbala, are undeniably of the same high order as those of the *egwugwu*, the male masked ancestral spirits. Also, it is significant that Chielo, in her priestly capacity, is cast as being in a superior position to even the male members of her society (64).

Ogwude is concerned that "serious gender concerns are trivialized when, for ideological reasons, critics look for loop-holes where there are none" (65). She insists that even in his first novel, it is wrong to accuse Achebe of doing a disservice to women because that novel holds up a mirror to the Igbo society of the day. What Ogwude is putting across is that Achebe has not painted an idyllic picture of pre-colonial Igbo society, and that Achebe should be commended for depicting that society in its stark nakedness.

With the myriad of opinions on Achebe's depiction of women in his novels, one is naturally curious to know how Achebe responds to the accusations. Not surprisingly, Achebe has shed light on the contentious issues in several interviews and conversations. Excerpts of some of the interviews are reproduced in this essay. Achebe offers insightful explanations but is neither defensive nor apologetic for his depiction of women in his novels.

Achebe in Interviews and Conversations

In an interview granted to Anna Rutherford in London on November 11, 1987, Rutherford asks Achebe what he thinks the role of women should be in the new African state. Perhaps, it is worthy of mention that this interview coincides with the nomination of Achebe's *Anthills of the Savannah* for the Booker Prize.

> **Rutherford:** Could we look at what you see the role of women to be in the new African state?
> **Achebe:** First of all let me say that, looking at the past and present, I think that we have been ambivalent, we have been deceitful even, about the role of the woman. We have sometimes said 'The woman is supreme – mother is supreme,' we have said all kinds of grandiloquent things about womanhood, but in our practical life the place of the woman has not been adequate. At the same time I'm not saying 'This is how it is going to

be from now on' because I am aware of my own limitations. In mapping out in detail what woman's role is going to be, I am aware that radical new thinking is required. The quality of compassion and humaneness which the woman brings to the world generally has not been given enough scope up till now to influence the way the world is run. We have created all kinds of myths to support the suppression of the woman, and what the group around Beatrice is saying is that the time has now come to put an end to that. I'm saying the woman herself will be in the forefront in designing what her new role is going to be, with the humble cooperation of men. The position of Beatrice as sensitive leader of that group is indicative of what I see as necessary in the transition to the kind of society which I think we should be aiming to create.

Rutherford: Have you changed your own ideas about what you think the role of women should be since you wrote *Things Fall Apart*?

Achebe: No, I haven't really ... I think the difference is this – that *Things Fall Apart* is dealing with a past period in our cultural history. This is where we were at that point in time. Even the novels that deal with the present, that is *No Longer at Ease* and *A Man of the People* were also descriptive of the role of women frozen in time. In *Anthills of the Savannah* there is more of looking into the future, not just for women but for society generally; how, for example, we can use our past creatively. I have always known that there was some crucial role which women played in times past, of which our ancestors have kept a memory but which, somehow, we have tried to suppress. There are so many folk stories telling you what catastrophe would be unleashed in the world if women were to get into power that you know that there is some kind of conspiracy going on; and I was always aware of that, but until this recent book I did not grapple with it centrally; that is the main difference. But then you grapple with things one at a time.

Rutherford: I was at the 1987 Stockholm Conference for African Writers, and there the women writers made a series of accusations which I thought were justified.

332

Achebe: I wasn't there but I read about it. That kind of thing does not interest me very much because I think these are women who are dealing with the problem from the position of the feminist movement in the West and I think this position is untenable. This is not what I am thinking about, I am thinking about something which is grounded in our own culture, something which you can actually derive from looking closely at our own culture. This culture is actually there and it recognizes the distinction between man and woman and doesn't aim to abolish it. The culture never says there is no difference; it says this difference does not authorize you, the man, to step on the woman, to make woman a second-class citizen.

It is noteworthy that in *Anthills of the Savannah*, Achebe's fifth novel, the female character has taken an upward turn, a sharp contrast to Achebe's earlier novels. This development has prompted feminists to acknowledge that Achebe, at long last, has salvaged the image of the African woman. They contend that Achebe is making amends in *Anthills of the Savannah* for his "mistakes" in *Things Fall Apart*. Published in 1987, *Anthills of the Savannah* features Achebe's strongest female character. During the interview with *Washington Post's* Bob Thompson, he specifically asks Achebe what he makes of the claim by feminists that in *Anthills of the Savannah* he has created the character Beatrice to make up for past mistakes. This very question, Thompson observes, and the sheer insistence on it, may have caused Achebe to show obvious irritation for the only time during the two-hour interview. This suggests that Achebe is clearly unhappy with the recurrent fielding of that question. Hear him:

> **Achebe:** I want to sort of scream that *Things Fall Apart* is on the side of women, and that Okonkwo is paying the penalty for his treatment of women; that all his problems, all the things he did wrong, can be seen as offenses against the feminine. To see Okonkwo beating his wives as something I have done is not to read fiction.

Achebe's explanation notwithstanding, Rose Mezu, a staunch critic of Achebe's female portraiture in his historical novels, maintains that:

> The inexorable winds of change have caused Achebe, a consummate pragmatist, to make a volte-face. The secret of his revisionist stance can be deduced from the central theme of his two tradition-based novels, *Things Fall Apart* and *Arrow of God* (1964): In a world of change, whoever is not flexible enough will be swept aside. Profiting from the mistakes of his tragic heroes, Achebe becomes flexible (5).

Mabel Segun reiterates that "Latter-day Chinua Achebe, trying to redeem his reputation as a literary wife-beater, has centred [sic] women and portrayed them in a more holistic manner in *Anthills of the Savannah*" (298). Theodora Ezeigbo, hailing this positive turn, affirms that some African male authors have joined in recreating women's experiences more constructively (52).

In another 2008 interview granted by Achebe to Okey Ndibe and Joyce Abunaw on behalf of the Association of Nigerian Authors (ANA) to commemorate the fiftieth anniversary of the publication of *Things Fall Apart*, the following questions are put to Achebe:

> **ANA:** If you have a chance of revising *Things Fall Apart*, where would your axe fall?
> **Achebe:** I wouldn't, I wouldn't bother with revising.
> **ANA:** Not even the incident with Chielo that some of us think that maybe ....
> **Achebe:** Well, many of you may think whatever you like. Yeah, I mean I have been told that I was a chauvinist. So people have different readings, but I trust the book, that it has enough spiritual power that it took care of many things that people may not yet understand. So I would leave it exactly as it is.

On his depiction of women in his novels, Achebe has this to say:

ANA: You've been accused by some critics of harboring an unflattering view of women in your novels. But to go back to again to the concept of balance, reading through *TFA* one sees the concept of spaces. We have male crop and female crop, male functions and female functions, ceremonies that are exclusive to women as well as ceremonies that are exclusive to men. And so it seems to me that there is a very intricate sense of balance in those arrangements. How do you see the place of women within the society you depict?

Achebe: There is a misreading of my fiction in that complaint. I think many people think that what I'm doing is praising the position of women. It's not; in fact, it's the very opposite. What I was doing was pointing out how unjust the Igbo society is to women. And how better to explore it than to make the hero of this story, Okonkwo... all his problems are problems that have to do with the feminine. There's nothing wrong with Okonkwo except his failure to understand that the gentleness, the compassion that we associate with women is even more important than strength. Now, people don't understand why I am showing these women who are not in charge. I'm showing them that way because that's how it is in this society I want to change. And that's what Okonkwo was not able to learn, and I want others after him to learn it: that women, compassion, music... these things are valuable, more valuable than war and violence.

ANA: One of the ironies is that Okonkwo the warrior misses out on two points. One is that the most important deity in this society, the earth goddess, is a female goddess. The other is that Agbala, the Oracle of the Hills and Caves, which has supervisory powers over wars, again, has a female principle at its core. Okonkwo, who is an extraordinary warrior, doesn't get that particular point and so continues to live under the illusion that the only thing that is important is the male and masculinity. Could you then talk about Unoka's importance in *TFA*?

Achebe: Well Unoka, if you like, you can place him with the women in the society. This is how Okonkwo saw him. But he's a very decent and nice person, not

335

successful in the sense of wealth and resources, or ability to look after his family and live big. All these things didn't work for him. One thing that worked for him was his flute, so in the view of the Igbo people he was a failure. And this is, in fact, where Okonkwo makes his biggest mistake, and Igbo culture is partly responsible because Igbo culture makes a lot of strength and power and success and Okonkwo heard this from his society. He heard it all the time, you know, this importance of strength and being manly and so on. Now Igbo society does not talk so loudly about the other side, but it talks gently. It's there, but you've got to make an effort to listen to hear it.... In a gentle voice the society is saying, "But also remember your children, but also remember the women, but also remember compassion." Why does it say, "Well if the gods have decided that this boy [Ikemefuna] should die, we can't stop them but I won't be there"? So cowardice is even a virtue. The Igbo society is saying that to Okonkwo. It is not only in the machete that there is virtue. There is virtue in sitting down and contemplating.

On February 26, 2008, the PEN American Center hosted a literary gala, co-sponsored by Anchor Books and Bard College, a tribute to Achebe on the fiftieth anniversary of the publication of *Things Fall Apart*. On the eve of the celebration, Achebe granted an interview to Carol Cooper of the *Voice*; obviously, Cooper does not seem to share feminists' sentiments on Achebe's female portraiture. Excerpts from the interview are reproduced below:

> **Cooper:** Your 1972 short story "Girls at War" is surprisingly feminist in its nuanced view of African women, yet it voices none of the stereotypical polemics common to Western feminism. Stylistically, how did you manage to compress so much information and insight into such a short narrative?
> **Achebe:** If you've been through a civil war and come close to all kinds of death, it's not very difficult to make a whole lot of talk organize itself into a strong, brief statement. One of the ideas behind this story is the humbug of powerful men in that difficult situation. Then there is

the innocence and idealism of school girls compared to the sickening cynicism of those "in charge." Put the two together and you have a very tragic story.

Cooper: The female characters who pop up in your fiction are always interesting because, even though they tend to speak softly, what they actually say and represent is always significant. Are you conscious of this when you are writing?

Achebe: Yes. Because what they stand for is the very thing which the male-dominated society does not consider. If you go back to *Things Fall Apart*, all the problems Okonkwo has from the beginning to end are related to ignoring the female. And that is where he is a flawed hero. Women stand for compassion.

In these interviews, Achebe speaks loudly and clearly on the woman question in his novels. He is passionate in his explanation that he is on the side of women, and that by portraying women "who are not in charge," he is actually helping to initiate awareness of the need for a full scale review of the position of women in the society and, hopefully, start the process that will lead to positive change. It does not now matter whether Achebe admits to "making amends" or not; the point is that amends have been made and women have been portrayed in ways that better reflect the multifarious roles that they play in society. Whether we believe Achebe's explanation or not, we must acknowledge that the women of *Things Fall Apart* belong to a different era in our cultural history when women were largely denied a voice.

Conclusion

So far, we have explored critics' reactions to Achebe's portraiture of women in his novels, in addition to Achebe's own responses to their accusations. However, we must admit that so much still remains to be done with respect to the situation of the woman in African societies. As we bask in the excitement of the debut of the new female character, we must remember that so much of her potential has not been actualized. This paper may well serve as a reminder to all women writers that a lot of work still remains to be done. They must continue to empower women through their fiction and help them "unlearn the lessons of the past, engendering in them a new dynamism born of their new awareness of their inherent strengths and potentialities for effecting change in their society as equal partners with men" (Segun 300). Achebe has made it clear that the woman herself must be at the forefront of this campaign, directing her own destiny and striving for inclusion in all societal decisions that directly affect her and her world. This is to say that the onus of designing what her new role is going to be rests solely with the woman.

Thus far, women have made significant contributions to the society at large and proven that, if given the opportunity, they have the tenacity to excel in all of their endeavors. This point is echoed by Rose Mezu as she chronicles some of the achievements of African women:

> African women are making meaningful contributions as lecturers, professors, and presidents of universities; as commissioners and ministers, senators and governors, and chairpersons of political parties; as directors and others involved in literary movements and campaigns against forced marriages, clitoridectomies, and obsolete widowhood practices. African women can outstrip their fictive counterparts to be partners with men in national progress and development, and to gain individual self-realization and fulfillment (7).

The source of these women's success is not far-fetched; their success lies in "their strong commitment to the general cause, their loyalty, selfless service, natural incorruptibility, their steadfastness and resilience" (Chukwuma 50). It is, therefore, imperative that all educated African women and men in positions of authority duly apply equity and the rule of law toward women. This will give women the desired boost to soar even higher in their pursuit of the common good because they possess a unique ability for nurturing and getting things done.

It is regrettable that the nations of Africa are assailed with incessant usurpation of power mostly by men the majority of who do not serve the masses' interest. They unashamedly defy accountability and due process and, almost always, fall short of standard expectations of moral decency. How can we alleviate the tremen-

dous burden that these nations bear in order to stem the inevitability of eventual collapse? Well, permit me to borrow a few words
of wisdom, even if ungrammatical, from a woman I much admire:
"The poor men seem to be all in confusion, and don't know what to
do. Why children, if you have woman's rights, give it to her and you
will feel better. You will have your own rights, and they won't be so
much trouble" (Sojourner Truth 247). Spoken in the 1800s, these
words are as poignant and relevant today as they were over a century
and half ago. They affirm the notion that women have so much to
contribute to contemporary society and their inclusion in decision-
making at all levels clearly assumes an immediate urgency that can
no longer be ignored or laughed off. Women must seek leadership
roles in governance and take their rightful place alongside the men
in the civil society. This is the surest way to ensure the success of the
democratic process in Africa and, if experience is anything to go by,
it is to the woman that we must look to bring back the glory of the
continent and restore equilibrium to a new social order.

Works Cited

Achebe, Chinua. *Things Fall Apart*. London: Heinemann, 1958.

_____. *No Longer at Ease*. London: Heinemann, 1960.

_____. *Arrow of God*. New York: Anchor Books, 1964.

_____. *A Man of the People*. New York: Anchor Books. 1966.

_____. *Anthills of the Savannah*. London: Heinemann, 1987.

_____. "The Novelist as Teacher." *Morning Yet on Creation Day*. London: Heinemann, 1975.

_____. *Girls at War*. New York: Anchor Books, 1991.

Acholonu, Rose. "The Female Predicament in the Nigerian Novel." *Feminism in African Literature: Essays on Criticism*. Ed. Helen Chukwuma. Port Harcourt: Pearl Publishers, 2003.

_____. "Feminist Discourse, Nigerian Literature and National Development." *A Journal of Nigerian Language and Culture* 3 (2002): 132-143.

Booker, Keith. *The African Novel in English: An Introduction*. Portsmouth: Heinemann, 1998.

Chukwuma, Helen. "Positivism and the Female Crisis: The Novels of Buchi Emecheta." *Nigerian Female Writers: A Critical Perspective*. Eds. Henrietta Otokunefor and Obiageli Nwodo. Lagos: Malthouse Press Ltd., 1989.

_____. *Women Writing: Feminism and National Development in Nigeria.* Port Harcourt: The University of Port Harcourt Press, 2004.

Cooper, Carol. Interview with Chinua Achebe. *Voice.* Annandale-on-Hudson. 25 Feb. 2008.

Ezeigbo, Theodora. "The Dynamics of African Womanhood in Ayi Kwei Armah's Novels." *Feminism in African Literature: Essays on Criticism.* Ed. Helen Chukwuma. Port Harcourt: Pearl Publishers, 2003.

Harrow, Kenneth W. "I'm not a (Western) feminist but ..." – A Review of Recent Critical Writings on African Women's Literature." *Research in African Literatures* Vol. 29, No. 3 (1998): 171-190.

Mezu, Rose. "Women in Achebe's World." *Womanist Theory and Research.* 1.2 (1995): 1-7. Online. http://www.uga.edu/ ~womanist/1995/mezu.html.

Nasser, Merun. "Achebe and His Women: A Social Science Perspective." *Africa Today* 27.3 (1980): 21-28.

Ndibe, Okey and Joyce Abunaw. Interview with Chinua Achebe. *Association of Nigerian Author's Review.* Annandale-on-Hudson, 15 Feb. 2008.

Ogwude, Sophia O. "Achebe on the Woman Question." *Literary Griot* 13.1 (2001): 62-69.

Ohale, Christine N. "The Evolution of the African Female Character: The Progressive Imaging of African Womanhood in African Literature." *Journal of the African Literature Association* Vol.2, No.1 (2008): 130-141.

Powell, Andrea. "Problematizing Polygyny in the Historical Novels of Chinua Achebe: The Role of the Western Feminist Scholar." *Research in African Literatures* Vol. 39, No.1 (2008): 166-184.

Rutherford, Anna. Interview with Chinua Achebe. Reproduced in *Kunapipi* Vol. ix, No. 2 (1987): 1-7.

Segun, Mabel. "Challenges of Being a Female Writer in a Male-Dominated Developing Society." *Matatu* 23-24 (2001): 295-302.

Stratton, Florence. *Contemporary African Literature and the politics of Gender.* London: Routledge, 1994.

Thompson, Bob. Interview with Chinua Achebe. Washington Post. Annandale-on-Hudson. 9 Mar. 2008.

Truth, Sojourner. "Ar'n't I a Woman? Speech to the Women's Rights Convention in Akron, Ohio, 1851." *The Norton Anthology of African American Literature.* Eds. Henry Louis Gates Jr. and Nellie Y. McKay. New York: W. W. Norton & Company, 2004.

Epilogue

FIFTY YEARS HENCE

Feminism, as most ideological tendencies, will run its course and end. But feminism like most ideological tendencies is informed by and derived from present-day realities. In the most basic form, feminism is a reaction which of course re-supposes an action. The position of women, therefore, in the world today, is the determinant factor on how far and whether feminism will go. The score sheet in writing by women is impressive and shows the issues that women contend with, and here, Igbo adage is relevant. *Obulu na akwu aguro na nti, nti ada ezuike.* Translation – as long as there are palm nuts in the cheek, the cheek will not rest. As long as there is female subjugation and marginalization so long will there be writing fora that address these issues.

Achebe has shown a remarkable sense of history and reality by showing the various developments of women through time. Angela Fubara, in her chapter, traced the development of women's assertion in Achebe's novels using the insect analogy that move from egg to pupa to larvae to butterfly. Now that the butterfly has flown, we need to chart its course and see how far it can go. Indeed, women still are in the majority in the world, but their positions do not reflect this reality. Writers must therefore probe into the success stories of women and see how far they have and can hold their own. It is remarkable that Achebe being male was able to present to the world the various statuses of women in Nigerian/ African society. It was his fiction that brought about the reaction of most women writers as Flora Nwapa, who sees the opportunity to salvage the image of the women. For indeed, who can tell your story better than yourself?

Achebe, in his novel *Anthills of the Savannah*, proffers a socio-political alternative to men's leadership. He makes Beatrice assume and perform the established role of man by christening Elewa's baby. She was the one who stepped in to fill the gap brought about by the men's absence. This means that women are indeed the "courts of final resort". This was the point underscored by Uzoechi Nwagbara in his submission in chapter nine. Women are assuming positions of responsibility in the affairs of the polity. This can only be seen as a demonstrable beginning. The population of women in the world (49-51 percent) demands that they should be given commensurate status and position in national and world affairs. Humanity suffers a disservice when more than half its population is under-utilized.

This text serves to show how women were able, even in pre-colonial times to the early years of colonialism where they were not exposed more than the homestead, were able, still, to navigate the patriarchal norm for a meaningful life. The chapters in their various ways have shown, if anything, that women's resilience and industry have brought them so far in asserting themselves. Achebe shows in a developmental manner how women have arrived to where they are today. The future therefore is indeed bright and the challenge rests on writers, male and female alike, who advance this cause of women to a logical conclusion which translates to a better humanity and better nationhood.

NOTES ON CONTRIBUTORS

Ada Uzoamaka Azodo, Professor, Purdue University, Calumet.

Blessing Diala-Ogamba is an Associate Professor of English in the Department of Humanities and Media Arts of Coppins State University, Baltimore, Maryland.

Patricia T. Emenyonu, formerly Associate Professor of English/ English Education at Imo State University and the university of Calabar in Nigeria, teaches in the departments of English and Africana studies in the University of Michigan-Flint.

Angela M. Fubara is a Senior Lecturer in the Department of Foundations of Rivers State University of Science and Technology, Port Harcourt, Nigeria.

Anthonia C. Kalu is a Professor in the Department of African and African American Studies of Ohio State University, Columbus, Ohio.

Caroline Mbonu, HHCJ, Department of Interdisciplinary Studies, University of California, Berkley, CA.

Laura Miller is an instructor in the Department of English and Modern Foreign Languages of Jackson State University, Jackson, MS.

Margaret Fafa Nutsukpo is a Senior Lecturer in the Department of English Studies at the University of Port Harcourt, Port Harcourt, Nigeria.

Uzoechi Nwagbara is a post graduate student Greenwich School of Management, London, United Kingdom.

Christine Ohale is a Professor of English in the Department of English, Communications, Media Arts, and Theatre of Chicago State University, Chicago, Illinois.

Chinyelu Ojukwu is a Senior lecturer in the dept. of English, University of Port Harcourt, Nigeria.

Chinyere Okafor is a Professor of English and Women's Studies in the Department of Women's Studies of Wichita State University, Kansas, U.S.A.

Chioma Opara is a Professor of English in the Department of Foundations of Rivers State University of Science and Technology, Port Harcourt, Nigeria.

Frances Orabueze is a Senior Lecturer in the Department of English of the University of Nigeria, Nsukka, Nigeria.

Irene Salami-Agunloye is a Professor of Drama and Theatre Arts in the Department of Theatre Arts of the University of Jos, Nigeria.

Onyemaechi Udumukwu is a Professor of English in the Department of English Studies of the University of Port Harcourt, Port Harcourt, Nigeria.

Paula T. Wingard is a doctoral student in the Department of English of the University of Arkansas, Fayetteville, Arkansas.

INDEX